D1555257

MIND, CODE AND CONTEXT

Essays in Pragmatics

T. Givón
University of Oregon

LEA LAWRENCE ERLBAUM ASSOCIATES, PUBLISHERS
1989 Hillsdale, New Jersey   London

Lawrence Erlbaum Associates, Inc., Publishers
365 Broadway
Hillsdale, New Jersey 07642

Library of Congress Cataloging in Publication Data

Givón, T., 1936-
    Mind, code, and context : essays in pragmatics / T. Givón
        p.   cm.
    Bibliography: p.
    Includes index.
    ISBN 0-89859-607-6. ISBN 0-8058-0482-X(pbk.)
    1. Pragmatics. I. Title.
B831.5.G58 1989
121'.68--dc19   88-21298
                                        CIP

PRINTED IN THE UNITED STATES OF AMERICA
10 9 8 7 6 5 4 3 2 1

To my parents, Victoria and Alexander Givón, who, by stranding me early in life between their abundant love and unbounded expectations, have inadvertently taught me the rudiments of pragmatics.

Contents

Preface

Pragmatics is an approach to description, to information processing, thus to the construction, interpretation and communication of experience. At its core lies the notion of *context*, and the axiom that reality and/or experience are not absolute fixed entities, but rather *frame-dependent*, contingent upon the observer's *perspective*.

Pragmatics traces its illustrious ancestry to the pre-Socratic Greek dialecticians, then via Aristotle to Locke, Kant and Peirce, eventually to 19th Century phenomenologists, and--last but not least--to Ludwig Wittgenstein. In cognitive psychology, pragmatics underlies figure-ground perception, primed storage and maleable recall, attended ('context-scanning') information processing, and flexible ('prototype') categorization. In linguistics, pragmatics animates the study of contextual meaning and metaphoric extension, frame semantics and the semeiotics of grammar-in-discourse, the sociology of language, and the acquisition of communicative competence. In anthropology, pragmatics is reflected in the exploration of cultural relativity, ethnomethodology and cross-cultural cognition.

In spite of such exalted lineage and wide applicability, the academic study of pragmatics remains narrow, insular and fractious. On the one hand, various formal schools have undertaken to keep pragmatics firmly attached to the very discipline which it purported to overthrow--formal deductive logic. On the other hand, a plethora of informal schools have taken the intoxicating freedom of contextual relativity as license for extreme methodological nihilism, unfettered intuitionism, and an *anything goes* rejection of sensible empirical constraints. What unites these extreme interpretations is, paradoxically, an antipragmatic faith in the Platonic excluded middle: *The lack of total order means a total lack of order; the lack of total understanding is a total lack of understanding.* In this way, the very essence of pragmatics is subverted by its most impassioned proponents.

Pragmatics, at its somewhat unadorned middle-ground best, closely reflects the evolutionary compromise practiced by biological organisms. In adapting to life in a less-than-ideal environment, bio-organisms have invariably opted for the proposition that half a loaf is infinitely better than none; that life is precariously suspended mid-way between absolute order and unmitigated chaos; that while full determinism is a dangerous evolutionary trap, unbounded freedom is an unrealistic evolutionary mirage. In their humble travail to adapt and survive, bio-organisms have recognized what contentious academics all too often ignore--that Goedel's observed limits on systems--neither fully consistent, nor ever complete--sum up rather well the pragmatic predicament of life and mind in a real environment.

The writing of this book was supported by a number of generous sources. I would like to take this opportunity and acknowledge their help. In order: the *Office of Naval Research*, research grant "Mechanisms of Cognitive Performance" (with S. Keele and M. Posner)(1983-1985), the *John Simon Guggenheim Memorial Foundation*, through a fellowship , "The pragmatics of human language" (1986); The *Fulbright-Hays Exchange Program*, through a visiting lectureship "The American Indian: Past and Present" (Auckland, 1986); *The National Endowment for the Humanities*, through research grants "Ute traditional Narratives and the pragmatics of word-order change" (Ignacio, 1980-1985); "Serial verbs and the mental reality of 'event': An empirical approach to the Sapir-Whorf Hypothesis" (Papua-New Guinea, 1985-1987; renewed 1988-1990); and the *Deutsche Forschung Gemeinschaft*, for a visiting fellowship "Lectures on pragmatics" (Köln, 1987). To make the picture complete, I would also like to acknowledge the consistent non-support of the *National Science Foundation*.

T. Givón
Eugene, Oregon

CHAPTER 1

INTRODUCTION

1.1. Instead of definition *

1.1.1. Context, frame and point of view

Pragmatics may be likened to a vast terrain whose boundaries are so distant that we perceive them only dimly, given our less-than-exalted vantage point. This is somewhat embarrassing for a discipline so intently focused upon the study of vantage points; although there is perhaps a certain measure of poetic justice involved in the embarrassment. As a serious empirical discipline, pragmatics is still in its infancy, clumsily attempting to grasp for its own meaning. It would thus be presumptive, and perhaps even alien to the very spirit of pragmatics, to saddle it prematurely with a rigid definition. Still, if there is a unifying theme to the entire enterprise, it must have at its very core the notion of **context**, or **frame**, or **point of view**.

Pragmatics as a method may be first likened to the way one goes about constructing a **description**. The reason why I've chosen 'description' as my first metaphor for pragmatics may trace back to dimly recalled times in military reconnaissance. When one was sent to draw a panoramic view of some Godforsaken hill, the resulting sketch-cum-commentary had to always specify the **map coordinates** of one's vantage point; that is where one stood when drawing the picture. Your description -- pictorial-cum-verbal, you were told -- was *useless* without those coordinates. The first metaphor for pragmatics as a method may thus be given as:

(1) **Description and point of view:**

> "The **description** of an entity is incomplete, indeed un-interpretable, unless it specifies the **point of view** from whence the description was undertaken".

*I am indebted to T.K. Bikson, Hartmut Haberland, Fred Kroon, Dennis Robinson and Martin Tweedale for many helpful suggestions concerning the early history of pragmatics. In revising this chapter, I benefitted greatly from having had the opportunity to present an earlier version at the Philosophy Department Colloquium, Auckland University.

The very same idea may be re-phrased in terms of a 'picture and frame' metaphor:

(2) **Picture and frame:**

"A **picture** is not fully specified unless its **frame** is also specified".

Pragmatics as a method may also be rendered in terms of the relation between meaning and context:

(3) **Meaning and context:**

"The **meaning** of an expression cannot be fully understood without understanding the **context** in which the expression is used".

As revealing as the three metaphors above may be, there is still a more general way of approaching the definition of pragmatics. Somewhat surprising, one may trace it back to the work of an eminent logician, Bertrand Russell.

1.1.2. **Systems and meta-levels: The two predicaments**

"...There was only one catch and that was Catch-22, which specified that a concern for one's own safety in the face of dangers that were real and immediate was the process of a rational mind. Orr was crazy and could be grounded. All he had to do was ask; and as soon as he did, he would no longer be crazy and would have to fly more missions. Orr would be crazy to fly more missions and sane if he didn't, but if he was sane he had to fly them. If he flew them he was crazy and didn't have to; but if he didn't want to he was sane and had to..."

J. Heller *Catch-22* (1962, p. 54)

The three core metaphors for the pragmatic method given above -- point of view, frame, context -- may be further generalized via the notions of **systems** and **meta-levels**. Let a system be, at its most general, a hierarchic arrangement of parts and sub-parts. When one undertakes to specify ('describe') a system, it is desirable, from a purely practical point of view, to impose some **limit** on the description, otherwise the descriptive task may be infinite. This requirement is the one we call **closure**.

The system, as a hierarchic entity, is made out of a progression of **levels**, each one acting as **meta-level** to the sub-level(s) embedded within it. Each meta level is thus the **context** for the sub-levels embedded within it. For purely practical reasons, if the system is to remain **finite** (i.e. describable within finite time, space and means), the last -- highest -- meta-level must remain **context-less**; it lacks its own meta-level. In terms of our picture metaphor, the last meta-level is the frame, yet itself remains un-framed, therefore not fully specified. And here lies our first predicament of pragmatics, that of **completeness**:

(4) **The predicament of completeness**:

"So long as the system is fully specified, i.e. closed, it must remain in principle incomplete".

Bertrand Russell in his *Introduction to Mathematical Philosophy* (1919), dealt with the second predicament, that of consistency. In his celebrated Theory of Types, he observed that the classical logical paradoxes, such as *the liar's paradox* ('I never tell the truth') are all instances of a more general phenomenon, that of self inclusion. That is, within the same description, one level acts as both the meta-level the sub-level. In other words, it 'includes itself'.[1] When such self-inclusion -- or 'crossing of meta-levels' -- is allowed, the system becomes **inconsistent**. And here lies the second predicament of pragmatics:

(5) **The predicament of consistence**:

"So long as one is allowed to switch meta-levels -- or points of view -- in the middle of a description, the description is logically inconsistent".

To bypass the predicament of inconsistency, Russell, in his *Theory of Types*, resorted to legislation. Logical descriptions, he insisted, must remain within the scope of **one specified meta-level**. In other words:

---

1   Russell formulated the general case of this paradox as: "The set of all the sets that don't include themselves; does it or doesn't it then include itself?"

(6) Russell's Constraint on systems:

> "A self-consistent (though in an obvious sense incomplete) logical description can only operate within a fixed point of view, context, meta-level".

In imposing his constraint, Russell, with one wave of his magic wand, exorcised the specter of pragmatics out of deductive logic. This exorcism yielded two results, the first intended, the second perhaps not altogether obvious to the exorcist himself at the time:

(a) Deductive logic was rescued as a closed, internally-consistent, coherent system.

(b) The instrument of deductive logic was removed, once and for all, as serious contender for modeling, describing or explaining human language -- or mind.

Put another way, Russell indeed saved the instrument, by giving up its original -- historic -- purpose.

Deductive logic for the moment aside, the pragmatically engendered predicaments of closure and consistence continue to haunt any attempt to describe language and mind. Neither language nor mind abides by the requirement of closure, except perhaps temporarily, for limited tasks. Both mind and language are necessarily **open systems** that constantly expand, add meta-levels, learn and modify themselves. Equally, both language and mind are notoriously promiscuous in violating Russell's constraint on self-inclusion and reflexivity. Consciousness is indeed forever adjusting its frame, shifting meta-levels; it keeps **re-framing** and reflexively framing itself. This propensity of consciousness is neither an aberration nor an accident. Rather, it is a necessary, adaptively motivated capacity; it stands at the very core of our perceptual and cognitive processing mechanisms. It is a precondition for the mind's ability to **select**, evaluate, file, contextualize and respond appropriately to mountains of information.

The key notions here are 'select', 'evaluate', 'contextualize' and 'appropriately'. In the immense, Herculean task of natural -- biological -- information processing, the bulk of the input is in fact blocked, i.e. deemed -- in the appropriate context -- to be either **irrelevant** or **not urgent**. Only small morsels of the input, judged to be either relevant or urgent in context, are let through for further processing. The selective exercise of the mind's **contextual judgement** -- the readjustment of the frame for the particular occasion and task -- is the *sine qua non* of natural, biological information processing, which is undertaken under severe limits: Finite time, finite storage capacity, finite means.

As we shall see throughout, it is the mind's pragmatic flexibility and open-endedness (i.e. 'incompleteness' and 'inconsistence'), its capacity to re-frame and re-contextualize, that enables it to perform -- sometimes concurrently, often selectively -- the multitude of its complex processing tasks.

1.2. The scope of pragmatics: Recurrent themes

As noted above, at the core of pragmatics lies the notion of context. Pragmatics is a **context-dependent** approach to analysis -- of behavior, of tasks, of systems, of meaning. A number of recurrent themes have been traditionally associated with pragmatics. All of them are mediated by -- or founded upon -- the core notion of context. In this section I will briefly survey pragmatics' most common *leitmotifs*.

1.2.1. Gradation, continuum and non-discreteness

As we shall see in Chapter 2, below, non-pragmatic approaches to description, thus to sub-levels within a hierarchic system, have always assumed that categories are **discrete**. In other words, membership in a category is governed by the strict rule of *the excluded middle*. A major feature of pragmatics has been, ever since its inception, that categories are not fully discrete, but may display shades and gradations. Not all exponents of non-discreteness have explicitly related it to the central notion of context. I would like to argue here that context is indeed the crucial *mediator* that makes non-discreteness both possible and necessary. The argument runs roughly as follows:

(a) The point of view -- being itself outside the picture -- cannot be constrained by the frame-internal system of discrete categories. Outside the upper meta-level of the system the context -- frame -- is undifferentiated.

(b) In principle, therefore, any adjustment in the ultimate point-of-view is bound to be non-discrete, it may be made gradually, without sharp categorial breaks.

(c) In principle, then, the system inside the frame will display the consequences of non-discrete adjustments of the frame.

This necessary connection between context and non-discreteness can only be broken by **discretizing** the notion of context. This has been attempted repeatedly in formal logic in the last four decades (see discussion in sections 1.7.4. and 1.7.5., below). However, the minute such gambit is accomplished, the erstwhile context ceases to be context. The erstwhile frame merely joins the system/picture on the inside. And on the outside -- *mutatis mutandis* -- there remains context, the last meta-level, open-ended, non-discrete, and as disdainful as ever of logic's slights of hand.

1.2.2. **Relevance and importance**

The two partly related notions of **importance** and **relevance** surface wherever one traffics in pragmatics. Both are a matter of **degree**, rather than of discrete choice. Both involve **contextual judgement** that can be captured neither by deductive nor inductive logic. Rather, the judgement involved in both is **abductive;**[2] reference must be made to the context relative to which something is judged to be either important or relevant.

1.2.3. **Similarity and analogy**

Much like importance and relevance, the notions of **similarity** and **analogy** are in principle impervious to deductive or inductive reasoning. Equally, they are non-discrete, a matter of degree. In principle, anything can be similar to anything else, and anything may be viewed by analogy to anything else -- provided the **appropriate** context, frame, or point of view is **construed**. And construing the appropriateness of context is, in principle, a purely abductive enterprise.

1.2.4. **Kind vs. degree: The arbitrariness of taxonomy**

Somewhat related to the question of non-discreteness of categories is the issue of supra-categories, meta-levels and thus -- in the universe of individual tokens -- the **hierarchy of types**. Typically, in a non-pragmatic ('Platonic') approach to the taxonomy of types and sub-types, one always assumes -- often implicitly [3] -- that it is somehow possible to tell a 'major' from a 'minor' property of individual tokens within a population by some algorithmic means. Individuals that differ from each other by only 'minor' properties are then said to differ only **by degree**; they therefore belong to the **same type**. In contrast, individuals that differ from each

---

2   See discussion directly below.
3   See for example Russell (1919).

other by a 'major' property are said to be different **in kind**; they belong to **different types**. We may illustrate this diagrammatically as follows:

(7) **Difference in kind and difference in degree**

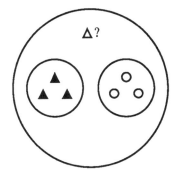

The fundamental distinction between 'degree' and 'kind' is the basis for all taxonomies -- pragmatic and non-pragmatic alike. The difference between the two approaches lies in their attitude toward the absoluteness of such a distinction. To the non-pragmatist, it is somehow a rigid, principled distinction that yields absolute categorial boundaries. The pragmatist merely points out the obvious, namely that the distinction between 'major' and 'minor' properties -- and thus between 'difference in kind' and 'difference in degree' -- is in principle **arbitrary**; it cannot be made on either deductive or inductive grounds. It is typically a matter of abductive judgement about the **context** -- often the **purpose** -- of the taxonomy. Only relative to that context can some properties or distinctions be deemed important, and others less so.

1.2.5. **Abductive inference and analogic reasoning**

The non-pragmatic tradition speaks of two modes of knowledge -- or modes of inference -- **deductive** and **inductive**. The first proceeds from the general rule to its specific instances. The second presumably proceeds from specific instances to the general rule. Pragmatically-based **abductive inference**[4] -- concerning appropriateness of context, importance, relevance, similarity or explanation -- is in principle a different kind of reasoning. It proceeds by **hypothesis, guesswork** or **intuition**, often by **analogy**. It is thus, in principle, unconstrained.

---

4   See discussion of Peirce, further below, as well as in Chapter 7, below.

1.2.6. **The semeiotic relation**

The discussion of the relation between a **sign** and its **designatum** almost always drags in pragmatics by either the front or the back door. This is due to the presence of the third term in the semeiotic equation, the silent partner -- the **interpretant**. The interpretant, as will be argued below,[5] turns out to involve the **perceived context**, within which the semeiotic relation holds for its perceiver. The semeiotic relation, of even the most abstract symbol, is thus in principle a **context dependent** entity, i.e. a matter of pragmatics.

1.2.7. **Purpose, function explanation and understanding**

As will be suggested further below,[6] **intent** is already a crypto-pragmatic notion, involving the mind of the intender as context for a proposition. In addition, the teleological notions of **purpose** and **function** -- in the philosophy of science as well as in the behavior of organisms -- are in principle pragmatic entities that cannot be captured by deductive or inductive means. They involve an abductive, analogical, context-dependent judgement. Further, these teleological entities often form the bulk of the context within which cognition, behavior and communication must be understood or explained. And 'explanation' is itself a pragmatic notion, since it involves relating an entity to its wider frame, its **context**.

1.2.8. **Norm, ground, saliency, frequency and markedness**

In the study of perception, cognition and communication, the notion of **norm** ('ground'), vis-a-vis which information (the 'figure') is salient, is a core notion. But 'norm' is itself a prime pragmatic construct: The norm in information processing is merely the **context** vis-a-vis which information is **salient**. As we shall see at a number of junctures below (in particular Chapters 2, 4 and 6), the notion of norm is inherently **distributional**; it is based on a certain skewing in the **relative frequency** of the 'figure' and the 'ground': The ground ('norm') is relatively frequent, while the figure ('counter-norm') is relatively rare. As we shall see later on, the substantive sense of **markedness** in natural language, perception and cognition is grounded in the pragmatics of norm vs. counter-norm and their skewed relative frequency.

---

5   See Chapter 3, below.
6   See Chapter 5, below.

1.3. **Early roots**

"...Any philosophical doctrine that should be completely new could hardly fail to prove completely false; but the rivulets at the head of the river of pragmatism are easily tracked back to almost any desired antiquity. Socrates bathed in these waters. Aristotle rejoiced when he could find them. They run, where one would least suspect them, beneath the dry rubbish-heaps of Spinoza. Those clean definitions that strew the pages of *Essay Concerning Humane Understanding* (I refuse to reform the spelling) had been washed out in these same pure springs. It was this medium, and not tar-water, that gave health and strength to Berkeley's earlier work... From it the general views of Kant derive such clearness as they have..."

C. S. Peirce, "Pragmatism in Retrospect:
The Last Formulation" [1940, p. 269]

1.3.1. **The dialecticians**

In these somewhat catty yet generous words, the founder of modern Pragmatism pays homage to his antecedents. These antecedents in fact go further back, to the pre-Socratic Dialecticians. Allen (1966) characterizes Anaximander's **dialectics** as follows:

"...The world, like a pendulum, maintains equilibrium through the alternation of its extremes..." [1966, p. 3]

And Diogenes Laertius ascribes to Heraclitus the following observation:

"...All things come into being by conflict of opposites, and the sum of things flows like a stream..." [1925, vol. II, p. 415]

The classical dictum also attributed to Heraclitus: "...You never step twice into the same river..." is also essentially pragmatic, presumably pointing out to the ever-changing context -- time, the river, the self. Similarly, in the anonymous manuscript *Divided Logi*, ascribed to the Protagoran tradition, we find the following observation: [7]

"...If we sat in a row and said 'I am an initiate', we would all say the same thing, but only I would speak the truth, since I really am one..."

---

7   Cited from Haberland (1985) after Diels (1969, vol. II).

A much fuller dialectic-pragmatic approach, apparently ignored by Peirce, is of course found in mystic Oriental philosophers, most succinctly in Lao Tse's *Tao Teh Ching*.[8] The mystic's route indeed remained an ever-present alternative to the two non-pragmatic reductionist schools -- empiricism and rationalism -- in the history of Western philosophy. But the mystics were easy to ignore in Western philosophy; they were inherently non-analytic; they also rejected the major tenet of Western epistemology -- the separation of Mind from World.

1.3.2. Socrates

The inclusion of Socrates in the roots of Pragmatism is at first surprising, given our largely Platonic access to his philosophy. However, in *Hippias Major* Socrates (or was it Plato?) adopts a Pragmatic -- indeed Wittgensteinean--approach in discussing the context relativity of the meaning of adjectives such as 'fine' and 'foul'. Indeed, Socrates invokes Heraclitus for that purpose:

"...Don't you know that what Heraclitus said holds good: The finest of monkeys is foul when put together with another class, and the finest of pots is foul when put together with the class of girls...If you put the class of girls together with the class of gods, won't the same thing happen as happened when the class of pots was put together with that of girls? Won't the finest girl be seen to be foul? And didn't Heraclitus (whom you bring in) say the same thing too, that 'the wisest of men is seen to be a monkey compared to god in wisdom and fineness and everything else'?..." [Woodruff, 1982, pp. 10-11]

1.3.3. Aristotle

Also somewhat surprising is Peirce's inclusion of Aristotle in the Pragmatist family tree. Surprising first because of Aristotle's extreme empiricist view of the source of mental categories, or 'forms'. According to Aristotle, 'forms' contain the entire categorial array (i.e. 'meaning') of perceived objects -- minus their existence. Aristotle's 'forms' -- though objective-external in origin, are just as fixed, absolute and universal as Plato's innate categories.[9] Like Plato, Aristotle views categories as discrete, requiring necessary-and-sufficient membership criteria.[10] Further, contrary to Morris's (1938) attribution, Aristotle's semeiotics shows no

8   Dealt with in some detail in Chapter 11, below.
9   See discussion of Aristotle's 'forms' as given in his *Metaphysics* in Tweedale (1986).
10 See Aristotle's *Categories*, in Ackrill (tr.& ed.,1963).

trace of Peirce's 'interpretant'.[11] Nonetheless, in four distinct areas Aristotle may be indeed shown to be an early exponent of pragmatics. We will take them up in order.

1.3.3.1. Non-discrete gradual change

This topic recurs in many of Aristotle's work, but is perhaps most clearly developed in the *Metaphysics*. The problem that necessitated a pragmatic departure for Aristotle arose from the inability of his absolute 'forms' to account for gradual change, such as 'coming-into-being' or 'passing away'. Aristotle rushed to the rescue of his 'forms' with the concept of *synolon*. As Tweedale (1986) observes:

"...The *synolon* is Aristotle's concession to the Heraclitean flux. It manages an existence of sorts even while it is coming-to-be or passing away. This is because it contains matter, the *sine qua non* for anything that undergoes a process of change..."[1986, p. 5][12]

1.3.3.2. 'The mean'

Aristotle's 'mean' (or 'the intermediate') in the *Ethics* may be interpreted as the pragmatist's Golden Mean, whereby the extreme, pure cases are to be eschewed in favor of the delicately balanced, hard to grasp thin line in-between.[13] Thus consider the following passage from the *Ethics* (McKeon, ed., 1941):

"...In everything that is continuous and divisible it is possible to take more, less or an equal amount, and that either in terms of the thing itself or relative to us; and the equal is an intermediate between excess and defect. By the intermediate *in the object* I mean that which is equidistant from each of the extremes, which is one and the same for all men; by intermediate *relative to us*, that which is neither too much nor too little -- and this is not one, nor the same for all. For instance, if ten is many and two is few, six is the intermediate, taken in terms of the object... But the intermediate relative to us is not to be taken so; if ten pounds is too much

11 See discussion in Chapter 3, below.
12 While forms are presumably immutable, absolute and undergo no flux. I owe my frail understanding of these issues to Martin Tweedale (in personal communication); see also Tweedale (1986).
13 I am again indebted to Martin Tweedale (in personal communication) for suggesting this area of Aristotle's pragmatism to me.

for a particular person to eat and two too little, it does not follow that the trainer will order six pounds..." [1941, pp. 957-958]

Aristotle is confronting here the problem of graded continuum, and also implicitly the problem of context, especially in making the intermediate 'relative to us' a contingent notion. This is even clearer in the next passage:

"...both fear and confidence and appetite and anger and pity and in general pleasure and pain may be felt both too much and too little, and in both cases not well; but to feel them at the right time, with reference to the right objects, toward the right people, with the right motive, and in the right way, is what is both intermediate and best..." [McKeon, ed., 1941, p. 958]

Aristotle thus enumerates the various elements of context upon which 'the intermediate for us' is contingent: time, object, participants, motive, manner. And while this is pragmatics in the realm of ethics, it is classical pragmatics nonetheless.

1.3.3.3. **Aristotle's functionalism**

Aristotle's approach to biology is suffused with functionalist teleology. His arguments are constructed first against an earlier **structuralist** tradition, manifest in the works of pre-Socratic materialists such as Empedocles. These materialist sought to describe and explain the nature of organisms in the same way as they described the nature of inorganic physical objects -- by reference to their component **elements**, or in the case of Democritus to their component **structures**. Aristotle begins his argument in *De Partibus Animalium* by advocating a move from Empedocles' elemental description to structural description, i.e. description in terms of the histology and anatomy of organs:

"...But if men and animals are natural phenomena, then natural philosophers must take into consideration not merely the ultimate substances of which they are made, but also flesh, bone, blood and all the other homogeneous parts; not only these but also the heterogenous parts, such as face, hand, foot..." [McKeon, ed., 1941, p. 647].

He then proceeds to argue that even such structuralist approach, such as that of Democritus, won't do:

"...Does, then, configuration and color constitute the essence of the various animals and their several parts? For if so, what Democritus says will be strictly correct... no hand of bronze or wood or constituted in any but the appropriate way can possibly be a hand in more than name. For like a physician in a painting, or like a flute in a sculpture, it will be unable to do *the office* which that name implies..." (*ibid*, p. 647; emphases are mine; TG)

Next, a teleological approach to biology is outlined, using the analogy of usable artifacts:

"...What, however, I would ask, are the forces by which the hand or the body was fashioned into its shape? The woodcarver will perhaps say, by the axe or the auger; the physiologist, by air and by earth. Of these two answers the artrificer's is the better, but it is nevertheless insufficient. For it is not enough for him to say that by the stroke of his tool this part was formed into a concavity, that into a flat surface; but he must state *the reasons* why he struck his blow in such a way as to affect this, and what *his final object* was..." [*ibid*, pp. 647-648; emphases are mine; TG]

The need for form-function correlation is now driven home, again by using the analogy of tools:

"...if a piece of wood is to be split with an axe, the axe must of necessity be hard; and, if hard, must of necessity be made of bronze or iron. Now exactly in the same way the body, which like the axe is an instrument -- for both the body as a whole and its several parts individually have definite operations for which they are made; just in the same way, I say, the body if it is to do its work, must of necessity be of such and such character..." [*ibid*, p. 650]

In outlining his functionalist argument, Aristotle rejects two extremist views of biology: The structuralist's anti-teleology, and Plato's abstract super-teleology (whereby all purposive phenomena -- in the inorganic and organic universe alike -- are attributed to some **higher purposive intelligence**). While not addressing himself specifically to language, Aristotle's functionalism in biology indeed presages an important ingredient of modern pragmatics.

1.3.3.4. Abductive inference

Hanson (1958) points out that Peirce's abductive inference, the 'third mode' of knowledge, was first described by Aristotle:

"...Aristotle lists the types of inferences. These are deductive, inductive and one other called *apagoge*. This is translated as 'reduction'. Peirce translates it as 'abduction' or 'retroduction'. What distinguishes this kind of argument for Aristotle is that the relation of the middle to the last term is uncertain, though equally or more probable than the conclusion; or again an argument in which the terms intermediate between the last term and the middle are few. For in any of these cases it turns out that we approach more nearly to knowledge... since we have taken a new term..." (1958, p. 85; cited from Aristotle's *Prior Analytic*, tr. by Jenkinson, ed. by Ross, Oxford, vol. II, p. 25)

In another reference, in the *Posterior Analytic*, Aristotle characterizes the mode of abduction as follows:

"...The particular facts are not merely brought together but there is a new element added to the combination by the very act of thought by which they are combined... The pearls are there, but they will not hang together till someone provides the string..." (*Posterior Analytic*, vol. II, p. 19; cf. Whewell, *Organum Renovatum*, pp. 72-73).

We will return to discuss the modes of inference, and abduction in particular, in Chapters 7 and 8, below.

1.4. **Kant**

1.4.1. **Extreme reductionism in Western Epistemology**

The nature of the categories of human mind, their origin, and what exactly they stand for, are persistent questions that have been with us since the dawn of Western thought. What is the **source** of all those entities that inhabit our mind? How did they get there? What do they stand for? Do we experience the world in a certain way because our mind is so pre-cast, chock-full of concepts that have been placed there by the **Deity** (as Descartes would have it)? Are those **innate ideas** there because of that latter-day deity, **Genetics** or 'the Bio-Program' (as Chomsky, 1966, 1968 or Bickerton, 1981, would)? Or do we, alternatively, owe our mental categories to **experience**? Has some real or perceived **outside world** been imprinted on our passive mind via sensory perception?

Ever since post-Socratic Greek philosophy began to contemplate the puzzle of mind vs. world (or 'in vs.out', or 'subject vs. object'), and until the latter part of the 18th Century, only two extreme answers to this eternal puzzle had been seriously contemplated in Western philosophy. **Rationalists**, from Plato down, had opted for the primacy of **innate categories** of the mind. **Empiricists**, from Aristotle onward, had argued for the primacy of **experience**, whether attributed to some putative **Real World** (the 'objectivist' option) or to the vagaries of our **senses** (the 'subjectivist' option).

It is perhaps not altogether an accident that the two extreme reductionist schools of Western epistemology, Rationalism and Empiricism, turn out nonetheless to share two of their most fundamental assumptions about the nature of mind:

(a) **Separateness of mind from world**: The mind and the world -- internal and external --are distinct and separate entities, allowing **no direct access** from one to the other.

(b) **Absoluteness of mental categories**: Categories of the mind -- be they Plato's innate ideas or Aristotle's perceived forms -- are discrete, universal and absolute, with membership adjudicated by rigid -- necessary and/or sufficient -- **criteria**, which members either do or do not possess.

With the first assumption (a), Western analytic philosophy detached itself from its old antecedence in the **mystic tradition**.[14] The second assumption (b) characterizes equally well rationalists from Plato to St. Augustine to Descartes to Chomsky, as it does empiricists from Aristotle to St. Thomas Aquinas to Hume to Skinner or Bloomfield. Its roots are presumably found in the logical doctrine of **the excluded middle**.[15]

The motivation for assumption (b) is both legitimate and, I believe, of some interest. Kant has alluded to it in his discussion of the potential infinity of the 'manifold multiplicity of intuitions' (i.e. 'sensations' of the outside world; see further below). Both Plato and Aristotle had to reckon with the very same problem. If reality is in principle unconstrained, nondiscrete and multifarious, and if the senses do not rigidly pre-select and constrain that multiplicity, then the understanding ('cognition') cannot match that unconstrained multifarious continuum without itself being infinite and unconstrained. Kant's solution to this dilemma was, I believe, the right one: Disengage 'the thing for itself' from 'the thing for us', by invoking the -- potentially discretizing -- **transcendental schema**. That schema is **pre-condition** to both perception and cognition. Plato, on the other hand, chose to ascribe the discretizing role to the innate categories of the mind.

Aristotle's position remains somewhat ambiguous. At first, glance he seems to have refused to acknowledge the problem. His mental categories -- the perceived 'forms' -- were said to correspond to actual objects *in all detail* -- except for actual existence. Presumably, if the world (or at least the world in process of change) is graduated and unconstrained, the 'forms' should be likewise. Thus, consider the following from *De Anima* (McKeon, ed., 1941):

---

14 See Chapter 11, below, for an illustration of that tradition, though from a non-Western source.

15 See Haberland (1985, p. 379) for a discussion of the history of the law of the excluded middle.

"...Actual knowledge is identical with its object... the mind which is actively thinking is the object which it thinks..." [pp. 593; 595]

If Aristotle had identified the dilemma, only two elegant ways out would have remained for him:

(a) Allow the mind an infinite capacity; or
(b) Construe the world itself as constrained, categorial, discrete.

Aristotle's way of scotching the problem was, as we have seen above, by postulating the *synolon*, which would account for the mind's ability to reflect the world's unconstrained flux. In terms of elegance, this is admittedly somewhat of a fudge.

1.4.2. Kant's middle-ground alternative

There are three main reasons, I believe, for considering Kant a pioneer of modern pragmatics. At issue are three major aspects of his epistemology. I will survey them in order.

1.4.2.1. The source of mental categories

Kant was clearly the first modern analytic philosopher to elucidate the **middle ground**, pragmatic alternative to the two extreme, reductionist schools of Western epistemology. I quote here from Kemp (1968), a rigorous interpreter:

"...Human knowledge arises through the joint functioning of intuition (the product of sensibility) [16] and concept (the product of understanding). Sensibility is a passive receptivity, the power of receiving representations of the objects by which understanding is an active spontaneity, the power of exercising thought over objects given us in sensible intuition. Neither by itself gives us knowledge: 'Thoughts without contents are empty', says

---

16 Kemp notes that Kant's *Anchaaung* means 'immediate apprehension' and is often translated as 'perception'. However, it subsumes not only 'sensory perception', but also 'pure intuition'. For this reason, Kemp prefers to render *Anchaaung* as 'intuition'. I personally feel that such a rendition is bound to be even more confusing, in that it suggests the exclusion of sensory perception from the meaning of the term.

Kant in a famous phrase (KRV A51 B75), 'intuitions without concepts are blind'..."[1968, p. 16] [17]

Kant's middle-ground epistemology stresses the **interactive**, mutually-dependent ('dialectic') relation between percepts and concepts. Concepts and percepts thus form the respective **context** for each other, a context within which each receives its respective interpretation. None is by itself a viable prime. [18] Kant's contribution thus lies in his attempt to do away with the artificial mind-vs.-world dilemma, via his **constructivist** interpretation of 'reality'. To quote Kemp again:

"...We do not find them [our sense impressions of the worlds; TG] already organized... but rather organize them ourselves..." [1968, p. 23]

And further:

"...'the order and regularity in the appearance, which we entitle *nature*, we introduce ourselves. We could never find them in appearance, had not we ourselves, or the nature of our mind, originally set them there' (A125)..." [1968, p. 32]

And finally:

"...Our empirical knowledge has two sources, sensibility and understanding. If our mind consisted of nothing but the passive ability to receive sensations, we should have a manifold multiplicity of intuitions, but no knowledge of what the manifold contained..." [1968, p. 23] [19]

17 I owe T.K. Bikson (in personal communication) an alternative -- and to my mind preferable -- rendition of Kant's dictum: "Concepts without percepts are empty, percepts without concepts are blind".

18 In much the same way, neither the chicken nor the egg, neither nature nor nurture, neither environment nor behavior, are independent primes. The Western intellectual tradition is replete with reductionist pseudo-puzzles.

19 Kant makes matters more complicated yet by observing that there must exist a mediating schema for matching categories of the understanding with sensible appearance, given that there is no guarantee that the two would be otherwise 'homogenous' -- i.e. isomorphic. This mediating function is presumably part of Kant's **apriori synthetic**, involving our space-time grid. Kant's transcendental schema is thus a precondition for matching concepts with percepts. To quote Kemp once again:
"...Now since there is no homogeneity between category and appearance, and since nevertheless the appearance has in the end to be subsumed under the category, there must, Kant says, be some third thing which is homogeneous both with the category and with the appearance, and which mediates between the two; this third thing, which must clearly be in one respect intelligible and in another sensible , consists in what Kant calls the transcendental schema. The key to this is the notion of time..." [1968, p. 30].
For a somewhat compatible view, see Givón (1979a, Ch. 8).

1.4.2.2. **Kant's analytic and apriori-synthetic**

First, Kant introduces the concept of **analytic** knowledge; that is, knowledge that comes to us by knowing the definitions of terms, the rules of logic, or the rules of games. Such knowledge is thus in principle **tautological.**[20] Analytic knowledge is in some sense thus **presupposed,** being true by convention.

Second, Kant introduces the notion of **apriori-synthetic** knowledge; that is, knowledge of facts that are always true of this world -- but not by analytic necessity. The latter is Kant's **transcendental schema** of space and time. That schema underlies our perceptual/conceptual apparatus itself as pre-condition to all possible experience of this world. Possible experience presupposes such a schema, rather than comprises it. Thus, consider the following passage from the *Critique of Pure Reason of Pure Reason* (Smith, 1929):

"...the representation of space must be presupposed. The representation of space cannot, therefore, be empirically obtained from the relations of outer appearance. On the contrary, this outer experience is itself possible at all only through that representation..." [p. 68]

It is possible to argue -- as I shall indeed argue later on [21] -- that Kant's analytic and apriori-synthetic are both early precursors of the pragmatic notion of **presupposition,** or **shared background.**

1.4.2.3. **The transcendental schema as a relative point-of-view**

In his discussion of the apriori-synthetic transcendental schema of space, Kant observes (Smith, 1929):

"....It is, therefore, only from the human standpoint that we can speak of space, of extended things etc. If we depart from the *subjective condition* under which we alone can have outer intuition...the representation of space stands for nothing whatsoever..." [p. 71; emphases are mine; TG]

Our point of view vis-a-vis the outside world is thus **relative.** Again, consider (Smith, 1929):

---

20 See discussion of Wittgenstein's *Tractatus* further below.
21 See further discussion in Chapter 4, below.

"...we cannot judge in regard to the intuitions of other thinking beings, whether they are bound by the same conditions as those which limit our intuition and which *for us* are universally valid. If we add to the concept of the *subject* of a judgement the *limitation* under which the judgement is made, the judgement is then unconditionally valid..." [p. 72]

In other words, a judgement -- knowledge, description -- is only unconditionally valid ('fully characterized') if the subject making it and his point of view -- or context -- are taken into account. This is certainly a clear articulation of a pragmatic, context-dependent theory of description.

1.4.2.4. **The world for us vs. the world for itself**

Given the discussion above, it is thus possible to view Kant's caution about the low likelihood of our ever coming to know 'the thing for itself' (as distinct from 'the thing for us') not as a mere species of healthy skepticism, but rather as an early precursor of the pragmatics of **gestalt** and **point of view**. Kant is willing to concede that there must be 'something out there' to stimulate our sensory perception. For a constructionist, that is a fairly safe abduction from the mere existence of experience, fine details notwithstanding. 'The thing for itself', however, remains unavailable to us, given our limited, relative point of view. Thus, in Kemp's discussion of Kant's *Transcendental Analytic* we find:

"...'the most the understanding can achieve *a priori* is to anticipate the form of a possible experience in general' (A246 B303). It does not give us knowledge of things as they are in themselves, but only of things as they appear to us..." [1968, p. 38]

I think we are entitled to read Kant as suggesting that it is our limited point of view -- the frame -- that determines the form of reality as it appears to us. Therefore, to discuss the nature of reality outside that frame -- or outside *any* frame (i.e. 'the thing for itself') -- really makes little sense. Kant thus anticipated the central theme of modern pragmatics. [22]

---

22 I am indebted to T. K. Bikson and Fred Kroon (in personal communication; but see also Kroon, 1981) for pointing out to me how Kant's 'transcendental schema', 'apriori synthetic' and 'the world for us' indeed presage a pragmatic approach to mind and meaning.

1.4.2.5. Kant the Platonist

There is no evidence in Kant's work to suggest a pragmatic approach to the formal nature of categories of the mind, i.e. a rejection of Platonic/Aristotelian discreteness and rigid criteria. For this, one must await Peirce or, more explicitly, Wittgenstein.

1.5. Peirce and Pragmatism

We turn now to consider, not for the last time, the acknowledged Godfather of modern pragmatics, Charles Sanders Peirce. His multiple insights range over major landmarks of the pragmatic agenda, often without being acknowledged by latter-day practitioners. At this point we will survey, rather briefly, the main areas of his contribution to pragmatics.[23] The first two -- abductive inference and semeiotics -- will be covered in greater detail in Chapters 3 and 7 below, respectively.

1.5.1. Abductive inference

The dichotomy between the two extreme schools of Western epistemology, empiricist and rationalist, was later echoed in the Philosophy of Science (see Chapter 8, below), in the discussion of modes of knowledge ('modes of inference'). Empiricists traditionally tended to emphasize induction as the prime mode of knowledge, while rationalists, quite predictably, have tended to emphasize deduction. Echoing Kant's rejection of both reductionist extremes, Peirce resuscitated Aristotle's third mode, which he rechristened abduction. This mode of **hypothesis** often involves **analogical reasoning**, and thus the pragmatic, context-dependent notions of *similarity* and *relevance*. As suggested earlier above, neither analogy nor similarity nor relevance may be characterized by inductive or dedutive means. All three also involve shades and gradations, again a characteristic feature of pragmatics.[24]

---

23 Such a short survey is both inadequate and presumptuous, given the enormous range of subjects Peirce had covered, his voluminous written output, and last but not least the considerable difficulty one experiences in penetrating his prose. I will thus not be surprised if in some dark corner of Peirce's writings further invaluable gems of pragmatic insight still lurk, waiting to be discovered. My own access to Peirce owes much to personal contact with a number of *bona fide* Peirceans, most particularly T. K. Bikson, Raimo Anttila, John Haiman and Michael Shapiro. The latter's book *The Sense of Grammar* (1983) was particularly helpful to me in my attempt to understand Peirce's semeiotics.

24 Deductive, inductive and abductive inference are further discussed in Chapters 7 and 8, below.

1.5.2. The interpretant as a third term in semeiotics

Peirce is responsible for introducing the notion of **interpretant** as the third term in the semeiotic relation, the term that binds the sign to its designatum in the minds of the interpreter. As will be suggested in Chapter 3, below, the interpretant is merely a stand-in for **perceived context**. Peirce thus took the non-pragmatic semeiotics that had prevailed since Aristotle and pointed out to its necessary pragmatic dimension.

1.5.3. Non-Platonic categorization

Peirce's well documented penchant for discrete trichotomies leaves off a distinct Platonic flavor. Nonetheless, in his explicit treatment of a number of sub-areas of pragmatics, he comes down -- in the final analysis -- on the side of non-discrete, context-dependent categorization.

Consider first Peirce's discussion of **iconic signs** (pictures, diagrams, metaphors), which hinges upon the concept of 'similarity'. In order for objects to resemble each other, the categories underlying them must be -- in principle -- non-Platonic. This is so because of two inherent features associated with 'resemblance':

(a) It may be infinitely and non-discretely **graded**; and
(b) it must be **contextually** mediated.

Implicitly, then, Peirce's semeiotics is founded upon non-Platonic categorization.

In two other respects, Peirce's discussion of categories goes considerably beyond Kant's Platonism, often presaging Wittgenstein. We will discuss the two in order.

1.5.3.1. The multi-dimensionality of semantic space

Peirce considered most natural (thus also linguistic) signs to be a mixture of three types of signs -- **symbol**, **index**, and **icon**. The three pure types are merely extreme facets of complex, multi-dimensional signs. Implicitly, Peirce thus pioneered the notion of 'impure categories', categories that are distributed along a multi-dimensional space.

1.5.3.2. **The non-discreteness of semantic dimensions**

Peirce's three types of icons -- **picture, diagram**, and **metaphor** -- are clearly three points along a continuum.[25] Whether we are fully entitled to interpret Peirce as an *explicit* non-Platonic categorizer remains to some degree a matter of conjecture. Buchler's interpretation seems to suggest contextually-mediate meaning:

"...A term has meaning, in other words, if it is definable by other terms describing sensible properties. The way in which, generally speaking, these other terms, which may not be in turn thus defined, acquire meaning, is by being *associated* or *correlated* in their *usage*, according to empirical conventions..." [1939, p. 113; emphases are mine; TG]

The reference to conventions and usage is decidedly Wittgensteinean. Further:

"...Peirce's emphasis on 'percept' and 'operation' is in effect an emphasis that meaning is something *public*. We properly explain the meaning of a term to someone not by eloquently attempting to evoke familiar images in his mind, but by prescribing how he can gain perceptual acquaintance with the word denoted. The appeal is not primarily to imagination but to tests that can be undertaken by everybody..." [1939, p. 115].

With sufficient leeway, one may read here a rendition of post-Wittgenstein Philosophy of Ordinary Language.
Further suggestions that Peirce may have considered categorial space to be scalar flow naturally from two key components upon which, he believed, meaning was founded -- **circumstances** and **habit**. Peirce clearly considers both to be graded and non-discrete. Thus:

"...Mill says that it means that if in all circumstances attending two phenomena are the same, they will be alike. But taken strictly this means absolutely nothing, since no two phenomena ever can happen in circumstances precisely alike, nor are two phenomena precisely alike..." [Peirce, 1940, p. 221]

And further:

"...Habits have grades of strength varying for complete dissociation to inseparable association. These grades are mixtures of promptitudes of

---

25 See further discussion in Chapter 3, below.

action, say excitability and other ingredients... Habit change oftenconsists of raising or lowering the strength of habit...." [Peirce, 1940, pp. 277-278]

Consider next Peirce's discussion of **vagueness**:

"...Logicians have too much neglected the study of *vagueness*, not suspecting the important part it plays in mathematical thought... Wherever degree or any other possibility of continuous variation subsists, absolute precision is impossible. Much else must be vague, because no man's interpretation of words is based on exactly the same experience as any other man's..." [Peirce, 1940, pp. 294-295]

If one reads 'experience' to mean 'context', then a clearly Wittgensteinean theory of meaning indeed emerges.

Finally, in his discussion of natural categories (such as biological classification), Peirce anticipates rather prophetically the current discussion of **prototype semantics** (see Chapter 2, below). The crucial ingredient is his observation on the role of **frequency distribution** and the **clustering** of populations around some **normative mean**:

"...It may be quite impossible to draw a sharp line of demarcation between two classes, although they are real and natural classes in strict truth. Namely, this will happen when the form about which the individuals of one class cluster is not so unlike the form about which the individuals of another class cluster, but the variations from each middling form may not precisely agree. In such a case, we may know in regard to any intermediate form what proportion of the objects of that form has one *purpose* and what proportion the other; but unless we have some supplementary information we cannot tell which one had one *purpose* and which one the other..." [Peirce, 1931, pp. 87-88; emphases are mine; TG]

1.6. Ludwig Wittgenstein

Wittgenstein's pragmatic approach to semantic categories will be discussed in considerable detail in Chapter 2, below. His flexible, non-discrete, context-dependent approach to meaning has had an enormous impact on the cognitive sciences -- in particular psychology, anthropology and linguistics.[26] In the space below I will merely summarize the two major points that constitute the core of Wittgenstein's contribution to the modern pragmatic agenda. One of those has been consistently ig-

---

26 Paradoxically, after two short decades of intense excitement, the interest in Wittgenstein within Philosophy seems to have degenerated into, largely, textual exegesis and cultish insularity.

nored, presumably because of its association with the 'early' Wittgenstein.

1.6.1. The rejection of deductive logic as a means for transacting new information

In his *Tractatus* (1918), a book often -- and to my mind mistakenly -- lumped together with Logical Positivism, Wittgenstein observes that the propositions of deductive logic can be all reduced to either tautologies or contradictions. Neither, he points out, could possibly serve to transact new knowledge. In rejecting deductive logic as possible model for communication, Wittgenstein--probably unintentionally-- came tantalizingly close to defining two major parameters of the pragmatics of communication, both anathemas to formal logic:

(a) The use of Language in communication is not a matter of truth or falsity of atomic propositions, but rather a process of transferring information from one mind to another.

(b) In communication, totally old (thus tautological to the receiver) information and **totally new** (thus incoherent to the receiver) information are equally useless. This is so because:

(i) Information that is totally old is totally redundant, it offers **no motivation** for the receiver to participate in the communicative transaction; and

(ii) Information that is totally new is totally incoherent, it offers **no overlap** with the receiver's existing knowledge, it thus **cannot be integrated** with it.

In order for information to be processed by some receiver -- i.e. integrated coherently into the receiver's pre-existing knowledge -- it must lie somewhere between these two extreme poles. Implicitly thus, the crucial role of the receiver in information processing, and thus of the receiver's **background knowledge**, which forms an important part of the transmitter's **discourse context**, is anticipated in the 'early' Wittgenstein. We will return to discuss this subject in Chapter 4, below.

One may argue, I think legitimately, that deductive logic, in setting up the notions of tautology and contradiction, has already made an incipient, covert move toward the pragmatics of context. This is so because tautology and contradiction are not properties of an atomic proposition, but rather of a proposition vis-a-vis another proposition. That other proposition may be considered the *context*. In the embryonic discourse called 'logical proof', the **premise(s)** is equivalent to our pragmatic notion of context. Deductive logic has thus been dealing with context implicitly -- surreptitiously -- all along. But the 'logical' context has always remained rigidly constrained, or **closed**. In the pragmatics of natural language, and thus of mind, context is, forever **open ended**.

1.6.2. The attack on Platonic categorization

Wittgenstein's contribution to pragmatics is of course much more intimately associated with his *Philosophical Investigations* (1953). Here one may observe three interlocking themes:

(a) The context-dependence of meaning;

(b) The flexibility, non-discreteness and scalarity of semantic dimensions; and

(c) The 'family resemblance' -- thus non-criterial -- nature of semantic categories.

We will return to discuss these three themes in considerable detail in Chapter 2, below.

1.7. Other strands of pragmatics

The pragmatic agenda in the second half of the 20th Century reminds one, in retrospect, of a dam burst. Many of the streams feeding into the swollen river, to borrow Peirce's metaphor, had been meandering, sluggishly and unobtrusively, for a long time. They had accumulated, slowly, leisurely, behind the dam of deductive logic. Somewhere along the way, the flow began to quicken, the tempo picked up. And all of a sudden the entire dam is threatened. In the space below I will briefly recount what seem to me to be some of the more obvious components of this pragmatic dam burst.

1.7.1. The language-and-culture tradition

With illustrious antecedents in philosophy, such as Kant, Peirce and Wittgenstein, it is easy to forget that other cognitive disciplines -- in their own way and within their own peculiar methodologies and preoccupations -- have also participated in the growth of modern pragmatics. At the intersection of linguistics and anthropology stands one such contribution, arising from the comparative study of cultures. The shared ('generic') **cultural world view** indeed constitutes the bulk of the background knowledge -- context -- vis-a-vis which inter-personal behavior and communication take place.

The balance between universality and specificity of human mind and human language easily translates into the question of how universal -- or how group-specific -- human culture is. Aristotle had already occupied himself with this issue, setting up the agenda for later work on universals.[27]

But the bulk of substantive contributions came from pioneer cross-cultural investigators, such as Whitney, von Humboldt, Boaz, Kroeber, Malinowski, Sapir and Whorf. The profound functionalism that permeated the work of these illustrious scholars is already, by definition, a brand of pragmatics (see section 1.7.2., below). Their consciousness of the intertwined nature of the language-and-culture complex enriched our understanding of culture as the ever-present context. Finally, their investigation into the balance between linguistic-cultural universality and specificity defined the agenda for a yet ongoing debate. We will return to discuss these issues in Chapter 9, below.

1.7.2. Early functionalism: The communicative context

The description of any structured instrument can be approached from two distinct points of view. It may be described purely in terms of its **structure**. In biology, this would amount to describing the **anatomy** of the various organs. Alternatively, the mere structural description of an instrument may be supplemented by a description of its correlated **function**. In biology, this would amount to describing the **physiology** of the organs. In biology, purely structural description, without seeking correlated function(s), has not been seriously entertained since Aristotle. Indeed, what would be the point? Likewise in the early history of linguistics, an implicit functionalism prevailed, beginning with the semantically motivated categories of Aristotle and the medieval *Modistae*, continuing with the implicit cognitive assumptions of the Cartesians,

---

27 In his *De Interpretatione*, Aristotle makes the following brief observation concerning the non-universal nature of the relation between language and mind, as compared with the universal relation between mind and world:

   "...Now spoken sounds are symbols of affections of the soul, and written marks symbols of spoken sounds. And just as written marks are not the same for all men, neither are spoken sounds. But what these are in the first place signs of -- affections of the soul -- are the same for all; and what these affections are likenesses of -- actual things -- are also the same..." [Ackrill, tr. & ed., 1963, p. 43].

and following with the mentalism of late 19th Century German Roman-
tics such as von Humboldt and Paul. Even the more structure-conscious
linguistic traditions, such as the 19th Century's Neo-Grammarians, or the
so-called 'Traditional Grammarians' such as Jespersen,[28] were profoundly functionalist in their interpretation of linguistic structure. Only in the
early 20th century, under the impact of behaviorism -- that extreme brand
of empiricism -- did explicit, unvarnished **structuralism** emerge upon the
linguistic scene, in the forceful person of Leonard Bloomfield.[29]

Bloomfield's extreme position, closely bound to his naive, dogmatic
empiricism, proclaimed that the instrument -- language -- may be
described without reference to its function -- meaning or communicative
use. It is indeed curious that the other modern school of linguistic structuralism, Generative Grammar, somehow contrives to trace its
philosophical roots to the philosophical rationalism of Descartes.[30]

The work of all 20th Century functionalist schools, from Jespersen and
Sapir onward,[31] falls squarely within the scope of pragmatics, insofar as
they have all insisted that the structure of language can only be understood and explained (rather than merely described) in the context of its
communicative use, i.e. its function. We will return to discuss some of
these issues in Chapters 7 and 10, below.

1.7.3. The Speech-act tradition: Purposive context

The 'late' Wittgenstein (1953) left behind as legacy the distinct British
school of **Ordinary Language Philosophy**. A sub-tradition of that school,
clustering around 'performative', 'speech-act' or 'illocutionary force'
analysis, has contributed massively to the recent pragmatic agenda,
beginning with Austin (1962) and continuing with Searle (1970), Grice
(1968/1975) and a veritable avalanche that came in their wake. This sub-
tradition occupies itself primarily with one important aspect of context -
- the goal or **purpose** of verbal acts. Still, many works within this tradition
branched out into the study of other important themes in pragmatics.[32]
We will return to this topic in more detail in Chapter 4, below.

---

28 See Jespersen's *Philosophy of Grammar* (1924).
29 See Bloomfield's *Language* (1933), as well as further discussion in Chapter 8, below.
30 This tracing back of antecedence was accomplished somewhat post-hoc in Chomsky (1966).
    Chomsky trained in linguistics under Z. Harris, a leading Bloomfieldian structuralist. His
    training in formal logic was also within a purely structuralist tradition, which his early
    book, *Syntactic Structures* (1957), clearly reflects.
31 One may list here at least the Prague School, Kenneth Pike, Dwight Bolinger and Michael
    Halliday.
32 See in particular Cole (ed., 1981).

1.7.4. **The presupposition tradition: Shared knowledge**

Formal logic, from its very inception a non-pragmatic, atomistic, context-free mode of semantic analysis, has been forced to gradually accommodate the pragmatic facts of life, as it wrestled with the complexities of natural language interpretation. The concept of presupposition, itself at least as old as Kant, was pressed into service to account for a range of context-related phenomena. The need for this arose from what was seen initially as a -- slight but disturbing -- 'distortion' in the interpretation of propositions of natural language. Some propositions -- or sometimes portions within them -- seemed to not be 'asserted' as true or false. Rather, they seemed to be 'presupposed', as **preconditions** for the meaningfulness (in logic truth or falsity) of other propositions.

The intuitive connection between 'logical' presupposition and the pragmatics of discourse context, communicative intent and speech act is of course obvious. Formal logicians from Strawson (1950) onward, however, have fought valiantly to constrain presupposition as a property of atomic propositions. They thus attempted to gloss over the obvious ontology of presupposition in the **speaker's communicative intent**, and in his/her context-bound assumptions about the **hearer's** communicative intent. This purging of speaker and hearer from the description of meaning is only a natural consequence of Russell's (1919) injunctions. It was transferred into linguistics beginning with Keenan (1969), thereby precipitating a litany of presuppositional literature in the 1970s and 1980's.[33] The main thrust of that literature has been, to this day, an attempt to sub-divide context on its multifarious shades and varieties into neat, discrete categories. The entire package is then to be grafted into a truth-conditional logic.[34] In this way, from having begun initially as an important opening toward pragmatics and the study of language in context, presuppositional analysis soon degenerated into a rear-guard action, purporting to reinforce the claim of a non-pragmatic instrument -- deductive logic -- on the semantic analysis of natural language. We will return to discuss these issues in Chapters 4 and 6, below.

---

33 See e.g. Fillmore (1971), Horn (1972), Karttunen (1974), *inter alia*. The seminal paper which triggered the linguistic world's interest in presupposition was actually rather detached from logic, Kiparski and Kiparski (1968).

34 See e.g. Keenan (1971), Gazdar (1979), Oh and Dinneen (eds, 1979), or Sperber and Wilson (1985), *inter alia*. The fatal attraction of the siren song of deductive logic to otherwise sober linguists, in the face of recurrent frustration and a veritable mountain of recalcitrant data, remains a great mystery.

1.7.5. Modal logic and possible worlds: The indexing of context

Modal logic began as a rather modest attempt to deal formally with non-fact propositional modalities such as 'possible' and 'future', with 'intended states' and 'tense', and most particularly with the problem of reference under the scope of such modalities.[35] Soon, however, **possible worlds logic** was pressed into service to deal wholesale with the problem of context. Consider, for example, the following lines from Montague (1970):

"...To interpret a pragmatic language L we must specify several things. In the first place, we must determine the set of all possible contexts of *use* -- or rather, of all complexes of *relevant aspects* of possible contexts of use; we may call such complexes *indices*, or to borrow Dana Scott's term, *points of reference*..." [p. 144; first two emphases are mine; TG]

As possible candidates for 'indices' only the indexical 'I' is explicitly mentioned, although in outlining the problem of context earlier, Montague refers to indexical expressions in general (i.e. person, time, place). The intractability of this list-approach, and the open endedness of 'possible contexts' and 'relevant aspects', somehow never seemed to daunt the late Montague. In his wake, others began to move in the obvious direction and enlarge the list of indices. Lewis (1972), for example listed eight types of context; so that a fully specified 'index' is now:

"...any octuple of which the first coordinate is *a possible world*, the second coordinate is *a moment of time*, the third coordinate is *a place*, the fourth coordinate is a set of persons (or other creatures capable of being *a speaker*), the fifth coordinate is a set of person (or other creatures capable of being *an audience*), the sixth coordinate is a set (possibly empty) of concrete things *capable of being pointed at*, the seventh coordinate is *a segment of discourse*, and the eighth coordinate an infinite sequence of things..." [1972, p. 176; emphases are mine; TG]

The considerable futility of such an enterprise -- the instability and open-endedness of each 'indexed' element of the context -- was glossed over at the time. In a later work, Lewis (1979) acknowledges the problem more explicitly, with detailed illustrations from a more realistic sample ap-

---

35 See e.g. Kripke (1963, 1972), Cocchiarella (1965), Hinttika (1967), Purtill (1968) or Scott (1970), *inter alia*.

proximating natural conversation. Similar misgivings were expressed earlier by Creswell (1972):

"...Writers who, like David Lewis[11], do try to give a bit more body to these notions, talk about time, place, speakers, hearers,...etc. and then go through agonies of conscience in trying to decide whether they have taken account of enough..." [p. 8] [36]

The logicians, again in Russell's well-motivated tradition, thus attempt to sanitize, constrain -- and sweep under the neat rug of a closed deductive system -- the intractable problem of context.

1.7.6. Ethnography of Speech: Social interaction as context

An important strand in modern pragmatics comes to us from the interface of sociology, anthropology and linguistics, via the works of Labov, Gumperz, Goffman, Sachs and Schegloff, Geerz, Garfinkel, Brown and Levinson, and many others, under various labels.[37] These works probe into the social, interactional and inter-personal context of communication and the face-to-face speech situation. Notions such as power, status gradients, politeness and deference, and control of the floor during communication (i.e. 'turn-taking') have been studied and elaborated. Many of those intersect rather naturally with the earlier pragmatic tradition of speech-act analysis. We will return to discuss a number of these topics in Chapter 4, below.

1.7.7. Developmental pragmatics

An important recent addition to the pragmatic agenda is the communicatively oriented study of child language acquisition.[38] An earlier rationalist-structuralist dogma[39] had held that the human language capacity is largely innate, and that therefore the role of linguistic input -- and thus of the communicative interaction and context -- in the acquisi-

36 Creswell (1972) goes on to suggest -- tongue in cheek -- that in interpreting the bar-room poem line 'Just fetch your Jim *another quart*' one might perhaps need to index "...a 'previous drinks' context...".
37 Sub-strands of this tradition have been called at one time or another 'Ethnolinguistics' (Gumperz, 1977,1982), 'Conversational Analysis' (Sacks, Schegloff and Jefferson, 1974; Brown and Levinson, 1978, 1979), 'Ethnomethodology' (Goffman, 1974, 1976; Garfinkel, 1972; Geertz, 1972), or 'Sociolinguistics' (Labov, 1972a, 1972b; Ochs, 1979a).
38 See for example Scollon (1974), Bates (1976), Keenan and Schieffelin (1976), Ochs (1979b), Ochs and Schieffelin (eds, 1979), *inter alia*.
39 As in, e.g., Chomsky (1968) and the long list of structuralist acquisition studies inspired thereby.

tion of language is minimal. Developmental pragmatics has evolved as an empirically-motivated reaction to that early dogma, endeavoring to study the acquisition of language in its natural, functional, communicative context.

1.7.8. **Pragmatics and machines: Plans, Goals, Scripts**

Within Artificial Intelligence (AI) there emerged a small but persistent pragmatic tradition, beginning with Winograd's (1970) attempt to incorporate speech-act notions into the algorithm, and continuing more recently with the scripts-plans-and-goals approach of Schank and Abelson (1977) or Levy (1979), *inter alia*. Since in principle pragmatics cannot be constrained within a closed algorithm without ceasing to be pragmatics, the various pragmatic moves within the AI community represent at least a tacit admission of the limits of the deductive algorithm as model for natural language, communication and behavior.

1.7.9. **Gestalt, prototypes and metaphors**

One must also note that pragmatics has had a vigorous presence within post-Behaviorist cognitive psychology, in the areas of gestalt and cognitive priming (see discussion in Chapter 3, below), and similarly in the psychology of perception (Attneave, 1959). More recently, a convergence has taken place between several disciplines looking at the nature of human categorization and **metaphoric meaning**, spanning Goguen's (1969) work on **fuzzy sets logic**, Rosch's (1973a, 1973b) work on **natural categories** in cognitive psychology, Ortonyi's (ed., 1979) work in the psychology of communication, Lakoff and Johnson's (1980) linguistic work on metaphor, and Johnson's (ed., 1981) work on metaphor in philosophy. This inter-disciplinary convergence, ascribed by some to 'late' Wittgensteinean influence, will be discussed in considerable detail in Chapter 2, below.

1.7.10. **Biology and evolution**

In the history of the study of the diversity of life forms, a certain parallel can be seen with the history of Western epistemology, with the balance shifting periodically between non-pragmatic and pragmatic schools of thought. Thus, creationist pre-evolutionary schools considered all extant biological species to be rigidly fixed -- much like Platonic/Aristotelian categories. In contrast, a dynamic, evolutionary, flux-like view of species is by itself already crypto-pragmatic.

Within the evolutionary camp itself, innatist non-pragmatic schools first predominated, expounding upon the wonders of **pre-ordained** speciation. The agent of such pre-ordination was the Deity itself, which mandated life to evolve toward some spiritual apex, and for the glory of God. (In the pinch, more recently, the secular deity of **molecular genetics** can also be pressed into the service of pre-determinism). An early version of this approach can be seen in Charles Bonnet's **preformation**,[40] which proposed to view all development as already present in the embryo (for ontogenesis), or in the earlier species (for phylogenesis). In somewhat the same vein, the late 18th Century German school of **Naturphilosophie** envisioned a universal, transcendental order governing evolution toward aesthetically and ethically higher peaks.[41]

A true, potentially pragmatic transformation eventually took place, first with Lamarck underlying interactive functionalism, later with Darwin's recognition of the role of the **environment** -- i.e., context -- in shaping the evolution of organisms. Here once again, one soon observes a familiar philosophical split.   On the one hand there is what Gould (1980) characterizes as the extreme **Neo-Darwinian** approach, according to which the role of environmental selection is fully deterministic, with the organism's purposive behavior having no role.   This school is rather reminiscent of extreme philosophical empiricism.   At the other extreme one finds **naive Lamarckians**,[42] according to whom the organism's purposive behavior is paramount in directing its own evolution. This school may be likened to extreme philosophical rationalism. As Gould (1980) points out, neither extreme is likely to be tenable. A more realistic approach is likely to be, once again, an **interactionist** -- thus pragmatic -- middle-ground. We will return to explore these issue in Chapter 10, below.

40 See discussion of Bonnet (1764) in Gould (1977, Ch. 2).
41 With august literary figures such as Schelling and Goethe, but also eminent biologists such as Kielmeyer and Meckel; for discussion again see Gould (1977, ch. 2) as well as Chapter 10, below.
42 Gould (1980) mentions in particular Koestler (1972).

1.8. Projections: Toward an integrated, pragmatics of organism, mind and behavior

In this book I will attempt to emulate pragmatics itself in one crucial respect: I will let the book remain unabashedly open-ended and incomplete. This flows rather naturally from my conviction that many of pragmatics' most profound ramifications have yet to be discovered, understood and articulated. It is, in addition, my suspicion that pragmatics -- as a method -- may hold the key to an integrated understanding of behavior and cognition, thus ultimately to an understanding of the evolution of biological organisms. Within this general context, pragmatics also hold the key to our understanding of language and mind. To the extent that so-called **Cognitive Science** is ever to become more than a political catch phrase, a passing fad, I suspect that pragmatics also holds the key to this yet-to-be unified field. Lastly, to the extent that the humanities have a realistic hope of becoming amenable to systematic investigation by some science-like method, pragmatics may hold the key to that as well.[43]

---

43 Feyerabend's (1975) wholesale rejection of all method, essentially on the grounds that no method *by itself* is 100% effective, is an unnecessarily extremist construction of science, in that it implicitly concedes the reductionists' passion for all-or-nothing solutions. In contrast, a pragmatic middle-ground of *methodological pluralism* has been taken for granted in the more 'messy' sciences such as biology and cognitive psychology (and, if Hanson (1958) is to be believed, also in physics). Indeed, earlier on, Feyerabend (1970) himself had advocated such pluralism. By 1975, Feyerabend had apparently opted for throwing the baby out with the bathwater, presumably on the theory that if one cannot have complete order, one might as well embrace total chaos. If cognizing and behaving organisms were to adopt the same methodological purism, their path to swift evolutionary extinction would be assured. These topics will be discussed at considerable length in chapters 7 and 8, below.

CHAPTER 2

CATEGORIES AND PROTOTYPES: BETWEEN PLATO AND WITTGENSTEIN

2.1. Discrete categories, fuzzy gradations and prototypes*

"There is a mysterious wisdom by which phenomena among themselves disparate can be called analogous names, just as divine things can be designated by terrestrial terms, and through equivocal symbols God can be called lion or leopard; and death can be called sword; joy, flame; flame, death; death, abyss; abyss, perdition; perdition, raving; and raving, passion...The more it is a dissimilar similitude and not literal, the more a metaphor reveals its truth..."

Umberto Eco,
The Name of the Rose (1980, p. 248)

2.1.1. Preamble

In the preceding chapter we surveyed the philosophical background upon which our discussion of mental categories can now proceed. From the dawn of Western epistemology, we noted, three traditional themes pervaded the discussion of mental categories:

(a) The **source** of categories; that is, whether they are **innate** ('conceptual', as rationalists would have it), or **external** ('perceptual', as empiricists would have it).

*I am indebted to Fr. Garth Hallett SJ, Michael Posner and John Verhaar for helpful comments and suggestions. An early precursor of this chapter was presented at the Symposium on Categorization and Noun Classification (Eugene, Oregon, September 1983), and benefitted greatly from the discussion there, in particular from comments by George Lakoff and Pete Becker.

(b) The **designatum** of mental categories; that is, what they stand for in the semeiotic relation.
(c) The **formal nature** of mental categories; i.e. whether they are discrete and absolute, or graded and context dependent.

Question (a) will not concern us here. Question (b) will be discussed in considerable detail in Chapter 3, below. In this chapter we will concern ourselves primarily with question (c).

2.1.2. **Extreme Platonic categorization**

As noted earlier,[1] both rationalists and empiricists, from Plato and Aristotle down, have subscribed to the view that mental categories are discrete and absolute. As we have also noted, both Plato (posing as Socrates) and Aristotle had their difficulties, or moments of pragmatist's doubt, concerning the absoluteness of categories. For brevity's sake, I will refer to the absolutist approach to categories from now on as the *Platonic* tradition. According to this tradition, membership in a category depends on the unambiguous possession or non-possession of some **criterial properties**. Such properties must be both **necessary** and **sufficient** in order to determine membership in a category. The possession or non-possession of a property is not a matter of degree or equivocation. **The law of the excluded middle** is strictly adhered to. Vagueness and indecision may invade the mental system due to insufficient information, but in principle, gradation and ambiguity have no theoretical status in this system. Such a system may be illustrated diagrammatically as:

(1) **Diagram of extreme Platonic categorization**

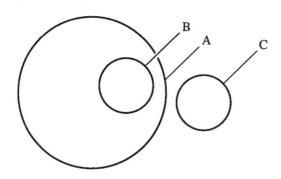

---

1   See Chapter 1, section 1.4.1.

In (1) above, A is the criterial property determining membership in the category. Individuals in sub-category B possess that property, and are thus members of A. Individuals in sub-category C do not possess that criterial property and are not members of A.

2.1.3. **Extreme Wittgensteinean categorization**

A second approach to categories, diametrically opposed to the Platonic, will be tentatively labeled as the extreme *Wittgensteinean,* after the 'late' Wittgenstein (1953). The question of whether Wittgenstein was indeed an extremist proponent of this approach will be discussed further below. According to this approach, categories are neither absolute nor discrete. To begin with, they are **relative,** or **contingent** upon **context** (use, purpose, point of view, general schema, etc.). Second, they are **fuzzy edged,** and the space defining them is a **continuum.** Category membership may be a matter of **degree.** Members of a category may relate to each other through **family resemblance** -- a non-logical, pragmatic notion. Member *a* may thus resemble member *b,* *b* may resemble *c,* *c* may resemble *d,* etc. But *a* and *z* may not resemble each other at all -- and still belong to the same category. This second extreme type of categorization may be illustrated diagrammatically as:

(2) **Diagram of extreme Wittgensteinean categorization**

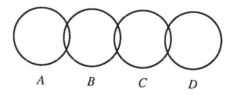

$$A \quad\quad B \quad\quad C \quad\quad D$$

In (2) above, sub-categories a,b,c,d, are equally members of a single meta-category, even though the intersection of shared properties (or 'similarities') between each adjacent pair is not the same as for the other pairs.

2.1.4. The prototype approach to categorization

It is important to recognize that both extreme approaches to categorization, represent important *aspects* of category formation, in cognition, language and behavior. There is indeed a certain *measure* of categorial discreteness in our perceptual, conceptual and linguistic organization. At the **sign** ('code') level, lexical items, morphemes, discrete syntactic structures and even *some* of the rules governing behavior and communication, all constitute -- up to a point -- a huge reservoir of *prima facie* evidence for the existence of such discreteness. At the same time, the very same phenomena in cognition, language and behavior, when studied closely and with sufficient care, furnish a large body of evidence in support of non-discreteness, fuzzy edgedness, scalarity and context relativity of categories and of the rules that govern their application. If one is then to be empirically responsible and philosophically honest, one could not subscribe to either extreme position in attempting to understand mind, language and behavior. Rather, one must recognize a middle ground, a **hybrid solution**, the pragmatic alternative.

The story of how the pragmatic alternative to the extremist approaches to categorization -- prototype theory -- came into being, is a happy case of convergence in Cognitive Science. As is often the case in empirical work, the philosophical lineage of this convergence may have been adopted largely *post hoc*, and it is not clear whether this adoptive lineage indeed played a significant role initially. The inception point of prototype categorization may be traced to experimental psychology, via Posner and Keele's (1968) work on the genesis of abstract ideas. Posner (1986) further credits, in retrospect, the works of Attneave (1959) in the psychology of perception, as well as Bransford and Franks (1971).[2] The thread was then picked up by Rosch (1973a, 1973b, 1975),[3] who was also responsible for suggesting the aptness of Wittgenstein's 'family resemblance' metaphor. Quite independently, Berlin and Kay's (1969) study of **folk taxonomies** and the cross-language distribution of color terms [4] brought Anthropology into the arena. And linguists soon joined the fray with Ross's work on squishes (1972, 1973, 1974) and Lakoff's on fuzzy concepts and hedges (1973, 1977, 1982).[5]

---

2   Posner (in personal communication) also points out that prototypes came into psychology from the notion of 'schema', via Kant, Head and Bartlett; then through Galton's idea of composite photographs representing different but related people. The notion of 'family resemblance' was discussed by Price in his *Thinking and Experience*, probably independently of Wittgenstein.

3   See also Rosch and Lloyd (eds, 1978).

4   See also Kay and McDaniel (1978) and Coleman and Kay (1981), *inter alia*.

5   See also Lakoff and Johnson (1980), *inter alia*.

Like the extreme Wittgensteinean approach, prototype semantics recognizes non-discrete categorial space both within and between categories.[6] Like Wittgenstein, again, it observes that natural mental categories are seldom defined in terms of one -- or even few -- necessary and sufficient criterial properties. Rather, natural categories are formed at the **intersection** of several 'characteristic', 'typical', 'normative' features. Such intersections, where significant **clustering** of individual members of the category's population is to be found, tend to be *relatively* stable and replicable, but not absolutely so. We may represent this third type of categorization, prototype clustering, by the following intersection diagram:

(3) **Diagram of prototype-clustering categorization**

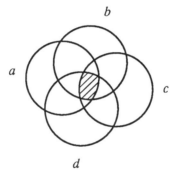

The shaded area in (3) represents the portion of the categorial space where individual members display the largest number of **characteristic features**. Individuals occupying that portion of the categorial space are the *most* **typical** members, the normative **exemplars** of the category, its **prototype**. Now, in other areas of the categorial space, fewer -- though

---

6 The expression 'within as well as between categories' can be, of course, translated as 'at various meta-levels of the categorial hierarchy'.

still 'enough' -- characteristic features intersect, say 3 out of 4. Such areas are still populated by many *fairly* typical individuals, ones that are *fairly* close to the category's prototype core. Certainly, individuals occupying those areas have stronger claim to categorial membership than those who occupy further outlying zones (say, at the intersection of only two properties, or one, or none). Membership is thus a matter of *degree*.

The characteristic gradation found in natural, prototype-like categories may be ascribed to two distinct sources:[7]

(a) Members may be ranked as to **how many** characteristic features they possess.
(b) The features themselves may be ranked according to their relative **importance** for defining the prototype.

Neither (a) nor (b) above can be determined by deductive or inductive means. Both involve context-dependent **abductive** judgement. By combining the gradation arising from both sources, one may derive an overall measure of degree of prototypicality, or distance from the prototype core, for each individual member of the category.

2.1.5. **Categorization and frequency distribution**

The way we have described prototype-like categorization thus far does not seem to diverge sufficiently, in some crucial respects, from our description of extreme Platonic categorization. Thus, in our diagram (3) above, individual members of the class either do or do not possess four, three, two, one or none of the features that define the class's prototype. What is missing is of course a crucial element of natural categorization, the element of **frequency distribution**. Put another way, nothing in the Venn diagram (3) guarantees that **a substantial majority** of the category's population will be *prototypical*, i.e. will display the largest number of the most important features. The notions of **norm** and **counter-norm**, so crucial in the phenomenology of natural categories, are completely missing. Indeed, Venn diagrams are, in principle, a **deductive** instrument. On

---

7   It is easy to show, of course, that the two factors are not really distinct from each other, but rather represent the application of the very same principle at two different meta-levels. This is so because in order to create gradation of types (b), in the rank-ordering of features according to their importance, one must resort to classifying features by their sub-features, how many of those each feature possesses, and of what importance. We have already noted (see Ch. 1) that *in principle* it is impossible to distinguish between a difference in **kind** and a difference in **degree**. Rather, it is the pragmatic **context** that makes possible such a distinction, whereby some features are considered 'more important' for the **purpose** at hand.

the other hand, natural categorization, at least at some level, requires an added **inductive** element.

In order to demonstrate how the prototype approach is indeed a real alternative to both the Platonic and Wittgensteinean extremes, one must note that a natural category, be it biological, behavioral, cognitive or linguistic, is characterized by the **degree of clustering** of its membership around the categorial **mean**, or **prototype core**. It requires characterization in terms of the **distribution** of its **population**. To illustrate this, let us return to the Platonic extreme; there, 100% of a category's population must distribute at exactly the same point of the categorial space, as in:

(4) **Frequency distribution of a population exhibiting extreme Platonic categorization**

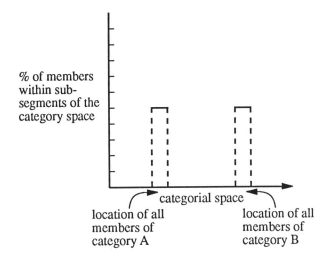

In contrast, the extreme Wittgensteinean approach to categorization would predict a uniform distribution of the population along the categorial space. This remains true regardless of whether individual members exhibit the possessed property to an equal or unequal degree. This type of categorization is illustrated in:

(5) **Frequency distribution of a population exhibiting extreme Wittgensteinean categorization**

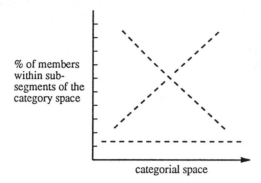

% of members within sub-segments of the category space

categorial space

One may now contrast both extremes with prototype-like categorization, whereby a certain *majority* of the population clusters somewhere near the categorial mean. Both 'majority' and 'near' are relative, context-dependent, terms. Their actual absolute values depend on the **saliency** relation of the category vis-a-vis its purposive pragmatic context. Such absolute values cannot be assigned deductively or inductively. This type of categorization may be illustrated as:

(6) **Frequency distribution of a population exhibiting prototype-like categorization**

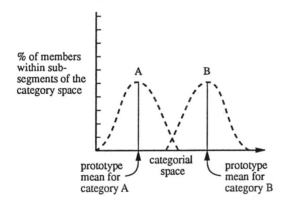

% of members within sub-segments of the category space

A   B

prototype   categorial   prototype
mean for   space   mean for
category A   category B

A number of details concerning this clustering distribution of natural populations around the categorial mean -- or prototype core -- must remain open. A bell-shaped distribution, whereby 2/3 of the population distributes within one standard deviation from the mean, is only one possible distribution. There are some grounds for suspecting that many -- perhaps most -- biological sub-systems, in neurology, perception, cognition, language or culture, require a sharper distribution curve, with a larger portion of the categorial population clustering closer to the mean. Such tighter clustering produces more salient categorial peaks. If this is indeed the case, it must surely be motivated by functional-adaptive considerations relative to each biological sub-domain. But whatever the functional context, the categorial peaks characteristic of prototype-like distribution must be *distinct enough* for the organism to associate a *substantial majority* of the category's population with its prototype.[8] Again, 'distinct enough' and 'substantial majority' cannot, in principle, be determined by deductive means.

2.2. Ludwig Wittgenstein and categorization

2.2.1. Preamble

As noted above, Rosch (1973a) adopted Wittgenstein's **family resemblance** metaphor in her work on natural categories and prototypes. However post-hoc this adoption may have been, it was far from accidental. Indeed, Wittgenstein's attack on Platonic categorization in his *Philosophical Investigations* (1953) had an exceptional trail-blazing impact on the modern pragmatic approach to categorization. This is particularly true because Peirce's earlier work on the subject has, until recently, gone almost entirely unnoticed, and is still ignored by the philosophical main stream.[9]

---

8   For an illuminating discussion of these issues, correlating the neuro-physiology of color perception and the semantic distribution of color terms in human languages, see Kay and McDaniel (1978). For an extensive review of the role of context, purpose and saliency in the construction and retention of classificatory schemata, see Medin and Schaffer (1978). The 'hybrid' prototype approach to categorization is defined there in terms that accommodate both 'analytic' and 'analogical' learning, i.e. both the Platonic and Wittgensteinean modes, respectively.

9   There is no evidence in the *Investigations* that Wittgenstein was at all aware of Peirce's work (Garth Hallett, in personal communication; but see also Hallett, 1977). Wittgenstein's attitude to antecedence is of course well documented: "...I do not wish to judge how far my efforts coincide with those of other philosophers. Indeed, what I have written here makes no claim to novelty in detail, and the reason why I give no sources is that it is a matter of indifference to me whether the thoughts that I have had have been anticipated by someone else..." (*Tractatus Logico-Philosophicus*, 1918, p. 3).

Whether one could also read a full-fledged prototype theory into Wittgenstein's work remains to some extent a moot question, given Wittgenstein's undeniable impact on cognitive psychology and linguistics. One must note, however, that it was in cognitive psychology, with its traditional -- largely methodological -- preoccupation with populations and frequency distribution, that an explicit prototype theory of categories arose. Wittgenstein's impact on Anthropology has been, on the other hand, far from unambiguous. His vigorous denial of Platonism has been often used in Anthropology to mean that if generalization cannot be absolute, no real generalizations exist.[10]

Like the other two Godfathers of modern pragmatics, Kant and Peirce, Wittgenstein's prose style is not always the epitome of clarity. As in the case of Kant and Peirce, his richly metaphoric style has over the years given rise to a veritable cottage industry of textual interpretation. In the following three sections I will discuss what seem to be Wittgenstein's three major themes in his attack on Platonic categorization.

2.2.2. The context-dependence of meaning

Technically speaking, one could easily conceive of an interpretation of context-dependent semantics that would be -- to all intent and purpose -- fully compatible with Platonic categorization. This would indeed be the case if one depicted the contexts themselves as absolute, discrete and sharply bounded. We could thus Platonically categorize all possible contexts; and as a consequence, if the **frame** is Platonically stable and discrete, the **picture** framed in it would be equally stable and discrete. We have already noted earlier why this solution to the problem of context is impractical, given the central predicaments of pragmatics. One may note that this solution has also been rejected historically. Both Plato and Aristotle, as noted earlier, refused to contend with the embarrassing messiness and open-endedness of real world context. Because of this

---

10 One must happily acknowledge, however, that at least some anthropologists who were profoundly touched by Wittgenstein's relativistic, context-dependent theory of meaning, nonetheless recognized the need to retain *some* measure of categoriality, both in our description of the subject matter and in our methodology. In referring to methodology, for example, C. Geertz writes: "...The besetting sin of interpretative approaches to anything -- literature, dreams, symptoms, culture -- is that they tend to resist, or to be permitted to resist, conceptual articulation and thus to escape systematic modes of assessment. You either grasp an interpretation or you do not, see the point of it or you do not, accept it or you do not. Imprisoned in the immediacy of its own detail, it is presented as self-validating... Any attempt to cast what it says in terms other than its own is regarded as a travesty -- as the anthropologist's severest term of moral abuse, ethnocentric..." (*The Interpretation of Cultures*, 1973, p. 24). And in referring to the subject matter: "...To abandon hope of finding the "logic" of cultural organization in some Pythagorean "realm of meaning" is not to abandon the hope of finding it at all. It is to turn our attention toward that which gives symbols their life: their use..." (*ibid.*, p. 405).

messiness and open-endedness of real world context. Because of this messiness, they idealized their categories (in Aristotle's case, the 'forms') and made them absolute and context free.

In modern linguistics, one may note striking parallels to the way Aristotle dealt with the predicament of pragmatics, i.e. by postulating a double system -- the *forms* and the *synolon*. One finds this, for example, in Saussure's distinction between *langue*, the idealized, Platonic, underlying **system** of the language, and *parole*, the messy universe of language **use** and language behavior.

Chomsky's distinction between linguistic 'competence' and linguistic 'performance' is a similar attempt to rescue Platonism by confining the discussion of linguistic categories to an idealized realm of the mind. And earlier, Bloomfield's rejection of the relevance of meaning to linguistic analysis was motivated, in no small measure, by a wish to avoid the pragmatic mess of the real world.[11]

History aside, there are good reasons why the theoretical possibility of Platonizing context is doomed from the very start. First, the number of potential distinct contexts in our experiential universe is in principle unbounded, thus potentially infinite. However large our storage capacity is, and however fast our retrieval system, they would never be large enough or fast enough, respectively, to store and retrieve all possible contexts. Second, contexts do not exist objectively, and thus cannot be objectively specified. Rather they are **construed** -- or **abduced** -- by the interpreter's mind, given specific goals, tasks, functions. This is, of course, the main reason why their number is potentially infinite. But it is also a good reason why they cannot be specified and stored *in advance* of experience, but rather must be construed by the experiencer *di novo*, for the occasion. Lastly, the process by which one construes the 'right' context, or ponders 'how right' it appears, is unspecifiable by deductive means. It involves abduction, which in turn hinges upon judgements of **relevance, similarity,** or **analogy.**

The best known and most often cited metaphor used by Wittgenstein (1953) to illustrate the context-dependent, nature of meaning is that of *games* [12]:

"...A move in chess doesn't consist simply in moving a piece in such-and-such way on the board -- nor yet in one's thoughts and feelings as one makes the move; but in the circumstances that we call "playing a game of chess", "solving a chess problem", and so on..." [33; p. 17].

---

11 This was so because Bloomfield, as a born-again empiricist, believed that meaning resided in the objective fabric of the Real World. The investigation of meaning was thus the proper domain of the natural sciences rather than of linguistics (see Bloomfield, 1933, pp. 139-140).

12 All quotations below are from the *Philosophical Investigations* (1953), and are identified by paragraph and page numbers, in that order.

"...When one shows someone the king in chess and says: "This is the king", this does not tell him the use of the piece -- unless he already knows the rules of the game up to this last point: the shape of the king... The shape of the chessmen corresponds here to the sound or shape of a word..." [31; p. 15].

Summarizing this point explicitly, Wittgenstein adds:

"...For a *large* class of cases -- though not for all -- in which we employ the word "meaning" it can be defined as thus: the meaning of a word is its use in language..." [43; p. 20].

Driving at the same point from another angle, Wittgenstein discusses the contrast between referring to a composite whole and referring to it through component parts:

"...Asking "Is this object a composite?" *outside* a particular language-game is like what a boy did once, who had to say whether the verbs in a certain sentence were in the active or the passive voice, and who racked his brain over the question whether the verb "to sleep" meant something active or passive. We use the word "composite" (and therefore the word "simple") in an enormous number of different and differently-related ways..." [47; p. 22].
The thrust of the argument is now given:

"...Suppose that instead of saying "Bring me the broom", you said "Bring me the broomstick and the brush which is fitted on it". -- Isn't the answer: "Do you want the broom? Why do you put it so oddly?"... Imagine a language-game in which someone is ordered to bring certain objects which are composed of several parts... and two ways of playing it: in one (a) the composite objects (brooms, chairs, tables etc.) have names... in the other (b) only the parts are given names and the wholes are described by means of them. In what sense is an order in the second game an analyzed form of an order in the first?..." [60; p. 30].

And in summary:

"...You may say: "The *point* of the two orders is the same". I should say so too. -- But it is not everywhere clear what should be called 'the point' of an order..." [62; p. 30].

Here Wittgenstein's 'point' is clearly the pragmatic context, or more specifically, the **relevant** portion of the potentially infinite number of different contexts that may be logically construed for each item, situation, event.

Another of Wittgenstein's ingenious metaphors for context should strike a familiar chord in the heart of travellers and mountaineers:

"...Language is a labyrinth of paths. You approach from one side and know your way about; you approach the same place from another side and no longer know your way about..." [203; p. 82].

Another equation of use with context is seen in a passing reference to **ostensive definitions**, where Wittgenstein -- presumably unawares -- echoes Peirce:

"...Whether the word "number" is necessarily in the ostensive definition depends on whether without it the other person takes the definition otherwise than I wish. And that will depend on the circumstances under which it is given, and on the person I give it to. And how he 'takes' the definition is seen in the use he makes of the word defined..." [29; p. 14].

Another observation yet equates context with **purpose** when one constructs a classificatory schema:

"...But how we group words into kinds will depend on the aim of the classification..." [17; p. 8].

Wittgenstein alludes to the public aspect of context in a way that is again reminiscent of Peirce:

"...Here the term language-*game* is meant to bring into prominence the fact that the *speaking* of language is part of an activity, or a form of life..." [23; p. 11].

Finally, Wittgenstein makes a number of memorable observations concerning the difficulty we seem to experience in understanding the 'real' meaning of words, and how deep we are mired in the mud of our old Platonic habit. While his language here is richly poetic, he nonetheless alludes to some of science's most ancient predicaments:

"...One thinks that one is tracing the outline of the thing's nature over and over again, and one is merely tracing round the frame through which we look at it..." [114; p. 48].

"...A main source of our failure to understand is that we do not *command clear view* of the use of words. -- Our grammar is lacking in this sort of

perspicuity. A perspicuous representation produces just that understanding which consists in 'seeing connexions'. Hence the importance of
finding and inventing *intermediate cases*..." [122; p. 49].

And:

"...(For the crystalline purity of logic was, of course, not the *result of
investigation*: it was a requirement). The conflict becomes intolerable; the
requirement is now in danger of becoming empty. -- We have got on the
slippery ice where there is no friction and so in a certain sense the
conditions are ideal, but also, just because of that, we are unable to walk.
We want to walk: so we need *friction*. Back to the rough ground..." [107;
p. 46].

2.2.3. The non-discreteness of meaning

The idea that context is the prime source of non-discreteness in our
mental categories had, of course, been expressed by Peirce, as in his
criticism of Mill:

"...since no two phenomena ever can happen in circumstances precisely
alike, nor are two phenomena precisely alike..." [1940, p. 221].

As noted above, the non-discreteness of context is not logically necessary,
but is in fact the case. Wittgenstein's depiction of the gradual, open-ended
nature of meaning is indeed brilliant. But like all frontal attacks against
a dominant dogma, it is often couched in equally extreme terms. This
clearly serves the useful purpose of highlighting one's differences with
the prevailing orthodoxy. Perhaps the reason why Wittgenstein *may* be
interpreted as an extremist on the issue of categories may be traced to the
historical context within which he had to elaborate his heretic views --
the preminence *of Logical Positivism in philosophy*.[13]
    Many of Wittgenstein's metaphors deal with the **open endedness** of
linguistic meaning, implicitly contrasting it with logic, which is closed
and internally-consistent:

"...ask yourself whether our language is complete; -- whether it was so
before the symbolism of chemistry and the notation of infinitesimal
calculus were incorporated into it; for these are, so to speak, the suburbs

---

13 For the Logical Positivists -- Frege, Russell, Carnap, Tarski, Montague -- Peirce apparently
   never existed. The same was apparently true for Wittgenstein. For all intent and purpose,
   then, Wittgenstein labored, within his own immediately-perceived intellectual environment, in the splendid isolation of a heretical pioneer.

of our language. (And how many houses or streets does it take before a town begins to be a town...)..." [18; p. 18].

"...But how many kinds of sentences are there? Say assertion, question, command? -- There are *countless* kinds: countless different kinds of use of what we call "symbols", "words", "sentences". And this multiplicity is not something fixed, given once and for all; but new types of language, new language-games, as we may say, come into existence, and others become obsolete and get forgotten..." [23; p. 11].

"...We call many different things "names"; the word "name" is used to characterize many different kind of usage of a word, related to one another in many different ways..." [38; p. 18-19].

Wittgenstein next makes the classical observation that the boundaries between **criterial** ('necessary', 'sufficient') and non-criterial properties for determining membership in a meaning category are not as sharp as the Platonic tradition would have them:

"...The essential thing is that this is a *lamp*, that it serves to give light; -- that it is an ornament to the room, fills an empty space, etc. is not essential. But there is not always a sharp distinction between essential and inessential..." [62; p. 30].

The discussion eventually leads to gradualism, then to the central metaphor of **family resemblance**:

"...[You may wish to challenge me by saying:] You talk about all sorts of language-games, but have nowhere said what the essence of a language-game, and hence of language, is: what is common to all these activities... And this is true. -- Instead of producing something common to all that we call language, I am saying that these phenomena have no one thing in common which makes us use one word for all, -- but they are *related* to one another in many different ways..." [65; p. 31].

"...(we) can see how similarities crop up and disappear. And the result of this examination is this: we see a complicated network of similarities overlapping and criss-crossing, sometimes overall similarities, sometimes similarities of detail. I can think of no better expression to characterize these similarities than "family resemblances"; for the various resemblances between members of a family: build, features, colour of eyes, gait, temperament etc. etc. overlap and criss-cross in the same way. -- And I shall say: 'games' form a family..." [66,67; p. 32].

Another of Wittgenstein's metaphors for the similarity bond between members of a category is the woven thread:

"...But someone wishes to say: "There is something in common to all the constructions -- namely the disjunction of their common properties" -- I should reply: Now you are only playing with words. One might as well say: "Something runs through the whole thread, namely the overlapping of those fibers..." [67; p. 32].

What Wittgenstein is presumably after is the idea that a *pattern* -- the whole -- cannot be defined by the sum of its constituent parts.

The fuzziness of inter-categorial boundaries is another major theme in Wittgenstein's argument:

"...How should we explain to someone what a game is? I imagine that we should describe *games* to him, we might add: "This *and similar things* are called 'game'". And do we know any more about it ourselves? Is it only other people whom we cannot tell exactly what a game is? -- But this is not ignorance. We do not know the boundaries because none have been drawn..." [69; p. 33].

"...One might say that the concept 'game' is a concept with blurred edges. -- "But is a blurred concept a concept at all? Is it even always an advantage to replace an indistinct picture by a sharp one? Isn't the indistinct one often exactly what we need?..." [71; p. 34].

"...Frege compares a concept to an area and says that an area with vague boundaries cannot be called an area at all. This presumably means that we cannot do anything with it. -- But is it senseless to say: "Stand roughly here"?..." [71; p. 34].

In his gentle admonition of Frege, Wittgenstein reminds us that the reason why fuzzy-edged concepts are not totally useless is the real-world context where they are employed. This is true when a concept's fuzziness does not impinge upon the **core function** it serves, upon the domain where it actually **applies**. Now, one may wish to argue that this is, at least implicitly, an articulation of prototype semantics. Indeed, in articulating a theory of prototypes, one must specify the areas of meaning that *can tolerate* fuzziness, and then contrast those with areas that *require* a higher degree of categorial stability; one must also explain why this is so, presumably in terms of the functional context. Wittgenstein's tantalizing references, suggestive though they may be, are never developed further. They are reiterated, suggestively, obliquely, through other metaphors:

"...[if you ask yourself] How did we *learn* the meaning of this word ("good" for instance)? From what sort of examples? In what language-game? then it will be easier for you to see that the word must have a family of meanings..." [77; p. 36].

"...I use the name "N" without a *fixed* meaning. (But that detracts little from its usefulness, as it detracts from that of a table that it stands on four legs instead of three and so sometimes wobbles..." [79; p. 37].

"...I said that the application of a word is not everywhere bounded by rules... A rule stands there like a sign-post. -- Does the sign-post leave no doubt open about the way I have to go? Does it show which direction I have to take when I've passed it; whether along the road or the footpath or cross-country?..." [84, 85; p. 39].

"...We understand what it means to set a pocket watch to the exact time or to regulate it to be exact. But... how nearly does it approach the ideal?... "Inexact" is really a reproach, and "exact" is praise. And that is to say that what is inexact attains its goal less perfectly than what is more exact. Thus the point here is what we call "goal". Am I inexact when I give our distance from the sun to the nearest foot, or tell a joiner the width of a table to the nearest thousandth of an inch?..." [88; pp. 44-45].

2.2.4. **Exemplars, norms and prototypes**

It is a bit harder to read into Wittgenstein's text an explicit elaboration of the prototype alternative to Platonic categories. In the space below, I have culled from the *Investigations* the strongest passages that suggest, at least under a sympathetic reading, something like a prototype approach. Let us begin with:

"...in certain cases, especially when one points 'to the shape' or 'to the number', there are *characteristic experiences* and ways of pointing -- characteristic because they recur often (not always) when shape or number are meant..." [35; p. 17; emphasis is mine; TG].

Taken at face value, 'characteristic experiences' that 'recur often' may be construed to mean **norms** based on **frequency**. In fact, however, Wittgenstein refers here to characteristic *mental* experiences the speaker may be having while 'pointing to a shape, number etc.'.
Consider next:

"...But then the use of the word is unregulated, the 'game' we play with it is unregulated". -- It is not everywhere circumscribed by rules; but no more are there any rules for how high one throws the ball in tennis, or how hard; yet tennis is a game for all that and has rules too..." [68; p. 33].

One can interpret this passage to mean that while some areas of meaning remain less regulated, others abide by stricter rules; and presumably then, the latter would require a higher *measure* of categoriality, perhaps prototype-like categories. But such an interpretation remains only implicit.
Consider next:

"...So I am shown various different leaves and told "This is 'a leaf'", I get an idea of the shape of a leaf, a picture of it in my mind. -- But what does the picture of a leaf look like when it does not show us any particular shape, but what is common to all shapes of leaf'? Which shade is the 'sample in my mind' of the colour green -- the sample of what is common to all shades of green? "But might there be no such 'general' sample? Say a schematic leaf, or a sample of *pure* green?" -- Certainly there might. But for such a schema to be understood as a *schema*, and not as the shape of a particular leaf, and for a slip of pure green to be understood as a sample of all that is greenish and not as a sample of pure green -- this in turn resides in the way the samples are used..." [73; p. 35].

This passage comes tantalizingly close to articulating a psychological notion of 'prototype' or 'typical exemplar' as a necessary ingredient in the formation of natural categories. But again, the interpretation remains implicit.
Consider next:

"...Here also belongs the idea that if you see this leaf as a sample of 'leaf shape in general' you *see* it differently from someone who regards it as, say, a sample of this particular shape..." [74; p. 35].

Wittgenstein argues two separate points here. First, he is recapitulating his position concerning the context-dependent nature of meaning. Second, he continues to attack the Platonic variant of 'idealized example'. A more explicit formulation of an alternative to Platonic categorization does not follow.
Consider next:

"...I want to say: we have here a *normal* case and abnormal cases. It is only in normal cases that the use of a word is clearly prescribed; we know, we are in no doubt, what to say in this or that case. The more abnormal a case, the more doubtful it becomes what we are to say... if there were for instance no characteristic expressions of pain, of fear, of joy; if rule became exception and exception became rule; or if both became phenomena of roughly equal frequency -- this would make our normal language-games lose their point..." [141, 142; p. 56].

This is, as far as I know, the most explicit elucidation in the *Investigations* of one fundamental prerequisite for a prototype theory -- as distinct from mere contextual gradualism: The correlation between **typicality** and **frequency** of an experience, and the attendant pragmatically-based notions of norm and counter-norm.[14]

Finally consider:

"...[a suggestive example that] is not meant to apply to anything but the examples given is different from that which *'points beyond'* them. "But then doesn't our understanding reach beyond all the examples?" -- A very queer expression, and a quite natural one! -- But is that *all*? Isn't there a deeper explanation; or mustn't at least the *understanding* of the explanation be deeper?... "But do you really explain to the other person what you yourself understand? Don't you get him to *guess* the essential thing? You give him examples, -- but he has to guess their drift, to guess your intention..." [208, 209, 210; pp. 83-84].

This passage echoes Peirce's notion of **abduction** or **pragmatic intuition** (Wittgenstein's 'guessing'), whereby the central features of *similarity*, *import* and *relevance* are -- in principle -- logically undefinable. One could also read into the text a prototype-semantic interpretation: General categories are inferred from typical exemplars, from normative cases. But, such a reading is only implicit in the text.

In one clear sense, Wittgenstein's contribution to the development of prototype semantics has already been acknowledged by Rosch and others, who considered him their inspiration in developing an empirically viable pragmatic alternative to Platonism.[15] But, to do justice to the spirit of a great master, one must also add that this interpretation of Wittgenstein serves to illustrate a central theme of Pragmatics, namely that for all practical purpose, meaning is the product of how you press it into use.

---

14 See discussion in Givón (1979a, Ch. 3).
15 Most of us cite Wittgenstein in ignorance of Peirce's work.

2.3. **Prototypes and metaphoric extension**

2.3.1. **Preamble**

The most prototypical member of a population ('category'), the one displaying the largest number of the most important characteristic features, is presumably the one that best approximates our mental concept of a prototype-like category. It is worth noting that Wittgenstein (1953) recognized this possibility, but did not explicitly resolve its seeming internal contradictions:

"...But for such a schema to be understood as a *schema*, and not as the shape of a particular leaf, and for a slip of pure green to be understood as a sample of all that is greenish but not as a sample of pure green -- this in turn resides in the way the samples are used..." [73; p. 35].

Indeed, the most striking feature of Rosch's work on natural categories is her demonstrating how our notion of 'class' -- the prototype -- evolves from repeated experience of **typical exemplars**. Members of a category can thus be ranked according to their distance from (or 'degree of resemblance to') the most typical exemplar -- the prototype *core*. And the core may be considered as something akin to the population's -- or the category's -- mean.[16]

The notion of resemblance or similarity is indeed the crux of how we form our mental categories. It is also crucial for understanding how we modify and extend existing prototype-like categories. One may call this process of extension **analogy** or **metaphor**.[17] There is nothing logically necessary, or Platonically discrete and absolute, about resemblance or 'being like'. Anything can, in principle, be said to 'be like' anything else, given the appropriate context. Analogy and metaphor are thus -- in principle -- pragmatic, open ended, context-dependent, abduction-driven notions.[18]

2.3.2. **Metaphoric induction into a lexical prototype**

The extension of category membership to new members is one of the most ubiquitous processes in human categorization, be it at the sensory,

---

16 See extensive discussion in Medin and Schaffer (1978).

17 These two names for the same phenomenon come to linguistics via two distinct traditions. 'Metaphor' comes to us via of literary analysis, while 'analogy' comes more directly from the philosophical tradition, most recently via Peirce. For a general discussion see Anttila (1977) and Lakoff and Johnson (1980).

18 See further discussion in Chapter 7, below, as well as in Givón (1982a).

cognitive or linguistic level. It is precisely the fuzzy-edged, prototype-like nature of mental categories that makes such extension possible. Through this process, *less typical* individuals may nonetheless join a category, given an appropriate (though 'less typical' or 'less frequent') context. Since the literature is rich with examples of such metaphoric extension of lexical meaning, one illustration here will suffice.[19]

Suppose one said:

(7)   George built a wall around himself

For (7) to be interpreted metaphorically, there must have been -- from the speaker's point of view -- something in George's behavior which resembled the literal meaning of *build a wall around oneself*. In principle, this could have involved the brick or mortar used, the characteristic wall-shape, wall-height, wall-color etc. But in this particular case, the analogy is likely to have involved the following two **pragmatic inferences** ('abductions') concerning the **normative** goals and consequences of literal wall-building:

(8)   a. **Goals:** Walls are often built for the purpose of *defending*
              oneself from outside threat;
        b. **Consequences:** Wall-building often results in undue *isolation*
              from the outside.

The metaphoric extension of the membership of the category 'wall-building' thus allowed *defensive and isolating behavior* to join the cluster of features characterizing it. These two features will remain, at least initially, less characteristic (less prototypical). They may at first define -- i.e. admit into the category -- marginal, less-typical, more exceptional members, ones judged to be included metaphorically rather than literally.

There is nothing *logically* necessary in selecting the two pragmatic inferences (8a) and (8b) over all others as the **relevant** or **important** inferences in this case. They are not endowed with such privileged status *in principle*. It is the purpose or context of this *particular* metaphoric extension of 'wall-building' that makes these two abductions relevant. It is of course true that some contexts are more frequent, normative or stable, given the general layout of the culture -- or of human cognition.

In this particular case, 'defensiveness' and 'isolation' are rather obvious metaphoric extensions, given the cluster of normal purposes of wall-building. But suppose the same physical walls were normatively built for an altogether different purpose, say laying siege to a citadel or reaching higher up. In the first instance, 'defensiveness' would change to 'offensiveness'; and 'isolation' will change its valence -- from reflexive

19 For a book-size collection, see Lakoff and Johnson (1980).

('isolating oneself') to transitive ('isolating someone else'). In the second, nothing related to either 'defensiveness' or 'isolation' would be relevant any more. Rather, one could construe another set of apt metaphors, such as *reaching up, ambition, self-improvement, intellectual growth* etc.

2.3.3. Metaphoric extension of a lexical prototype

The flexibility, open-endedness and context-sensitivity of prototype-like categories also provide for the eventual change in the definition of the prototype itself. Such change is the common end product of the process we have just discussed, i.e. metaphoric induction of new members into a category. The cumulative impact of this influx of new and less-prototypical members inevitably leads to either the re-definition of the prototype core features, or to changes in their relative ranking. Metaphoric extension is indeed the major source of diachronic change in lexicon, phonology, morphology and grammar. We will discuss only one case from lexical semantics as illustration.

The English verbs *know* and *can* may be traced back to the same Indo-European root, with the meaning 'know' being presumably the older one.[20] The extension from *know* to *can* is due to one less-central sense of *know* -- 'know how (to do)'. And presumably this less-central sense extended itself via the following pragmatic inference:

(9)   '*know* how to do' ⊃ 'be better *able* to do'

Now, not all uses of *know* involve the sense of 'know how'; two other senses are presumably more central to the prototype definition of *know*:

(10)   a.   '*know* that P is true/false'
         b.   '*be familiar* with N'[21]

Next, *can* as we know it now involves not only the sense 'know how', but also another -- more central -- sense, 'have *power* to act'. When *can* completed its historical divergence from *know*, along the line taking advantage of a fortuitous phonological variation, the newer sense of 'have power to act' became more central to its prototype definition; while the sense of 'know how' -- which came from *know* as the historical 'bridge' in the original metaphoric extension, became less central to the newly-assembled prototype definition of *can*.

---

20 I owe the details of this example to Raimo Anttila (in personal communication).
21 Where 'P' stands for 'proposition' and 'N' for 'individual entity'.

To take the example a bit further, *can* soon developed a rather predictable deontic sense, that of 'be *permitted* to act'. This extension occurred, presumably, through the following chain of pragmatic inferences:

(11) a. 'have the *power* to act' ⊃ '*not* be *restrained* from acting'
   b. '*not* be *restrained* from acting ⊃ 'be *permitted* to act'

There is nothing deductively necessary about inferences (11a,b). The consequent in (11a) is only one of many possible reasons why one may 'have power to act'. And the consequent in (11b) is only one possible reason why one may be 'not restrained from acting'. It is the specific context which motivated the choice of these particular abductions as **relevant** in this case.

Finally, *can* quite commonly also develops an epistemic sense, that of *probability*, presumably via the pragmatic inference:

(12) '*ability* to act' ⊃ '*higher probability* of acting'

And although this epistemic sense may not be central for the current prototype definition of *can*, it is clearly recognized by speakers and may even be on the ascendance.[22] In this way, each new sense of *know*, and of *can* after it split from *know*, re-defines the old prototype to some degree, by extending membership to new items that had been excluded from the category before. The process of inducting new members into a category is thus the very same process that eventually modifies the category's prototype core.

2.3.4. Prototypes, metaphoric extension and grammaticalization

Metaphoric extension of prototype-like categories is also central to the process known as **grammaticalization**, through which lexical words become grammatical morphemes (and eventually inflectional morphology). I will illustrate this process here with one widely-attested change, where the verb *go* and *come* give rise, respectively, to the modalities 'future' and 'perfective'.[23] This change involves a metaphoric extension of the sense of spatial motion of *go* and *come* to temporal motion, a rather common type of **semantic bleaching**.[24]

---

22 See discussion, and some experimental results, in Givón (1979a, ch. 3).
23 For grammaticalization in general see Givón (1971, 1975a; 1979a, ch. 6).
24 See discussion in Givón (1979a, ch. 8). The connection between grammaticalization and metaphoric extension is also noted in Claudi and Heine (1984) and Heine and Reh (1984). The original discussion of the widespread transformation of 'go' and 'come' into tense-aspect markers can be found in Givón (1973a). A related discussion may be also found in Traugott (1974).

One may construe this change as a metaphoric switch from *spatial* to *temporal* deixis. As is well known, *go* and *come* differ, in addition to their semantic features of motion from some source or toward some goal, also by their pragmatic feature of **deixis**, whereby *go* is used when the motion is away from the position of the speaker, *come* is used when the mostion is toward the speaker's position. The metaphoric extension that occurs in grammaticalization may thus hinge upon the following pragmatic inference:

(13) (a) GO = 'move away from *this place'* ⊃
         FUTURE = 'move away from *this time'*
     (b) COME = 'move toward *this place'* ⊃
         PERFECTIVE = 'move toward *this time'*

Two semantic elements of the verbs *go* and *come* have been preserved in the metaphoric transformation above: (a) the sense of **motion to/from**; and (b) the **deixis**. Both have been transformed from space to time. But in addition, another transformation also occurs. Spatial motion is not uni-directional; one could go or come either to or from a place. But temporal motion is unidirectional. So that the erstwhile *go* as a 'future' modality could only mean going **away from** the present. While the erstwhile *come* as a 'perfective' modality could only mean coming **toward** the present. And the features 'away from' and 'toward' were inherited from the deixis feature of the erstwhile verbs.

The inferences in (13) are typically abductive. Many other semantic features of *go* and *come* were deemed **irrelevant** for this particular metaphoric extension. Motion in time is indeed an inseperable ingredient of motion in space, but may not be the **core** of the prototype *go* or *come*. In this metaphoric extension, however, it was **relevant** to to the **purpose** of the extension, and became a **core** feature of the prototypes of 'future' and 'perfective'.

To drive the latter point home, consider the equally common grammaticalization of the serial verbs *go* and *come* into the locational case-markers 'to' and 'from', respectively.[25] *This process may be summarized as:*

(14) a. GO = 'He walked *going* (to the) market' >
         TO = 'He walked *to* (the) market'
     b. COME = 'He walked *coming* (from the) market' >
         FROM = 'He walked *from* (the) market'

Unlike the metaphoric extension in (13), in (14) it is not the deixis feature of *go* and *come* that have been preserved, but rather the semantic features of 'motion toward a goal' and 'motion away from a source', respectively.

---

25 For the grammaticalization of serial verbs into case markers, see Givón (1975a).

Further, the directionality of *go* and *come* as case-markers is exactly the opposite of their directionality as tense-aspect markers. In other words, for the **purpose** of the latter metaphoric extensions, other features of the verbs were judged **more relevant**, and those are the ones that became the prototype **core** of the new grammatical morphemes.

2.4. Prototypes and metaphoric extension in the grammar of transitivity

Prototype-like categorization and metaphoric extension are just as pervasive in grammar as they are in the lexicon and inflectional morphology. In the space below I will illustrate this by citing a number of metaphoric extensions in the grammar of transitivity.

In grammar -- and grammars -- the notion of transitivity is central to our understanding of *events* and *actions*, and how these two differ from mere *states*. The prototype definition of 'event' involves three core features:[26]

(15) a. **Agency:** An event is a change involving a highly visible/salient, volitional, controlling, acting *agent/cause*;

b. **Affectedness:** An event is a change involving a highly visible/ salient, non-volitional, non-acting affected *patient/effect*;

c. **Rate of change:** An event is a change that is highly visible/salient in terms of *rate of change* over time.

Note first that the three conditions in (15) can each be couched in terms of **degree**; indeed, many intermediates may be found on these three scales. Further gradation may also arise when an event scores high on one or two of these scales but not on the other(s). Finally, gradation -- and fuzzy-edgedness -- may also arise from the fact that these three features are only the most **important** features in defining the transitive prototype; other -- less central -- features may still exist.

In a broad sense, features (15a,b,c) refer to the prototypical agent, patient and verb, respectively, involved in the transitive event. Some examples of prototypical transitive events are:

---

26 For further discussion see Hopper and Thompson (1980; 1982 eds) or Givón (1984, chapters 4,5,8,11).

(16) a. Mary cut the meat
    b. John destroyed the house
    c. They killed the goat
    d. She broke the chair

Many events involve objects that are less-than-prototypical patients. That is, in terms of our prototype feature (15b) they themselves are either less concrete, less visible, less salient; or the effect of the event on them may be less salient; or the entire change may be relatively slow (feature (15c)) and thus again less salient.[27] Some of these less-prototypical objects are not really patients by the strictest definition. They do not -- 'objectively speaking' -- undergo any visible change during the event. Nonetheless, grammars often offer the option of construing such patients -- metaphorically -- as *patient-like*. They are then marked grammatically as *direct objects*, the most common way of coding prototypical patients. This option offered in grammars is not trivial; it reflects subtle differences in the way an event may be **viewed, construed, contextualized**. To illustrate this, consider first the following paired expressions, each involving the same lexical verb. Each expression renders the -- 'objectively same' -- event as either intransitive (on the left) or transitive (on the right). And in a clear sense, the transitive version is a metaphoric extension of the intransitive:

(17)	literal sense (intransitive)	metaphoric sense (transitive)
	a. He rode *on* the horse	He rode *the horse*
	b. He swam *across* the channel	He swam *the channel*
	c. They entered *into* the citadel	They entered *the citadel*
	d. She took the money *from* him	She robbed *him* of his money
	e. She walked *with* her dog	She walked *her dog*

The horse in (17a) on the left is construed as a *location*; it is less affected, less controlled. On the right it is construed as an affected, manipulated, controlled *patient*. The channel in (17b) on the left is mere geographic *space* to be crossed. On the right it is an *adversary* to be conquered, subdued, tamed. The citadel in (17c) on the left is a *location* to be entered. On the right it is construed as a *target*, to be breached and taken over. In (17d) on the left 'he' is construed as the *source* from which money was removed. On the right 'he' is the affected, aggrieved *victim*. Finally, the dog in (17e) on the left is a *companion*, a self-controlling partner. But on the right the dog is a controlled, manipulated *patient*. Thus, regardless of the near

---

27 Saliency or affectedness of the patient (condition (17b)) and rate of change (condition (17c)) are not totally independent of each other.

identity of the 'objective' physical event, one can construe these non-patients metaphorically as 'patient-like', then code them syntactically as one would prototypical patients. Consequently, the entire clause is coded as a prototypical transitive clause.

In the grammar of transitivity, the exact opposite metaphoric extension can also take place. That is, one can *demote* an object that is 'objectively' a prototypical patient, by construing it as if it were 'not quite a patient'. It is then stripped of direct object status, and the entire clause is coded as intransitive. As an illustration of this process, consider the following paired expressions. In each pair, the 'original' transitive appears on the left and the metaphoric ('derived') intransitive on the right:

(18)   original transitive   derived intransitive
        with prototype patient   with 'demoted' patient
        ------------------------   ------------------------
        a. She ate *the fish*   She ate (regularly)
        b. They hunted *the deer*   They hunt (each fall)
        c. She hunted *the deer*   She went deer-hunting
        d. He drank *his beer*   He drinks (excessively)
        e. He fought *Joe Lewis*   He fights (for a living)
        f. She shot only *one bullet*   She started shooting

The 'logical' object in the expressions in (18) is expressed on the right as either *zero* or an 'incorporated' part of the verb. Both are syntactic devices used to demote the object and render the clause intransitive. The reason for this demotion is that the object is *non-specific* ('non-referential'); it's type is predictable, it is highly **stereotyped**. Thus, one stereotypically eats 'food', drinks 'liquor', hunts 'game animals' or 'deer', fights 'prize fighters' or shoots 'bullets'. The stereotypicality and non-specificity of the object make it cognitively **less salient**, thus lowering the transitivity of the clause (recall condition (15b) above).[28]

It is also quite common in language to metaphorically construe events in which -- strictly speaking -- the subject is not a prototypical agent (and thus the event does not abide by condition (15a) above) *as if* they were transitive events. As illustrations consider:

(19) a. He saw the mountain
     b. She knew the answer
     c. He heard the song
     d   She feared him
     e. He wanted a sandwich
     f. She remembered the conversation

---

28 In many languages, the transitivity of the clause is coded morphologically on both the subject and the verb. In such languages, traditionally referred to as 'ergative', the expressions on the right hand side in (18) will exhibit intransitive morphology.

Examples (19a-f) violate all three prototype transitivity conditions in (15). First, the subject is neither volitional nor active nor a causer; second, the object is not visibly affected and thus not a prototype patient; and third, the change is neither fast nor salient. In fact these expressions code, strictly speaking, *states* rather than events. In many languages, especially those that display an *ergative* or *active-stative* morphology,[29] the expressions in (19) would be coded syntactically as intransitive clauses. English allows coding them *as if* they were transitive, i.e. with subject and direct object. In construing them as transitives, English seems to be relaxing an important part of the definition of 'agent' in (15a), moving from the stricter condition of 'having volition, control and decision-to-act' to a weaker condition of 'having conscious mental activity'. Such extension is again an instance of generalization or *semantic bleaching*, based on the fact that both volition and decision-to-act are themselves mental activities. The pragmatic inferences involved in this generalization may be given as:

(20) a. 'subject capable of *mental activity*' ⊃
                'subject capable of *volition* and *decision*'

     b. 'subject capable of *volition* and *decision*' ⊃
                'subject capable of *acting* as *agent*'

Consider next the converse case, where an event is semantically quite transitive -- with prototypical agent (and patient); but the agent is *unimportant, unknown, stereotyped/predictable, non-referential* or communicatively *irrelevant*. Under such conditions the agent may be metaphorically *downgraded*, and the clause is then coded as *passive* or *impersonal*, as in:[30]

(21) a. The window was broken yesterday (*by John*)
     b. *They* found him dead on the beach
     c. *You* buy newspapers from a vending machine
     d. English is spoken here
     e. *One* doesn't do this sort of a thing any more
     f. He got killed in a traffic accident
     g. *Everybody* knows him well around here

---

29 In ergative languages, the morpho-syntax is sensitive to all three prototype conditions in (15). In active-stative languages, clausal morpho-syntax is sensitive primarily to condition (15a). For further discussion see Givón (1984a, Ch. 5).

30 This downgrading closely parallels the situation of objects-patients in (18), above. Constructions with stereotyped, downgraded patients, as in (18), are often referred to as 'antipassive'.

These English expressions are grammatically quite diverse, and the 'irrelevant' agent in them is suppressed by a variety of means. The agent is *demoted* via the use of oblique case-marking in (21a). It is left unexpressed altogether in (21d,f). Or it is expressed as a non-referential, impersonal pronoun in (21b,c,e,g). Such passive-impersonal constructions are often used to convey a state resulting from an event, rather than the event itself (which is more commonly coded as an transitive active clause). Impersonal-passive clauses as in (21) may be viewed as 'metaphorically intransitive'.[31]

The last example involves what linguists somewhat implausibly call 'raising', and are fond of discussing in purely syntactic terms. Consider the following two pairs of English sentences, each with alternating verbs that are semantically rather close:

(22) a. He *wished* that *she* would visit
b. He *wanted her* to visit

c. She *agreed* that *he* could leave
d. She *let him* leave

Verbs of volition or permission as in (22) above are not prototypically transitive. They involve mental rather than physical processes, no discernible action by an agent, and little if any visible physical effect on the object. In fact, strictly speaking the verbs in (22) are intransitives, they 'have no object'. In the variants (22b,d), however, a syntactic object -- the so-called 'raised' one -- appears. It is, strictly speaking, the subject of the complement verb. But there is a subtle difference in meaning between the transitive (object-taking) and the intransitive (objectless) member of each pair. In (22a) a purely internal 'wishing' took place, with no hint of contact or communication between the two participants. The subject of *visit* -- 'she' -- could have been miles away, and thus not likely to have been manipulated by the subject of *wish*.'She' is coded as subject, thus emphasizing her possible independence as a decision-making agent. In (22b), on the other hand, there is a higher likelihood that the wish was actually communicated, that there was *direct contact* between subject and object -- and thus an opportunity for the subject to manipulate the object. Syntactically this is expressed by the 'raising'. That is, the logical subject of the complement verb is coded *as if* it were a manipulated object of *want*. It is thus treated metaphorically like a prototype patient.

In the same vein, the subject of *leave* in (22c) may not even be there and may not be aware of what went on in the mind of the subject of *agree*. There is thus no implication that he actually left. In contrast, in (22d) there is a stronger implication of communicative -- or even physical -- contact

31 See further discussion in Givón (1981a).

between the two participants, and also an implication that the object of
let in fact left. The subject of *leave* is thus construed, metaphorically, as
more like a patient, and coded syntactically as an object. The pragmatic
inferences involved in these metaphoric extensions may be given as:[32]

(23) a. If the subject of 'wish' (or *agree*) establishes *physical contact* with
a person whose action they desire (or agree to), the probability
of *communicating* their wish (or agreement) to that person increases;

b. If you *communicate* to another person your desire (or agreement)
that they take an action, the probability of their *taking action* is
higher than if you did not;

c. The more you *adjust your actions* to the motives of another
person, the less you act as an independent agent; and the more
you resemble a *manipulated patient.*

None of these inferences are deductively necessary. They are probabilistic, abductive, pragmatic.

2.5. The functional motivation for a hybrid system of categories

"...The solution to great arguments is usually close
to the golden mean..."

S.J. Gould,
Ontogeny and Phylogeny, (1977, p. 18)

It is reasonably clear that the philosophical poles of Platonic rigidity
and Wittgensteinean flexibility represent two extreme *aspects* of the cognitive and neurological tool-box possessed by living organisms. Under
specific task conditions, blends of the two -- at various ratios -- are both
possible and necessary. In summarizing the history of recent experimental research into these issues, my colleague Michael Posner characterized
the pragmatic, hybrid nature of human categorization -- and the function-

---

32 For more discussion of the semantics and pragmatics of manipulative verbs in relation to
the syntax of their complements, see Givón (1975b, 1980a).

"...The major lesson of this research seems to me to lie in its confirmation of the general information processing tenet of **bounded rationality** (March and Simon, 1958). The constraints imposed upon information processing by the nature of the human brain lead to some heuristics that provide means for allowing us to operate efficiently in the world to which we are adapted..." (1986, p. 9 of ms)

Linguistic or mental categories, or rules of grammar, are seldom totally discrete and exceptionless. Still, linguistic and mental categories -- and rules of grammar -- do exist. And among them, those that display high **frequency** -- and thus presumably high **functional load**, i.e. those that are more **predictable**, turn out to also be more **stable** and more **discrete**, given their functional context.

As will be noted in Chapter 7, the same imperfect but manageable blend between stronger and weaker categoriality also characterizes information processing in general, in humans as well as in other biological organisms. In the functional domains of neurology, motor-control, attention and memory, the interplay between **automated** (more category-dependent, less context-scanning) and **attended** (less category-dependent, more context-scanning) processing is well documented. Within this biological hybrid system, the relative flexibility and open-endedness of categories is just as important as their relative stability, distinctness and saliency. The more Wittgensteinean aspects of the system, at whatever level, allow the organism to perform **context-sensitive, feedback-dependent** tasks. Such tasks require finer discriminations of shades and gradations in the scanned context; they also demand the exercise of subtle and contingent judgement in interpreting the phenomenological continuum. This type of information processing tends to depend on using more narrow, sequential, analytic, time consuming, **conscious, attended** processing channels. Neither the use of human language, nor its analogy-driven adaptive change over ontogeny, phylogeny and history, could ever proceed without this flexible component of our categorization system.

It may be argued that the flexibility required by the organism in processing information at whatever level may be theoretically achieved through assigning discrete categorial status to all imaginable contexts. But, as we have already noted above, such Platonization of context is both logically and psychologically a mirage, and for a number of reasons:

(i) **Memory storage capacity:**

The number of theoretically possible contexts is in principle both undenumerable and unspecifiable. Anything at all can be the context for anything else, given some judgement of **relevance**. And as already noted, relevance -- or the similarity decisions that underlie judgements of relevance -- are both open-ended entities.

(ii) Processing time:

Our lexicon, for all its Wittgensteinean open-endedness, is still finite and largely discrete at any particular point in time. This allows the organism to embark upon search-and-retrieval operations that can be concluded, at least in principle, within finite time. But to search through, and retrieve from, a potentially infinite pool of discrete contexts would be a futile procedure. It is precisely because contexts can be **construed** upon contingency, or **abduced** for the occasion, that meaning is processable at all.

(iii) Expansion and modification:

The acquisition and integration of new information into an existing knowledge-base is in principle impossible within a full discrete, deductive system. Any non-trivial change in a knowledge-base must rely on analogy, abduction, metaphor and judgements of relevance. None of these could operate -- or even be defined -- within a system of discretized context.[33]

While a processing system must incorporate a considerable measure of Wittgensteinean flexibility, equally well some decisions made by organisms -- or tasks performed at various levels -- must proceed at high speed, categorially, unattended, in parallel, and with little regard to finer shades and gradations. Under task conditions that demand such categoriality, the context itself must be construed in starker, discrete, Platonic terms. Task that are highly **repetitious**, thus **predictable**, are carried out that way, as well as tasks that require, **high speed response**. Thus, if a deer must decide -- within a fraction of a second -- whether a potential predator is too small to worry about (say a bobcat), or large

---

33 For an extensive discussion of the relevant literature in the psychology of learning, see Medin and Schaffer (1978). Hyman and Frost (1975) also suggested that during earlier stages in the acquisition of a new category, actual instances -- **exemplars** -- are stored as mental representation of the category (see also Hintzman and Ludlam, 1980; Hintzman, 1983). But later on such exemplars are converted into **prototypes**; and later still, prototype-like categories are converted into more discrete **Platonic categories**. The philosophical literature, from Peirce to (even the early) Wittgenstein (1918), had of course made similar observations, although on less firm empirical grounds.

enough to run away from (say a cougar), the categorization supporting such a decision is likely to be rather discrete and Platonic. Such categorization would tend to compress all potential intermediates on the scale into either one extreme or the other. And it would tend to pay much less attention to fine shades of context.

A hybrid, prototype-like system of categories is thus, most likely, a necessary **optimal solution** to the real-world task environment within which organisms process information. It allows them to make gross discriminations and snap decisions whenever necessary. Still, the system retains an ingrained potential for flexibility, context-sensitivity and extendability, to be used when such features are called for. [34]

2.6. **Closure**

The hybrid solution to the problem of categorization -- the theory of prototypes -- in a way recapitulates Kant's anti-reductionist approach to epistemology: Neither concepts nor percepts are by themselves viable as sole source of our mental categories. Only together, **interactively**, can they give rise to our mental representation -- **construction** -- of experience. Posner's 'bounded rationality' -- rational enough to allow some categorial stability, yet incomplete and flexible -- is a similar kind of pragmatic compromise. Within such a framework, both extreme features of the system -- the Platonic and the Wittgensteinean -- are equally necessary, in order for the organism to perform adaptive tasks.

I would like to close this chapter with Gould's comment on another futile argument between two reductionist extremes, this one in the history of biology:

"...I doubt that such a controversy could have arisen
unless both positions were valid (though incomplete)..."

S.J. Gould
Ontogeny and Phylogeny (1977, p. 59)

---

34 As Posner and Warren (1972) note, more rigid and discrete categories are a crucial prerequisite for automated, unattended processing. Conversely, more flexible prototype-like categories must be involved in analytic, attended processing. In the discussion of the three modes of inference -- induction, deduction and abduction (Chapters 7 and 8) -- we will return to this subject in some detail. In discussing the nature of human categorization, we thus introduce a number of *leitmotifs* that will remain with us throughout much of this book.

Chapter 3

THE LINGUISTIC CODE AND
THE ICONICITY OF GRAMMAR

"...A sign is something by knowing which
we know something more..."

C.S. Peirce

3.1. **Preamble***

In this chapter we return to discuss the justification for treating human language as a **system of signs**, or a **code**. I will use these two terms interchangeably. Our discussion of this rather complex subject will be divided into three headings:

(a) The role of the **interpretant** -- or **context** -- in binding the sign and the designatum together in the semeiotic relation;

(b) The identification of the linguistic **designator** ('sign'), the **designatum** of language, and the notion of 'code';

(c) The **Iconicity** of the linguistic code, its non-arbitrary nature, particularly in so far as grammar ('syntax') is concerned.

An attempt will be made to support the latter with a certain body of evidence illustrating the pervasive iconicity found in the grammar of natural language. In a summary section, some broader bio-adaptive implications of the iconicity of natural language will be outlined.

*I am indebted to T.K. Bikson, John Haiman, Michael Shapiro, Martin Tweedale and John Verhaar for many helpful comments and suggestions. This chapter also benefitted from the general discussion at the Symposium on Iconicity, Stanford University, May 1983; particularly from comments by Henning Andersen, Joseph Greenberg and Dan Slobin.

3.2. **The interpretant as context**

3.2.1. **Background**

As noted in Chapter 1, above, the semeiotic relation between a sign and its designatum must be taken as a *trichotomy* , demanding a third term -- the **interpretant**. The notion that the coding relation is triadic rather than (as is superficially more pleasing) diadic, is attributed by Morris (1938) to Aristotle, but the relevant passage in *De Interpretatione* does not support this attribution. 'Interpretant' has always been -- and still remains -- somewhat of a murky concept. Morris (1938), for example, suggests that the **interpreter** -- the mind that perceives the significance of the semeiotic relation -- is a *fourth* term in the semeiotic relation:

"...These three components in the semeiosis may be called, respectively, the *sign vehicle* , the *designatum* , and the *interpretant* ; the *interpreter* may be included as a fourth factor..." [1938, p. 3].

However, in another passage Morris seems to identify 'interpretant' with the mind of the interpreter:

"...The interpretant of the sign is the mind; the interpretant is a thought or concept..." [1938, p. 30]

In one of his more desperate attempts to give a coherent definition of 'interpretant', Peirce identifies it as an **effect** upon the interpreter:

"...I define a Sign as anything which is so determined by something else, called its Object [i.e. the designatum; TG], and so determines an effect upon a person, which effect I call its Interpretant... My insertion of 'upon a person' is a sop to Cerebrus, because I despair of making my own broader conception understood (H 80-1)..." [Shapiro, 1983, p. 47].

Citing Aristotle again, Morris also seems to define 'interpretant' as the **generic-lexical knowledge** of all entities and their properties, held in common by members of the speech community (i.e. 'culture'):

"...The interpretant is a thought or concept; these thoughts or concepts are common to all men and arise from the apprehension by the mind of objects and their properties..." [1938, p. 30].

And citing Peirce, Morris also defines the 'interpretant' as a set of shared **habits** and rules of **usage**:

"...Charles S. Peirce, whose work is second to none in the history of semeiotic, came to the conclusion that in the end the interpretant of a symbol must reside in a *habit* and not in the immediate physiological reaction which the sign vehicle evoked or in the attendant image or emotion -- a doctrine which prepared the way for the contemporary emphasis on *rules of usage* ..." [1938, p. 31; emphases are mine; TG]

Morris's somewhat narrow definition of 'interpretant' is perhaps understandable, given that his (and Aristotle's) discussion is confined, to the most arbitrary type of sign, the **symbol**. Within human language, this type of sign is confined, almost exclusively, to the **lexicon**. Morris makes this rather clear in his discussion:

"...the interpretant is a thought or concept; these thoughts or concepts are common to all men and arise from the apprehension by the mind of objects and their properties; uttered words are then given by the mind the function of directly representing these concepts, and indirectly the corresponding things; the sounds chosen for this purpose are arbitrary and vary from social group to social group; the relations between the sounds are not arbitrary but correspond to the relations of concepts and so of things..." [1938, p. 30].

Morris's oblique reference to 'relations between sounds', which may probably be translated as 'relations between words within the proposition', is but a faint echo of Peirce's own discussion of iconicity in grammar.

We are, I believe, again indebted to Peirce for providing the critical mass in identifying 'interpretant' with **context**. This is so because, unlike Aristotle and Morris, Peirce discusses not only **symbols** but also **indices** and **icons**. For each of these three types of sign, he identifies a wide range of possible *types* of interpretant. Further, Peirce's recognized *complex signs*, especially in our grammatical code. And within those complex signs, a mixture of symbolic (i.e. 'more arbitrary'), indexical and iconic *sign-elements* can be observed. Each sign-element, in turn, may motivate a different *interpretant-element* in the complex sign. The precise internal structure of this multiplicity, and its potential Wittgensteinean scalarity, is often obscured by rather Platonic proclivities of Peirce's expository style, which is indeed replete with discrete trichotomies and the trichotomies of trichotomies. (See Peirce, 1940, pp. 115-118, as well as Shapiro, 1983, pp. 63-65). But it is perhaps possible to

interpret Peirce's discrete trichotomies as standing for a scalar continuum.[1]

As for the *function* of the Peirce's 'interpretant', Shapiro (1983) offers
the following observation:

"...It is only the genuine triadic relation obtaining between sign, object
and interpretant that enables the sign to *offer assurance* to the interpretant that the object for which it stands is simultaneously identical
with the object of the sign the interpretant interprets..." (1983, p. 61).

The 'interpretant' here seems to be equated with the interpreter.
'Assurance of interpretation' is thus guaranteed by having the appropriate interpretant (or, in my terminology, the **relevant context**) assigned to the sign:object diad as its third member. Peirce himself
proceeds to give here one more trichotomy, of the types of 'assurances
of interpretation'.[2]

Perhaps the most suggestive rendition of Peirce's 'interpretant' as
'context' is to be found in the following passage (Shapiro, 1983):

"...Each sign has one *immediate interpretant*, but any finite number of
dynamic interpretants, beginning with zero. Peirce's theory of interpretants argues that semeiosis is *teleological*, that interpretation is
shaped by a normative *goal* ..." (1983, p. 55; emphases are mine; TG).

An equally suggestive rendition is given by Short (1981) in his discussion of 'immediate', 'dynamic' and 'final' interpretants:

"...First, the idea of *immediate interpretant* presupposes that of a *ground*
of interpretation: the significance of a sign is its immediate interpretant
and this is its *grounded* interpretability, which the sign possesses regardless of whether it is actually interpreted. Second, the idea of a *final interpretant* presupposes that of a *goal* of interpretation. For, apart from such
a goal, consideration of a sign would not lead the interpreter to any
'destined' conclusion... any conclusion should remain just as good..."
(1981, p. 214; emphases are mine; TG).

---

1   I owe this suggestion to T.K. Bikson (in personal communication).
2   Assurance by *instinct* , by *experience* and by *form* ; see Shapiro (1983, p. 60). If I am not
    mistaken these three correspond to the Kantian propositional modalities, 'possible truth',
    'factual truth' and 'analytic truth', and thus presumably also to Peirce's 'abduction',
    'induction' and 'deduction, respectively. For further discussion of those, see Chapter 4,
    below.

Rather than follow the elaborate sub-classification of signs and their interpretants offered by Peirce and later interpreters, I will suggest in the following section that Peirce's notion of 'interpretant' be equated with a Wittgensteinean notion of 'context'.

3.2.2. **Steps to an ecology of contexts** [3]

In this section I propose to integrate Wittgenstein's notion of context-dependent meaning with Peirce's notion of 'interpretant'. I will do so initially *by fiat*, declaring them to be one and the same. This will be done through an *axiom* concerning the application of 'context' (or 'inter-pretant') to a cognitively-based[4] theory of communication ('information processing'):

(1) **Axiom concerning the pragmatics of 'relevant context':**

(a) The relevant context for the communication of knowledge ('information', 'belief') from one mind to another is not some *objective context* ; nor is it a *set of propositions* about such objective context.

(b) Rather, the relevant context for the communication of knowledge ('information', 'belief') is itself some knowledge, information or **belief** held by some **interpreter**, i.e. by some **participant** ('speaker', 'hearer') in the communication.

As one can see, axiom (1) makes it easy to understand why Peirce's 'interpretant' has received such a wide range of potentially conflicting renditions. Once again we have come face to face with the three prover-bial blind men describing the 'same' elephant. One may, on the one hand, choose to dwell on the fact that the 'relevant interpretant' is not independent of the mind of the interpreter. Given such a choice, it would be easy to equate the two. But this merely defers enumerating all the highly specific *types of context* that figure as the most normative ('likely', 'important') interpretants. In doing so, one downplays the 'more objective' aspect of 'interpretant'.

One may, on the other hand, choose to dwell on the contexts *themsel-ves,* for the moment ignoring the fact that those contexts can only play

---

3   With obvious indebtedness for the title of this section to Gregory Bateson's *Steps to an Ecology of Mind* (1972).

4   By 'cognitive-based' I mean a theory of information processing that emphasizes the fact that information is transferred from the *mind* of one organism to the *mind* of another. Such a theory must thus take into account the cognitive and perceptual mechanisms that constrain the way the mind/brain processes information.

their 'interpretant role' inside the mind of the interpreter. In doing so, one tends to underplay the role of the interpreter's mind -- i.e. the 'more subjective' aspect of 'interpretant'.

The obvious resolution to this artificial dilemma must again be Kantian in nature. It must involve the recognition that 'interpretant' -- the *relevant* context for communication -- is an *interactive* product, to which both mind and environment contribute in liberal measures.[5]

Let us turn now to consider the major sub-divisions of context relevant for the use of language in communication. One must recognize that this list is to some extent open ended, and rightly so. Nonetheless, both the specific categories and the three major *foci* under which they are grouped are highly stable and well attested in the traditional linguistic literature.[6]

(a) The generic focus: Shared world and culture

(i) Knowledge of (and beliefs concerning) the so-called real world (including **society** and **culture**), assumed by the speaker to be held by hearer, as member of the same speech community ('culture'), and manifest first and foremost in the commonly-held **lexicon**.[7] This tacitly subsumes whatever universal cognitive constraints that underlie the human mind, including any universal capacities for logical inference.[8] It also subsumes whatever perceptual universals that underlie the human sensory apparatus.[9] At least in principle, it thus also subsumes Kant's **Transcendental Schema** of time-and-space.[10]

---

5   It is reasonably clear that Peirce occupied himself, on different occasions and in different contexts, with different aspects of 'interpretant', a fact that perhaps explains the great variety of definitions of this elusive entity he seems to have produced.

6   See for example Cole and Morgan (eds, 1975), Cole (ed. 1978, ed. 1981) or Levinson (1983), *inter alia* .

7   The lexicon -- dictionary -- is the most conspicuous repository of the shared generic knowledge of the (relatively stable) properties of entities, institutions, customs, beliefs etc. Much of Aristotle's 'interpretant' in his *De Interpretatione* boils down to generic, lexically-coded knowledge.

8   This corresponds, broadly, to Kant's *analytic* knowledge. See Johnson-Laird (1983) for an extensive survey of such universal capacities from an experimental psychologist's point of view. I suspect Johnson-Laird has over-estimated by a considerable margin the scope and universality of these components of our shared generic background. But some capacities to do deduction and induction (and obviously also abduction, on which Johnson-Laird is silent) are surely cognitively based and human-universal.

9   See for example the discussion of color perception and its linguistic significance in Kay and McDaniel (1978).

10   I.e. Kant's *apriori synthetic*.

(b) The deictic focus: Shared speech situation

(ii) Deixis:

The knowledge, shared by the speaker and hearer in a **particular speech act** and by virtue of being together on the same **scene** at the same **time**, of the **immediate** ('deictic') speech situation. This includes, among others, the shared reference for 'I' and 'you', 'now' and 'then', 'this' and 'that', or 'here' and 'there'.

(iii) Socio-personal relations:

Knowledge, shared by the speaker and hearer, *in their respective roles* , of their respective socio-personal relation. This includes respective power, status, long-term social goals, obligations, entitlements, needs and **expectations**, most specifically as they are relevant to the communicative transaction *at hand* .

(iv) Speech-act Teleology:

The shifting **goals** of the communicative transaction, clause by clause, primarily from the speaker's perspective. The more *localized* , linguistically coded **speech act** designation of clauses (declarative, interrogative, manipulative, etc.). This may or may not also include the speaker's **information-processing goals**, such as foregrounding vs. backgrounding, focus, emphasis or contrast, and the designation of **important topics**. [11]

(c) The discourse focus: Shared prior text

(v) Overt and covert propositions:

Knowledge, shared by the speaker and hearer in a particular communication transaction, of the **specific discourse** that has been transacted, in particular the **immediately** preceding discourse.[12] This includes the specific propositions comprising the uttered text, but also whatever other entailed

---

11 See discussion in Levy (1979) as well as further below. Whether one wishes to include here detailed information-processing goals remains a thorny issue. Such goals are *hierarchically layered* and tend to open the door for infinite meta-regress. Further, speakers are increasingly less conscious of harboring these increasingly more abstract processing goals. One must recognize here the potential for another Wittgensteinean continuum. For further discussion of 'degree of consciousness', see Chapter 7, below.

12 Pete Becker (in personal communication) refers to this as 'prior text'.

propositions the speaker assumes that the hearer can derive from the text by whatever means. It also includes such entailed propositions the speaker assumes that the hearer can derive from the thematic structure of the text, again by whatever means.

(vii) **Meta-propositional modalities:**
Knowledge, held by the speaker and hearer and shared to various degrees (and not always symmetrically), of the **strength** of their respective **belief, certainty, evidential support** or valuative **preferences,** all pertaining to the propositions comprising the specific discourse (or entailed from it). This also includes some **probabilistic assessment** of the strength of *each other's* beliefs and preferences.[13]

One must, finally, own up to the existence of an irreducible residue, a recalcitrant *escape clause* concerning the open-endedness of 'context'. This residue can never be fully captured, however exhaustive and refined one's taxonomy may be. I refer here to the provision, seemingly unprincipled yet *sine qua non* of any empirical pragmatics, which *in principle* admits any information at all as legitimate context (or 'interpretant') in natural communication, provided the speaker deems it **relevant** to the transaction -- on whatever grounds -- and **available** to the hearer, by whatever means.[14]

3.3. 'Code' and 'designatum'

We now turn to deal with the other two components of the semeiotic relation, sign and designatum. We will begin by discussing a question that has traditionally been rather controversial, namely, what precisely is the **designatum** of the linguistic sign.

3.3.1. The designatum: Some background

"...Now spoken sounds are symbols of affections in the soul, and written marks are symbol of spoken sounds. And just as written marks are not the same for all men, neither are spoken sounds.

---

13 See discussion in Chapter 4, below.
14 One's private mental life, Divine revelation, hunches, intuitions, inspiration and the like are all perfectly legitimate grounds for assuming the relevance of some context. Whether -- and to what degree -- such sources insure successful communication is a separate, empirical, issue. But there is no principled grounds on which this open-endedness of context can be ruled out, nor is it particularly desirable to attempt such strict delimitation.

But what these are in the first place signs of -- affections of the soul -- are the same for all; and what these affections are likenesses of -- actual things -- are also the same..."

> Aristotle, *De Interpretatione*
> (J.L. Ackrill, tr., 1963)

In this terse passage Aristotle opened, for all eternity, the agenda of Western semeiotics. The arbitrariness of the linguistic symbol -- the sound code -- is declared boldly. The two-step coding relation is outlined, between 'sounds', 'affections of soul' and 'actual things'. And an iconic relation -- **likeness** -- is posited between mental entities and the external reality they stand for. (This 'likeness' was expressed through Aristotle's 'forms'; see Chapter 1, above). What is more, the relation between mind and reality is said to be **universal**.

Aristotle's two-step coding relation has survived to this day in the discussion of language by both philosophers and linguists. It is commonly given as:

(2)   LANGUAGE---THOUGHT---REALITY

Consider, for example, the following rendition from Haiman (1980):

"...Since the transformational revolution, it has been claimed that the structure of *language* reflects the structure of *thought* , and that its study provides a window on the mind... I contend that the structure of thought in its turn reflects the structure of *reality* to an extent greater than is now fashionable to recognize... (1980, p. 537)

In this passage Haiman argues specifically against Chomsky's dismissal of any systematic coding relationship between 'mind, and 'reality'. Chomsky's position is to some extent predictable from his Cartesian rationalism. Implicitly, Chomsky construes the linguistic code (see in particular Chomsky, 1968) as involving a *bi-partite* coding relationship between 'language' and 'thought/mind', without worrying about whether thoughts may code some 'reality':

"...our interpretation of the world is based in part on representational systems that derive from the structure of the mind itself and do not mirror in any direction the form of things in the external world..." (Chomsky, 1981, p. 3)

At another point, Haiman seems to be throwing in a skeptical -- perhaps a Kantian or Lockean -- hedge, suggesting that perhaps 'external reality' is not an issue here, but rather *perceived reality* :

"...many linguistic universals reflect, in a rather obvious way, our common *perceptions* about our world..." (to appear, p. 3)

However, this passage may be also read with 'our common perceptions' standing for 'thought', thus allowing at least tacitly for the second coding relationship, the one between 'thought' and 'external reality'.

A different, more expanded and more explicit argument for a *bi-partite* Aristotelian coding relation has been advanced by Verhaar (1983). Verhaar considers first a *triadic* code, with two coding relations.

(a) 'Internal': The relation of **sound** to **meaning**; and
(b) 'External': The relation of **meaning** to some **X**.

I will henceforth refer to these two relations as, respectively:

(a) The **sign-relation** ('S-relation' for short); and
(b) The **experience-relation** ('X-relation' for short).

Verhaar points out, I think correctly, that -- at least for the **lexical code** -- the S-relation is rather trivial. The more interesting and difficult issue concerning the lexicon is the precise nature of the X-relation, more specifically, what exactly is the designatum 'X':

"...The "target" of consciousness is some "X"..." (1983, ms, p. 2)

Verhaar next proceeds to discuss a number of cases where a *triadic* relation is not feasible, and where the linguistic code seems to boil down to a *diadic* relation. His first case involves the well-known *self-inclusion paradox* , or 'consciousness of consciousness':

"...Now, it is by all means possible to be conscious of one's being conscious of X, but in such a state of consciousness, the original X has disappeared "out of the picture"...the original consciousness, of which one is now conscious, has lost its intentionality and therefore also its X..." (1983, ms, p. 2).

There are two issues that Verhaar neglects to consider in his argument. First, while the X of self-reflection may not be the *same* X ('external/perceived reality'), a definite *new* X has come into being via self-reflection, namely 'the "being conscious" of which one is now conscious'. The X --

and with it the X-relation -- is not lost but only shifted. Second, the difficulty in identifying the X here is not specific to self-reflection, but is rather a feature of all predications reporting *mental events, as in:*

(3) a. Mary *knew* that John went to Seattle.
    b. John *felt* a great pain.
    c. John *contemplated* the apple.

The designatum ('X') of (3a) is not the external event of John's going to Seattle, but rather the internal mental event of Mary's knowing it. Similarly, the 'X' of (3b) is not the pain itself, but rather John's feeling it. And the 'X' of (3c) is not the apple, but rather John's contemplating it. As we shall see further below, the fact that the 'X' in an X-relation (or even one of the terms in the S-relation) is a 'subjective' mental entity in no way disqualifies it from being a legitimate designatum, nor does it impinge upon the more-than-diadic nature of the linguistic coding relation.

The second argument used by Verhaar, in his attempt to challenge triadic Aristotelian semeiotics, involves the grammatical coding of the pragmatic function of 'topic:

"...There is, in syntax, a kind of genuine X-relatedness that is *not* "iconic": That of topicalization. It is not "iconic" because topicalization is not "triadic", but dyadic: it is like "pointing", and comprises therefore *only* (of) that pointing and that which is being pointed at..." (1983, ms, pp. 4-5)

As we shall see further below, Verhaar's perceptive comments on topicalization in fact pertain to the entire functional realm of discourse-pragmatics, as coded by morpho-syntax. When we discuss this issue more fully, I will attempt to sketch out the reasons why the absence of an obvious -- even conscious -- mental designatum, should not in itself be taken to mean the total lack of such a designatum.

The third argument raised by Verhaar against Aristotle's triadic semeiotics revolves around the issue of *language and culture* . In this connection, while acknowledging the Sapir-Whorf Hypothesis, Verhaar quotes Cassierer's (1933) account of the way children acquire their first language:

"...language does not just come into a world of objective perceptions which are already there... [it] is itself a mediator in the formation of objects; it is, to a certain extent, the mediator *par excellence* , the most important and precious instrument for the conquest and construction of a true world of objects..." (Cassierer, 1933, p. 33)

This argument is indeed Verhaar's most general, and thus presumably the most challenging. It is framed primarily in terms of the **lexical code**. It opens the door, potentially, for a would-be Wittgensteinean rejection of either the distinctness of language from thought (if one goes by the *Investigations*), or of the distinctness of thought and/or language from 'reality' (if one goes by the *Tractatus*). In the former, Wittgenstein characterizes Augustine's Platonic approach to the linguistic code as follows:

"...Every word has a meaning. This meaning is correlated with the word. It is the object for which the word stands..." (1953; 1; p. 2)

This approach seems to dispense with Verhaar's X-relation. (Much like Chomsky, Augustine's faith in a systematic relation between 'reality' and 'mind' was indeed weak). The bulk of the *Investigations* argues against such Platonism; but it is apparently possible to construe the argument not only as a rejection of absolute categories, but also of *all* categories. And if so, one must also dispense with Verhaar's S-relation.

To compound matters, an extreme would-be 'late' Wittgensteinean could also argue for giving up Verhaar's X-relation, roughly along the following lines:

(a) Meaning does not map extensionally to some objective reality; rather, it maps onto a contextually-mediated -- thus highly subjective -- reality.
(b) Since the external 'X' cannot be defined rigorously, the X-relation between meaning and 'X' lacks a proper designatum; therefore such a relation does not exist.

I myself feel that such an extreme interpretation is unsupported by 'late' Wittgenstein's text, which does not argue for a *total* contextualization of meaning, nor for *total* subjectivization of all external designata. In this connection one may recall the following passage from the *Investigations* :

"...But then the use of the word is unregulated, the 'game' we play with it is unregulated". -- It is not *everywhere* circumscribed by rules; but no more are there rules for how high one throws the ball in tennis... yet tennis is a game for all that and has rules too..." (1953; 68; p. 33; emphasis is mine; TG)

One may perhaps infer a rejection of the 'X' -- and thus of the X-relation -- from the following passage of the *Tractatus*:

"...the limits of my language means the limits of my world..." (1918, p. 115)

arguing that 'since language and world are one and the same' there is no sense in talking about a relation between 'X' and itself, unless it was a rather strange reflexive relation. Again, I find this an unnecessarily extreme reading of the 'early' Wittgenstein. Let us turn now to outline a more realistic approach to language as a communicative code.

3.3.2. Language as a complex coding system

In the discussion thus far I have deliberately followed a tradition that must now be transcended. That tradition, in discussing language as semeiotics ('coding system'), has been for a long time beclouded by almost total disregard for some rather fundamental facts concerning human language. Chief among those is the fact that language is a *complex, multi-level* code, rather than a relatively simple matching of sound sequences with lexical meanings. The reason why the complexity of the linguistic code is so crucial for our discussion of the designatum -- and the nature of both the S-relation and X-relation -- involves all three aspects of the semeiotics of language:

(a) **The sign level**:

Each of the three major *functional realms* of language -- lexicon, propositional semantics and discourse pragmatics -- displays its own highly specific coding properties (or 'coding processes'). It is thus incumbent upon us to define the S-relation in language three separate times, in terms that are highly specific to each functional realm.

(b) **The mind level and the S-relation**:

   (i) The 'internal', mental entity associated with the linguistic sign in the S-relation is highly specific to each of the three functional realms. Our discussion of this mental entity -- and of its S-relation -- must be thus highly specific to the functional realm under study.

   (ii) The S-relation between the linguistic sign at one end and the mental entity at the other is *not a single* coding step. Rather, it involves *several* successive steps of coding and re-coding. And this complex process of successive coding is highly specific -- cognitively and neurologically -- to each of the three functional realms.

(c) **The level of experienced reality:**

(i) The external 'X', paired with the mental entity through the X-relation, is itself highly specific to each of the three functional realms. Our discussion of this 'X' and its X-relation must be thus highly specific to the functional realm under discussion.

(ii) Finally, the X-relation between the external 'X' and whatever mental entity it may code, may also be a **multi-step coding process**. It may involve highly specific perceptual, neurological and cognitive steps.

The complex, multi-coding nature of both our S-relation and X-relation, while well documented in the neurology and psychology of both cognition and perception, is largely outside the immediate scope of our discussion here. We will thus proceed to discuss the three functional realms coded in human language.

3.3.3. Functional realms coded by language

"...When one shows someone the king in chess and says: "This is the king", this does not tell him the use of the piece -- unless he already knows the rules of the game up to this last point: the shape of the king... The shape of the chessmen corresponds here to the sound or shape of a word..."

L. Wittgenstein,
Philosophical Investigations
(1953; 31; p. 15)

In the above passage Wittgenstein coined, perhaps unintentionally,[15] a lovely metaphor for both the reality and complexity of the linguistic code. The complex, multi-level meaning system underlying the game of chess, and the codes used to make that system manipulable by the

---

15 Wittgenstein -- unlike Peirce -- deals almost always with the most obvious level of semeiology, the sound-coding of lexical meaning. However, Wittgenstein's reference to 'rules' is clearly not limited to lexical-semantic regularities (as in the definition of the chessmen's "roles"). Rather, it also pertains to the rules governing possible board positions, moves, and coherent move sequences ('Sicilian Defense', 'King's Pawn Opening'). Extending Wittgenstein's discussion to the other two functional realms coded by language -- propositional semantics and discourse pragmatics -- is thus natural.

players, indeed mirror, in a simplified *microcosm,* the multi-level functional system of language and its S-related codes:

(i) Lexical meaning:

Taken broadly, the chess pieces are all lexical **words;** so are the definition of the various *locations* ('squares') and their *properties* ('colors'). Complex spatial *configurations* of squares, where pieces may make well-defined *clusters* , are then **complex lexical items** ('compounds', 'derived vocabulary'). And this again mirrors an important property of the human lexicon.

The *shape* of the king is not, per se, an expression of its lexical meaning (i.e. its role in the game). Rather, it is the **code-expression** ('sign') of that role, a highly concrete visual code standing in this metaphor for our **sound code.** Unlike the predominantly symbolic-arbitrary sound-code of the human lexicon ('king', 'König', 'shah', etc.), the visual shape of the king is to some extent -- residually -- iconic; although many chess-sets use a much more abstract -- increasingly arbitrary -- lexical code for the chessmen.

(ii) Propositional information:

The spatial positions of the individual chess pieces are **states,** and their descriptions are **state propositions.** The moves made by individual pieces from one spatial positions to another are **events,** and their descriptions are **event propositions.**

In the human mind, then, information about specific states or events, concerning specific individuals at specific times and places, is coded by **propositions.** And human language, in turn, codes those mental propositions by **syntax;** syntax specifies how words are combined, together with **grammatical morphemes** to make **sentences;** and sentences are the signs that stand in an S-relation to mental propositions.

(iii) Discourse-pragmatic function:

The concatenations of individual moves into well-defined move-sequences, the hierarchic meta-structure of those combinations from the lowest *local* level, through increasingly *global* ('tactical' or 'strategic') levels, is governed by **discourse pragmatics.** Through discourse-pragmatic conventions or rules, propositions expressing individual states ('positions') and events ('moves') receive their **thematic coherence;** they become meaningful within the multi-propositional structure of the discourse -- the game.

The functional realm of discourse-pragmatics is **jointly coded** in human language, together with propositional-semantics, by sentence-level syntax. One may, to quite an extent, identify within sentential syntax the code elements that bear specific responsibility for coding propositional-semantic **information**, and those that are more specifically responsible for coding discourse-pragmatic **function**.

If we are to identify the **designatum** ('X') associated with human language, and at the same time understand the complex, multi-level coding relation of 'X', 'language' and 'mind', we must pursue the investigation separately for the three main functional realms, (i) **meaning**, (ii) **information**, and (iii) **function**.

3.3.4. In search of the designatum

> "...Enormous simplifications were possibly necessary to carry a deeper truth on the surface of a mass of unsorted detail. That was, after all, what happened when history was written; many, if not most, of the true facts discarded..."
>
> A. Powell *Temporary Kings*
> (1973, p. 27)

In this section we will consider further the questions raised by Verhaar (1983) concerning the S-relation and X-relation that bind together the linguistic code, its mental designatum and the latter's experiential designatum. We will treat each functional realm separately.

3.3.4.1. The lexical code

a) The S-relation

The nature of the sound-code via which the mental lexicon of concepts is coded is relatively well understood empirically. It is also perhaps slightly less controversial philosophically. Cross-cultural diversity in lexical-semantic organization indicates that the **mental designatum** associated with the S-relation (and thus the **experiential designatum** that stands in a X-relation to it) is in part culturally mediated. Culture as a context for meaning is indeed one sub-category of context (see above); we will discuss it more fully in Chapter 9, below.

Whatever one may choose to say about the existence and nature of the experiential designatum, the meaning of a word -- whatever it may be --

must itself be a **mental entity**. Each lexical mental entity ('concept') thus has some **sound-code label** attached to it.[16]

For the speaker, the lexical code-label serves in the retrieval and transmission of intended lexical meanings. For the hearer, the code-label evokes lexical meanings intended by the speaker, together with, presumably, other meanings that were not necessarily intended by the speaker. Presumably, the code-label also serves as a major **mnemonic device** for the storage (and retrieval) of conceptual knowledge in the mind/brain. (The other major mnemonic device is of course **meaning** itself, which presumably is represented in the mind not as an unordered, and thus unretrievable list, but rather as a *system* of semantic interrelations).

Finally, an enormous body of experimental psycho-linguistic literature demonstrates, through specific behavioral consequences, the mental reality of both the sound code and mental lexical meaning that partake in the lexical S-relation. [17]

(b) The X-relation

While the reality of the S-relation associated with the lexicon is relatively well established, Verhaar's X-relation -- and thus the question of what is the **experiential designatum** of mental lexical item -- remains controversial. The cleavage lines in this controversy follow the predictable philosophical division:

16 The sound-label can be substituted by other 'superficial coding' labels. It can be changed into an alphabetic code that represents the sounds more abstractly, with a wide latitude as to how faithful the written code is to the spoken one. Further, lexical meaning can be coded *pictographically* or -- as often evolves from pictographic codes -- *ideographically* . Finally, lexical meaning (as well as the entire language) may be also coded *gesturally* , as in ASL. Thus, if the same person is a fluent speaker, a literate writer and also a user of ASL, that person is capable of controlling potentially many codes pertaining to the very same mental entities.

17 For an exhaustive up-to-date review of the literature on what psychologists call 'lexical access', in terms of the mental reality -- and experimental- behavioral consequences -- of both the code-labels and lexical meanings, see Carr (1985). For details concerning the storage and retrieval of words and mental categories, see Rosch and Lloyd (eds,1978), Smith and Medin (1981), Anderson and Bower (1973), Neely (1976, 1977), Nissen (1976) or Kintsch (1974), *inter alia* . For many details concerning the neurological reality of the lexicon and its sound-code, see Patterson and Marcel (1977), Pirozzolo and Rayner (1977), Saffran and Marin (1977), Searleman (1977), Shallice & Warrington (1975), Whittaker (1983), *inter alia* . For details of the mental reality and behavioral consequences of the sound-code itself, see Adams (1979), Cole and Rudnicky (1983), Ganong (1980), Klatt (1979), Luce and Pisoni (1984), Nooteboom (1981), Cohen and Nooteboom (eds, 1975), Pollatsek and Carr (1979), *inter alia* .

(i) For extreme **rationalists**, the X-relation is trivial, presumably because of the primacy of innate ideas (the mental designatum), and also because of the alleged lack of systematic isomorphism between mind and reality. Thus, language may indeed be 'the mirror of mind', but mind is not 'the mirror of reality'.

(ii) For extreme **empiricists**, the X-relation between external (or 'perceived') reality and mental entities is taken for granted, given the primacy of world (or 'percept') over concept. At its extreme logical-positivist, experiential designata are referential, real-world entities standing in an **extensional** relation to mental concepts.

(iii) For **Kantian constructivists**, the X-relation is presumably highly systematic, complex, bi-directional and interactive. It is -- to add the Peircean-Wittgensteinean element -- also a context-mediated relation.

But what is then the experiential designatum of our mental lexicon? The bulk of our generically-shared mental-lexical concepts could not possibly stand in an X-relation to referential designata, but only to **classes** of **potential** experiential designata. Still, mental concepts are formed, contextually, interactively, through the experience of individual referential instances.[18] It is thus primarily when placed in the context of **specific proposition**, about specific individuals partaking in specific states or events, anchored at specific times and places, that lexical items stand in an X-relation to experiential designata. Therefore, in order to determine the experiential designata of lexical items ('concepts'), one must study the experiential designata of **propositional information**.

3.3.4.2. The propositional code

(a) **The S-relation**

As noted above, propositional-semantic information is coded in human language by syntactic structure. 'Structure' is a much more abstract and complex coding instrument than the sound-code. At its most concrete, syntactic structure is made out of the following three **coding devices:**

---

18 See discussion in Ch. 2, above, concerning the role of typical referential exemplars in constructing prototype-like generic categories.

    (i)   grammatical morphemes
    (ii) intonation contours
    (iii) linear order

Grammatical morphemes are phonologically coded much like the lexicon (from whence they evolve over time). Their 'meaning' however, is not lexical but much more general and abstract.[19] Further, most grammatical morphemes -- much like the bulk of word-order and intonational devices that make up syntax -- are not involved in the coding of propositional **information**, but rather in the coding of discourse-pragmatic **function**.

The propositional information coded by syntax pertains primarily to three major aspects of the state or event:

(4) (a) Designating the **roles** of the **participants** in the state or event (agent, patient, recipient, instrument, associate, beneficiary, manner, possessor, predicate, time, place etc.);

     (b) Designating the **predication type** ('verbal' vs. 'adjectival' vs. 'nominal' predicate); and

     (c) Identifying the **transitivity value** of the proposition ('transitive' vs. 'intransitive'; 'state' vs. 'process' vs. 'action').

When combined together, aspects (4a,b,c) above make up the **propositional frame**, sometimes referred to by philosophers as 'logical syntax' or 'logical structure' (see e.g. Carnap, 1959). When further combined with specific lexical items, propositional frames are transformed into full-fledged propositions, bearing **information** concerning the state or event (i.e. who did what to whom, where, when, with what, for whom, with whom, how, why or under what circumstances, etc.).

Sentences (or 'clauses'), which are syntactically-coded propositions, are thus the **signs** that stand in an **S-relation** to propositions. And propositions are, in turn, the **mental entities** coded by sentences. Since both linguistics and psychology have established the independent reality of both sentences and propositions beyond any reasonable doubt, we will forego belaboring the point here.[20]

(b) The X-relation

At first glance, an **X-relation** between mental propositions and some **experiential designatum** ('states', 'events') seems a safe bet. This seems

---

19 For an extensive discussion of the relation between lexicon and grammatical morphology, see Givón (1984a, Ch. 3).

20 For extensive surveys of the linguistic evidence, see Chafe (1970, 1979, 1980, ed.), Langacker (1984) or Givón (1984a), *inter alia* . For an equally extensive surveys of the experimental psychological literature, see Kintsch (1974, 1977), Kintsch and Keenan (1973), Kintsch and van Dijk (1978), van Dijk and Kintsch (1983) or Johnson-Laird (1983), *inter alia* .

true even in spite of the somewhat murky status of the triadic relation between language, thought and reality. In the space below I will attempt to illustrate how the experiential designatum of propositions, much like that of lexical items, is a context-dependent, pragmatically-mediated entity.

Consider the following, eminently transparent, proposition describing a rather concrete event:

(5) A man was beating a dog

Suppose you reported event (5) to me; suppose the mental proposition expressed in (5) referred ('stood in an X-relation') to some real event;[21] suppose, further, that you meant to report that event, which you had in fact witnessed, truthfully and accurately. The mental proposition coded by (5) refers to *what* ('beating') some *agent* ('a man') did to some *patient* ('a dog'). There seems to be, at first glance, a simple isomorphic X-relation between the proposition in (5) and the event it purports to code. But this seeming isomorphism dissolves rather quickly under the glare of even the most cursory inspection.

Suppose you witnessed that event from about 100 yards away, with the following details registering on your retinas rather sharply:

(6) (a) The man was beating the dog with a stick, which he held in his left hand;
   (b) The dog was tied to a tree, with a yellow leash;
   (c) The man kept raising and lowering the stick at certain intervals (say every 3 seconds);
   (d) The dog kept yelping, rather pitifully, producinga thin, high-pitched, rather unnerving wail;
   (e) The man was tall, dark-haired, athletic, dressed in a green jogging outfit;
   (f) The dog was a small, black-and-white off-spaniel mutt;
   (g) It was a bright, cool, breezy day, the 29th of October, around 10:27 am;
   (h) The whole scene was located on a green lawn, in the park above the river;
   (i) You were standing 107 yards away, to the south-east, at the bottom of the fir-covered butte.
   (j) There was another man watching the scene from about 70 yards on the opposite side; a woman holding the

---

21 See further discussion in Chapter 5, below, concerning the domain of reference of linguistically-coded information, the so-called 'Real World', and its relation to the 'Universe of Discourse'. Verhaar's first exception to the straight-forward X-relation between 'thought' and 'reality' indeed involves thought as the object ('designatum') of thought.

hand of a small child was walking diagonally across the lawn, coming up to about 40 yards from the man-and-dog scene, then slowly withdrawing toward the public bathrooms; other people -- both adults and children -- were playing all over the park;

(k) On the freeway in the background, about half a mile away, cars were zooming along at a fast clip.

Your reporting (5) to me was prompted by my inquiring: "What happened at the park?". All you told me, upon a certain reflection, was (5). Yet, it turns out that you also saw, at the very same time and place and from the same vantage point, all of the details in (6a-k) above. I know this because when I indeed persisted in asking, you readily volunteered all the added details. And you could have, had I persisted further, added even more. In fact, the sky is the limit·to what you could have added. Still, to begin with, you contended yourself with reporting only (5). Why?

The point of the exercise is by now transparent:

(i) There is, in principle, no limit to the detail that *could have been* included in your description of that rather concrete, perceptually transparent, seemingly unambiguous 'single event' that you saw. We quit at (6k) for lack of time and space, but could have gone on forever.

(ii) In principle, the choice of what to include and what to exclude in descriptions depends on one's pragmatic **framing**, i.e. on one's judgements of saliency, relevance, importance. None of these judgements are 'objective'; nor can they be arrived at deductively or inductively; they are all are a matter of **point of view**; of **context**; or the relevant **interpretant**.

There is a vast chasm, in principle, between the mental *propositional* representation of states and events and the 'real' (or 'experienced') states or events they purport to code. There is an equally vast chasm between mental *pictorial* representation of states and events and what actually registers on the eye's retina.[22] The mind/brain is highly selective about what it sees, retains or reports. And this selectivity is pragmatically controlled, except when processing has become fully automated.[23]

---

22 Viz Pylyshyn's (1973) "What the mind's eye tells the mind's brain". The problem we have here with propositionally-coded information about 'experience' is in no way unique. The Interpretant is ubiquitously here, as it is at other levels of information processing.

23 See Chapter 7, below, for extensive discussion of the automation ('routinization') of information processing at various levels.

What we noted above should in no way impel us to beat a hasty retreat for the illusory safety of Platonic (or Chomskyan) idealism. The lack of *total* iconic systematicity in the X-relation between mind and experience in no way means a *total lack* of such systematicity. One's rejection of naive, empiricist **objectivism** concerning 'reality' does not automatically commit one to embracing an equally extreme Wittgensteinean mush. In this connection, one may recall Geertz:

"...To abandon the hope of finding the "logic" of cultural organization in some Pythagorean "realm of meaning" is not to abandon the hope of finding it at all. It is to turn our attention toward that which gives symbols their life: Their use..." (*The Interpretation of Cultures* , 1973, p. 405)

Once again, a pragmatic middle-ground is the only empirically viable alternative to both extremes. The mind and reality **interact** in the **construction** of a **mental analog** -- or **isomorph** -- of some 'experienced reality'. That analog is only **similar**, but never identical, to whatever it purports to code. And similarity, the cornerstone of iconic-isomorphic representation, is a pragmatic, **context-mediated** relation. The context or 'interpretant', whether invoked or uninvoked, [24] is thus the ubiquitous silent partner in any coding relation.

Note, finally, that much empirical evidence from experimental psychology demonstrates how **selective** people are in constructing mental representations of states and events. This pertains to directly-witnessed states and events, as well as to those derived from reading or oral presentation. The mental representation of states and events is shown to be highly context-dependent, sensitive to many types of contextual **priming**. Finally, mental representation of states and events may remain, under some task conditions, visual rather than verbal-propositional.[25]

---

24 An apocryphal account has it that Xenophon, seeking a favorable omen from the Delphic oracle concerning his projected Persian Expedition, tried to outwit the God by not invoking its name directly. The Pythia came back with the sobering observation: "Invoked or uninvoked, the God will be there". The interpretant -- invoked or univoked -- is just as ubiquitous.

25 For the details of verbal accounts of witnessed events, see -- most conspicuously -- Loftus (1980), as well as many details in Paivio (1971), Potter et al (1977), Tversky (1969, 1975), or Pylyshyn (1973), *inter alia* . For various aspects of the context-dependent nature of the storage and retrieval of propositionally-coded experience, see Mandler and Johnson (1977), Mandler (1978), Kintsch (1974), Kintsch and Green (1978), Rumelhart (1977), Rumelhart and Ortony (1977), Anderson and Paulson (1978), Anderson and Pichert (1978), Anderson, Garrod and Sanford (1983), Perfetti and Goldman (1974) or Schank and Abelson (1977), *inter alia* . For similar suggestions reported by linguists, see Labov and Waletzky (1967) or Chafe (1980), *inter alia*.

3.3.4.3. **The discourse-pragmatic code**

3.3.4.3.1. **Preamble**

We return now to deal with the full impact of Verhaar's (1983) observations concerning 'topicalization'. Traditionally, philosophers and linguists have tended to take for granted their direct, intuitive access to lexical meaning and propositional information. Both were taken to be mental entities of which one is **conscious**. The same has never been true for discourse pragmatic functions. Both their mental designata and their experiential designata remain unexplored. Linguists have only recently begun to understand, just barely, how syntax codes various discourse-pragmatic functions; how the coding of such functions is distinct from the coding of propositional information; even what discourse-pragmatic functions are all about. This is of course natural. Discourse-pragmatics is a set of highly abstract **meta-phenomenological operations** and **processing instructions**. The processor is often unconscious of using them in processing the text. What is presented below is, therefore, only an incomplete sketch.

3.3.4.3.2. **Discourse-pragmatic functions**

In this section I list the major discourse-pragmatic functions that tend to be morpho-syntactically coded in natural language. The list is not exhaustive, nor is it the final formulation, given the rather tentative present state of our understanding.

(7) **Major discourse-pragmatic functions**

(a) **Topicality and reference functions:**

(i)   The assignment of (relative) **topic importance** to clausal participants ('subjects', 'objects'), presumably in a way that is sensitive to their **thematic importance** in the discourse; this often intersects with the marking of **semantic referentiality** (see Chapter 5, below).

(ii)   The **referential tracking** of clausal participants ('referents') as they are introduced into the discourse for the first time ('indefinite') or re-introduced ('definite'); the marking of **anaphoric predictability** (or 'accessibility') of clausal participants; the assignment of **coreference** relations in the discourse (see Chapter 6, below).

(iii)   The assignment of **contrastive** or **emphatic** status to clausal participants.

This cluster of function is performed by a large number of grammatical devices, such as case-marking of subject and object, the syntax of transitivity, passivization and anti-passivization, articles, demonstratives, pronouns and agreement, word-order and intonation.

(b) **Propositional modality functions:**

(iv)   The assignment of temporal, aspectual, epistemic, evidential, evaluative or speech-act **modality** to propositions, all involving various aspects of the **speaker's attitude** toward the proposition (see Chapter 4, below).

Syntactically, these functions are coded primarily by verb morphology, occasionally also with some participation of word-order and intonation.

(c) **Thematic coherence functions:**

(v)   Coding coherence relations between propositions, and between larger units, in discourse. This may be done first, anaphorically, in terms of **thematic predictability** and **thematic coherence** of propositions vis-a-vis the preceding discourse. Second, it may done cataphorically, in terms of **thematic importance** and **thematic predictability** of propositions vis-a-vis the following discourse.

(vi)   Coding **foreground-background** status to propositions, i.e. which ones constitute the **gist** of the message and which are **peripheral,** respectively.

(vii)   Coding more specific local **inter-clausal relations,** such as sequentiality or counter-sequentiality, temporality, conditionality, causality, contrast etc.

Syntactically, these functions are coded by either verb morphology or subordinating or coordinating conjunctions, as well as by word-order and intonation.

(d) **Socio-personal functions:**

(viii)   Coding the **socio-affective relations** between speaker and hearer, in terms of affect, status, obligations, power, needs, entitlements etc.

Syntactically, these functions may be coded together with speech-acts (see (iv) above). It is more common, however, for the bulk of these functions to be coded primarily by intonation, gesture and facial expression.

As should be obvious, discourse-pragmatic functions represent -- without exception -- various facets of the speakers' **attitude, perspective,** or **point of view.** They may 'be about' the reported propositional information; they may 'be about' various aspects of the **context** -- cultural, situational or textual -- that are relevant to how these propositions are to be integrated into coherent communication; they may even 'be about' some discourse-pragmatic functions themselves. Discourse-pragmatic functions are **mental meta-operations, meta comments,** or even **processing instructions.**[26] Such mental operations can be -- and often are -- highly abstract; they are clearly 'mental'; they are clearly coded by syntax; they are clearly, therefore, **mental designata** standing in an S-relation to some portion of the linguistic code. Their S-relation, as we will note below, is also highly **isomorphic-iconic.** Still, their S-relation is complex and abstract, it is much less accessible to conscious inspection than the S-relation holding between mental propositions and their syntactic code. [27]

3.3.4.3.3. The experiential designatum of discourse-pragmatic function: In search of a missing X-relation

As noted earlier, Verhaar (1983) suggests that the semeiotic relation of discourse-pragmatic function (his 'topicalization') is not tri-partite but rather *bi-partite* . That is, there is no experiential designatum ('X') in these mental operations, and thus no X-relation. On the face of it, this observation seems rather sound. Unlike for lexical concepts and mental propositions, one is hard-pressed to identify some real-world or experiential 'X' that might correspond to discourse-pragmatic functions. While I do not propose to resolve this problem for eternity at this point, one word of caution is in order. In the realm of propositional information too, the experiential 'X' need not have real-world extension. It could have, and often does have, a **discourse-universe** extension (see Chapter 5, below). Further, this designatum may also have a **purely internal** mental extension, as in the case of propositions involving verbs of thinking, knowing, wanting or feeling (see discussion of Verhaar's

---

26 In this sense, they are also akin to Verhaar's (1983, p. 2) self-reflection paradox, although perhaps in a sense that Verhaar himself did not anticipate; and certainly not in a sense that depletes meaning, as 'knowing that one knows...' indeed seems to do.

27 The syntactic structure that codes these operations is also more abstract. In this sense, a clear *meta-iconic* relation seems to hold between the degree of complexity/abstractness of the designatum and the degree of complexity/abstraction of the code.

reflexivity argument and example (3), above). It is, I believe, premature to rule out the possibility that discourse-pragmatic mental operations stand in some X-relation to some -- likewise **internal, mental** -- designata.

3.4. Iconicity and isomorphism in grammar

3.4.1. Background

> "...every animal communication system that is known...either consists of a fixed, finite number of signals, each associated with a specific range of behavior...or it makes use of a fixed, finite number of linguistic dimensions, each of which is associated with a particular non-linguistic dimension in such a way that selection of a point along the linguistic dimension determines and signals a certain point along the associated non-linguistic dimension... When I make an arbitrary statement in a human language... I am not selecting a point along some linguistic dimension that signals a corresponding point along an associated non-linguistic dimension..."
>
> N. Chomsky, *Language and Mind*
> (1968, pp. 69-70)

In surveying the history of our preoccupation with language as semeiology, one is struck by the persistent clustering of certain philosophical propensities, a clustering that seems less-than-accidental and yet not quite logically necessary. These propensities may be given as the following pre-empirical postulates:

(i)   There is an **evolutionary dis-continuity** between pre-human and human communication (cf. Chomsky, 1968);

(ii)   Language is a **separate module** of the mind/brain, not part of 'general cognition' (cf. Chomsky, 1968; see also Chomsky's various contributions in Piattelli-Palmarini ed., 1979);

(iii)   **Structuralism** in the analysis of language; that is, language structure can be analyzed **independently** of its communicative function (cf. Saussure, 1915; Bloomfield, 1933; Chomsky, 1957, *inter alia*);

(iv)   Some **abstract, idealized** entity -- be it *langue* or *competence* -- is the 'object' of linguistic analysis (cf. Saussure, 1915; Chomsky, 1964);

(v)   The **synchronic** facts of language must be studied in strict separation from **diachronic** facts (Saussure, 1915);

(vi)   The **sign-relation** between the linguistic code and its mental designatum is **arbitrary**, unlike the obvious iconicity seen in pre-human communication (Saussure, 1915; Chomsky, 1968).

The **Uniqueness of Man** doctrine expressed in (i) and (vi) was espoused by Descartes on religious grounds, and is closely connected with his belief in **innate ideas** and their divine source.[28] Innate ideas, those Platonic absolutes underlying the human mind, are presumably also at the bottom of the **idealization** of the object of linguistic investigation (iv). And that idealization of the data-base (iv) is reflected in the further idealization in (v), where 'steady state' is abstracted from the ever-present process of change. The so-called **modular** approach to language and cognition (ii) is an unprecedented non-Cartesian elaboration by latter-day structuralists, closely linked to the view of language structure as **autonomous** from language function (iii).

We come at last to the presumed **arbitrariness** of the human linguistic code. It seems to be intimately bound with all the other components of the cluster:

(a) The arbitrariness doctrine is surely implicit in the anti-evolutionary and anti-developmental approach of the structuralists (i), as well as in the strict separation of synchronic state from diachronic change (v). (It is only through the three developmental processes -- phylogeny, ontogeny and diachrony -- that the isomorphic pairing of language code and language function is mediated).

(b) The arbitrariness doctrine is consistent with the modular separation of language and cognition (ii), since cognition is a major functional parameter underlying language.

(c) The arbitrariness doctrine is virtually a logical consequence of the structuralist's insistence on separating the study of

---

28 Chomsky (1968) and Bickerton (1980) merely substitute *DNA* for the *Divine*. See discussion of the history of evolutionary thinking in Chapter 10, below.

structure and function (iii); functional considerations -- i.e. the needs for coherent storage and quick retrieval -- furnish the most obvious motivation for an iconic relation between code and meaning.

(d) Finally, the arbitrariness doctrine is also an implicit consequence of the idealized data base (iv, v). This is so because only in studying structures and functions in their communicative context -- i.e. in language use -- can we begin to appreciate the nature and extent of their isomorphic-iconic S-relation.

3.4.2. Preliminaries

3.4.2.1. Iconicity and isomorphism

'Iconicity' presupposes 'isomorphism'. An iconic code is necessarily one that displays an isomorphism to its designatum. As Peirce has noted, an *icon* is a sign that bears some **similarity** to its designatum. 'Iconicity' and 'similarity' are thus closely linked. Here is what Aristotle had to say on this matter:

"...Things are "alike" [*hómoios*] when, though they are not absolutely the same and though they are different individuals, they nevertheless have the *same form* ..." (*Metaphysics* , p. 206)

And our dictionary defines 'isomorphism' as "...similarity in form..." (Morris, ed., 1969, pp. 694-695). And form, in turn, involves two components:

(a) A matching number of corresponding **points**; and
(b) A matching number of corresponding **relations**.

Isomorphism is thus neither an explanation of nor motivation for iconic coding, but simply part of its *definition*.[29]

---

29 In this I am diverging from Haiman (to appear), who asserts that 'isomorphic' representation requires only the matching of points, while 'diagrammatic' representation requires the matching of both points and relations. I find this distinction arbitrary; it is supported by neither precedent nor argument. The same goes for Haiman's (1983) attempt to view iconicity as a 'motivation' ('explanation') for isomorphism.

3.4.2.2. **Motivation and explanation**

The motivation for the existence, or for the rise, of iconic code-relations in any sub-system within a biological organism falls within the same domain as all other explanations in biology. It must be first and foremost **functionally** explained.[30] This is true either for our *ultimate* understanding of the synchronic structure of a system through its bio-cognitive context, or for our understanding of the developmental mechanisms by which the system has evolved.[31] In biology, this functionalist approach to explanation has been taken for granted ever since Aristotle. Thus, consider the following from a standard textbook of anatomy:

> "...anatomy is the science that deals with the structure of the body... physiology is defined as the science of function. Anatomy and physiology *have more meaning* when studied together..." (Crouch, 1978, pp. 9-10; emphases are mine; TG)

The first layer of explanation of iconicity in language is not strictly empirical; rather it is a pre-empirical, common-sensical postulate, a *meta-assumption* concerning the use of human language as a communicative tool. In one guise or another, it has been with linguistics since its very beginning.

(8) **The iconic imperative:**

> "All other things being equal, a coded experience is easier to store, retrieve and communicate if the code is **maximally isomorphic** to the experience".

Wherever language and its mental representation may have their experiential designatum, postulate (8) pertains to both Verhaar's 'S-relation' and 'X-relation'. Otherwise, it always pertains to the S-relation between the linguistic code and its mental designatum.[32]

Haiman (to appear) points out that principle (8) is a version of the traditional *one form one meaning* or *one-to-one correlation* between form and meaning principle. Bolinger renders this principle as:

---

30 In this connection, note Posner's (1985) discussion of the functional-adaptive motivation for the hybrid prototype categorization (Chapter 2, section 2.6., above). See also discussion in Givón (1979, Ch. 1; 1984a, Ch. 2), as well as Chapter 8, below.

31 In language, these developmental mechanisms include evolution, ontogeny and diachrony.

32 Since it is fairly clear that many more perceptual, neurological and cognitive coding steps (or 'mapping relations') occur in the production and perception of language (and in mental representation of experience in general), one must assume that principle (8) also pertains to those other mapping relations.

"...The natural condition of language is to preserve one form for one meaning, and one meaning for one form..." (1977, p. x)

As suggested earlier, language processing probably involves multiple coding steps. Within each step, principle (8) manifests itself in ways that are specific to the processing level involved. Further, the three functional realms coded by language may exhibit the motivating power of principle (8) in ways that are specific to their processing mode (cf. sections 3.3.3, 3.3.4, above). Thus, whenever economy is invoked as a motivating principle, it must be considered relative to the level and mode of real-time physiological and mental processing associated with each coding level.[33]

3.4.2.3. Degree of conscious access to iconic code relations

Andersen (1983), in a Peircean vein, points out that the notion of 'similarity' requires the **consciousness** of similarity in the mind of some interpreter. In our re-formulated terms (see axiom (1), section 3.2.2., above), this follows naturally from the observation that the relevant **interpretant** -- or **context** -- for similarity relations is always a mental construct in the mind of some interpreter. However, 'being in the mind' may involve different **degrees** of consciousness. One's degree (and mode) of consciousness vis-a-vis the three coded realms of language -- lexicon, propositional meaning and discourse-pragmatics function -- may be radically different. One is, no doubt, quite conscious of the S-relation *cum* X-relation of at least *some* lexical concepts. One may be much less conscious of the S-relation and X-relation of propositional information. Although it is still possible to point out those relations, at least in more concrete cases, to the naive speaker. Finally, one is, on the whole, quite unaware of either the existence of *any* mental or experiential designata of the syntactic structure that codes discourse-pragmatic function, or of the nature of either its S-relation or X-relation. The reasons for this differential awareness are transparent. They may be summarized here as follows:[34]

(a) The experiential designata of lexical items are more concrete and obvious than those of propositions; and those of pro-

---

33 Haiman (1983, to appear) attempts to separate iconic from economic motivation. As I have argued elsewhere (Givón, 1984b), I think this is a confusing dichotomy. Rather, economy of mental, neurological or sensory processing ultimately motivates *all* cases of isomorphic coding. Postulate (8) is thus as pertinent to cognition, perception, neurology and biology as it is to language.

34 These three facts concerning the code, the coded and their relation are themselves meta-iconically matched.

positions are in turn more concrete and obvious than those of discourse-pragmatic function;

(b) Whatever one-to-one coding relation existing between code and designatum is thus most transparent for lexical items, less so for propositions, and least so for discourse-pragmatic functions;

(c) The code level itself is most concrete for the lexicon (strings of sounds), less concrete for propositional meaning, and most abstract for discourse-pragmatic function.

What this gradation implies for the Peircean 'interpretant' remains for the moment somewhat open. Both Andersen (1983) and Haiman (1983) seem to reject the abstract iconic relations matching syntax with discourse-pragmatic function as legitimate extensions of Peirce's concept of icon. They do so in part because of the unclear nature of 'consciousness' and 'interpretant' associated with this isomorphic code. My own inclination, derived at least in part from recent neuropsychological studies of **levels of attention**,[35] is to resist such apriori delimitation of the subject matter. It may yet turn out that unwarranted rigidity will lead us to disregard the most interesting if least obvious iconic code associated with human language. Many other mental coding operations are equally unavailable to conscious perusal. The fact that the discourse-pragmatic code is more complex, abstract, and less given to conscious scrutiny is no reason for ignoring its existence, its specific properties and its broader cognitive and biological implications.

3.4.3. **Isomorphism, abstraction and prototypicality**

"...Hypoicons may be roughly divided according to the mode of Firstness of which they partake. Those which partake of simple qualities, or First Firstness, are *images* ; those which represent the relations, mainly diadic, or so regarded, of the parts of one thing by analogous relations in their own parts, are *diagrams*; those which represent the representative character of a representamen by representing a parallelism in something else, are *metaphors* ...."

C.S. Peirce (1940, p. 105)

In this section I propose to recapitulate the obvious, namely that the Peircean **icon** and **symbol** are merely two extreme poles on a con-

35 See Posner (1985), as well as Chapter 7, below.

tinuum, one that represents the degree of **abstraction** in coding relations. The increase of abstraction along this scale means, perforce, an increase in **arbitrariness** of the code. There is nothing particularly earthshaking about these observations; they are akin to Bateson's (1979) note concerning 'patterns and patterns of patterns'.[36] Haiman also recognizes a similar gradation between image and diagram:

"...Although Peirce himself did not emphasize this point, it should be clear that the distinction between an icon that is an *image* (like a photograph), and one that is a *diagram* (like a stick figure), is also mainly a matter of degree..." (to appear; p. 16 of ms)

To illustrate with a simple example the continuum between iconic and symbolic representation, consider the gradual evolution of the letter *A* in our alphabet. To judge from its Semitic etymology,[37] *A* is derived historically from a pictograph representing 'bull' or 'cattle' (Hebrew *?lf*). The first step in the abstraction process had already occurred when the head alone -- rather than the entire body -- was used to represent the entire animal:

(9)

---

36 Bateson (1979) views this issue, I think correctly, as a matter of increasingly more *general* meta-levels of description, deriving his formulation from Russell's (1919) *Theory of Types* .

37 The earliest attestation of the script is usually ascribed to Phoenician. However, the name of the pictograph *?alef* has the requisite meaning in Hebrew rather than in Phoenician.

Presumably, the head was considered the most relevant, important, **prototypical** part of the body. And this, in turn, expresses a clear hierarchic ('taxonomic') judgement at two distinct levels:[38]

(a) A **functional-biological** judgement concerning the crucial, governing role the head plays vis-a-vis the body; and

(b) A **perceptual** judgement concerning what are the most salient visual features of a bull, especially in terms of the need to distinguish it from other domestic quadrupeds of a roughly similar shape.

In addition, the representation of the animal's head in (9) already involves considerable abstraction, dispensing with more minor structural features such as hair, skin folds or exact detail of the eye, ear, nose etc. Bateson considers such abstraction or simplification, inherent in the modeling ('representation') of any phenomenon, "...in principle distortive of the phenomena to be mapped..." (1979, p. 53). But such 'distortion' is inherent in all processes of generalization, abstraction, and concept formation; or, for that matter, in all coding and representation.

The taxonomic-hierarchic decision referred to above is just as obvious in the next step of abstraction, where again more minor details are dispensed with:

(10)

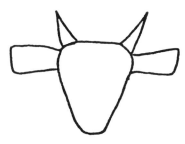

---

38 While the two considerations -- functional and structural -- are formally distinct, it is most likely that the mind does not keep them apart, leastwise operationally. And this is probably another manifestation of our postulate (8).

Curving lines are gradually regularized and straightened, to conform to their prototypical extension. The head now displays the more abstract iconism of a *triangle* , carrying the original difference between the wider top and narrower bottom to its ultimate prototypical conclusion. From here the path is indeed short to a recognizable version of the letter ?alef.

(11)

What keeps version (11) residually iconic, i.e. isomorphic to the original bull's head, is its vertical orientation vis-a-vis the scanning eye, an orientation that preserves the spatial arrangement of the bulls head in its prototypical posture. But the number of isomorphic points, thus also of their inter-*relations*, has shrunk to a bare minimum (horns, ears, crown, snout). The isomorphism in *pattern* is still there. The next, historically attested, development in the Phoenician/Hebrew script effectively pulled the rug from under this residual iconicity, by turning the ?alef on its side:

(12)

And once the inherent iconism of the prototypical spatial orientation has been removed, the transition to the Greek *alpha* -- via further inversion of the capital letter -- is relatively trivial:

(13)

The magic of iconic-isomorphic representation is lost altogether, and we have a unitary symbol standing for a unitary sound or concept.

The gradual process of abstraction seen above may be summarized as follows:

(i) **Number of isomorphic points:**
The abstraction of signs involves a gradual reduction in the number of points in the sign that map onto points in the designatum, all the way to the absolute minimum that still allows an S-relation -- one. Presumably, this depletion proceeds up the *hierarchy of generality* . That is, more specific ('minor') points are removed first; more generic ('major') points, those found at higher meta-levels of the classificatory hierarchy, survive longer.

(ii) **Pattern of relations between points:**
When the number of points is reduced, the number of inter-point relations is also reduced. The pattern is thus gradually abstracted or generalized. But however abstract and elusive, an isomorphic pattern of relation must remain there, since the points alone, even when matching the designatum point by point, do not guarantee isomorphism.

The end-point in the transition of a sign from **icon** to **symbol** displays two related features. First, only a single point now stands in an S-relation—trivially isomorphic—with the designatum. Second, the symbol displays no obvious pattern of inter-point relation isomorphism with the designatum. One may thus concede that symbolic representation, as an extreme pole on the continuum of **degree of iconicity**, is indeed strikingly different from the imagic extreme. But if we now insist on viewing this as a difference in *kind* rather than in *degree*, we are bound to ignore two fundamental points, one methodological, the other ontological:

(a) **Methodological:**
There is no principled way by which one can decide at what point, on the graded continuum between image and symbol, one has traversed the boundary between iconic and symbolic representation.

(b) **Ontological:**
In some fundamental way, a one-point symbolic sign is just as isomorphic to its designatum as an n-point diagram or image. It is isomorphic, however, at the appropriate meta-level of abstraction. That is, it stands for the designatum *as a whole* .

One may of course wish to dismiss point (b) as sheer sophistry. However, our lexicon and its phonological representation constitute a large body of *prima facie* evidence in support of precisely such single-point iconic representation (see discussion further below). In sum, the degree of abstractness of the isomorphic relation between linguistic signs and their mental or experiential designata, should not prejudice our study of the complex, abstract iconicity of the grammatical code.

3.4.4. Iconicity in syntax: Case studies

3.4.4.1. Propositions and temporal order

Two relatively concrete, transparent types of iconicity in syntax will be mentioned here without much detail. The first involves the rather superficial isomorphism between components of the proposition and components of a state or event. Thus, in the sentence

(14) John cut the meat for Mary with a knife

each noun phrase corresponds to a participant in the 'event' (or rather, in the mental proposition). The same line of reasoning would, presumably, also suggest that the verb itself corresponds to one element in the proposition, the 'action'. As one can see, however, both the S-relation and X-relation of the verb are much more abstract and *constructed* than those of the nominal arguments.[39]

Another relatively transparent case of iconicity in grammar is discussed by Haiman (1985; to appear). It involves the fact that events tend to be coded, by propositions, in the same temporal order in which they occurred in real time. Thus, in (15) below, (15a) is a more preferred order of reporting. And (15b), while possible, is a more *marked* order:[40] Preposed clauses are preferred over post-posed ones regardless of temporal order in the coded experience. The principle controlling such preference is discourse-pragmatic, having to do with the strategies by which earlier discourse is recalled back at a relevant point later in the discourse.

(15) a. Having finished his dinner, John left.
    b. John left, having finished his dinner.

A more trivial case of such iconicity involves the simple concatenation of propositions, as in:

(16) a. John got up and left.
    b. ?John left and got up.

---

39 See discussion in section 3.3.4., above, concerning the designatum of propositions.
40 For some text-based quantified studies of the frequency of pre-posed and post-posed adverbial clauses, see Thompson (1985) and Ramsay (1985). The problem is not as simple as it first appears.

3.4.4.2. Quantity scales in the grammar of referential identification

In a series of cross-linguistic studies (Givón, ed.,1983; 1984c; see also Chapter 6, below) it was noted that the most common topic-coding anaphoric devices used in languages may be ranked along a scale of **referential predictability** ('accessibility', 'continuity'). The points on the scale that are most stable cross-linguistically are:

(17) **most predictable/continuous**
    a. zero anaphora
    b. unstressed pronoun
    c. stressed pronoun
    d. definite noun
    e. restrictively modified definite noun
    least predictable/continuous

Let us illustrate these anaphoric devices with simple examples from English. Respectively:

(18) a. John came in, [ø] looked around and [ø] gasped.
    b. John talked to Bill; then *he* left. (= John left)
    c. John talked to Bill; then *he* left. (=Bill left).
    d. John came in and paused. *The woman* got up.
    e. *The tall woman* remained in the room. Later on, *the man who had been hiding under the couch* emerged.

The grounds on which a referent may be more predictable ('accessible') may vary, with the most obvious ones being:

(a) Gap of absence from the previous appearance in discourse
(b) Referential complexity of the preceding discourse
(c) Available 'redundant' propositional-semantic information
(d) Available 'redundant' discourse-thematic information

And at least two of these, (a) and (b) above, can be measured quantitatively in text-based studies or in psycho-linguistic experiments.[41]

---

41 For the text-based studies, see Givón (ed., 1983) as well as Chapter 6, below. For the growing psycho-linguistic literature see Fletcher (1982), Dahl and Gundel (1982), Tomlin (1985), Givón *et al* (1985) and Gernsbacher and Hargreaves (1986), *inter alia* .

The coding principle underlying the scale in (17) is rather transparent, and may be summarized first as:

(19) **Code-quantity and informational predictability:**
"The less predictable the information is, the more coding material is used coding it"

Since psycho-linguistic evidence [42] suggests a clear correlation between the predictability of information and the amount of **mental effort** used in processing it, one may re-phrase (19) in a more general way, as a correlation between code quantity and mental effort:

(20) **Code-quantity and mental effort:**
"The more mental effort is used in processing information, the more coding material will be used in representing the information in language".

Note first that the designatum of the pragmatic function 'degree of referential predictability', i.e. the mental dimension underlying scale (17), is itself neither a mental concept of some real-world entity, nor a mental proposition concerning some experienced state or event. Rather, the designatum is itself an **abstract mental process**, having to do with the speaker's assessment as to how accessible the referent is to the hearer. The linguist may reflect upon the use of the anaphoric devices in (17/18), and may indeed conclude that they are ranked along a scale of mental accessibility or retieval effort.[43] But it is reasonably safe to assume that speakers are largely unaware of the rather simple iconic relation existing there.

Further, the scale in (17/18) is merely one of many instances where principle (19/20) manifests itself in language. For example, lexical morphemes bear more (and more specific) information than grammatical morphemes, and are on the whole phonologically larger. In the pragmatic use of intonation to designate degree of informational **novelty** ('contrast', 'surprise'), perceptually more prominent intonation (higher pitch, louder amplitude, longer duration) always codes less predictable information (cf. Bolinger, 1978, 1984).[44]

Note also that the code-quantity scale in (17) and its clear iconic rela-

---

42 Dahl and Gundel (1982), Chang (1980), Corbett and Chang (1983), Garrod and Sanford (1977), Anderson, Garrod and Sanford (1983), Dell, McKoon and Ratcliff (1983), Ratcliff and McKoon (1980), McKoon & Ratcliff (1980), Givón *et al* (1985), *inter alia* .

43 As, for example, in Givón (1979, ch. 2).

44 In our scale (17) we have a partial reflection of this fact, in that in many languages -- English included -- the difference between unstressed pronouns ('clitic pronouns', 'verb agreement') and stressed ('independent', 'contrastive') pronouns is coded primarily by stressing the latter.

tion with some mental dimension is clearly at odds with Chomsky's characterization of human grammatical structure as non-iconic, non-scalar, non-matching:

"...When I make some arbitrary statement in human language,...I am not selecting a point along some linguistic dimension that signals a corresponding point along an associated non-linguistic dimension..." (1968, p. 70)

Bolinger (1984) has pointed out that the use of intonation in human language is a natural extension -- in his word, part and parcel -- of the **gestural** inventory used in human communication. This is the very subsystem that Chomsky himself concedes resembles animal communication:

"...The examples of animal communication that have been examined to date do share many of the properties of human gestural systems, and it might be reasonable to explore the possibility of direct [i.e. evolutionary; TG] connection there..." (1968, p. 70)

Principle (18/19), underlying the grammar of referential tracking in human language, thus seems a natural extension of the phylogenetically older gestural coding system found in pre-human communication.

3.4.4.3. The use of word-order in the grammar of referential identification

In a number of recent studies (see Chapter 6, below),[45] it was shown that the pragmatic use of flexible word-order in language, with particular reference to the position of the subject and object vis-a-vis the verb, is highly sensitive to both the relative **predictability** ('continuity', 'accessibility') and relative **importance** of those nominal referents

---

45 See summary in Givón (ed., 1983a). The cross-linguistic evidence on the discourse-pragmatic conditioning of word-order flexibility now includes text-based studies of Ute (Givón, ed., 1983a), Spanish (Bentivoglio, 1983), Biblical Hebrew (Fox, 1983; Givón, 1977), Yagua (Payne, 1983), Papago (Payne, 1984), Tagalog (Fox, 1985), Iroquois (Mithun, 1985), Mandarin Chinese (Sun and Givón, 1985), Indonesian (Verhaar, 1984; Rafferty, 1985), Chamorro (Cooreman, 1985), Nez Perce (Rude, 1985), Hixkaryana (Derbyshire, 1985) and Pidgin English (Givón, 1984b).

('topics') in discourse. The correlation between topic predictability, topic importance and word-order can be summarized initially as:[46]

(21) a. "More **unpredictable/inaccessible** referents tend to be fronted"

b. "More **important** referents tend to be fronted"

It is possible, further, to integrate (21a,b) into a single formulation, by noting their common denominator -- **task urgency**:[47]

(22) "When a referent is either **less accessible** or **more** important in the discourse, the communicative task of coding it well ('strongly', 'distinctly') is more urgent".

And once (22) is granted, it is possible to express (21) as the unitary cognitive principle (see also Chapter 6, below):

(23) "Attend first to the most urgent task"

Much like principle (19/20), which motivates the S-relation between the syntactic code and some internal operation of mental effort, principle (23) suggests an isomorphic S-relation between the syntactic code and some mental dimension of **task urgency**. Both of these **internal designata**, which may ultimately reflect the very same mental process, are highly abstract. They involve the inner workings of the **processor** itself, rather than any coded experience *per se* . Both are relatively inaccessible to conscious reflection (compared to propositional information or lexical concepts).

3.4.4.4. **The grammatical coding of complement clauses**

There exists a systematic correlation between the semantic properties of complement-taking verbs, most specifically the type of semantic *bond*

---

46 While English is a rigid SVO language, it still reflects this principle in dislocated constructions. Thus compare: a. *L-dislocation* :John, I saw him yesterday; b. *Neutral order;* I was John yesterday; c. *R-dislocation* I saw him yesterday, John. In quantified text sudies (Givón, ed., 1983a) it was shown that (a) is characteristic of large referential gaps, (b) of intermediate ones and (c) of smaller ones.

47 For the initial suggestion see Givón (ed. 1983a, 1984b). See also further discussion in Chapters 5 and 6, below.

they display vis-a-vis their complement clause, and the syntactic structure of that complement clause. The semantic properties involved, subsumed originally under the label of **binding**,[48] can be expressed in terms of three major scalar features:

(24) a. **Control**: "The higher the main verb is on the binding scale, the stronger is the control exerted by its agent over the agent of the complement clause".

b. **Success**: "The higher the main verb is on the binding scale, the more likely it is that the intended manipulation was successful, and the more likely it is that the event/state coded in the event coded in the complement indeed occurred".

c. **Independence**: "The higher the main verb is on the binding scale, the less likely it is that the agent of the complement clause can act independently".

The binding scale thus ranks **manipulative** over non-manipulative verbs, **implicative** ('successful') over non-implicative manipulations, **intended** over unintended manipulations, and **direct** over mediated manipulations.[49]

The syntactic structure of complement clauses involves four distinct elements that together code the degree of binding exerted by the main verb over its complement clause:

(25) a. **Subject/agent case-marking**: "The higher the main verb is on the binding scale, the less likely is the subject/agent of the complement to display the case-marking characteristic of subjects/agents of main clauses".

b. **Verb modalities**: "The higher the main verb is on the binding scale, the less likely is the complement verb to display the tense-aspect-modality markings characteristic of main-clause verbs".

---

48 Givón (1980a), with some of the semantic details due to an earlier work (Givón, 1975b). Since that account was written, Chomsky has come out with his own 'binding', which has nothing to do with the topic discussed here. Unlike Peirce, I do not feel compelled to change the name of my brain-child in order to save it from kidnappers.

49 That is, 'order' >'wish', 'cause'>'order', 'make'>'cause', 'make'>'have', respectively.

c. **Fusion or co-lexicalization**: "The higher the main verb is on the binding scale, the more likely is the complement verb to co-lexicalize with the main verb".

d. **Separation**: "The higher the main verb is on the binding scale, the less likely it is that a subordinating morpheme would separate the complement clause from the main clause".

The coding correlates (25a,b,c,d) are rather transparent iconic-isomorphic expressions of three major **transitivity** properties of the complement clause:

(25a)   codes the **agent** of the complement as either being or not being an independent, willful, controlling initiator of the event;

(25b)   codes the **action/verb** of the complement as either being or not being independent in time, perfective in aspect and realis in mode;

(25c,d) jointly code the independent status, or lack thereof, of the **event** expressed in the complement clause.

Note next that the isomorphism between the syntactic devices in (25) and the transitivity properties of complement clause derives its power from two radically different sources. Both coding principles (25a) and (25b) derive their power -- at least in part -- from some *system-internal*, abstract norms, or *rules of grammar* . Only because these system-internal norms for case-marking and tense-aspect marking have already been established for the grammar of main clauses, can coding correlations (25a,b) assume their iconic power. The main components of these system-internal norms are highly universal, and may be summarized as follows:

(26)   a. **Universal norms for subject-marking in transitive clauses:**

"Given the case-role hierarchy:[50]

AGENT > DATIVE > PATIENT > OTHERS

---

[50] For a detailed discussion of the various case-role hierarchies, see Givón (1984a, Chapters 4,5).

the more the subject case-marking resembles the one normally displayed by the highest-ranking term of this hierarchy (i.e. the *agent*), the more is the event likely to be an independent transitive event".

b. **Universal norms for verb-marking in transitive clauses:**

"Given the verb-modality hierarchies:[51]
PERFECTIVE > IMPERFECTIVE
SEQUENTIAL > PERFECT/ANTERIOR
COMPACT > DURATIVE
REALIS > IRREALIS

the closer the verb morphology of the clause is to the higher-ranking term in these hierarchies, the more likely is the event to be an independent transitive event".

While the universal hierarchies in (26a,b) are widely attested cross-linguistically, and while they are no doubt themselves founded upon general cognitive, communicative and socio-cultural principles, the actual grammar of case-marking and tense-aspect-modality is highly *language-specific*. It involves *partially arbitrary* language-specific considerations of rigid word-order, of morphology, of diachronic attrition, etc. In contrast, the iconic power of coding correlates (25c,d) derives rather transparently from a general cognitive principle, one that may be given as:

(27) **The proximity principle:**
"The closer two mental entities are to each other semantically or functionally, the more likely they are to be placed together, in linear proximity, in the linguistic code".

Haiman (to appear) renders principle (27) as:

"...linguistic fusion signals conceptual fusion; linguistic independence signals conceptual independence..." [p. 209, ms]

The overt linguistic code is substantially *linear*. What principle (27) does is establish an iconic relation between linear proximity at the code level and **conceptual proximity** (of a great variety of types) at the mental designatum level. Both the co-lexicalization of verbs (i.e. (25c), also

---

51 For a detailed discussion of these hierarchies, see Hopper & Thompson (1980) and Givón (1982b, 1984a ch. 8).

called 'predicate raising') and the absence of a subordinating morpheme (25d), are thus coding manifestations of greater conceptual proximity ('affinity', 'unity') of the two propositions (main and complement). The use of these devices signals that the speaker construes the two propositions as **a single event**. The first device, (25c) is manifest at the lexical level. The second, (25d), is manifest at a wider-scoped syntactic level.

Note, in passing, that principle (27) also predicts the co-lexicalization of derivational affixes with their relevant stems, the co-lexicalization or adjacency of grammatical operators with their operand lexical stems, the proximity of operator words to their operand words, and the correlation between linear proximity and conceptual scope.

The combined syntactic coding scale that corresponds, in a particular language, to the conceptual scale of 'degree of binding' between main and complement clauses, is indeed complex. It involves the case-marking system, the tense-aspect-modality system, morphemic subordinator and the *degree* of co-lexicalization.[52] To illustrate this briefly, consider the following examples from English:

(28) a.	He *let-go* of her	(pred-raising)
b.	He *let* her *go*	(bare-stem comp.)
c.	He *wanted* her *to go*	(infinitive comp.)
d.	He *wished* that she *would go*	(subjunctive comp., nominative subject, subordinator)
e.	He *thought* that she *had gone*	(finite comp., nominative subject, subordinator)

This syntactic scale is totally *integrated* , with the highly abstract, grammar-dependent code elements such as case-marking and verb modality (25a,b) interspersed throughout with the more concrete, cognitively-transparent coding devices (25c,d). This suggests, at least tentatively, that in spite of the disparate cluster of motivations that give rise to the iconicity of the syntactic code, at some level this code may assume a *unified mental reality* .

3.4.4.5. Passivization and the coding of transitivity

Passivization is a complex phenomenon, ranging over at least three major functional domains:[53]

---

52 While (25c) is formulated here in categorial (either/or) terms, there is good cross-language evidence in support of a *scalar* interpretation of this feature as well. For details see Givón (1980a).

53 For the original formulation of this cluster approach to passivization, see Givón (1981a).

(29) **Functional domains of passivization:**

(a) **Topic assignment:**
"Marking some non-agent -- most commonly an object -- as the **primary topic** of the clause";

(b) **Impersonalization:**
"Downgrading the **importance** or **topicality** of the subject/agent of the event";

(c) **Stativization:**
"Construing the event as the **resulting state** of an action".

As one can see, as a pragmatic operation of re-orienting the speaker's point of view vis-a-vis an event, passivization tampers with all three major components of transitivity.[54] It suppresses the saliency of the agent-cause, upgrades the saliency of the patient-effect, and focuses on the resulting state of the event, rather than on the change ('process') itself.

Each of the three functional domains of passivization (29a,b,c) is associated with a distinct grammatical coding-feature that stands in a transparently iconic S-relation to it. The three coding features of passivization are respectively:

(30) **Coding features of passivization:**

a. **Non-agent promotion:**
"Some non-agent (most commonly 'object') argument of the transitive event receives in the passive clause the type of case-marking (in terms of word-order, morphology and grammatical agreement)[55] that in the active clause characterizes the agent of the event. That is, given the case hierarchy:
AGT > DAT > PAT > OTHER,
the promoted non-agent is 'moved', syntactically, up to the top of the hierarchy".

b. **Agent/subject demotion:**
"The agent/subject of the active clause receives in the passive clause the type of case-marking characteristic of

---

54 See also discussion of transitivity in Chapter 2, section 2.5.1..
55 See discussion in Keenan (1975).

a lower positions on the case hierarchy. Most commonly, this involves either **oblique** or **unmarked** case, or
total **deletion**".

c. **Verb stativization:**
"The verb in the passive clause is likely to display syntactic characteristics more commonly associated with
stative or adjectival predicates, in terms of the auxiliary
'be', **adjectival** or **gerund** morphology, and **perfect** or
imperfective aspectual morphology".

To illustrate some of these grammatical features briefly, consider the following examples from English:

(31) a. Mary found John on the beach   (active)
     b. John was found *by Mary* on the beach   (passive with
                                           oblique AGT)
     c. John was found on the beach   (passive with
                                           deleted AGT)

Each syntactic feature of the passive, as given in (30), corresponds to
one functional feature in (29). Most of the detailed features in (30a,b,c)
depend for their iconic power on abstract, system-internal structural
norms that are highly specific in the grammar of particular languages.
For example, feature (30a) isomorphically matches **non-agent topicalization** only because of the norm that establishes the prototype syntactic
status of agents/subjects as occupying the top of the case hierarchy. It is
only vis-a-vis this abstract norm that the promotion of the non-agent to
subject-of-passive is truly iconic. In the same vein, feature (30c) receives
its iconic power from specific grammatical norms for marking stative
predicates. In contrast, coding feature (30b) -- isomorphic to **agent suppression** (29b) -- derives its iconic power from two distinct sources.
First, the assignment of oblique case-marking again depends on language-specific grammatical norms. But second, total agent deletion (by
far the most common means of agent-demotion in passive clauses cross
languages)[56] is iconic in a much more concrete and cognitively transparent sense, abiding by the following coding principle:

---

56 In most human languages, the agent of the event cannot appear overtly in the passive
    clause. For discussion and many details, see Givón (1979, Ch. 2; 1981a).

(32) **The relevance or importance principle**:

"A piece of information that is either unimportant or irrelevant receives less over coding".

Note now that the participation of principle (32) in the coding of the passive is integrated into a **scale** of *degree of agent demotion*, where total deletion appears as the most extreme coding device:[57]

(33) **Scale of agent demotion in passivization**:

    a. object-like linear position
    b. object-like case-marking morphology
    c. total deletion

And it is again possible that scale (33) is treated as a *unified* mental entity, isomorphic to the functional scale of *agent suppression*, regardless of the divergent source of its iconic power.

3.4.4.6. Antipassivization and the coding of transitivity

We have discussed at a number of points above the three major components of **semantic** transitivity, involving the prototypical agent, patient, and verb modality.[58] As we have already seen in the discussion of passives, the grammatical coding of these three main components of transitivity is highly iconic. When the functional text-distribution of semantically-transitive clauses is studied, other facets of iconicity in the grammatical code are revealed, ones that involve more clearly discourse-pragmatic function.

In a series of quantified text studies covering a number of languages,[59] the degree of **topicality** ('predictability' and 'importance') of agents and patients of semantically-transitive clauses was measured, using quantitative text-based methods. In particular, the **ergative-transitive** clause in these languages was compared with both the **passive** and **antipassive** clause-type. The relative topicality, and semantic referentiality, of the agent and patient arguments in these clauses may be summarized as follows:

---

57 The scalarity observation here is due to Keenan (1975).
58 See discussion in the preceding section, as well as in Ch. 2, above. More extensive treatments can be found in Hopper and Thompson (1980) and Givón (1984a, Chapters 4,5).
59 See Cooreman (1982a, 1982b) for Chamorro; Cooreman, Fox and Givón (1983) for Tagalog; Rude (1983) for Nez Perce; Cooreman (1985) for Dyirbal. For more details of the measurements, see Chapter 6, below.

(34) **Topicality of clause types:**

clause type	topicality	referentiality
TRANS-ergative	AGT>PAT	both AGT & PAT highly REF
INTRANS-passive	PAT>>AGT	AGT mostly NON-REF
INTRANS-antipass	AGT>>PAT	PAT mostly NON-REF

In the **transitive-ergative** clause both agent and patient tend to be highly referential, and the agent is more topical ('continuous', 'important') in the discourse than the patient. In contrast, the agent in the **passive** clause tends to be highly non-referential and non-topical; and the patient in the **antipassive** clause tends to be highly non-referential and non-topical. The use of the passive and antipassive constructions to code discourse-pragmatic function is thus determined by the relative topicality, and referentiality, of the agent and patient of the clause.

In the ergative languages that were studied, the morphology of agent, patient and verb is sensitive to the **degree of transitivity** of the clause. In such languages, the syntactic coding of passivization and antipassivization, in particular as it pertains to the marking of agent and patient, may be summarized as follows (see also section 3.4.4.5., above for passivization):

(35) (a) **Passive:**
The agent either assumes oblique-case morphology or, more commonly, is left unexpressed. In addition, if the verb had any transitive morphology, it is lost in passivization.

(b) **Antipassive:**
The patient loses its direct-object morphology. It may then assume oblique-case morphology; or it may be incorporated into the verb ('co-lexicalized'); or, most commonly, it may be left unexpressed. Again, if the verb had any transitive morphology, it is lost in anti-passivization.

The iconic-isomorphic S-relation between the semantic-pragmatic properties of agents and patients (as given in (34)) and their syntactic coding properties (as given in (35)) is rather transparent. We have already discussed the passive earlier above. For the antipassive, we find a reminiscent scale, involving the **degree of demotion** of the patient when it is low in topicality and/or referentiality:

(36)   **least demoted**
   a. Direct-object marking
   b. Loss of direct-object case-marking; sometimes assumption of oblique case-marking
   c. Co-lexicalization with the verb ('incorporation')
   d. Total deletion ('zero coding')
   most demoted

Of the four coding points on scale (36), two -- (36a,b) -- receive their iconic power via more abstract grammar-dependent norms. The other two, however -- (36c,d) -- are cognitively transparent, bringing to mind immediately coding principle (32), the one that relates the strength ('saliency') of the code with the importance or relevance of the coded meaning/function. Principle (32) may be recast in slightly more general terms as (37):

(37) **The saliency isomorphism principle:**

   "The degree of **perceptual/ mental saliency** of the code tends to be isomorphic to the degree of **communicative** saliency of the message".

The only coding device the antipassive added, above and beyond what was seen in the passive, is co-lexicalization (36c), whereby an object low in topicality or referentiality may become part of the verbal word (as prefix or suffix), and thus receive less independent coding. As examples of English constructions that are functionally equivalent to the antipassive of ergative languages, consider:

(38)   a. **Transitive:**
        He shot *the target*

       b. **Antipassive, object incorporation:**
        He went *target*-shooting

       c. **Antipassive, zero object:**
        He went shooting

3.4.4.7. Stereotypicality, predictability and coding saliency

The very same process of morphological incorporation or zero expression ('deletion') governed by principle (37) is seen in the case of *instrumentals* and *manner adverbs* . As illustration consider:

(39) **Instrumentals:**

    a. **Independent coding:**
       John fished *with a fly-hook*

    b. **Morphological incorporation:**
       John went *fly*-fishing

    c. **Semantic incorporation (zero coding):**
       Mary slapped John (implied: 'with her hand')

(40) **Manner adverbs:**

    a. **Independent coding:**
       Mary stitched the pillow *cross-wise*

    b. **Morphological incorporation:**
       Mary *cross*-stitched the pillow

    c. **Semantic incorporation (zero coding):**
       Mary murdered John (implied: 'deliberately')

Here, the element that receives less salient coding is highly predictable or **stereotyped**. One may suggest that our code-quantity principle (19) is involved, by which more predictable information receives less (or less salient) coding.

3.4.4.8. Linear ordering, proximity and scope

The most common device in grammar for indicating scope relations and conceptual (or functional) proximity, is via linear ordering and/or linear proximity. This coding behavior is virtually dictated by the narrow, **single-channel** nature of the linguistic code. To illustrate this phenomenon at the syntactic level, consider the rigid ordering of the pre-verbal auxiliaries in Creole languages.[60] The relative ordering of these auxiliaries tends to be:

(41)   (PERFECT) (MODAL) (DURATIVE) VERB

Of the three auxiliaries, 'durative' has the narrowest -- **lexical-semantic** -- scope, ranging over the verb itself. 'Modal' ('irrealis') has a wider --

---

60 See originally in Bickerton (1975, 1981), as well as further discussion in Givón (1982b).

propositional -- scope. And 'perfect' ('anterior') has the widest -- **discourse-pragmatic** scope, ranging over a chunk of discourse larger than the single proposition. The relative ordering of these pre-verbal auxiliaries in the morpho-syntax of Creoles, thus their relative proximity to the verb, reflects rather iconically the relative semantic or pragmatic scope of these operators, and their relative relevance to the verb. This iconic relation is another manifestation of our proximity principle (27).

Another illustration of principle (27) may be seen in the grammar of negation in Russian. This example involves the correlation between the syntactic position of the negative marker, and the contrastive focus associated with negation. Thus consider:[61]

(42) a. Ivan jego *ne*-ubil
          Ivan him NEG-killed
          'Ivan didn't *kill* him' (neutral or V-focus)

      b. Ivan ubil *ne*-jego
          Ivan killed NEG-him
          'Ivan didn't kill *him* ' (OBJ-focus)

      c. Jego ubil *ne*-Ivan
          him killed NEG-Ivan
          '*Ivan* didn't kill him' (SUBJ-focus)

What one can see in (42) is an interaction between a rather abstract grammatical norm in Russian, one that requires the placing of a focused element *at the end* of the clause, and the cognitively-transparent proximity principle (27), through which the negative marker is placed *nearest* the element under the scope of contrastive negation. Once again, the grammatical code integrates norm-dependent and cognitively-transparent iconicity principles.

To illustrate the contrast between the relative arbitrariness of the specific word-order norm in Russian negation and the naturalness of the proximity principle (27), consider the very same process occurring in a *verb-first* language, Bikol. In this language, the more abstract grammatical word-order norm places focused elements at the *beginning* of the clause. Still, the negative marker in focused negation is placed *next to* that fronted element:[62]

---

61 After Dreizin (1980).
62 For the Bikol examples and discussion, see Givón (1984a, ch. 9).

(43)   a. **Affirmative:**
   nag-gadan 'ang-lalake ning-kanding
   AGT-kill SUBJ-man OBJ-goat
   'The man killed a goat'

  b. **Neutral (or V-focus) negation:**
   da'i nag-gadan 'ang-lalake ning-kanding
   NEG AGT-kill SUBJ-man OBJ-goat
   'The man didn't *kill* a goat'

  c. **SUBJ-focus negation:**
   da'i 'ang-lalake nag-gadan ning-kanding
   NEG SUBJ-man   AGT-kill OBJ-goat
   'The *man* didn't kill the goat'

  d. **OBJ-focus negation:**
   da'i ning-kanding nag-gadan 'ang-lalake
   NEG OBJ-goat   AGT-kill SUBJ-man
   'The man didn't kill the *goat* '

Finally, principle (27) is also apparent at the morpho-tactic level, where it governs the relative order and proximity of grammatical/inflectional and derivational morphemes vis-a-vis lexical stems.[63]

3.4.5. Some meta-iconicity considerations

Most of the iconicity principles surveyed above, with the exception of meta-principle (8), are concrete, cognitively transparent rules for assembling together morpho-syntactic structure. In this section we will deal briefly with a number of more general meta-iconic considerations.

3.4.5.1. Arbitrary grammatical norms vs. natural iconic principles

As seen in the discussion of negation in Russian and Bikol, above, a certain relation exists between the abstract, often language-specific grammatical norms, and the more universal, concrete, cognitively-transparent iconicity principle. This relation may be expressed as the following meta-iconic prediction:

---

63 For many cross-language examples and an extensive discussion, see Bybee (1985).

(44) **Meta-iconic principle of universality:**

"The more concrete and cognitively transparent a coding principle is, the more it is likely to be universally manifest in the grammars of all human languages".

As we shall see further below, cognitively transparent iconicity principles are also more likely to be manifest in pre-human communication.

3.4.5.2. Conflicts between iconicity principles

One of the most concrete, cognitively transparent iconicity principles involves the isomorphism between the temporal order of experiences and the temporal order of their coded-expression in communication.[64] In this connection, one case where the sentence-internal ordering of constituents seems to reflect temporal ordering, has been discussed widely in the psycho-linguistic literature.[65] It pertains to the relative ordering of agent ('cause') and patient ('effect'). As Sridhar (1980) puts it:

(45) **The cause-before-effect principle:**

"...nominals denoting figure-of-state and agent-of-action precede those denoting ground and patient..." (1980, p. ix)

Now, of the rigid word-order types found in human language, the most common ones -- in terms of cross-language distribution -- are SVO, VSO and SOV. In all three, the agent ('subject') indeed precedes the patient ('object'), thus presumably upholding principle (45). However, there exist two other well-attested word-order types, VOS[66] and OVS.[67] Of these two, one (VOS) is just as rigid as can be found.[68] The word-order of VOS and OVS languages, one may now argue, is obviously not governed by the *semantic* principle (45). Rather, it is governed by the *pragmatic* principle (21/23) above. That principle, recall, orders more topical ('predictable') information *after* less-topical/predictable information. Now, the subject is most commonly more topical ('predictable' and 'important') in discourse than the object -- and the agent is assigned the subject role much more frequently in discourse than the patient.[69]

---

64 See extensive discussion in Haiman (1983; to appear), as well as section 3.4.4.1., above.
65 See Osgood (1971) and Sridhar (1980), *inter alia*.
66 As in Malagasy (Keenan, 1976).
67 As in Carib languages, cf. Derbyshire and Pullum (1981).
68 Word-order rigidity is often a matter of degree. For an extensive discussion, see Givón (1984a, ch. 6), as well as Chapter 6, below.
69 See discussion in section 3.4.4.3., above, as well as in Givón (ed. 1983a).

Therefore, VOS and OVS languages seem to reflect -- iconically -- principle (21/23). The gist of the argument is this: When two equally natural coding principles predict conflicting results, the resolution of such conflict in any particular language is not always predictable from general considerations.

3.5. Some bio-adaptive considerations

3.5.1. The difference of Man[70]

We have surveyed above clear and ample illustrations of precisely what Chomsky said is not to be found in human language:

> "...the selection of a point along a linguistic dimension determines and signals a certain point along an associated non-linguistic dimension..." (1968, pp. 69-70)

We have seen that an extremely small number of cognitively-transparent principles, pertaining to sequential **order**, code **quantity/saliency**, and relative **proximity** of the code units, underlie the syntax of natural human languages. We have seen how these principles govern an array of systematic, isomorphic-iconic relations between the units of the syntactic code and message properties such as informational **predictability**, **importance**, conceptual **relevance** or **precedence**.

It is of course true that the grammar of human languages incorporates many more abstract, arbitrary grammatical norms, and those turn out to be much more language specific. But such less-iconic norms are well integrated, in syntax, with the more natural, universal, cognitively-transparent principles. And quite often these seemingly arbitrary norms turn out to be themselves motivated either cognitively or socio-culturally.[71]

One may perhaps suggest that the introduction of increasingly non-iconic ('more arbitrary') codes into communication is the unique evolutionary hallmark of human language. It can be shown, however, that the mixing of more cognitively-transparent ('natural') codes with less transparent, ('arbitrary') codes within the same complex coding scale is a feature of primate communication as well. To illustrate this, consider the

---

70 With indebtedness, for the title, to Mortimer Adler (1967). Like Descartes and Chomsky, Adler considers human language to be non-contiguous with animal communication, thus making 'The difference of Man'.

71 See extensive discussion in Slobin (1973), Langacker (1984) or Givón (1984a), *inter alia* .

scale that codes the dominant-subordinate message in Bonnet Macaques (after Simonds, 1974):

(46) **Dominant-subordinate coding scale in Bonnet Macaques:**

	6 Attack
	5 Lunge
dominant	4 Open-mouth threat
signals	3 Eyelid threat
	2 Stare
	1 Look

---

	1 Lip-smack slowly
	2 Lip-smack rapidly
subordinate	3 Grimace
signals	4 Grimace widely
	5 Grimace and present
	6 Run off, grimace and tail-whip

On the dominant portion of the scale, an increase in **code intensity**, abiding by our importance principle (32), is clearly discernible from point 1 to 2 to 3, all involving eye-signal intensity. But the transition from 3 to 4 involves switching to another code element, the open mouth. And while the escalation is natural and obvious, the integration of eye-signal and mouth-signal into the same scale involves a higher level of symbolic -- i.e. more arbitrary -- representation.

A similar mix of naturalness and arbitrariness can be seen when one compares the coding of aggression and submission in dogs and horses. Dogs raise their head and prop their ears up to display aggression. Horses lower their head and flatten their ears back to display aggression. Both, however, display a similar **quantity scale** in coding the degree of aggression.

3.5.2. The biological basis of isomorphic coding

3.5.2.1. Function, teleology and organisms

In sounding out the major themes in the study of organisms, Eckert and Randall (1978) write in their introduction to animal physiology:

"...The movement of an animal during locomotion depends on the structure of muscles and skeletal elements (e.g. bones). The movement produced by a contracting muscle depends on how it is attached to these elements and how they articulate with each other. In such a relatively familiar example, the relation between *structure* and *function* is obvious. The dependence of function on structure becomes more subtle, but no less real, as we direct our attention to the lower levels of organization -- tissue, cell, organelle, and so on... The principle that *structure is the basis of function* applies to biochemical events as well. The interaction of an enzyme with its substrates, for example, depends on the configuration and electron distributions of the interacting molecules. Changing the shape of an enzyme molecule (i.e. denaturing it) by heating it above 40° C is generally sufficient to render it biologically nonfunctional *by altering its shape* ..." (1978, pp. 2-3; emphases are mine; TG)

The isomorphic coding of functions, at whatever level, is the oldest fact of biological organization. Even the most primitive organismic fragment -- the virus -- has at least one coding relation that is fully isomorphic, matching sequences of nucleotides in its DNA (or RNA for some viruses) with sequences of amino acid in its protein.[72] The critical element that makes something *a biological code* (i.e. in Peirce's words "...something by knowing of which we know something more...") is the presence of some **teleology, purpose** (or, for a less-conscious organism, **function**), i.e. an **interpretant**. And the notion of function, in turn, is the *sine qua non* of the definition of 'biological organism'.[73]

3.5.2.2. Ontogeny, phylogeny, language change and the iconicity of language

All biological codes are constructed, and eventually modified and remodified, by evolutionary processes. And all evolutionary processes are interactions between an organism and its environment. The context for evolutionary interaction is always functional-adaptive. The matching of structure and function in biology is always mediated by evolutionary change.

The same must hold for the communicative code. Its pervasive iconicity arise -- and is constantly modified -- via three functionally-mediated developmental processes: Diachronic change, language learning and language evolution. The evolutionary accretion of a communicative code (the 'S-relation') to a pre-existing perceptual, neural and cognitive coding of experience (the 'X-relation') is only one episode in a long biological scenario. Within that scenario, the increased complexity and

---

72 This seeming single-step coding relation is in fact functionally more complex. In order for the virus to replicate and perpetuate itself, it must penetrate a host cell, where the virus DNA code is first interpreted by the host-cell's enzymes, who then translate it into amino acid sequences as well as virus DNA.

73 See further discussion in Chapter 8, below.

abstractness of human communicative functions and their code, is a natural adaptively extension of pre-existing functions, structures and, above all, pre-existing coding principles.

3.5.2.3. From icon to symbol

The increasing abstractness of the human linguistic code -- from multi-point iconicity to one-point symbolism -- has not substantially transformed its pervasive isomorphism. There is no cogent reason why this increasing abstraction should not be considered as part and parcel of function-driven evolutionary change.[74] This integration of symbolic ('arbitrary) and iconic ('natural') elements in the human linguistic code was indeed noted by Peirce:

"...Particularly deserving of notice are icons in which the likeness is aided by conventional rules..." (1940, p. 105)

While Peirce did not intend his observation developmentally, it is just as relevant today as when first made. The addition of abstract ('conventional') elements to our mental and communicative codes does not alter their inherent iconicity. When confronted with seemingly arbitrary relations between code and designatum, the human organism -- like all others -- strives to discover, impose or construe a maximal measure of non-arbitrariness. In following our iconic meta-imperative, we strive to retain and reinforce the magic that makes it so much easier to store, retrieve and communicate information within finite time and finite neural resources -- the magic of an isomorphic-iconic code.

---

74 In the same vein, the highly iconic second-language Pidgin, and early childhood **pragmatic mode** of communication (Givón, 1979, Chapters 5, 7), eventually give rise to the more abstract -- thus more *symbolic* -- **syntactic mode**. Iconic-pictographic writing systems eventually evolve into more arbitrary alphabets (see section 3.4.3., above). At the ontogenetic, evolutionary or diachronic levels, increased abstraction of the code is indeed a recurrent theme.

CHAPTER 4

PROPOSITIONAL MODALITIES: TRUTH, CERTAINTY, INTENT, AND INFORMATION

4.1. Propositions, sentences and information

The proposition -- or its equivalent in natural language, the sentences or clause[1] -- has always been considered, whether on intuitive or formal grounds, the basic information-processing unit in human language. Words may have **meaning**, but only propositions carry **information**. Even when it appears, *prima facia*, that a single word bears information, on further inspection that word turns out to stand in for an entire proposition. For example, in (1) below the curt one-word response (1b) stands for the fuller proposition (1c):

(1) a. Who killed the butler?
    b. The maid.
    c. The maid killed the butler.

In this chapter we will not concern ourselves with the specific information carried by individual propositions. As noted in Chapter 3, above, propositional information in language is assembled together from two distinct sources:

(a) The actual **lexical words**[2] used; and
(b) The **propositional frame** within which the words are assembled.

Thus, proposition (1c) above combines the lexical words 'maid', 'kill' and 'butler'. They are assembled into a transitive propositional frame

---

1   For the purpose of the discussion here I will disregard the difference between 'clause' and 'sentence'.
2   Sentences in natural language contain, in addition to lexical words, also grammatical words ('grammatical morphemes'). Thus, the two definite articles 'the' in (1c) are 'grammatical words' associated with the discourse-pragmatics of coreference; while the past tense '-ed' is a grammatical morpheme. For the purpose of this discussion, we need not concern ourselves with these grammatical operators.

that assigns to 'maid' the role of **agent** of 'kill', and to 'butler' the role of **patient** of 'kill'.

We will, from here onward, concern ourselves primarily with certain **meta-operators** on propositions, namely the **propositional modalities** under whose scope the entire proposition falls. Propositions in human language, so long as they are embedded within some **communicative context**, always fall under some modality (quite often under more than one). Once communicative context is taken into account, the severe limits of the traditional logical approach to propositional modalities become apparent. Thus, in departing from the logical tradition, we will sketch out a discourse-pragmatic approach to propositional modalities.

4.2. Epistemic modalities: The logico-semantic tradition

In the logical tradition,[3] propositions are treated as **atomic** entities, existing apart from speaker, hearer and discourse context. Likewise, propositional modalities in this tradition pertain ('belong') to the proposition itself. Further, these modalities are judged to be purely **epistemic**, i.e. pertaining to the **truth** of the proposition. This approach can be traced back at least as far as Aristotle's *De Interpretatione*, where the following four propositional modalities were recognized:

(2) **Epistemic modalities:**

    (a) Necessary truth: true by definition
    (b) Factual truth: true as fact
    (c) Possibly truth: true by hypothesis
    (d) Non-truth: false

The distinction between (a) and (b) above overlaps to quite an extent with Kant's distinction between **analytic** and **synthetic** truth, respectively. Roughly speaking,[4] a proposition is analytically true if it follows *by definition* from the internal properties of the representational system, such as mathematics, language or a game. Such propositions are, for example:

(3) a. Two plus two equals four
    b. A bachelor is an unmarried adult male
    c. To win at chess, you must capture the king

---

3 Cole (ed., 1981, Introduction) uses the term *semantic* for the logical tradition, to contrast with *pragmatic*. There is a certain intuitive justification for this, in that semantics in human language has traditionally dealt with the two least context-dependent realms of the linguistic message, *lexical-semantics* and *propositional frames* (see discussion in Givo'n, 1984a, ch. 2).

4 For some detail, see discussion of Kant's epistemology in Chapter 1, above.

In contrast, a proposition is synthetically true if it expresses a non-analytic fact about the world.

As noted in Chapter 1, above, analytic truth is already a *crypto-prag-matic* modality. This is so because analyticity rests implicitly upon **conventions**, which must then be **shared** ('subscribed to') by the **parties** to a **contract**. Traditional philosophers have masked this inherently **social** aspect of language, by arbitrarily restricting the contract's parties to *a single mind*. This restriction then made it possible to ascribe all modalities to the proposition itself.

There is another reason why Kant's epistemic modes should be interpreted as crypto-pragmatic. The analytic and the synthetic are also **modes of knowledge**, indicating one's **source of information**: Knowledge is obtained analytically through learning the conventions of language, logic, games. Knowledge is obtained synthetically by discovering what the world is like. And in natural language, the epistemics of source shades into the epistemics of **evidence**, in determining the communicative mode of propositions.

As noted above, it has been traditionally assumed (as in, for example, Carnap, 1947) that the four epistemic modalities pertained to the proposition itself. Even as such, these modes already echo -- faintly, implicitly -- the four major epistemic modalities of natural language.[5] In human language, however, the four modalities are defined *pragmatically*, i.e. with explicit reference to the speaker, to the hearer, and to their respective **communicative intent**.

4.3. Epistemic modalities and the communicative contract

4.3.1. Preamble: Epistemic vs. other modalities

Human communication involves an intricate network of conventions concerning what speakers and hearers are entitled to expect of each other when carrying out their respective roles in communication.[6] Within this vast network, which is all part and parcel of the pragmatics of language, only a small portion deals with strictly epistemic matters of

---

5 There are obviously many more propositional *sub-modalities* in natural language, some clearly epistemic. Many of those are explicitly coded in the grammar of particular languages. Each of the three 'truth' modes has many sub-modes (or sub-clauses in the communicative contract).

6 Some of the conventions subsumed under the communicative contract pertain to non-informative speech acts, such as command, request or query (cf. Austin, 1962 or Searle, 1970, *inter alia*). Others involve various other aspects of the declarative speech-act (cf. Grice, 1968/1975, Cole and Morgan, eds, 1975 or Gordon and Lakoff, 1971, *inter alia*). For the moment, we shall deal primarily with the portion of the communicative contract that govern the epistemic aspect of the transaction.

truth or subjective certainty. Rather, even those modes that are primarily epistemic tend to shade gradually into other -- intentional, social or manipulative -- modes. This gradual progression may be represented as follows:

(4) **Shading of communicative modalities:**

   (a) epistemic modes of **truth**, or **probability**
   (b) psychological modes of **subjective certainty**
   (c) intentional modes of **wish, ability** or **need**
   (d) social modes of **status, authority, power** or **obligation**
   (e) action modes of **causation** or **manipulation**

The latter modes, (4d) and (4e), shade further into the vast area of **non-verbal interaction**. A clearer cleavage may be perhaps suggested between the epistemic-psychological cluster of modes (4a,b,c), the intentional-social-action cluster (4d,e), and other inter-personal modes; but such a cleavage is to quite an extent a Platonic mirage. It may merely highlight, along the graduated modal space, three somewhat idealized *prototype peaks*.

4.3.2. The epistemic space and evidentiality

4.3.2.1. The communicative contract

Epistemic modalities, like all other propositional modalities in human language, are governed by the **communicative contract** between the speaker and hearer. At the epistemic extreme of the modal range (see (4a), above), the contract governs the speaker's responsibilities concerning the **evidentiary justification** of propositional information, according to its **source** and **reliability**. At the psychological sub-range (4b), the contract governs the **subjective certainty** that speakers assign to the communicated information. At the intentional, inter-personal and social sub-ranges (4c,d,e), the contract governs the **interaction** between speaker and hearer concerning the epistemic status of the communicated information: The hearer's reaction -- from challenge to tacit assent to affirmation; the speaker's reaction to that reaction; etc. All these facets of communication are presumably governed by various clauses and sub-clauses of the communicative contract. The various clauses and sub-clauses are not altogether independent of each other. Often they display predictable interactions ('redundancies'). Such redundancies make it impossible to separate sharply epistemic from intentional, intentional from manipulative, and manipulative from other social, inter-personal modalities. At their prototypical core, the various modes on the epis-temic range may display sharp -- Platonic -- categorial peaks. At the same time, they also display considerable Wittgensteinean gradation and overlapping similarities.

4.3.2.2. Evidentiality and epistemic modes

The study of evidentiality in the grammar of human languages[7] allows us to re-define the four epistemic modalities (2a,b,c,d) in discourse-prag-matic terms. Respectively:

(5) Pragmatically re-defined epistemic modalities:

  a. **Presupposition:** Presupposed or backgrounded infor-mation
  b. **Realis-Assertion:** Strongly-asserted information
  c. **Irrealis-Assertion:** Weakly asserted information
  d. **NEG-assertion:** Strongly-asserted denial of information

The pragmatics of the NEG-assertion mode (5d), above and beyond its being a strong assertion, will be dealt with separately below. It is in some ways a hybrid mode, displaying some of the pragmatic properties of R-assertion (5b), and Presupposition (5a), as well as some of the semantic properties of IRR-assertion (5c). We will discuss the other three modalities below, according to the various clauses of the communica-tive contract. First, however, let us consider briefly the way these three modes are coded -- or 'distributed' -- in grammar.

4.3.2.2. The grammatical distribution of the three epistemic modalities

The distribution of the three modalities -- presupposition, R-assertion and IRR-assertion -- in the grammar of natural languages is quite pre-dictable and universal; what follows is a brief summary.[8]

---

7 For full discussion and survey of the cross-language evidence, see Chafe and Nichols (eds, 1986) or Givón (1982c).
8 For the original observation, see Givón (1973b); for further detail see Givón (1984a, chs 8, 11).

4.3.2.2.1. **Presuppositional clauses**

The following grammatical[9] environments tend to harbor, rather consistently, presupposed clauses. In some of these environments clauses
are obligatorily presuppositional, while in others they are optionally so.

(6) (a) Restrictive relative clauses:
         The man *I saw yesterday...*

    (b) Complements of cognition verbs:
         I knew that *she was there*

    (c) Complements of evaluative adjectives:
         It's terrible that *he drinks so much*

    (d) Adverbial clauses:
         Because *she didn't show up...*

    (e) Participial-adverbial clauses:
         Having finished dinner, he got up and left

    (f) Nominalized subject clauses:
         His killing the chicken surprised me

    (g) Nominalized object clause:
         I respect *his decision to quit*

    (h) WH-questions:
         Who *killed John?*

    (i) Cleft/focus clauses:
         It was Mary *who killed John*

In addition, in many languages there is a high correlation between
presuppositionality of clauses and the use of the **perfect** ('anterior')
aspect, as in:

(7) a. He knew that *she had done it*
    b. *Having finished*, she left.
    c. *His having left* surprised no one
    d. The man *who had done it...*

---

9 While we describe these as 'grammatical' environment, they are equally well also
   'functional', given the high degree of systematic pairing, in natural language, of specific
   structures with particular functions.

4.3.2.2.2. Irrealis clauses

The following grammatical environments tend to display the scope of an irrealis modality:

(8) a. The future tense:
> She **will** *remember*

b. Conditional ('if') clauses:
> **If** *he comes back,...*

c. Complements of non-implicative modal verbs:
> He **wanted** *to leave*
> She **must** *see him*

d. Complements of non-implicative manipulation verbs:
> She **told** him *to leave*
> He **asked** her *to help him*

e. Complements of non-factive cognition verbs:
> He **thought** *that she didn't love him*

f. The scope of epistemic adverbs:
> **Maybe** *he did it*
> **Presumably** *she left*

g. Non declarative speech-acts:
> *Leave immediately!*
> *Was she there?*

4.3.2.2.3. Realis clauses

The R-assertion mode distributes in grammatical environments contrasting with those given in (6), (7) or (8) above. That is, it typically is to be found in **main, declarative, affirmative** clauses with a **past/perfective** tense-aspect, and where neither the irrealis environments in (8), nor the presuppositional environments in (6) or (7), are involved.

4.3.2.3. Subjective certainty

The evidence from the study of natural language strongly suggests that our three modes of information are ranked according to the subjective certainty of the speaker. The ranking is of course transparent:

(9) **Epistemic modes and subjective certainty:**

presupposition > R-assertion > IRR-assertion

Thus, for example, predicates that code the highest subjective certainty are also most likely to also be presuppositional, as can be seen from the following descending scale of subjective certainty in English:

(10) a. I *know* she was here.
      b. I *am sure* she was here.
      c. I *think* she was here.
      d. I *believe* she was here
      e. I *see* she was here.
      f. I *hear* she was here.
      g. I *guess* she was here.
      h. They *say* she was here.

These verbs, often used with the first person subject, tend to function as **epistemic quantifiers** on the subsequent proposition. In many languages, these verbs become grammaticalized as **evidentiary particles**.[10] But if any of the verbs on this scale can be used presuppositionally, it is always the verb 'know', the highest on the scale of subjective certainty.

In some languages, such as KinyaRwanda or Thai, 'know' and 'think' are the same lexical verb, but a special *complementizer particle* signals that the complement clause is presupposed. When that particle is used, the verb is translated as 'know'. When another particle is used, the verb is translated as 'think'. To illustrate this, consider the following from KinyaRwanda[11]:

(11) a. ya-ri   a-zi   *ko* amazi yari mare-mare
       he/PAST-be he-believe *that* water was deep-deep
       'He *knew* that the water was very deep'
       (and indeed it was)

      b. ya-ri   a-zi   *ngo* amazi yari mare-mare
       he/PAST-be he-believe *that* water was deep-deep
       'He *thought* that the water was very deep'
       (but it may have not been)

However, at a lower portion of the subjective certainty scale, where no presuppositionality is involved, the very same contrast between *ko* and

---

10 See various descriptions in Chafe and Nichols (eds, 1986).
11 See detail in Givón (1982c) and Givón and Kimenyi (1974).

ngo codes the degree of **certainty** or **doubt** the speaker holds vis-a-vis the quoted information:

(12) a. ya-mu-bgiye   *ko*   u-a-kora-ga   cyaane
          he/PAST-him-tell *that* you-PAST-work-HAB hard
          'He told him that you worked hard'
          (and I don't doubt it)

      b. ya-mu-bgiye   *ngo* u-a-kora-ga   cyaane
          he/PAST-him-tell *that* you-PAST-work-HAB hard
          'He told him that you worked hard'
          (but I doubt it)

The contrast between *ko* and *ngo* complements is thus primarily a matter of **certainty** or **evidentiality**. Only at the very top of the certainty range do complements coded by *ko* turn presuppositional.

4.3.2.4. **Source of information and defensibility**

At the very core of the epistemics of evidentiality in human language lies the differentiation between various sources of information. In this section we will survey briefly how this feature applies to the three main epistemic modalities.

4.3.2.4.1. **Presupposition**

We will continue to use the traditional name of 'presupposition' to refer to this epistemic modality, although it is clear that the term **unchallengeable information** is more accurate. The communicative contract treats presupposed information as assumed by the speaker to be either **known to, familiar to** or otherwise **unlikely to be challenged by** the hearer. The sources of this unchallengeability may be attributed to a number of sub-clauses, all grouped under the three major sub-divisions of context ('shared background', see Chapter 3, above).

(13) **Sources of presupposed information:**

   a. **Shared situational context:**
       (i) The information is **deictically obvious** to the hearer in the immediate speech environment;
       (ii) The speaker was a direct **participant** -- as subject or object -- in the reported event or state;

b. **Shared generic context:**
   (iii) The information is **universally shared**, by all members of the speech community, as part of their knowledge of their **world** and **culture**, most of it (but not all) coded in the shared **lexicon**;
   (iv) The information pertains to agreed-upon **conventions, rules** or **games** (including logic) to which both speaker and hearer   normally subscribe;
   (iv) The information is given by **divine revelation**, with the speaker and hearer subscribing to the same higher being(s);

c. **Shared discourse context:**
   (v) The information was asserted earlier **in the discourse** by the speaker, and the hearer did not then challenge it.

To the contract clauses in (13) above one must add the following **escape clause:**

(14) **Escape clause for presupposed information:**

"The information is **presupposed** by the speaker -- for whatever reason, to be either:
   (i) somehow **known to the hearer**, by whatever means;
or
   (ii) otherwise **acceptable to the hearer** without challenge, for whatever reason".

This escape clause is necessary to account for intuitive, inspired or telepathic sources of information about other minds. It is also required to account for *ersatz* presupposition, of the type Lewis (1979) describes as follows:

"...If at time *t* something is said that requires presupposition P to be acceptable, and if P is not presupposed just before *t*, then -- *ceteris paribus* and within certain limits -- presupposition P comes into existence at *t*..." (1979, p. 340)

Presumably part of Lewis's 'within certain limits' involved the non-challenging behavior of the hearer.

As one can see, the presupposition mode includes the traditional *necessary, analytic* and *apriori-synthetic* truth, as well as presupposition and more. At the core of this modality is then the speaker's reasonable belief that the hearer will refrain from challenging the information, and thus that the information requires **no justification, no defense.**

4.3.2.4.2. Realis-assertion

Under this mode, information is strongly asserted, yet it remains **open to challenge** by the hearer. The speaker must then be prepared to **defend** the information, by citing the **source of evidence.** Most typically, the source tends to be one of the following:

(15) **Sources of evidence in defense of R-asserted information:**

    (a) **Direct experience,** by various sensory modalities;
    (b) **Hearsay,** i.e. the communicated experience of others;
    (c) **Inference** -- direct or circuitous -- from direct or communicated experience.

4.3.2.4.3. Irrealis-assertion

Under the scope of the IRR-assertion mode, information is weakly asserted, as hypothesis, possibility, probability, supposition, conjecture, prediction or guess. The source of the information is thus largely **irrelevant,** since the speaker does not intend to defend the information too vigorously against challenge. In fact, often the speaker volunteers the information under the irrealis mode precisely in order to solicit challenge, correction or corroboration.

4.3.2.5. Rules of evidence

The phenomenon of **evidentiality** in the grammar of natural languages most commonly skips over presupposed and IRR-asserted clauses. It thus pertains primarily to R-asserted clauses.[12] One may thus

---

12 Hargreaves (1983) reports that in Newari the grammar of evidentiality pertains to at least one irrealis clause, the future tense. This is relatively rare. Further, though the same grammatical markers may be used, the distinctions become those of *degree of subjective certainty,* as in (10) above. The contrast between *ko* and *ngo* in KinyaRwanda is another case in point. A similar case is also found in Sango (H. Pasch, in personal communication), where the presence of a complementizer particle at the top of the certainty scale codes the difference between 'know' and 'think'. Toward the bottom of the scale, the same complementizer codes only degree of subjective certainty.

suggest that presupposed clauses are considered -- per the communicative contract -- **self evident**.[13] IRR-asserted clauses, in turn, are asserted weakly and without sufficient evidentiary support, and without intent to strongly defend the verity of the proffered information. Only in the case of R-asserted clauses is evidence assumed to be both *available* and *expected*.

When a language marks evidentiality in its grammar, most commonly the following distinction are observed, ranked according to the degree of **evidentiary strength**, thus corresponding closely to **subjective certainty**:

(16) **Scale of evidentiary strength of source:**

    a. Direct sensory experience
    b. Inference from direct sensory experience
    c. Indirect inference
    d. Hearsay

In languages which further differentiate among several possible sensory sources of direct evidence, the grammar of evidentiality tends to rank the senses according to their **reliability** as source of evidence:

(17) **Scale of reliability of sensory evidence:**

    a. Visual experience
    b. Auditory experience
    c. Other sensory experience

In the grammar of evidentiality, one also finds the ranking of the participants in the event according to person:

(18) **Scale of participants in event:**

    a. Speaker
    b. Hearer
    c. Third party

This ranking exempts from the burden of evidence -- and thus from the grammar of evidentiality -- reports about events/states in which the speaker was a participant. By the same token, it is considered odd to inform hearers about events in which they participated -- unless the speech act is not informative, but rather a *complaint, accusation* or *question*. Thus, evidentiary particles are most commonly found in clauses

---

13 See DuBois (1985).

reporting states or events with third-party participants, in particular third person subjects.

In a number of languages, the grammar of evidentiality also ranks the **spatial proximity** of the reported event/state to the speech situation, again in terms of evidentiary strength:

(19) **Scale of spatial proximity:**

    a. Near the speech situation
    b. Away from the speech situation

This scale, in a sense, is not entirely independent of scale (18) above, since the speaker's proximity to the reported event raises the probability of direct sensory access.

Finally, the grammar of evidentiality also tends to rank the **temporal proximity** of the reported event to the speech time, in a rather predictable way:

(20) **Scale of temporal proximity:**

    a. Nearer to speech time
    b. Farther away from speech time

Thus, of the two major realis tenses, *present-progressive* and *past*, the former is much more often exempt from evidentiality marking, while the latter is much more likely to require evidentiary marking. Again, this deictic scale is not altogether independent of scales (18) and (19) above, since temporal proximity of the event to speech *time* is often associated with spatial proximity to speech *place*, thus with the speaker's direct presence at the reported scene.

4.3.2.6. **Certainty, challenge and response**

As one would expect from the discussion above, the three epistemic modalities -- presupposition, R-assertion and IRR-assertion -- receive rather different treatment under the last clause of the communicative contract, the one dealing with the legitimacy of challenge by the hearer, and the appropriate reaction by the speaker to such challenge. As noted above, presupposed information is proffered with the expectation of no forthcoming challenge -- and thus no need for evidentiary defense. The reaction to a challenge, if and when one comes, may of course depend on the contractual sub-clause the speaker assumes has been violated. When the violated sub-clause involves shared **textual** information, about some specific event, the reaction to challenge may range from faint surprise to mild protest to extreme indignation, depending on the real-world pragmatic consequences of the misunderstanding. To illustrate this, consider the same propositional information, proffered by speaker A in (21) as presupposition, and in (22) as R-assertion:

(21) A: Joe is really depressed over *Marion leaving him.*
      B: Hold it -- Marion left Joe? When?
      A: You mean you didn't know? I thought you did, it's all over town; she left him Thursday, they say it was quite a scene.

(22) A: Marion left Joe.
      B: She did? When?
      A: Last Thursday, they say it was quite a scene.

A's reaction to B's ignorance will be, typically, much milder in (22) than in (21).

A misunderstanding arising from the sub-clause pertaining to shared ('deictic') **situation** could cause quite an irritable reaction. Thus consider:

(23) A: Pass me *that* monkey-wrench, will ya.
      B: Which one? Where?
      A: There's only one monkey-wrench right there next to you! What's the matter, can't you see?

Considerable irritation may be also provoked by a misunderstanding arising from the sub-clause that governs **generic** shared knowledge, as in:

(24) A: Pass me a medium-size *monkey-wrench*, will you.
      B: Monkey-wrench, monkey-wrench...what's that?
      A: A monkey wrench! No, not that, that's a lock-spanner! Don't you know what a monkey-wrench is?

The examples above are only suggestive, but the challenge and reaction behavior of speakers and hearers can also be investigated empirically. In a recent study, Tsuchihashi (1983) observed speaker's and hearer's challenge and reaction behavior in transcripts of Japanese conversation. In Japanese grammar, propositions may be marked by either one of 15 verb-final speech-act particles. These particles rank the proposition all the way from prototypical strong assertion through weak assertion, hedged assertion and tentative request for confirmation, down to a prototypical yes/no question. In her study, Tsuchihashi found the following three correlations:

(a) Propositions on the strong-assertion end had the highest probability of **the speaker being a participant** in the reported event; that probability decreased gradually through the weak-assertion portion of the scale, and was the lowest at the question end of the scale.

(b) The probability of **assertive intervention from the hearer** was lowest at the strong-assertion end of the scale; it increased gradually through the weak-assertion portion of the scale, and was the highest at the question end of the scale.

(c) The probability of **the speaker responding in a contrary manner** to the hearer's intervention was highest at the strong assertion end of the scale decreased through the weak-assertion portion of the scale, and was lowest at the question end of the scale.

Tsuchihashi thus confirmed the suggestions made above concerning the pragmatics of epistemic modalities. In addition, her study also furnished strong support for another pragmatic challenge to the logical tradition of propositional modalities: It clearly suggests that these modalities may be on a **graduated scale**, rather than discretely categorized in a Platonic fashion.[14] We will deal with this subject further below.

4.4. **The continuum space of propositional modalities**

4.4.1. **Preliminaries**

So far we have treated the three epistemic propositional modalities -- presupposition, R-assertion, IRR-assertion -- as discrete entities, each with its own behavior vis-a-vis various sub-clauses of the communicative contract. In this section I will survey evidence suggesting that such rigid discreteness -- while justified in the most gross features -- is not always compatible with other facts of natural language. We will see how epistemic modalities shade gradually into one another. We will also see how epistemic modalities may shade into non-epistemic ones, such as manipulative speech acts. This gradual shading, so typical of a prag-

---

14 See also Givón (1982a, 1984e).

matically-based system, eventually force us to reassess the nature of the semantic/pragmatic space underlying all propositional modalities. The reassessment is, of course, in line with the prototype approach to categorization, outlined in Chapter 2, above.

Gradation within as well as between propositional modalities should be expected, if one accepts the validity of the underlying parameters suggested in our pragmatic treatment of epistemic modalities, above. These parameters may be recapitulated, together with a some added ones, as:

(25) **Parameters underlying the mental space of propositional modalities:**

    (a) Subjective certainty
    (b) Trust in the reliability of evidence
    (c) Willingness to entertain challenge
    (d) Propensity to respond to challenge
    (e) Gradient of authority/power
    (f) Strength of intent to act, or to manipulate others to act

Of these six parameters, the first four -- (25a-d) -- involve primarily the pragmatics of epistemic modalities. The last two -- (25e,f) -- shade into non-epistemic modes. All six parameters are, at least in principle, non-discrete **psychological** dimensions. As noted in Chapter 2, above, human categorization, be it in grammar, perception or cognition, is more often than not a **hybrid**, a functionally motivated compromise between Wittgensteinean gradation and Platonic discreteness. Discovering a similar balance between discreteness and scalarity in the domain of epistemic modalities is thus only to be expected.

4.4.2. The non-discreteness of presupposition

4.4.2.1. General considerations

Scalarity within the various types of presupposition may arise from a large number of sources, depending on the sub-clause in the communicative contract through which presupposition arises (see (13) above). In order:

(a) **Deictic obviousness:** What is present within the field of vision may be closer or more remote, more obvious or less obvious; the hearer may be an acute, a careless, or an impaired observer, raptly attending or momentarily distracted. Considerable information concerning all this is available to the speaker, in his/her assignment of probabilities concerning the hearer's belief.

(b) **Speaker participant:** The speaker may have been an active, central, closely-located participant in the reported event, or a passive, peripheral, remotely-located one. The speaker's first-hand access to the information may thus vary.

(c) **Generic information:** Every social group displays some hierarchic sub-divisions, with sub-groups and sub-sub-groups. The degree of generality of information within the entire population thus varies. Speakers are conscious of such variation, which presumably figures in their assessment of what the hearer is likely to know on general grounds.

(d) **Divine revelation:** The Divine is presumably held in absolute awe, but even there a culture may observe a number of divinities, ranked as to their strength and omniscience.

(e) **Mention in prior discourse:** Here there are a number of reason for scalarity. First, the time-lag within which the hearer is entitled to legitimately challenge a strong assertion may be flexibly graded. Second, the time-gap between a strong assertion and the current time of speech may vary, giving rise to memory gradation. Lastly, information that is thematically more central in the discourse is retained longer than less central information.[15] But thematic centrality is often a matter of degree.

(f) **Rules, games, conventions:** Rules are typically rigid, but as Wittgenstein (1953) has pointed out, the scope of their applicability may vary, as would the degree of their centrality to the game. Further, since they are generically-shared conventions, what was said in (c) above also holds here.

(g) **Unpredictable information:** The source of specific information the speaker has about what the hearer knows may vary in reliability. In addition, what applied to prior-text, (e) above, also applies here.

In sum, then, none of the sources from which presupposed information arises is immune to scalarity.

---

15 For an empirical study of this, see Anderson, Garrod and Sanford (1983).

4.4.2.2. Truth, Knowledge, belief or familiarity?

The grammar of many languages treats a number of clause-types that are logically *not* presuppositional as if they were presupposed. Those clauses are then contrasted with R-asserted clauses. Most conspicuous among such clause-types are:

(a) Conditionals
(b) yes-no-questions
(c) NEG-assertions

Concerning the first, Haiman (1978) cites much cross-language evidence in support of the *topical* status of hypothetical conditional. Now, since conditionals are irrealis clauses, they could not be *logically* presupposed. Nonetheless, they must be considered **background** clauses, in the sense that the information carried in them has been **discussed** or **entertained as possibility** in the preceding discourse. The speaker takes for granted the **accessibility** of that information to the hearer; but he does not assume that the hearer *believes* in it, nor that the hearer *knows* they to be *true*.[16]

Concerning the second, Bolinger (1978) has shown that yes/no-question, which logically **have no truth value** (and were listed in (8) above as a sub-type of *irrealis*), nonetheless are presuppositional in the following sense: The speaker has a considerable **bias** toward either the affirmative or the negative, a bias that is reflected consistently in the grammatical form of the question. Thus, consider:

(26) a. Was Elsa there?
      b. Wasn't Elsa there?
      c. No, she wasn't there.
      d. Yes, she was there.

Bolinger argues, I think convincingly, that in uttering (26a) one is more prone to expect the negative response (26c); while in uttering (26b) be one is more prone to expect the positive response (26d).

Concerning the third, it has been shown[17] that NEG-assertions, which have a NEG-truth value, are typically used in discourse contexts where the corresponding affirmative had either been mentioned, discussed, entertained, contemplated or raised as a possibility. To illustrate this briefly, compare (27) and (28) below:

---

16 Further empirical, text-based support for this may be found in Ramsay (1987), where it was shown that Haiman's generalization applies to pre-posed ADV-clauses, but not to post-posed ones. A similar suggestion was made in Givón (1982a).
17 Givón (1979a, ch. 3); see discussion further below.

(27) A: Hey, what's new?
       B: Well, let's see -- my boy graduated yesterday.
       A: Congratulations!

(28) A: Hey, what's new?
       B: Well, let's see -- my boy *didn't* graduate yesterday.
       A: Was he supposed to? I didn't know he was that old.

Affirmative R-assertions, it seems, are expressed on the background of the hearer's **relative ignorance**.[18] NEG-assertions, on the other hand, are expressed on the much richer background of expectations, namely that the corresponding affirmative is at least **familiar** to the hearer, and more typically that the hearer is indeed **disposed to believe** in the corresponding affirmative. But this is clearly not a presupposition in the *logical* sense (i.e. the speaker 'believing in the truth' of the corresponding affirmative). If that were the case, the speaker would have been caught in the bind of presupposing the truth of p while asserting its falsity.

The gist of this discussion is as follows: Logicians have traditionally defined the epistemic mode of *presupposition* either in terms of the truth of p,[19] or at the very least -- if a measure of pragmatics has been allowed to prevail [20] -- in terms of the speaker's **belief** in the truth of p. When hard-pressed by the increasingly recalcitrant data of human language, logicians embarked upon various rear-guard operations, splitting presupposition into an increasing number of discrete categories: Logical presupposition, pragmatic presupposition, conventional implicature, conversational postulates and what not.[21] Natural language, on the other hand, seems to treat presupposition pragmatically from the very start, in at least two distinct senses:

(a) Presupposition is a matter of the speaker's belief **about** the hearer's state of mind, not about the truth of some proposition; and

(b) Presupposition pertains not only to the hearer's strong beliefs, but also to the hearer's **weaker beliefs, assumptions, predispositions** or even vague **familiarity** with a proposition.

---

18 Information is never transacted on the background of *total* ignorance, or lack of *any* presumptions about the hearer's beliefs. For discussion, see Givón (1984a, ch. 7).
19 As in, for example, Keenan (1969, 1971); Horn (1972), Oh and Dinneen (eds, 1979), *inter alia*.
20 As in, for example, Karttunen (1974).
21 See, Gazdar (1979), *inter alia*.

One could then easily scale various grammatical constructions according to strength of presuppositionality, roughly as follows:

(29) **Scale of presuppositional strength:**

    a. **Strongest:** Complements of 'regret', 'be happy', 'be good'
    b. **Strong:** WH-questions, cleft-clauses, relative clauses; Complements of 'know', 'discover', 'forget'
    c. **Weaker:** Various nominalized clauses; Realis adverbial clauses
    d. **Weakest:** conditionals, negatives, yes/no-questions

One may similarly scale *know*, *believe in* and *be familiar with* on a sliding scale. While the top of these hierarchies tends to display the so-called 'logical' presupposition, far below the top some **pragmatic** presupposition may persist.

4.4.2.3. Presupposition vs. backgroundedness

As suggested in (6), above, restrictive relative clauses are, typically, strongly presuppositional. Consider now the contrast between an RR-clause modifying a *definite* head noun, and an RR-clause modifying an *indefinite* head noun:

(29) a. **Definite head:**
        The man *we hired yesterday* came in this morning and resigned.
    b. **Indefinite head:**
        A man *we hired yesterday* came in this morning and resigned.

While a sentence such as (29a) is uttered normally under an expectation that the hearer *shares the information* that 'we hired that man yesterday', the same is not true of (29b). This is so because when the speaker uses an indefinite noun, he does *not* assume that the hearer is familiar with that noun.[22] Therefore, the hearer could not be familiar with an event -- coded in the RR-clause -- in which that noun was a participant. Still, the RR-clause in (29b) is *not* strongly asserted, even though it is clearly new to the hearer. Rather, the information in the RR-clause is **backgrounded**. But why is that information coded by a structure that, in other contexts, when the head is definite, codes shared background information?

---

22 See discussion in chapter 6, below.

The common denominator for employing RR-clauses in (29a,b) is this pragmatic notion of *backgroundedness*. The more logical sense of presupposition arise as a stronger, more restricted *special case* under some discourse conditions. The pragmatic notion of backgroundedness entails that the speaker expects that the hearer will **not challenge** the information.[23] In the stronger case of presupposed old information, no challenge is expected because of presumed shared knowledge. In the weaker case of backgrounded new information, the speaker invites the hearer not to challenge the information by coding it as subsidiary, non-central, **less important**. The speaker thus gives a **cataphoric blank check** to the hearer, promising that the information will indeed not be of great thematic importance in the **subsequent** discourse. As we shall see in Chapter 5, above, marking information in such cataphoric terms is a major feature of discourse pragmatics.

4.4.3. The non-discreteness of assertions

We have already noted that the grammar of evidentiality scales R-assertions according to **evidentiary strength** (and thus also subjective certainty; see (15) through (20), above). IRR-assertions are likewise scaled for **subjective certainty** (see (10), above). In scaling both R-assertions and IRR-assertions in English, a wide variety of grammatical means may be used:

(30) a. **Modal verbs**: will, may, must, should, can, might
      b. **Cognition verbs**: believe, assume, presume, guess, suspect, think, suppose, surmise, doubt, be sure
      c. **Adjectives**: possible, probable, likely, true, false, alleged, presumed,
      d. **Adverbs**: maybe, perhaps, probably, possibly, presumably, necessarily, truly, really, most likely, allegedly

Finally, as already noted earlier above, the transition between R-assertion and IRR-assertion is often gradual, and such graduality is expressed quite often in the grammar of natural languages. Various *tags* may be use to temper the strength of R-assertions. Such tags are often augmented with intonation, as well as with various *irrealis* operators. Thus consider:

---

23 Lewis (1979) notes the role of this *no challenge* assumption in the 'creation' of presupposition, observing: "...presupposition evolves according to a rule of accommodation specifying that any presuppositions that are required by what is said straightaway come into existence, provided that nobody objects..." (1979, p. 347)

(31) **strongest assertion**
    a. He's home.
    b. He's home I think.
    c. , He's home, I think...
    d. He may be home.
    e. He's home, isn't he.
    f. He's home, right?
    g. He *is* home isn't he?
    h. He *is* home, right?
    i. He *is* home, or is he?
  weakest assertion

As we shall see directly below, this gradation from strong to weak assertion may proceed on toward questions -- i.e. toward non-declarative speech acts.

4.4.4. Epistemic modalities and manipulative speech-acts

4.4.4.1. Preamble

The traditional discussion of propositional modalities, from Aristotle down, has taken for granted a clear division of epistemic from non-epistemic modes. A cursory look at the distribution of epistemic modalities in the grammar of human languages, most particularly the distribution of *IRR-assertion* (8), reveals that this clean break can only be maintained by considerable idealization of the facts. As a conspicuous example, non-declarative speech acts systematically partake in the mode of *irrealis* -- even though they are not assertions. In this section we will consider a range of facts, all pointing to systematic shading from the epistemic through the intentional and toward the manipulative.

In a sense, the basis for such shading has already been laid down in our discussion of the pragmatics of epistemic modalities, above. Notions such as *certainty* and *probability of challenge* already shade into the province of **intent, power** and **action**. This shading is not logically necessary. Rather, it involves pragmatic inferences about **likelihood** and **normativity**. We will begin with a discussion of the connection between irrealis and intentionality.

4.4.4.2. From irrealis to intent to power

One of the most typical irrealis contexts is the scope of verbs of intent, ability and obligation, as in:

(32)　a.　She *wanted* to leave.
　　　b.　He *was able* to work.
　　　c.　They *had* to come in.

Take *want* first. Intent is presumably a purely-internal motivation. But intent to change the state of the world from that which exists to that which does not yet, invites considerations of one's **ability**, thus one's **power** to affect the change.

Next, *ability* may be either internally engendered, or facilitated by lack of external restraint. Either way, it implies some -- internal or external -- **restraints**, as well as the **power** to overcome them. Further, external restraints -- when consciously acknowledged -- shade into the notion of **obligation**.

Finally, *obligation* may be either internally or externally motivated. Either way it involves **power** relations vis-a-vis some other participant. Within the seemingly most innocuous intentional scopes, then, the notion of **power**, thus also of **power gradients** vis-a-vis others, is already implicit.

The power gradient vis-a-vis an external agent is even more apparent in another typical irrealis context, the scope of (non-implicative) manipulative verbs, as in:

(33)　a.　She *wanted* him to leave.
　　　b.　He *told* her to go.
　　　c.　She *asked* him to do it.

Examples (33) all involve -- under the scope of a manipulative verb -- an embedded irrealis clause. And the semantic interpretation of that embedded clause depends on various socio-pragmatic notions, such as manipulation, power gradients, obligations, propensity to act etc.

4.4.4.3. Subjunctives: From certainty to manipulation

Consider next the distribution of another wide-spread irrealis clause, the **subjunctive**. In Spanish, one finds this clause-type most commonly in two embedded complement clauses:

(34)　a.　**The subjunctive of uncertainty:**

　　　　　no *sé*　　　*si*　　*venga*
　　　　　no know-I　if　come-she-SUB
　　　　　'I don't know *if* she's coming'

b. The subjunctive of manipulation:

Le dije   que   *viniera*
her said-I   that   come-she-PAST/SUB
'I told her that she *should* come'

The same grammatical form thus seems to span the space from the epistemics of *uncertainty* to *attempted manipulation*. The very same form is also used in the polite imperative, a non-declarative speech act:

(35) *venga*!
     come-you/SUB
     'Come!'

The same sharing of a subjunctive form can be shown in English, in the systematic triple-use of 'should' and 'must': First as epistemic-modal subjunctives; second as manipulative subjunctives; and third in manipulative speech acts:

(36) (i) **Epistemic-modal:**
          a. He *must* have done it.
          b. She *should* be here in five minutes

     (ii) **Obligative-manipulative:**
          c. She told him that he *must* leave.
          d. He told her she *should* go.

     (iii) **Manipulative speech act:**
          e. You *must* leave immediately!
          f. You *shouldn't* stand there!

Many other languages show this systematic pattern. In natural language, this systematic sharing of grammatical form is most commonly the footprint of the historical process of *analogic extension*. Through such a process, the *functional scope* of one structure is extended, to code other functions that were not previously coded by the same structure. Such extension almost always involves the judgements of *similarity* of the two functions. And when many -- typologically and genetically unrelated -- languages exhibit the very same pattern of analogical extension, one is entitled to conclude that the human mind perceives the two functions involved as similar or related.[24]

---

24 Analogical extension can also proceed by *structural* similarity. For some discussion of the historical processes through which systematic coding correlations may be achieved, see Givón (1984a, Ch. 2).

4.4.5. The speech act continuum

4.4.5.1. Preamble

The speech-act mode of propositions has been a notorious stumbling block in the logical tradition's attempt to represent human language. The **purposive context** cannot easily be represented as a semantic property of the proposition itself, it fairly reeks of the pragmatics of speaker, hearer and context. It is thus not surprising to find that pre-Socratic philosophers, such as the *sophists*, were both familiar with and interested in non-declarative speech-acts. In this connection, Haberland (1985) observes:

"...Protagoras distinguishes four parts of discourse..., namely "wish, question, answer and command"...Protagoras seems to have been interested in *speech acts*, not sentences in modern parlance. But... it is *statements* Plato is interested in..." (1985, p. 381; emphases are mine; TG)

Plato's role in narrowing the focus of philosophical interest to the study of declarative propositions alone is well documented. Haberland identifies the reason for Plato's diminished focus as follows:

"...For Plato...true knowledge -- which, as he argues in this connection, does not coincide with perception -- cannot aim at context-dependent truths; the truth of a sentence should not depend on who says it, in which situation, and to whom, and it should not, more specifically, depend on what the sentence is an answer to... But this interest of Plato's in statements...is again only understandable from a series of premises that are no longer self-evident. The first of these is that *truth is the main concern of the philosopher*. The second is that *analysis of language is ancillary to philosophical pursuits*. As a corollary from these two premises, we get that *linguistic analysis is mainly concerned with truth* as well. The third premise is that *truth is timeless and independent of context*..." (1985, pp. 381-382; emphases are mine; TG).

Eventually, Ordinary Language Philosophers (cf. Austin, 1962), shifted the focus away from the mere **truth** of linguistic expressions, and back to their **felicity**, or **appropriateness** in context. Subsequently, speech-acts have been intensely investigated through 25 years of modern pragmatics, producing a vast literature.[25] In the discussion here, we will not attempt to recapitulate that literature. Rather, we will confine ourselves largely to three issues:

25 For more recent discussion, see many of the contributions in Cole and Morgan (eds, 1975) and Cole (ed., 1981), *inter alia*.

(a) The functional-semantic continuum underlying speech acts
(b) The systematic shading between speech acts
(c) The systematic shading between non-declarative speech acts and the irrealis epistemic modality.

A growing body of cross-language typological studies indicate that three or four syntactic constructions consistently code the same three or four major speech-act *prototypes* in human languages.[26] These prototypes are:

(37) a. **Declarative:** Goal = imparting information
      b. **Imperative:** Goal = eliciting action
      c. **Interrogative:** Goal = eliciting information...
         (i) **WH-question:** ...to confirm the identity of an item
         (ii) **Y/N-question:** ... to confirm the truth of a proposition

It is hard to find a language in which these four speech-act prototypes are not coded explicitly, via distinct syntactic constructions. Traditional speech-act analysis has tended to describe these functions as absolute and discrete.[27] This tradition, of studying the *prototype peaks* without paying attention to the graded terrain between them, incurs certain empirical costs. These costs are especially visible in the analysis of the so-called **indirect speech acts**.

Explicitly or implicitly, the literature on indirect speech-acts identifies those as 'meaning one thing while masquerading as another',[28] bizarre *coding infelicities* that perform the function of one speech act while assuming the syntactic structure of another. This is in spite of a considerable body of data (see survey in Brown and Levinson, 1978) suggesting that the so-called 'masquerade' is surprisingly systematic cross-linguistically. That is, that the same range of 'indirect' constructions are used in unrelated languages to perform the same range of speech-act functions. Still, the bulk of traditional attempts to deal with this *chimera* presupposes the discreteness of speech-acts.[29]

There are strong factual grounds for suspecting that the three-or-four major syntactically-coded speech acts (37) are just the most common,

---

26 For many cross-language details, see Sadock and Zwicky (1985). For interrogatives, see Chisholm (ed., 1984).
27 See for example Austin (1962), Searle (1970), Grice (1968/1975), *inter alia*.
28 See e.g. Sadock (1970), Green (1970, 1975), Gordon and Lakoff (1971), Searle (1975) or Davison (1975), *inter alia*.
29 See discussion in Levinson (1983), pp. 263-278. The lone exception seems to be Lyons (1977, pp. 753-768), where the shading from epistemic doubt (i.e. *irrealis*) to interrogative speech-acts is acknowledged, and where questions are considered 'grammaticalized features of doubt'.

conventionalized (thus 'grammaticalized') *prototype peaks*, spanning a multi-dimensional mental space, one made of several *non-discrete* **socio-psychological** dimensions. This multi-dimensional continuum underlies the entire functional domain of speaker-hearer interaction, i.e. our communicative contract. Within this continuum, the various speech-act prototypes shade into each other. In the following sections some of this shading will be illustrated.

4.4.5.2. **From imperative to interrogative**

Consider first the continuum in (38) below, between prototypical imperative and interrogative speech acts:

(38)　**most prototypical imperative**
　　a. Pass the salt.
　　b. Please pass the salt.
　　c. Pass the salt, would you please?
　　d. Would you please pass the salt?
　　e. Could you please pass the salt?
　　f. Can you pass the salt?
　　g. Do you see the salt?
　　h. Is there any salt around?
　　i. Was there any salt there?
　　most prototypical interrogative

The extreme points of scale (38) correspond to the well-coded prototypes. The mid-points on the scale -- (38c,d,e) -- exhibit intermediate features both functionally and syntactically. Finally, intermediate (38b) is more like the imperative prototype (38a), and intermediates (38f,g,h) are closer to the interrogative prototype (38i).

One may consider the intermediate points in (38) as a continuum of **metaphoric extensions** between the prototypes of imperative and interrogative. Felicity conditions under which such extensions are appropriate have been discussed in the speech-act literature.[30] The exact nature of the socio-psychological dimensions that underlie the continuum in (38) is yet to be empirically determined, by methods which sooner or later must transcend the traditional arsenal of linguistics and philosophy. As a weak hypothesis, the following dimensions may be suggested:[31]

---

30 See e.g. Grice (1968/1975) or Gordon and Lakoff (1971), *inter alia*.
31 These are similar to various features suggested in, e.g., Grice (1968/1975), Gordon and Lakoff (1971) or Searle (1975). One should not consider these features to be strictly linguistic. They are perhaps primarily socio-psychological, governing human interaction in general. As such, they are of course available to mediate verbal interaction.

(39) a. The **power (authority) gradient** between speaker and hearer

  b. The degree of the **speaker's ignorance** concerning a state of affairs about which he wishes to learn

  c. The degree of the **speaker's sense of urgency** or deter- **mination** vis-a-vis the attempted manipulation

All three parameters are scalar, thus representing a multi-dimensional space. One takes it for granted that not all the logically-possible slots within that space are actually instantiated in natural languages. The relatively small sub-set that tends to get coded more-or-less systemati- cally are constrained, presumably, in part by cognitive universal, in part by human-universals real-world adaptive tasks, in part by culture- specific adaptive considerations.

4.4.5.3. **From imperative to declarative**

Consider next the scale in (40) below, spanning the continuum be- tween the prototypes of imperative and declarative:

(40) **most prototypical imperative**
  a. Wash the dishes.
  b. You better wash the dishes.
  c. You might as well wash the dishes.
  d. I suggest you wash the dishes.
  e. It would be nice if you could wash the dishes.
  f. It would be nice if someone could wash the dishes.
  g. The dishes need to be washed.
  h. The dishes are dirty.
  i. The dishes were dirty.
  most prototypical declarative

Expression (40a) is syntactically a prototype imperative, with the agent left unexpressed, being predictable from the speech situation. Inter- mediates (40b,c,d,e) explicitly code the subject/agent 'you'. The manip- ulative force of the speech-act gradually recedes, as the syntactic form is slowly transformed toward the declarative prototype. In (40f) 'you' is replaced by 'someone', an impersonalization that further decreases the manipulative power. The impersonalization is further underscored with the passive form (40g). Finally, both (40h,i) are, syntactically, fairly prototypical declarative. And the shift to past tense in (40i) makes a situation-bound imperative interpretation virtually untenable.[32]

Of the underlying socio-pragmatic dimensions in (39), the two pertaining to imperatives -- (39a,c) -- are presumably also involved in the continuum in (40). In addition, the following features are likely to also be involved:

(41) a. The speaker's **subjective certainty** of the information
      b. The speaker's assessment of the **hearer's ignorance** of that information
      c. The speaker's assessment of the strength of the **hearer's motivation** to learn that information

Presumably, degree of similarity in form along the scale (40) represents, isomorphically, degree of similarity along the relevant functional dimensions.

4.4.5.4. From declarative to interrogative

One may as well note that a similar continuum exists between the prototypes of declarative and interrogative. Consider first the scale involving Y/N-questions:

(42) **most prototypical declarative**
     a. Joe is at home.
     b. Joe is at home, I think.
     c. Joe is at home, right?
     d. Joe is at home, isn't he?
     e. Is Joe at home?
    most prototypical interrogative

This continuum involves, among other features, a clear decrease in the speaker's subjective certainty concerning the information in his/her possession. It thus involves the *irrealis* -- doubt -- modality as an intermediate point (e.g. (42b) on the scale between R-assertion and Y/N-question. The number of well-coded morpho-syntactic points on this scale may be much larger, in English as well as in other languages.[33]

Finally, consider the continuum between declarative and WH-question:

---

32 This is obviously not the entire story. Other types of thematic and real-world pragmatic 'redundant' information are also involved in determining the likelihood of manipulative interpretation.

33 See Tsuchihashi's (1983) description of this continuum in Japanese.

(43) **most prototypical declarative**
    a. Joe called, and...
    b. What's-his-name called, and...
    c. Whoever it was that called, tell them...
    d. I don't know who called.
    e. Who knows who called.
    f. Who called?
    most prototypical interrogative

A similar gradation is seen here as in (42), from R-assertion ('certainty') through IRR-assertion ('uncertainty') to question.[34]

In sum, neither the socio-pragmatic space underlying speech-acts, nor the syntactic structures that code them, isolate them completely from other propositional modalities, or from each other. One can indeed discern clear *prototypes* in both the epistemic ('declarative') and manipulative ('interrogative', 'imperative') regions of our modal space. However, to account for both the functional organization and syntactic coding of the space, one must adopt a partially-flexible, partially open-ended pragmatic approach.

4.5. The pragmatics of NEG-assertion

4.5.1. Preamble

As suggested earlier, NEG-assertion is, in some ways, a *hybrid* epistemic modality. It shares some features of each of the other three modes. First, in terms of **subjective certainty**, thus the pragmatics of challenge and defense, it resembles R-assertion, being also a **strong assertion**. Second, in terms of the **referential opacity** vis-a-vis nominals under its scope, it resembles IRR-assertion. Finally, in terms of the pragmatics of **shared background**, it resembles the modality of **presupposition**. We will begin the discussion here by outlining this last aspect of the pragmatics of negation.

4.5.2. Negation as a speech act

The logical tradition has always considered negation to be a purely semantic operation, one which merely reversed the **truth value** of a

---

34 The use of WH forms to code epistemic uncertainty is wide-spread. Thus, for example, in Ute any WH pronoun can be use in low-certainty declarative sentences, if the speaker is unsure of either the token-identity of a nominal, or of its type-identity. Such expressions are usually translated into English as: 'what's-his-name', 'what-cha-ma-call-it', 'who knows' etc.

proposition. In that way, negation in language resembles the negative operator in math. As suggested above, however, negation also carries a distinct pragmatic component. NEG-assertions are in some sense presuppositional, though clearly not logically so. They are used when the speaker assumes that the hearer either **believes in the truth** of the corresponding affirmative proposition; or perhaps **entertains the possibility** of its being true; or that the corresponding affirmative had been established as **background expectation** in the discourse. The latter condition, the weakest of the three, is probably their common denominator.

NEG-assertions are used, most often, as a distinct *speech act*. While R-assertions purport to **inform**, NEG-assertions aim to **contradict, correct** or **deny**. What is denied is the background expectation, the corresponding affirmative.

Establishing the corresponding affirmative as background for a NEG-assertion may be accomplished explicitly in the preceding discourse, as in:

(44) **Background:** Joe told me that he won ten grand in the lottery...
NEG-assertion: ...tho later I found out *he didn't*

In (44) the speaker himself/herself sets up the affirmative expectation, then contradicts it. Background expectations may also be due to the interlocutor, as in:

(45) **Background**: A: I understand you're leaving tomorrow.
NEG-assertion: B: No, I'm *not*. Who told you that?

The speaker may rely, in assuming background expectations, on specific knowledge about the hearer's state of affairs or state of mind. To illustrate this, consider the felicity of the three responses to the NEG-assertion below:

(46) A: So *you didn't leave* after all.
B(i): No, it turned out to be unnecessary.
B(ii): Who said I was going to leave?
B(iii): How did *you* know I was going to?

Response (46Bi) suggests that the hearer accepted the corresponding affirmative as shared information. Response (46Bii) suggests that the hearer believes the speaker is mislead. In response (46Biii), the hearer registers surprise at how the information leaked out to the speaker, by inference thus conceding its truth.

Finally, background expectations to a NEG-assertion can also be traced to **generically shared** information. To illustrate this, consider:

(47) a. There was once a man who had no head
      b. ?There was once a man who had one head
      c. ?There was once a man who didn't look like a frog
      d. There was once a man who looked like a frog

The reason why the negative (47a) is pragmatically felicitous is because it reports a **break from the norm**. The reason why (47b) is pragmatically odd is because it merely echoes that norm, and is thus tautological. Conversely, the negative (47c) paraphrases the norm and is thus pragmatically odd; while the affirmative (47d) breaks the norm, and is thus pragmatically felicitous. The background norm thus turns out to be crucial ingredient for understanding the **pragmatic felicity** of propositions. If we were to live in a universe where men had no heads, or where they most commonly resembled frogs, both felicity contrasts in (47) would have been reversed.

But if both the affirmative and negative can be, equally, expected background, why do we consider NEG-assertions to be somehow special, more presuppositional, *marked*? In order to answer this, one must consider the ontological status of non-states and non-events. We will do that under two separate headings:

(a) Explicit vs. implicit normative expectations
(b) The skewed pragmatics of states and events

4.5.3. **Explicit and implicit normative expectations**

An *affirmative* background assumption for (47a), above, is **relatively explicit**;[35] it is derived from our generic knowledge of 'man' as stored in our shared lexicon. Namely, *All men have one head*. The pragmatic felicity of (47a) is thus achieved on the background of this -- more explicit -- assumption. But there are, in addition, potentially an infinite number of **implicit inferences** that one can derive from the prototype 'man'. And some of those are **negative implicit inferences**. This explains the pragmatic oddity of the NEG-proposition (47c): It paraphrases an *implicit* norm, *Men do not look like frogs*. And it is precisely this implicit norm that makes the affirmative (47d) pragmatically felicitous.

The derivation of implicit background inferences most likely proceeds gradually and indirectly. The chain of assumptions in (48) below may illustrate this likelihood, whereby (48e) is derived by a chain of inferences:

35 If features of meaning are indeed clustered, prototype-like entities (as suggested in Ch. 2, above), then the difference between explicit and implicit inferences from 'core' meaning must be a matter of degree, rather than of kind.

(48) a. Men look, normally, like men.
　 b. Other species (including frogs) normally look like them-
　　 selves.
　 c. Entities are classified -- among other things -- by visual
　　 similarity.
　 d. Since men are not frogs,
　 e. therefore men don't look like frogs.

One major difference -- or skewing -- between affirmative and negative propositions is that *explicit* normative information tends to be affirmative. Negative background inferences tend to be more *implicit*. But
by observing this, we have not answered the question concerning the
skewed status of NEG-asserted information. Rather, we have merely re-
formulated it.

4.5.4. The ontology of negatives states and events

4.5.4.1. The pragmatic status of negative events

Events are *changes* in an otherwise inert universe. It is a law of physics
-- **inertia** -- that motivate this facet of our constructed experience, i.e. the
skewed frequency of *happening* and *not-happening*. Events are, prob-
abilistically, **much less expected**, much **less frequent**, than non-events.
Inertia is the background norm, it requires **less energy**. Breaking the inertia is the exception, the **counter-norm**; it requires more energy. It is because of this probabilistic skewing that events -- changes -- are more informative, salient -- **foreground** -- than non-events. For this very reason,
non-events -- stasis -- tend to be the normative **background** upon which
events appear salient. Negation is a pun, a reversal, a play upon the
norm. It is used when -- much more rarely in normal communication --
one establishes the event as background expectation. On that background, the non-event becomes salient, informative. But this is still the
exception to the norm, a relative rarity in discourse.[36]
　Let us illustrate this with a number of simple examples. Consider first:

(49) a. A man came into my office yesterday and said...
　 b. *A man *didn't* come into my office yesterday and said...
　 c. ?*Nobody* came into my office yesterday and said...

---

36 Text counts reveal that in common narrative or conversation, the percent of NEG-assertions
　 as compared to affirmative assertions seldom exceeds 5 percent (see figures and discussion
　 in Givón, 1979a, ch. 3).

The non-event (49b) is pragmatically -- and indeed grammatically[37] -- the oddest. This must be so because if an event did not occur *at all*, why should one bother to talk about a referring, specific individual that was then 'involved' in that non-event?

While more grammatical, (49c) is still pragmatically unlikely. This is so because the norm of my everyday routine is *not* that *All people visit my office at all times*, but rather that *Most people don't ever visit my office*. Visits to my office are thus selective, more rare than non-visits. This is what makes them events. On the background of such a norm of non-events, (49a) is indeed pragmatically more felicitous.

Consider next:

(50) a. The man you *met* yesterday is a crook.
      b. ?The man you *didn't meet* yesterday is a crook.

Normatively, you meet only a few men in a given day. So, to identify a person by an event -- coded in the REL-clause in (50a) -- is indeed informative, salient, an apt way of distinguishing him from the xillion men you did not meet that day. Given the norm, (50b) is indeed pragmatically odd. Unless the foreground-background relations are reversed, as in, for example:

(51) You were supposed to meet four men yesterday.
      Three showed up, the last one never did.

On the background of (51), the non-event (50b) is indeed salient and pragmatically felicitous.

Next, consider:

(52) a. Where did you leave the keys?
      b. ?Where *didn't* you leave the keys?

In general, WH-questions are presuppositional, so that the entire clause, excepting the WH-element, is taken to be background information. The affirmative (52a) is pragmatically felicitous because *normally* there are a xillion possible places where your keys were *not* left, but only one place (at a time) where they were. For that very reason, the negative (52b) is pragmatically bizarre. Even supposing that the background expectations were somehow reversed, say with *I didn't leave my keys any place*, (52b) remains odd. This is so because, given that a potentially infinite number of places would qualify for the correct answer, the purpose of asking -- to elicit a specific location response -- cannot be fulfilled. In-

---

37 As noted in Givón, (1979a, ch. 3), referential-indefinite arguments are systematically excluded from NEG-assertions; see further discussion in section 4.5.5., below.

asking -- to elicit a specific location response -- cannot be fulfilled. Indeed, (52b) is only pragmatically felicitous as an *echo question*, where one heard a NEG-assertion -- a denial -- but has somehow missed the location part.

Finally, consider:

(53) a. When John comes, I'll leave.
      b. ?When John *doesn't* come, I'll leave

The affirmative (53a) is felicitous because the time when John comes, on a particular occasion, can be specified; but the xillion times when John doesn't come are not exactly denumerable. For that reason, the negative (53b) is odd -- unless one modifies the background, as in:

(54) I waited and waited there. Finally, when John didn't come, I left.

What makes (54) felicitous is that it establishes a *unique* reference point in time, by which John *had not* come (in the process masking the meaning of the *plu-perfect* with an overt use of the past tense). Once such a point becomes specifiable, the use of the negative in the time-adverb clause becomes felicitous.

4.5.4.2. The pragmatics of negative states

It had been observed elsewhere [38] that in paired antonymous adjectives, most typically of size, extension, elevation, texture, loudness, brightness, speed, weight etc., the positive member of the pair stands for both the possession of the property (i.e. the *positive* extreme) and the generic designation of the property (i.e. the *unmarked*). The negative member, on the other hand, stands only for the negative extreme -- of not possessing the property. This systematic bias is not logically predictable, since in logic both of the following equations are of equal status:

(55) a. not alive = dead
      b. not dead = alive

The systematic bias in paired adjectives in human language arises from an equally systematic skewing of their **perceptual saliency**: The positive

---

38 See Bierwisch (1967) and Givón (1970), *inter alia*; for some psycho-linguistic support, see H. Clark (1970) and E. Clark (1971).

(56) **paired adjectives**

positive	negative	perceptual property
big	small	ease of visual perception
long	short	" " " "
tall	short	" " " "
wide	narrow	" " " "
thick	thin	" " " "
light	dark	" " " "
high	low	" " " " above ground
fast	slow	ease of visual perception of rate of change over stationary ground
loud	quiet	ease of auditory perception
high note	low note	ease of auditory perception
sharp	dull	ease of tactile perception
heavy	light	ease of gravity/tactile perception
rough	smooth	ease of tactile perception
hard	soft	ease of tactile perception
spicy	bland	ease of savory perception
strong	weak	ease of olfactory perception

Much like non-events, negative qualities tend to form the normative **background** -- in terms of the frequency of pervasive **absence** -- vis-a-vis which the more rare **presence** of qualities is salient.

4.5.5. Negation and irrealis

So far we have surveyed evidence suggesting that the mode of NEG-assertion shares some of the pragmatic characteristics of presupposition, namely some **backgroundedness**. In this section we will briefly outline how NEG-assertion also shares some of the *semantic* properties of IRR-assertion.

The evidence will be discussed in more detail in Ch. 5, below. It has to do with *referential opacity* of propositions, and with the possibility of assigning a *non-referential* interpretation to nominal arguments within opaque propositions. Briefly, under the scope of R-assertion and presupposition, nominal arguments may only be interpreted referentially. Thus consider the following examples from English, a language in which indefinite NPs may be interpreted either referentially or non-referentially:

(57) a. John saw *a movie*   (R-asserted)
         (⊃ there's a *particular* movie that John saw)

      b. It is good that John saw *a movie*   (presupposed)
         (⊃ there's a *particular* movie that John saw)

In contrast, under the scope of IRR-assertions one may obtain a *non-referential* interpretation of an indefinite NP (as well as, for many IRR-clause types, also a referential-definite interpretation). Thus consider:

(58) John may go to see *a movie* tomorrow   (IRR-asserted)
      (i)   There's a *particular* movie that John plans to see.
      (ii) John plans to see *some* movie, tho neither he nor I have
            in mind any particular movie.

Under the scope of negation, a non-referential interpretation of indefinites is allowed (as under IRR-assertion), but a REF-indefinite interpretation is odd. Rather, if an argument under NEG-scope is referential, it must be *definite*:

(59) a. John didn't see *a movie*
          (i)   there exists *no movie* such as John saw it
          (ii) * ⊃ there exists a *particular* movie such as John
                didn't see it.

      b. John didn't see *the movie*
         (⊃ there exists *a particular* movie such as John didn't see
          it)

It has been suggested[39] that the reason why REF-indefinites are barred from the scope of negation has to do with the presuppositional status of negation. Briefly, if a NEG-assertion is uttered in the context of the corresponding affirmative proposition being background knowledge or expectation, then a fairly obvious inference must hold:

(60) "If a proposition is familiar to the hearer, the identity of the
      referring arguments within that proposition must also be
      familiar to the hearer; the argument must thus be definite".

This pragmatically-motivated restriction aside, NEG-assertions still share with IRR-assertions the semantic property of allowing referential opacity under their scope.

---

39 Givón (1979a, ch. 3).

4.6. Certainty, power and deference

4.6.1. Preamble

In several sections above we noted that there exist some inferential connections among various propositional modalities, so that the purely epistemic modes shade gradually into socio-manipulative modes. These connections may be summarized as the following one-way inferences:

(61) a. truth ⊃ knowledge
      b. knowledge ⊃ certainty
      c. certainty ⊃ status
      d. status ⊃ power

None of these inferences is logically necessary. Rather, they are **pragmatic norms** associated with the communicative contract. The communicative contract, it seems, is itself embedded within a wider context, a well-regulated matrix of **socio-personal interaction**. In this section we will briefly survey some of the socio-personal dimensions that seem to be consistently associated with the communicative contract.

4.6.2. Certainty and authority

As suggested above, the communicative contract inexorably ties together the more epistemic dimensions of knowledge and subjective certainty, with the more socio-personal dimensions of authority, status and power. Thus, for example, in the grammar of Japanese (Tsuchihashi, 1983), women are assigned a special verb-marking R-assertion particle, one that ranks consistently below the prototypical male-used R-assertion particles, in degree of subjective certainty, or determination to beat down a challenge from the hearer.

More generally, Syder and Pawley (1974) observe that in facing an interlocutor of higher power ('status', 'authority'), speakers tend to **scale down** their expression of certainty, by using hedges that place assertions in a lower -- *irrealis* -- epistemic range. This is not done, necessarily, because of perceiving a contrary attitude on the part of the high-status interlocutor. Rather, the tone-down may be a hedge against the *possibility* that the higher authority *might* hold a contrary belief. Such **epistemic deference** to power realities is a pervasive feature of many, perhaps all cultures.[40]

---

40 See Brown and Levinson (1978).

4.6.3. **Authority, negation and politeness**

As noted above, NEG-assertion is a contrary, denying speech-act. One would thus expect its use to be extremely sensitive to the perceived social position of the interlocutor. This is indeed the case, seemingly universally, in the use of NEG-assertions in the context when the interlocutor is perceived to be of higher status or power. Under such conditions, speakers tend to tone down their disagreement, they couch their contrary opinion in a variety of 'softening' devices. Many of these devices are sub-varieties of *irrealis*, as in:

(62) a. Quite, quite.
    b. Yes, I see.
    c. I see what you mean.
    d. I suppose you got a point there.
    e. Perhaps not quite so.
    f. Perhaps you may wish to consider an alternative.
    g. Well, I'm not sure about that, maybe...
    h. Now if it were up to me, I would suggest...

In more traditional cultures it is often not easy to find any overtly-marked negation in speech directed toward perceived superiors or outsiders.

Somewhat paradoxically, negation can itself be used as a **softening** operator in the face of perceived higher authority. This **toning down** function of negation seems to apply to both epistemic and manipulative modes. Thus consider:

(63) a. *Won't* you come in please?
        (= Do come in)
    b. I suppose he *isn't* done yet.
        (= I wonder if he's done)
    c. I *don't* suppose he's done yet?
        (= I wonder if he's done)
    d. *Wouldn't* it be better if...
        (= It'd be better if...)
    e. I suppose you *couldn't* spare a fiver...
        (= I wish you would)

This use of negation -- often in conjunction with *irrealis* operators, including modals, subjunctives, conditionals and yes/no question markers -- is wide-spread cross-linguistically, perhaps universal.[41] I suspect its polite-

---

41 See Goody (ed., 1978), especially Brown and Levinson (1978). See also Salisbury (1986).

ness, deference value derives from the overlap between negation and ir-realis, along the psychological dimension of **subjective certainty**

4.6.4. Certainty, modesty and politeness

Questions of politeness and deference, with their complex culture-specific -- and presumably some universal -- details, shade rather persistently into the epistemic range of our modal space. Thus, for example, Syder and Pawley (1974) note that some cultures seem to put a certain prime on the so-called *modesty principle*, by which speakers as a matter of course claim to know less than they do, especially when the information may reflect favorably on their personal stature. It may well be that this culture-specific tendency is another reflection of a more universal principle, already noted above:

(64) **Subjective certainty and higher authority:**

"In communicating to an interlocutor of higher status, one downgrades one's own subjective certainty".

Lewis (1979) makes a similar observation couched in terms of a putative slave-master relationship.

4.6.5. Knowledge, certainty, responsibility and blame

In many cultures, perhaps in most, claiming **direct personal responsibility** for conveyed information may be a serious social error, to be strictly avoided in any but the most intimate -- thus well protected -- social contexts. Strong claims to *direct authorship* of transmitted information, with the attendant marking of high *subjective certainty* and strong *evidential support*, are all to be avoided. In carrying out communication under these cultural constraints, a variety of highly conventionalized strategies are used, including **indirection,** disclaimer, oblique attribution, impersonalization, couching R-assertions as yes/no questions, negation and irrealis. While the structural devices may be the same as in some of the cases cited above, the guiding principle is perhaps different. That principle is roughly this:

(65) **The hazardous information principle:**

    a. Knowledge is power, but power is responsibility.
    b. Information may be coveted, it may also be hazardous and socially destabilizing.

   c. Transmitting new information may yield a clear social advantage, but it also incurs some risks.

   d. Therefore, being identified explicitly as the author of information may be unwise, must be avoided.

The operation of this principle is particularly conspicuous in small, rural, geographically scattered communities, where residents of isolated homesteads are adept at cajoling fresh gossip, preferably malicious, out of the occasional visitor. In spite of their geographic scatter, such communities are often **intimate** social units, where one's business is everybody's business, and where most mundane news disseminates with lightning speed. The transmission of fresh gossip may indeed be the real purpose of a visit. Yet the would be transmitter must tread lightly, lest he be soon pointed at -- often accusingly and by the very same host who warmed the information out of him -- as the explicit author.

4.7. The hybrid nature of propositions: Between Tautology and contradiction

> "...The propositions of logic are tautologies.
> Therefore the propositions of logic say nothing..."
>
> L. Wittgenstein,
> *Tractatus Logico Philosophicus* (1918, p. 121)

In discussing epistemic modalities earlier above, we proceeded as if propositions are either asserted (R-asserted, IRR-asserted, NEG-asserted) or presupposed. In following this line, we have tacitly shared the traditional assumptions of logical semantics. But in this respect too, the logical-semantic tradition grossly misrepresents the facts of *use* of natural language. In actual communication, all propositions tend to be **informational hybrids,** carrying some presupposed ('old') and some asserted ('new') information. In order to understand why this *must* be the case, one must acknowledge two general properties of human discourse:

   (a) Every new proposition that is transacted in human discourse presupposes an enormous amount of shared **background information,** some generic-lexical, some situational-deictic, some text-specific.

   (b) Human discourse is overwhelmingly **multi-propositional.** That is, it is seldom the case that the message spans only a single proposition. Rather, it spans some multi-propositional

sequence. In other words, it has multi-propositional **coherence**.

Each proposition in discourse must thus be *coherent* with respect to all three contexts -- the *generic* (culturally-shared), the *deictic* (situationally-shared), and the *textual* (discourse-shared). Achieving such coherence requires that not all the information in the proposition be new. Rather, some of it must recapitulate -- or allude to -- shared background information, in order to cohere with it.

Coherence vis-a-vis a larger system is achieved by **partial overlap** of information. The best -- albeit negative -- metaphor for this may be found in Wittgenstein's (1918) discussion of the two logical extremes of **tautology** and **contradiction**:[42]

"...A tautology has no truth conditions, since it is unconditionally true; and a contradiction is true on no condition. Tautologies and contradictions lack sense..." (1918, p. 69)

A proposition is tautological if it repeats the information already given in another proposition. A proposition is contradictory if it is logically incompatible with the information given in another proposition. Both extremes yield communicative disasters:

(a) Total informational **redundancy** = tautology = **no interest**
(b) Total informational **incompatibility** = contradiction = **no coherence**

Human communication is necessarily a hybrid system, a compromise between the two logical extremes.[43]

The most common data type supporting this concept of the hybrid nature of propositions comes from the study of the pragmatic properties of grammatical subjects. In most languages, the grammatical subject of a clause must be definite -- i.e. presupposed to be known to the hearer. Even in languages -- such as English -- that tolerate indefinite subjects, referential-indefinite subjects are rare in text, seldom above 5%-10%.[44]

In many languages, direct objects also tend to be definite, 'old',

---

42 See further discussion in Chapter 7, section 7.2.2., below.
43 As Wittgenstein (1918) has pointed out, all the propositions of deductive logic can be reduced to either tautology or contradiction. Deductive logic is thus, in principle, the wrong means for incrementing *new* knowledge into a system.
44 See text-counts and discussion in Givón (1979a, ch. 2).

'topical' information.[45] Text counts in English[46] suggest about 50% definiteness for direct objects.

As we noted earlier above, many grammatical clause-types are largely presupposed. Such *background clauses* are not very frequent in text, being pragmatically *marked*. But their cumulative frequency in many text-types, or styles, may easily exceed 50% (as against asserted *foregrounded clauses*).

In a recent quantified study,[47] the average number of new-information-bearing words (subjects, objects, verbs, adjectives, adverbs) per clause was calculated for a written English text. The clauses ranged in length between 3 and 10 lexical words, with the average around 5 words per clause. The results may be couched in terms of the following principle:

(66) **Ratio of incremented information in text:**

   (a) **The one-chunk per clause ratio:**

   "The average number of new-information-bearing words per clause is 1.4 words, i.e. approximating *one* chunk of new information per proposition".[48]

   (b) **The 25% per clause ratio:**

   "On the average, about 25% of all lexical words in a clause -- thus in the text at large -- are new information words; the rest is old information".

These results suggest that human language utilizes a highly **incremental** approach to information processing. The bulk of the information in the clause ('proposition') is *old, background, shared, presupposed*. Only a relatively small portion of the clause is new information.

The functional explanation for such an information processing system is relatively transparent: The 75% old information packed into most clauses is used to established the **coherence** -- and thus **relevance** -- of each chunk of new information vis-a-vis the already stored information. The old information chunk are the **addressing** mechanism. Such a processing system is motivated, in turn, by the two main features of human discourse already outlined above:

---

45 See Givón (1984d).
46 Givón (1979a, ch. 2).
47 Givón (1984a, ch. 7).
48 This principle was first suggested in Givón (1975c).

(a) The multi-propositional nature of human discourse and its coherence;
(b) The large, complex ever-present context that is required in order to interpret chunks of new information.

The old information packed into propositions in natural communication is needed to perform **anchoring, coherence, relevance** functions vis-a-vis the multi-propositional prior text, and prior context.

4.8. The negotiation of modality

Even the most pragmatic approach to meaning and communication often clings to one *shibboleth* of our venerable logical tradition: Speakers know what is in their own mind; their lexical meanings are fully specified; their propositions concerning states and events are explicit; their modalities are deliberately chosen. We cling to these conventions as to dear life, often in the face of much *prima facie* evidence to the contrary. Lewis' (1979) charming anecdotal discussion of 'score-keeping in a language game' is one account of how one **negotiates** truth, presupposition, definiteness, and incidentally also meaning. Unfortunately, the implications of Lewis' account for our analytic approach have gone largely ignored.

This vast, potentially explosive issue must ultimately be resolved through the empirical study of actual communicative behavior. At this point I would like to simply illustrate the problem with two textual examples. Both are taken from the same work of fiction. The two participants in the negotiation are **Mrs. Phillip J. King** and **Momma**. In the first passage, the shifting peaks of negotiated meaning are boldfaced; the manipulated epistemic modality is given in italics:

"...Mrs. Phillip J. King said he had been **dashing**, but Momma would not go along with dashing and said *to her mind* he had been **not unattractive**, but Mrs. Phillip J. King couldn't see fit to drop all the way from dashing to not unattractive, so her and Momma negotiated a description and arrived at **reasonably good looking**, which was mutually agreeable though it seemed for a minute or two that Mrs. Phillip J. King might hold out to have the reasonably struck from the official version. But Momma went on to tell her how she *thought* **his nose had a fanciful bend to it** which distracted Mrs. Phillip J. King away from the reasonably because, as she told Momma back, she *had always thought* his nose had a fanciful bend to it herself. Mrs. Phillip J. King called it **a Roman nose** and she said there wasn't anything uppity or snotty about it but it was purely **a sign of nobility**. And Momma said he *certainly* carried himself **like a Roman**, which sparked Mrs. Phillip J. King to *wonder if maybe* he had*n't* **come from Romans,** *if maybe* that was*n't* why he was **a Republican.** But Momma said she *recalled* he was **a notable Democrat.** And Mrs. Phillip J. King said, "*Maybe* he was". And Momma said she *believed* so. And Mrs. Phillip J. King said "*Maybe* he was" again...I was not present when Mrs. Phillip J. King decided she couldn't let **reasonably good looking** rest peacefully and resurrected the whole business with the argument that **a moustache under that fancifully bent nose** *would have most certainly* made for **dashing.** But Momma could not see clear to allow for a moustache since there had not been one actually; however, Mrs. Phillip J. King *insisted* that *if* Momma *could just imagine* a **finely manicured and dignified Douglas Fairbanks-style moustache** under that Roman nose then all of the rest of the features *would surely* come together and *pretty much* scream **Dashing** at her. But even with a moustache thrown in Momma could not sit still for any degree of dashing though Mrs. Phillip J. King campaigned rather fiercely for **Considerably Dashing** and then **Somewhat Dashing** and then **A Touch Dashing,** so Momma for her part felt obliged to retreat some from **reasonably good looking** and her and Mrs. Phillip J. King settled on **passably handsome** with Mrs. Phillip J. King supplying the **handsome** and Momma of course supplying the **passably...**"

T.R. Pearson, *Short History of a Small Place*
(1985, pp. 191-192)

The second passage is noteworthy for the wide range of evidentials, as well as other epistemic operators, used in the progressive upgrading of 'truth':

"..."Pepsi Cola" she said. "Yes, I **believe** it was Pepsi Cola because **I'm near certain** it was Mr. Womble who ran the Nehi outfit". And Momma sat straight up and said, "Helen?"... But Mrs. Phillip J. King just went straight on and said, "It **had to be** Pepsi Cola. He owned the bottling plant **you know** in Burlington. **I mean** his daddy, **now I don'** think he ever owned it himself, but his daddy did and made a killing putting out Pepsi Cola until he sold the business and made another killing doing that. **Momma said** it was just a ton of money that changed hands. **She was brought up in Burlington you know**". "But Helen", said Momma... "And **they tell me** his wife was just a gorgeous woman but not from around here...**Momma said** he went out and got one all the way from Delaware or Ohio, **she couldn't ever remember** exactly which, but **I imagine** it was Delaware since **P.J. tells me**...that Delaware is one of your urban states...and **P.J. says** there's plenty of money in Delaware mostly on account of the Duponts, and she **might have even been** a Dupont herself, anyway **I don't know** that she **wasn't** and she was **probably** from Delaware **I imagine**, which is where they all come from..." "Wasn't it cookies instead of Pepsi-Cola?" Momma wanted to know. "Didn't Mr. Alton's Daddy make those savannahs with white cream filling and those little oval shortbread cakes that came in the blue sack?" And Mrs. Phillip J. King got a little hot on account of the cream-filled savannahs and the shortbread cakes and she said to Momma, "Now Inez, he **might have** dabbled in cookies later but **I can tell you for a fact** it was Pepsi-Cola at the first because **Momma said** it was Mr. Womble at the Nehi and Mr. Foster at the Coca-Cola and Mr. Todd W. Smith at the Sundrop and Mr. Nance at the Pepsi-Cola, and **Momma herself told me** it was Pepsi-Cola that made him his money but **I don't ever recall** a whisper of cookies **passing her lips**..."..."

T.R. Pearson, *A Short History of a Small Place*
(1985, pp. 193-195)

CHAPTER 5

THE PRAGMATICS OF REFERENCE: EXISTENCE, REFERENTIAL INTENT AND THEMATIC IMPORT

5.1. Reference and existence*

5.1.1. The Real World vs. the Universe of Discourse

The treatment of reference in linguistics developed historically as the by-product of a long-established logical tradition. Within that tradition, one formulation (admittedly now somewhat of a straw-man; but see Russell, 1905, 1919; Strawson, 1950 or Carnap, 1958) holds that reference (or *denotation*) is a mapping relation between linguistic terms and entities which **exist** in the **Real World**. Therefore, the **truth** of sentences containing referring expressions depends, *inter alia*, on whether the referring expressions inside them denote or do not denote in the real world. To illustrate this approach, consider the sentences (1) and (2) below:

(1) a. *The king of France* is bald
      b. *The queen of England* is bald
      c. I rode *a unicorn* yesterday
      d. I rode *a horse* yesterday

(2) a. There is a king of France (and only one)
      b. There is nothing which is both king of France and bald
      c. There is a queen of England (and only one)
      d. There is something which is both queen of England and bald

According to Russell's approach to reference (see Strawson, 1950), in asserting (1a) one asserts two contradictory propositions: The false (2a), and

* I am indebted to Martin Tweedale, Frank Lichtenberk, Dwight Bolinger and Paul Otto for many helpful comments. This chapter also benefited from early presentation at the Georgetown Round Table on Linguistics (Wahington, DC,1984), S.I.L. Grammar Workshop (Ukarumpa, Papua-New Guinea, 1985), the Linguistics Colloquium at Auckland University (Auckland, 1986), and the Linguistics Colloquium, Australian National University (Canberra, 1986).

the true (2b). Further, the falsity of (2a) is due to *failure of denotation*. In asserting (1b), on the other hand, no contradiction is present. One asserts the true proposition (2c) -- true due to *proper denotation* -- and the factually false (2d). Similarly, (1c) is a false assertion because of failure of denotation; while (1d) may be true because proper denotation may be obtained.

It is nonetheless remarkable that human languages tend to code the nominals in (1a,b) and (1c,d), respectively, with exactly the same grammatical devices, paying no heed to the fine distinction of real world denotation and truth. Is the grammar of human language -- and the mind behind it -- confused, misleading or capricious? Or is it perhaps marching to the beat of a different drum? Reference in human language seems to *not* be a mapping from linguistic terms to individuals existing in The Real World, but rather a mapping from linguistic terms to individuals **established verbally** -- for whatever purpose -- in the **Universe of Discourse.**

It is of course true that the Universe of Discourse and The Real World display a considerable overlap in normal human discourse, which tends to deal with extant human individuals and their everyday affairs. But when the two worlds do not overlap, the grammar of reference cheerfully disregards Real-World denotation, abiding instead by denotation in the universe of discourse.

The grammar of reference may also disregard denotation altogether, as can be seen from (3) below:

(3)   a. John is looking for *a horse*; *it* escaped last Friday
       b. John is looking for *a horse*; *it* better be white

The horse in (3a) denotes a specific individual entity in the universe of discourse. The one in (3b) does not. Still, the grammar of English applies the anaphoric pronoun *it* to both the real horse in (3a) and the hypothetical horse in (3b).

5.1.2. **Reference vs. referential intent**

It is of course possible, for a logic-based description of reference, to concede the point and make every universe of discourse -- in fact, the multiplicity of **possible universes of discourse** -- a separate realm of denotation for linguistic terms. In a very clear sense, **Possible Worlds Semantics**[1] is a formal attempt to accomplished just that. As we shall see later on, problems will persist even with this approach.

---

1   See e.g. Kripke (1963, 1972), Cocchiarella (1965), Hinttika (1967), Purtill (1968), Scott (1970), Montague (1970) or Lewis (1972), *inter alia*; also discussion in Chapter 1, above. Whether the 'indexing' that proliferated under Possible Worlds Semantics accomplishes much more than merely *labeling* some major areas of pragmatics that are impervious to a truth-conditional treatment, remains to be seen.

Reference in a Universe of Discourse is already a *crypto pragmatic* affair. This is so because every universe of discourse is *opened* ('established') -- for whatever purpose -- by a **speaker**. And that speaker then **intends** entities in that universe of discourse to either refer or not refer. And it seems that in human language it is that **referential intent** of the speaker that controls the grammar of reference. Thus, *a horse* in (3) above is, by itself, a **referentially opaque** term. It could either refer to a horse in the universe of discourse in (3a), or it could have no such reference (or else refer to the **type** *horse*) as in (3b). And in the absence of The Real World as arbiter of denotation, the speaker's referential intent seems to be all one may have to go by.

While crypto-pragmatic in this one sense, a treatment of reference based primarily on referential intent is still *semantic* in another sense: It makes no reference to extra-propositional context, above and beyond the speaker who utters the proposition. Thus, if the speaker can be *abstracted* and thus ignored, as has been done matter of factly in logic since Plato, reference would remain essentially limited to the scope of the atomic proposition. In the next section we will discuss reference in natural language from such a semantic perspective. We will note the predictable relation between propositional modalities and referentiality of nominals under their scope. We will also see why, given natural language facts, a purely semantic approach to reference can achieve only partial characterization of the facts.

5.2. The semantics of indefinite reference [2]

5.2.1. Referential opacity

The term **referential opacity** is originally due to Quine (1953), in a context that actually does not concern us directly here. His original observations concerned examples like (4a,b) below[3]:

(4) a. Managua is
          (i) Julia's home town
          (ii) the capital of Nicaragua
     b. Harry knows that Managua is
          (i) Julia's home town
          (ii) the capital of Nicaragua

---

2 The treatment of reference given below was first suggested in Givón (1973b). A somewhat similar account may be found in Jackendoff (1971).
3 I am indebted to Martin Tweedale (in personal communication) for discussing with me the history of the treatment of reference in philosophy, as well as the history of the term 'referential opacity'.

Assuming that (the speaker knows that) the nominal expressions (i) and (ii) above refer to the same city (Managua), the substitution of (i) and (ii) in (4a) does not change the truth value of the proposition. An environment such as (4a) will thus be called **referentially transparent**. In contrast, (4b) is a **referentially opaque** environment, because the substitution of (i) and (ii) there seems to change the truth value of the proposition. That is, Harry may know those two facts about Managua without necessarily knowing that they refer to the very same city.

One may argue, something Quine did not choose to pursue, that what is at the bottom of the referential opacity of (4b) is the interjection of **another mind** -- thus **another perspective**. And only when the knowledge of that other mind does not match the *speaker's* knowledge does one obtain this type of referential opacity.

The term referential opacity was also extended by Quine to the environments that concern us more directly here. As Aristotle noted in *De Sophisticis Elenchis* (McKeon, ed., 1941), in some linguistic environments one can obtain an ambiguity between the *sensus divisus* ('referential') and *sensus compositus* ('generic', 'attributive', 'non-referential') of a nominal expression.[4] To illustrate this, consider the following expressions, the first one by Quine's definition referentially transparent, the second referentially opaque:

(5) a. John married *a rich woman.*
　　 b. John wanted to marry *a rich woman,*
　　　　 i. ...but *she* refused him.
　　　　 ii....but he couldn't find *any.*

The speaker uttering (5a) is **committed** to the referential existence -- in the universe of discourse -- of some rich woman that John married. In other words, the following implication must hold:

(6) If John married one, *that particular one* must have existed.

Expression (5a) is thus referentially **transparent** in the sense we will be using here. Expression (5b), on the other hand, is in this sense referentially **opaque**. In uttering it, the speaker may or may not have made a referential commitment. Two interpretations of *a rich woman* are possible:

---

4 Medieval philosophers persisted in using Aristotle's terminology. In the 20th century the terms *de re* and *de dicto* were used to denote 'referential' and 'non-referential, respectively. Donellan (1966) is responsible for recasting those, at least for some grammatical environments, as 'referential' and 'attributive', respectively. Finally, linguists have also used the terms 'specific' and 'generic', respectively.

(7) a. John -- and thus the speaker -- has *a particular woman* in
         mind; he wishes to marry **her.**
     b. John -- and thus the speaker -- has *no particular woman* in
         mind; he wishes to marry someone of that **type.**

Interpretation (7a) is compatible with ending (5bi) above; and Interpretation (7b) is compatible with ending (5bii).

Since the indefinite noun is opaque in (5b) but transparent in (5a), this
type of referential opacity is not signalled in English by the presence (vs.
absence) of the indefinite article itself. Rather, it is somehow due to the
propositional modality under whose scope the indefinite expression
falls.

5.2.2. **Reference and propositional modalities**

In this section I will recapitulate the earlier discussion[5] concerning
how the second type of referential opacity (i.e. as in (5b) above), more
specifically of indefinite nominals, is systematically predictable from
the propositional modality under whose scope the nominal falls. For
this purpose, the four major propositional modalities discussed in Ch. 4
above, may be grouped into two pairs:

(8) a. FACT: Presupposition
                   R-assertion
     b. NON-FACT: IRR-assertion
                   NEG-assertion

To the **non-fact** category one must add two linguistic environments that
were not discussed in ch. 4, above:

(9) a. HABITUAL:
         John meets *a woman* every Tuesday at the pub
     b. NOMINAL PREDICATE:
         John is *a man*
         John is *my friend*

The common denominator of irrealis, negation, habitual and nominal
predication is fairly obvious: *None* of these modes refers to the *occurrence
of a particular event at a particular point in time.* This is, presumably, the
common feature of non-fact.

The rule for (this type) referential opacity is then given as:

---

5   This was discussed briefly in Ch. 4, section 4.5.5., above. See also Givón, (1972a, 1973b).

(10) a. "Under the scope of FACT modalities, nominals can only be interpreted as referential".

       b. "Under the scope of NON-FACT modalities, nominals may be interpreted as either referential or non-referential".

The most common FACT and NON-FACT modalities in human language were listed in Ch. 4, above. Since human discourse, most particularly everyday narrative or conversation, seems to employ NON-FACT modalities rather sparingly,[6] it is possible to render (10) above more realistically as a *markedness* expression:

(11) "Nominals **may** be interpreted non-referentially only if they are under a NON-FACT scope. Otherwise they **must** be interpreted referentially".

One short note must be added here concerning the markedness -- skewed -- relation between the referring and non-referring sense of nominals. Formal logicians 'handled' the description with two quantifiers, the **existential** to mark referring senses, and the **universal** to mark non-referring ones. There are two things that are odd in this formalization. First, it considers both the referential and non-referential equally marked, whereas the distributional facts of natural language strongly suggest that the non-referential is the *marked* category. Second, in using the universal quantifier to mark non-referring nominals, logicians lump together two distinct senses of 'not referring'. To show this, consider examples (12a,b,c) below:

(12) a. John thinks *a girl* in his class is willing to marry him.

       b. John thinks *some girl* in his class will eventually agree to marry him.

       c. John thinks *all girls* might be willing to marry him.

While 'girls' in neither (12b) nor (12c) refers to a specific individual, their sense of *not referring* is rather distinct. In (12b), a **possible** single individual is hypothesized. In (12c) an entire **multiple group** is referred to, or perhaps the **type**. The universal quantifier may perhaps characterize (12c), but clearly not (12b).

---

6 We have already discussed in Ch. 4, above, why NEG-assertions are relatively rare in normal discourse. The irrealis mode is also less common, except in specialized discourse such as (among others) law codicils, exam questions, or academic discussions.

5.2.3. The grammatical marking of indefinite reference

As we have seen above, English indefinite nouns are potentially ambiguous as to whether they refer or do not refer to an entity in the universe of discourse. The indefinite article simply marks the fact that the term is being introduced into the discourse for the first time -- and without any **speaker's presumption of hearer's familiarity.** Such presumption -- or presupposition -- is in fact the major requirement for marking nominals as **definite.**[7] The article system of English marks rather sharply the contrast between definite and indefinite. In many languages, on the other hand, the grammar distinguishes just as sharply between referential and non-referential indefinites. And in predicting referential opacity, such languages abide by the very same rules (10, 11) as English. To illustrate this, consider the following examples from Hawaii Creole, where the numeral *one* marks referential-indefinite nouns, while *zero* marks non-referential nouns:[8]

(13) R-ASSERTION:

    a. i rid wan-buk
       he read one-book
       'He read a book' ($\supset$ a specific book)

    b. *i rid buk
       he read book   (*$\supset$ no specific book)

(14) PRESUPPOSITION:

    a. i hapi i rid wan-buk
       he happy he read one-book
       'He's happy that he read a book' ($\supset$ a specific book)

    b. *i hapi i rid buk
       he happy he read book (*$\supset$ no specific book)

---

7 See extensive discussion in Ch. 6.
8 Following Bickerton (1975). Other languages with a similar contrast marked by *one* vs. *zero* are: All Creoles, Turkish, Sherpa, Nepali, spoken Hebrew, Old English, Old German, Old Spanish, Old French, Mandarin Chinese, and literally scores of others; see discussion in Givón, (1978a; 1981b).

(15) IRR-ASSERTION:

    a. i want rid wan-buk
       he want read one-book
       'He wanted to read a book' ($\supset$ a specific book)

    b. i want rid buk
       he want read book
       'He wanted to read a book' ($\supset$ no specific book)

(16) NEG-ASSERTION:

    a. i no-rid buk
       he no-read book
       'He didn't read a/any book' ($\supset$ no specific book)

    b. i no-rid di buk
       he no-read the book
       'He didn't read *the* book' ($\supset$ a specific-DEF book)

    c. *i no-rid wan-buk
       he no-read one-book (*$\supset$ a specific -INDEF book)

Some languages mark in their grammar only the contrast of referential vs. non-referential, with definiteness left unmarked. Such languages
still abide by rules (10, 11) as English or Creoles. For example, in Bemba
(Bantu) the VCV- form of the noun prefix codes referential nouns
regardless of definiteness; while the CV- form codes non-referential
nouns. Thus consider: [9]

(17) R-ASSERTION:

    a. a-a-somene *ici*-tabo
       he-PAST-read REF-book
       'He read *a/the* book' ($\supset$ a specific book)

    b. *a-a-somene *ci*-tabo
       he-PAST-read NREF-book (*$\supset$ no specific book)

---

9 For details see Givón (1972a, 1973b). Generic subjects in Bemba are considered definite,
    and thus marked as referential. This is another argument for the inadequacy of the
    traditional lumping together of all 'non-referring' nominals under the universal quantifier.
    Bemba, like many other languages, distinguishes clearly between a nominal that has
    potential individual reference under the scope of NON-FACT, and a nominal that *refers to the*
    type.

(18) IRR-ASSERTION:

    a. a-a-fwaayile uku-soma *ici*-tabo
        he-PAST-want INF-read REF-book
        'He wanted to read *the/a* book' ($\supset$ a specific book)

    b. a-a-fwaayile uku-soma *ci*-tabo
        he-PAST-want INF-read NREF-book
        'He wanted to read *a* book'   ($\supset$ no specific book)

(19) NEG-ASSERTION:
    a. ta-a-a-somene *ici*-tabo
        NEG-he-PAST-read REF-book
        'He didn't read *the* book'   ($\supset$ a specific-DEF one)
                                    (*$\supset$ a specific-INDEF one)

    b. ta-a-a-somene *ci*-tabo
        NEG-he-PAST-read NREF-book
        'He didn't read *a/any* book' ($\supset$ no specific book)

In sum, the correlation between propositional modality and referential opacity seems -- or at least seemed at the time the original studies were conducted -- a matter of straight-forward *semantic* description. Those studies, however, were conducted on isolated, out-of-context sentences.

5.3. The pragmatics of reference: Denotation vs.referential import

5.3.1. The numeral 'one' in Hebrew

Spoken Hebrew is one of the languages to which the description of Hawaii Creole, above, seemed to apply in all detail. That is, when Hebrew sentences were studied in isolation, the numeral *one* seemed to mark semantically referential indefinites, while *zero* marked non-referential indefinites. However, when sentences were placed in discourse context, some semantically-referential nouns were nonetheless marked by *zero*. To illustrate this, consider:[10]

---

10 Givón (1978a, 1981b).

(20)

a.

...az nixnasti le-xanut sfarim ve-kaniti sefer- *xad*;
then entered-I to-store-of books and-bought-I book- *one*
'...so I went into a bookstore and bought *a book*;

ve-ratsti habayta ve-karati oto,
and-ran-I home and-read-I it
and I ran home and read it,

ve-ze beemet haya sefer metsuyan...
and-it truly was-it book excellent...
and it was indeed an excellent book...'

b.

...az nixnasti le-xanut sfarim ve-kaniti sefer;
so entered-I to-store-of books and-bought-I book
...so I went into a bookstore and bought *a book*;

ve-ratsti habayta ve-axalti aruxat erev ve-halaxti	li-shon...
and-ran-I home and-ate-I meal-of evening and-went-I	to-sleep
and I ran home and ate supper and went to	sleep...'

In both (20a) and (20b) *book* is semantically referential. Nonetheless, the subsequent discourse context makes it more natural to use the REF-indefinite marker *one* in (20a), and not to use it in (20b). But why? The answer is reasonably transparent: In (20a) one runs home and proceeds to read the book and discuss it. The specific referential identity of the book **matters** in the subsequent discourse. In (20b), on the other hand, one does some book-buying, then goes about one's routine; the book is never discussed again, its specific ('referential') identity **does not matter** in the subsequent discourse.

In discussing (20a,b) above we relied, admittedly, on intuitive judgement. That intuition was nonetheless suggestive: The grammar of reference in language seems all of a sudden to be sensitive not to the semantics of reference, but rather to its pragmatics. That is, the grammar marks nominals as 'referential' not merely because the speaker intended them to **exist** in the universe of discourse, but rather because their specific referential identity was **important** in that universe. In the following sections I will describe briefly three empirical studies that seem to confirm this early intuition. The first two concern the grammatical contrast between the indefinite *one* and *zero*. The third involves the contrast, in spoken American English, between the indefinite use of *this* and *a*.

5.3.2 **Methodological preliminaries: The empirical measurement of the importance of referents in discourse**

The importance of a nominal topic in discourse may be assessed empirically along three distinct lines:

(a) **Intuitive judgement**: One may solicit the subjective judgement of a sufficient number of naive judges, asking them to rank the nominal topics in a discourse according to **centrality** or **importance**. Such informal judgements tend to be highly uniform.

(b) **Text frequency**: One may make the reasonable assumption that in human discourse important participants are mentioned more frequently. The importance of nominal topics can be thus assessed indirectly, through their frequency in text.

(c) **Psychometric measures**: It is possible, finally, to assess the importance of nominals in discourse by a variety of direct or less direct experimental psychometric methods. For example, one may measure the amount of **attention** paid to a noun as it is processed, or the amount of **mental effort** expended in processing it. One may also measure the **recall** of nominal topics, in terms or speed or error, assuming -- with considerable empirical justification [11] -- that thematically important topics are recalled faster and more accurately than thematically incidental ones.

5.3.3. **The numeral 'one' in Krio**

Krio is an English-based Creole language spoken in Sierra Leone. When studied in isolated sentences, the contrast between the numeral *one* and *zero* in the marking of indefinite nouns in Krio abides, just as in Hawaii Creole above, by the rules of semantic referentiality (10, 11). In a recent text-based quantified study, the distribution of *one*-marked and *zero*-marked indefinite nominals in four Krio narrative texts was investigated. The grammatical sub-categories investigated were:[12]

---

11 See Anderson, Garrod and Sanford (1983).
12 From Givón (1985a), where further discussion can be found. The tabulation below is based on the raw data reported there.

(21)　a.　*one*-marked REF-indefinite:
　　　　　...pas nomoh foh *wan eykuru dog* wey dey-fen yamyam...
　　　　　pass no-more for *one mangy dog* that PROG-search food
　　　　　'...except for *a mangy dog* that was searching for food...'

　　　b.　*one*-marked NON-REF-indefinite:
　　　　　...i tan lek *wan ol mami* dey-redi foh dai...
　　　　　it stood like *one old woman* PROG-ready for die
　　　　　'...it stood like *an old woman* ready to die...'

　　　c.　*zero*-marked REF-indefinite:
　　　　　...so di chif put-am na *blok*...
　　　　　so the chief put-him in *cell*
　　　　　'...so the chief put him in *a cell*...'

　　　d.　*zero*-marked NON-REF-indefinite:
　　　　　...di moni wey denh go-gi-am foh *grachuiti*...
　　　　　the money that they FUT-give-him for *gratuity*
　　　　　'...the money that they were going to give him as *gratuity*...'

The following properties were then determined for each *one*-marked and *zero*-marked indefinite noun in the text:

(a) **Semantic status:**
　　(i)　　Referential
　　(ii)　Non-referential
(b) **Thematic importance:**
　　(i)　　Major participant in the story
　　(ii)　Minor participant that:
　　　　　(A) is related to major one
　　　　　(B) appears at crucial thematic juncture
　　(iii)　Minor participant
(c) **Total occurrence in the text**

Thematic importance was judged in this case on purely intuitive grounds. The results of these measures, in percentages and average values, are tabulated in (22) below.

(22) Correlation between grammatical marking and semantic status, thematic importance and text frequency of indefinite nouns in written Krio narrative

	one-marked		*zero*- marked		total	
	N	%	N	%	N	%
tokens in text	20	42%	28	58%	48	100%
Semantic status:						
REF	18	90%	4	14%		
N-REF	2	10%	24	86%		
TOTAL	20	100%	28	100%		
Thematic status:						
MAJOR	16	80%	/	/		
MIN-THEM	4	20%	10	36%		
MINOR	/	/	18	64%		
TOTAL	20	100%	28	100%		
Average text frequency:	15.1 occur.		1.17 occur.			

The results can be summarized as follows:

(a) **Correlation between grammar and semantic status**:
Indefinites marked by *one* are 90% semantically referential. Indefinite marked by *zero* are 86% semantically non-referential.

(b) **Correlation between grammar and thematic importance**:
Of the *one*-marked indefinites, 80% are major participants; 20% are minor participants with some *local* thematic import; none are strictly minor. Of the *zero*-marked indefinites 64% are minor participants; the remaining 36% are minor participants with some local thematic import; none are major participants.

(c) **Correlation between grammar and text-frequency**:
One-marked indefinites appear in the text, on the average, 15.1 times. *Zero*-marked indefinites appear in the text, on the average, 1.17 times.

(d) **The text-frequency of semi-minor participants:**
None of the members of this category occurred more than twice (2) in the text, regardless of their grammatical marking. Whatever thematic importance these nouns carry is thus purely **local.**

In spite of the considerable overlap -- 80% to 90% -- between semantic and pragmatic referentiality, the results suggest that the grammar of indefiniteness in Krio is sensitive primarily to the **pragmatics** of reference, i.e. to **referential importance.** This is so because of the patterns of exceptions:

(a) Semantically referential indefinites that were pragmatically (thematically) unimportant, were marked by *zero* -- much like the bulk of the semantically non-referential indefinites.

(b) Semantically non-referential indefinites that were pragmatically (thematically) important, were marked by *one* -- much like the bulk of the semantically referential indefinites.

Thus, in the 10%-20% of cases where the semantics and pragmatics of reference conflicted, the grammar chose to abide by the pragmatics of reference, completely disregarding the semantics.

5.3.4. **The numeral one in Mandarin Chinese**

Mandarin Chinese uses the contrast between *one* and *zero* exactly as spoken Hebrew or Creole, to signal at the semantic level the difference between referential and non-referential nouns. To illustrate this briefly, consider the following discourse-less sentences:[13]

(23) a. **R-assertion (FACT):**
      ta mai-le *yi*-ben shu   (REF-INDEF; *one*-marked)
      he buy-PERF *one*-CL book
      'He bought *a book*'

   b. **IRR-assertion (NON-FACT):**
      (i)ta hui mai *yi*-ben shu   (REF-INDEF; *one*-marked)
         he MOD buy *one*-CL book
         'He may buy *a (specific) book*'
      (ii)ta hui mai shu-de   (NON-REF; *zero*-marked)
         he MOD buy book-NOM
         'He may buy *some book(s)*'

---

13 Huang (1985).

c. **NEG-assertion (NON-FACT):**
   ta mei mai shu   (NON-REF; *zero*-marked)
   he NEG buy book
   'He didn't buy *a/any book*'

In such isolated sentences, then, the contrast between *one* and *zero* marking of indefinite nouns seems to be predictable on purely semantic grounds.

In a recent quantified discourse study,[14] *one*-marked and *zero*-marked indefinite nouns in five narrative texts of written Mandarin were compared as to the following measurable properties:

(a) **Semantic referentiality**;
(b) **Text frequency**: Total no. of occurrences in the text;
(c) **Persistence**: Number of recurrences in the ten clauses directly following the first occurrence in the discourse;
(d) **Thematic importance**: as judged by four native speakers of Mandarin, provided that the judgement of at least 3 out of the 4 agreed;

The results are tabulated in (24) below.

(24) Correlation between grammatical marking, semantic referentiality, thematic importance and text frequency in written Mandarin Chinese narrative

| | *one*-marked | | *zero*-marked | | | | | |
| | | | REF-INDEF | | NON-REF | | TOTAL | |
	N	%	N	%	N	%	N	%
total N in text:	40	100%	20	31%	45	69%	65	100%
semantic status:								
ref-indef	39	97.5%						
non-ref	1	2.5%						
thematic status:								
major	19	47.5%	/	/	2	5%	2	3.5%
minor-thematic	17	42.5%	/	/	1	2%	1	1.5%
minor	4	10.0%	20	100%	42	93%	62	95.0%
average total # of occurrences in the text:	14.5		2.15		1.75		1.87	
average persistence per 10 clauses after first occurrence:	3.10		0.30		0.20		0.23	

14 The results presented below were re-tabulated from the data in Huang (1985).

The results tabulated in (24) above may be summarized as follows:

(a) **Semantic referentiality:**
The overwhelming majority of the *one*-marked indefinites --
97.5% -- are semantically referential. Only a single token was
an exception to this otherwise categorial distribution. In contrast, the *zero*-marked indefinites contain a significant number of referential indefinites -- 31%.

(b) **Total occurrences in the text:**
On the average, a *one*-marked indefinite recurred 14.5 times
in the text. In contrast, a *zero*-marked indefinite recurred on
the average only 2.15 times in the text. And the difference between referential and non-referential *zero*-marked indefinites
is rather negligible (2.15 vs. 1.75, respectively). Grammatical
marking thus correlates well with pragmatic importance,
but not at all well with semantic status.

(c) **Persistence in the next 10 clauses after first occurrence:**
On the average, a *one*-marked indefinite appears 3.10 times
in the 10 clauses directly following its first introduction into
the text. In contrast, a *zero*-marked indefinite appears on the
average only 0.23 times in the 10 clauses directly following
its introduction. Again, the difference between semantically
referential and semantically non-referential *zero*-marked indefinites in negligible (0.3 vs. 0.2, respectively).

(d) **Thematic importance:**
Of the *one*-marked indefinites, 47.5% were judged to be major
participants in the narrative. Another 42.5% were judged
minor, but either of thematic importance **locally**, or related --
as kin, part-of-whole, etc. -- to an important participant. Only
10% were judged to be strictly minor. In sharp contrast, of the
zero-marked indefinites, 95% were judged strictly minor. Of
those that were semantically referential, 100% were strictly
minor. And of the semantically non-referential, 93% were
strictly minor. In other words, semantic referentiality does
not at all correlate with *zero*-marking, nor with thematic importance. Thematic importance, on the other hand, correlates
rather well -- negatively -- with *zero*-marking.

It is clear, then, that the grammatical contrast between *one* and *zero* in introducing indefinite nouns for the first time into Mandarin discourse
codes the pragmatics of **referential importance,** rather than the semantics of denotation.

Once again, it is not an accident that the overwhelming majority of *one*-marked -- pragmatically important -- nouns are also semantically referential. The Mandarin texts studied were folk stories about everyday life of simple people. But this overlap between the semantics and the pragmatics of reference should not obscure the fact that when the two are in conflict, the grammar opts to code the pragmatics.

5.3.5. The unstressed indefinite *this* in spoken English

The use of the unstressed demonstrative *this* as an indefinite article in spoken English has been noted informally for a long time.[15] As an indefinite article, *this* contrasts with the unstressed *that*, which seems to serve as a definite article. Again intuitively, it seems that the indefinite *this* marks primarily semantically referential indefinites. This may be illustrated informally in:

(25)   a. *this* under the scope of FACT:

I saw *this* girl yesterday, and...

(the speaker has a particular girl in mind, but *does not* assume that the hearer can identify her; i.e. REF-indefinite)

b. *this* under the scope of NON-FACT:

I was looking for *this* girl yesterday, and...

(same inference as in a. above)

c. *a* under the scope of NON-FACT:

I was looking fo *a* girl yesterday, and...

(the speaker may *either* have or not have a particular girl in mind)

The English indefininite article *a(n)* (Old English 'one') thus marks referentially opaque indefinite nominals, regardless of their semantic-

---

15 Dwight Bolinger (in personal communication) notes that the use of the unstressed *this* as an indefinite article did not begin to impinge on his sharp normative ear until the early 1950s. The transcripts of spoken rural Western American English of a 60-year old male studied in Givón (1983b) show no significant use of the indefinite this. Prince (1981) comes, on the basis of informal data, to the same conclusion reported here, as does Wald (1983).

referential indefinites. It thus seems to penetrate the grammar at the very same point where *one* did in Old English, as a marker of referentiality. But is it semantic or **pragmatic** referentiality?

To illustrate how *this* indeed marks the pragmatics of reference in colloquial English discourse, consider the following letter that appeared a few years ago in the Dear Abby column:[16]

(26) "Dear Abby: There's *this guy* I've been going with for near three years. Well, the problem is that he hits me. He started last year. He has done it only four or five times, but each time it was worse than before. Every time he hit me it was because he thought I was flirting (I wasn't).

Last time he accused me of coming on to *a friend* of his. First he called me a lot of dirty names, then he punched my face so bad it left me with a black eye and black-and-blue bruises over half of my face. It was very noticeable, so I told my folks that the car I was riding in stopped suddenly and my face hit the windshield.

Abby, he's 19 and I'm 17, and already I feel like *an old married lady* who lets her husband push her around. I haven't spoken to him since this happened. He keeps bugging me to give him one more chance. I think I've given him enough chances. Should I keep avoiding him or what?

Black and Blue".

The following features in the use of the unstressed *this* vs. *a(n)* in (26) are striking:

(a) The REF-indefinite participant introduced by *this* recurs throughout the text and is obviously the other important participant (together with the narrator);
(b) The REF-indefinite participant introduced by *a(n)* never recurs; his specific identity is obviously incidental to the story;
(c) The only other indefinite introduced by *a(n)* is a NON-REF attributive noun.

In an effort to obtain firmer empirical validation of the anecdotal evidence, a recent study[17] analyzed the recorded speech of six 8-10 year old native American English speakers, chatting among themselves in-

---

16 This advice column is one of the few places where one can find this recent innovation of English grammar in writing, tho only occasionally. Only young people seem to use it.
17 Shroyer (1985). See also Wright and Givón (1987).

formally. Four narratives in all were collected and analyzed, and four grammatical categories were studied:

(27) a. *this*-SUBJECT: *'...there's these two guys...'*
     b. *this*-NON-SUBJECT: *'...he saw this great bear...'*
     c. *a(n)*-SUBJECT: *'...and there was a fly to third base...'*
     d. *a(n)*-NON-SUBJECT: *'...he saw this monkey holding a candy bar...'*

The **topic persistence** (TP) of referents -- i.e. the number of times a referent was mentioned in the 10 clauses immediately following its introduction into the discourse -- was measured for the four grammatical categories (27). The numerical distribution of the four categories in the combined texts, and their average TP measure are tabulated in (28) below.

(28) **Text distribution of grammatical categories marking indefinite nouns, and average Topic Persistence (TP) of tokens within each category measures**

	Subject			Non-Subject			Total		
	N	%	TP	N	%	TP	N	%	TP
'this'	28	65%	6.95	15	35%	2.40	43	100%	5.32
'a(n)'	13	12%	1.5	94	88%	0.56	107	00%	0.68

As can be seen, *this*-marked indefinites typically:
(a) tend to appear in the subject position;
(b) tend to have a much greater TP value; they are thus, presumably, more important in the discourse.

In contrast, *a(n)*-marked indefinites typically:
(a) appear overwhelmingly in the object position;
(b) tend to have a much smaller TP value; they are thus, presumably, less important in the discourse.

The total text-distribution of *high-persistence tokens* (TP > 2) and *low-persistence tokens* (TP = 0-2) in the four grammatical categories was also analyzed.[18] The results are summarized in (29) on the following page.

---

18 In plotting the distribution of the various persistence levels for the total population of indefinite nouns in the text, Shroyer (1985) observed a very sharp break in the distribution curve, occurring between the TP values of 2 and 3. The cutting point between 'important' and 'unimportant' indefinites was decided on this heuristic basis.

(29) **Distribution of the high-persistence (TP > 2) and low-persistence (TP = 0-2) tokens within the four grammatical categories**

	THIS						A					
	Subject		Non-Subj		Total		Subject		Non-Subj		Total	
TP	N	%	N	%	N	%	N	%	N	%	N	%
0–2	4	14.2	10	66.6	14	32.5	10	76.9	89	94.6	99	92.5
>2	24	85.8	5	33.4	29	67.5	3	23.1	5	5.4	8	7.5

The distribution figures in (29) may be summarized as follows:

(a) *this*-SUBJ-marked indefinites are prototypically -- 85.8% -- high-persistence topics;
(b) *a(n)*-NON-SUBJ-marked indefinites are prototypically -- 94.6% -- low-persistence topics;
(c) *this*-marked indefinites are in general -- 67.5% -- high-persistence topics;
(d) *a(n)*-marked indefinites are overwhelmingly -- 92.5% -- low-persistence topics.

The only substantial exception to an otherwise rather striking correlation between grammatical marking and pragmatic referentiality, are the 32.5% of the *this*-marked category that exhibit low-persistence. The obvious, though tentative, explanation is that thematic importance and text frequency, while correlating well over the long run, never correlate 100%. Grammatical marking of indefinites by *this* is ultimately sensitive to the psychological dimension of importance, not to mere text frequency.

In innovating, fairly recently, the grammatical distinction between referential and non-referential indefinites, English has chosen -- just like it chose 900 years ago with the numeral *one*, and much like Mandarin and Krio have -- to code the pragmatic feature of **thematic importance**, rather than the semantic distinction of denotation in the universe of discourse.

5.4. Normative action and referential interpretation: The context-sensitivity of referential intent

While noting, as in rules (10), (11), that under the scope of non-fact modalities both referential and non-referential interpretation of indefinite nominals (in English) is possible, we haven't quite told the entire story of the semantics of reference. A distinctly pragmatic flavor is added even to so-called semantic referential intent when one considers the question of **normativity**. Consider first the following contrast between two verb-object combinations:

(30) a. He's going to take *a woman* out to dinner, then...
      b. He's going to take *a bus* back home, then...

The propositional modality -- irrealis -- is the same in (30a) and (30b). Nevertheless, *a woman* in (30a) is most likely to be interpreted as referential, while *a bus* in (30b) is most likely to be interpreted as non-referential. This is so because **as a norm** a man is more likely to plan an evening out with a *specific* woman; while going home we takes *whatever* bus that may come along, as long as the destination is right.

Consider next the contrast between two friends of mine, one a learned philosopher who spends much of his life reading in his chosen subject, the other a rancher who reads himself to sleep every night with a paperback Western. Suppose each said to me, before turning in for the night:

(31) I'm going to retire now and read *a book*.

The probability is rather high that I would assign a *referential* interpretation to *a book* in (31) when uttered by the *philosopher*, and a *nonreferential* one to *a book* when uttered by the *rancher*. I know their personal habits, the reason why each reads book, and the role that a book's specific identity is likely to play in the reading habits of either. I also know that if I asked my rancher friend what book he read last night, he'd be hard pressed to remember the title.

In a language like Krio or Bemba (see section 5.2.3., above), the speaker uttering (30a,b) and (31) above would surely use the appropriate grammatical marking to cue us into their **referential intent**. But even in an under-coded language such as standard English, our knowledge of normativity guides us in assigning referring on non-referring interpretation to nominals in such potentially opaque contexts.

5.5. The non-discreteness of reference and definiteness

5.5.1. Preamble

In the preceding sections we surveyed a range of facts (and arguments) all pointing out to the conclusion that in human language the grammatical markers that code referentiality do not abide by the semantics of denotation, but rather by the pragmatics of referential importance. Importance -- or **relevance** -- is indeed a central notion in pragmatics. There is no way for deciding relevance or importance on purely deductive grounds.[19] It is simply up to the speaker's context-mediated judgement.

Another major facet of pragmatics that manifests itself in the grammar of reference and indefiniteness is **non-discreteness**. Traditional deductive logic shudders at the specter of non-discreteness, and for obvious reasons: Clear-cut, truth-conditional decisions cannot be made when categories such as denotation or definiteness turn mushy. Nonetheless, the study of human language suggests that such mushiness persists, at least at the margins of seemingly discrete coding systems.

5.5.2. Non-discreteness of reference: Vague speaker's intent

Consider the -- presumably referentially opaque -- use of indefinite nominals in the following yes/no questions:[20]

(32) a. Did you see *anything* there?
      b. Did you see *anybody* there?
      c. Did you see *any man* there?
      d. Did you see *some man* there?
      e. Did you see *a man* there?
      f. Did you see *a tall man* there?
      g. Did you see *a man wearing a blue shirt* there?
      h. Did you see *a man* there *wearing a blue shirt and sitting on a red barrel and twirling a silver baton in his left hand?*

There is a gradation from (32a) through (32h), one that seems to proceed along a speaker-oriented **psychological** dimension:

(a) "How strongly the speaker intends to suggest that he/she is referring to a particular individual"

The gradation may be also described, alternatively, as proceeding along a **probabilistic** dimension, concerning what the hearer is entitled to infer:

(b) "What the probability is that the speaker referred to a specific individual"

Be the ultimate dimension as it may, it is clearly non-discrete. Further, the grammar of English seems to code this progression through the use of three major devices which, when combined, yield finer gradation:

---

19 In this sense, both 'importance' and 'relevance' are akin to the pragmatic notion of similarity, see discussion in Chapters 2 and 3.
20 This gradation was described earlier in Givón (1982a).

(33) **Coding of the scale of referential strength**

  (a) The scale of indefinite articles:
       any ⊃ *some* ⊃ *a*
  (b) The scale of restrictive modification:
       less ⊃ more
  (c) The scale of noun specification:
       thing ⊃ person ⊃ specific noun

Segment (32a,b,c) illustrates coding device (33c). Segment (32c,d,e) illustrates coding device (33a). While segment (32e,f,g,h) illustrates coding device (33b). It is clear, further, that devices (33b) and (33c) represent a single scale of **increased semantic specification**. And the higher an indefinite expression appears on any of the coding scales (33a,b,c), the more it is likely that the speaker meant it to be non-referential.

Consider next the case of WH-questions in Ute, a Uto-Aztecan language spoken in Utah and Colorado. Most commonly, interrogative pronouns in Ute distinguish between *type*-identity (non-referential) and *token*-identity (referential) questions. Thus consider:[21]

(34)   a. **Token-identity question:**
          'a-'ara 'ina ta'waci?
          WH-be   this man
          ' *Who* is this man?'
          (= please *identify* him)

       b. **Type-identity question:**
          'ini-'ara 'ina ta'waci?
          WH-be   this man
          ' *What kind* (of a person) is this man?'
          (=please *describe* him)

This neat division is muddied up, however, by a further distinction within the *type*-identity question category, that of **degree of type description**. Thus consider:

(35)   a. 'ini-'ara 'ina?
          WH-be   this
          'What kind (of a *person*) is this?'

       b. 'ini-kwa 'ara-'ay 'ina?
          WH-MOD be-IMM this
          'What kind (of a *creature*) could this possibly be?'

21 For full detail see Givón (1980b, ch. 12).

The difference between (35a) and (35b) has to do with the degree of the speaker's uncertainty concerning the type-description of the entity under question. In (35a) the speaker has some hunch but requests further information. In (35b) the speaker is completely baffled.

5.5.3. Gradation of referential intent

Earlier above we noted that propositional modalities have a systematic effect on the referential status of nouns under their scope. Consider now the effect of various propositional modalities -- all but the last one irrealis -- on the interpretation of indefinite objects in English:

(36)   a. John wants to buy *a house*, but can't find *any*
       b. John usually buys *a house* in June; *it's* cheaper then
       c. John usually buys *a house* in June; *it* is cheaper then;
       d. John usually buys *a house* in June, then sells *it* in July.
       e. John would buy *a house* in June, then sell *it* in July.
       f. John bought *a house* in June, then sold *it* in July

Semantically, the probability that *a house* in (36a) refers to a specific house is minimal, in (36f) maximal. And (36b,c,d,e) seem to represent intermediate degrees of specific reference. But such gradation cannot be captured by deductive, truth-conditional means.

Reconsider now the contrast between *a* and *some*:

(37)   a. John wants to buy *a house*
       b. John wants to buy *some house*
       c. John wants to buy *some house near his Mom's home*

The probability of specific referential intent by the speaker is highest in (37c), lowest in (37a) and intermediate in (37b).

Consider next the effect of pluralization on the reference of indefinite objects:

(38)   a. John wants to buy *a house*
       b. John wants to buy *some houses*
       c. John wants to buy *houses*

As noted earlier above, the interpretation of (38a) may be either referential or non-referential. But somehow the probability of a referential interpretation is highest in (38a), lower in (38b) and lowest in (38c).

The effect of pluralization can be further shown in the following contrast:

(39) a. *John buys *a house* for a living
      b. John buys *houses* for a living

The singular *a house* is less compatible with an extreme non-referential interpretation; whereas the use of the plural *houses* is natural with such a non-referential interpretation
    Consider, finally, the interaction between word-order and pluralization:

(40) a. John buys *houses* in June; he sells *them* in July
      b. John buys *houses* in June; in July he sells *them*.

Somehow, (40a) imparts a stronger probability that the *very same* houses are involved, and thus a stronger referential intent by the speaker. On the other hand, (40b) imparts a weaker probability that the *same* houses are involved, thus seemingly a weaker referential intent. Referential intent, it seems, is not always a matter of either or. Like other psychological dimensions manipulated by the speaker, it is on occasion subject to finer gradations.

5.5.4. Scales of definiteness: Degree of specification

Somewhat similar scales may be observed in the grammar of definite description. In Spanish, for example, one finds a gradation in the **degree of genericity** of nouns; or, conversely, in the degree of **specificity of definite description**. To illustrate this, consider:

(41) a. Maria siempre habla con brujos
          'Maria always speaks with *sorcerers*'   (NON-REF)
      b. Maria siempre habla con los brujos
              (i)'Maria always speaks with
                  (the) sorcerers'   ('SEMI-DEF')
              (ii)'Maria always speaks with
                  the sorcerers   (DEF)

In (41a) *sorcerers* is least referential. But (41b) has two distinct interpretations: Either fully *definite*, as in (41bii), where the speaker indeed refers to specific sorcerers identifiable to the hearer. Or the *semi-definite* in (41bi), where the group that may fit the description is smaller than in (41a) but larger than in (41bii).
    A similar scalarity of definite description may be shown in English. Thus consider:

(42) The person who killed Smith is insane
    a. I know exactly who killed Smith; that person is insane.
    b. Someone killed Smith, I don't know who, all I know is
        that the killer is insane

As Donellan (1966) has noted, interpretation (42b) is **attributive**, thus in some funny sense **less-referential** -- in spite of the speaker's obvious commitment to believe that a **specific** individual indeed killed Smith. But interpretation (42b) can be slowly tipped toward definiteness, as in (42a), by gradually loading more and more descriptive attributes on the semi-definite noun:

(43)   a. The *person* who killed Smith is insane
        b. The *woman* who killed Smith is insane
        c. The *young woman* who killed Smith is insane
        d. The *beautiful young woman* who killed Smith is insane

With the addition of each further description, the probability of the speaker **intending** the definite noun attributively -- rather than referentially -- decreases. The device used to achieve this gradation -- further semantic specification -- is the same seen in (32), (33) above.

5.6. Coreference, topicality and evocation: The pragmatic grey margins of Russell's Type Theory

5.6.1. Preamble

In the final section of this chapter we will survey what at first appeared to be merely one more pragmatic facet of reference. Namely, that in human discourse the so-called relation of **coreference** between linguistic expressions often cannot be defined in strict terms of **sharing the same referent**. As it turns out, the pragmatics of coreference in natural language impels us to re-invoke to the discussion of categorization (see Chapter 2). And that, in turn, leads in short order to the subject of a hierarchic **theory of types**. We will open with a brief exposition of how pragmatics invades the realm of coreference.

5.6.2. The pragmatics of coreference

We have dealt earlier in this chapter with five parameters of the pragmatics of reference. First, we saw how reference was a mapping from language onto a **universe of discourse**. Second, we saw how it must involve the speaker's **referential intent**. Third, we saw how it must involve **thematic importance** in the discourse context. Fourth, we saw how it often involves the pragmatic notion of **norm**, thus perforce also its underlying base, **frequency**. And fifth, we saw how it often involves **gradation**. In this section we will deal with another facet of the pragmatics of reference, one that manifests itself most succinctly in linguistic expressions of coreference. A more specific treatment of the pragmatics of coreference -- particularly **anaphoric** reference -- can be found in Chapter 6.

The term coreference is traditionally reserved for instances where the *same entity* is referred to, following its first introduction (or subsequent re-introduction) into the discourse. Coreference in natural language is thus closely related to anaphora and definiteness. In the clearest -- and presumably most common -- cases, a *definite description* is used after a prior mention of the entity establishes it as referring in the universe of discourse. If, on the other hand, the prior mention is non-referential, an *indefinite* pronoun may be used, either referentially or attributively. Thus consider:

(44) John decided to marry *a rich girl;*

(a) ...but *she* rejected him.   (DEF-anaphoric)
(b) ...and he finally found *one.*   (INDEF-referential)
(c) ...he kept looking for *one.*   (INDEF-attributive)

One might of course insist that of the three examples in (44), only the anaphoric 'she' in (44a) is strictly coreferential. The indefinite 'one' in (44b) is merely *referential*. While 'one' in (44c) is *non-referential*. Logically, it indeed seems, the pronouns in (44a,b,c) bear different relations to their antecedent. In (44a) 'she' refers to **the same token**. In (44b) 'one' refers to **a token** of the **same type**. While in (44c) 'one' refers only to the **same type** as the antecedent, without referring to any particular token. Yet, in some sense, however vague, *a rich girl* in (44) is the proper **antecedent** for all three expressions that follow, it **evokes** all three equally well. Yet, can such 'evocation' be specified logically?

One way of handling this type of data while still remaining within the bounds of some logic, is by means of a Russellian **Theory of Types**.[22] One could, for example, note that the common denominator to all three types of co-reference in (44) is the relation of **type identity**. One could then note the following, eminently sensible, one-way implication:

(45) token identity $\supset$ type identity

One could then posit the equally sensible grammatical rule:

---

22 Whether this Theory of Types is close to Russell's (1919) remains to be seen.

(46) "An *anaphoric* pronoun will be used only when the antecedent is *token*-identical. When the antecedent is only *type*-identical, an *indefinite* pronoun will be used".

A cursory look at some more data quickly reveals that the situation is a bit more complicated: Type-token relations in coreference seem to work both ways. A non-referential ('type') antecedent may evoke either type or token coreference; and much the same way, a referential ('token') antecedent may evoke either type or token coreference. Thus consider:

(47)   a. John was looking for *a white horse;*
      b. ...I was looking for *one* too.
      c. ...he didn't like *the one* he had.

      d. John was looking for *his white horse;*
      e. ...I didn't have *any horse,* so I rode a mule.
      f. ...and I was looking for *mine.*

Rules (45, 46), so it appears, must be modified to allow for fully symmetrical co-reference: From type to token as in (47c); from token to type as in (47e); from type to type as in (47b); and finally from one token to *another* token of the same type, and thus in *some* sense again from type to type, as in (47f).

In the same vein, consider (48) below:

(48) John wanted to marry *a rich girl,*
      a. ...but *she* had to be pretty.
      b. ...but *the girl* he finally married wasn't.

The pronoun *she* in (48a) is non-referential. And the definite noun in (48b), while denoting a referential individual, corefers only to the type of the antecedent *girl*, especially since the antecedent was itself non-referential. Still, the non-referring expression *a rich girl* in (48) is, in some sense, the proper antecedent to both *she* in (48a) and *the girl* in (43b). Our grammar rule (46) is not much help in accounting for (48a,b).

We might, in a desperate attempt to save the spirit if not the actual letter of rule (46), construct a more complex rule that will still purport to abide by some Russellian Theory of Types. But our problems becomes further compounded when we turn to considers the next set of examples:

(49) Mary was looking for *a house* to rent,
    (a) ...but *the neighborhood* was too run down.
    (b) ...but *the rents* were getting too high.
    (c) ...but *the landlords* were all greedy.
    (d) ...but *all the yards* were too small.
    (e) ... *her roommate* was getting married.
    (f) ... *her rose garden* was overflowing.
    (g) ... *her boa constrictor* was getting too big.

All the anaphoric definite expressions in (49a-g) are referential. They are all evoked, rather transparently, by the **non-referential** antecedent *a house*. In all cases, one may say that there remains an **elliptical** thread of coreference between the antecedent and the subsequent anaphoric expression, one that can be reconstructed back to the stereotype -- prototype -- notion of *rental housing*.[23] But these threads -- or inferences from the prototype -- are, as Wittgenstein would have observed, on a descending scale of **centrality** vis-a-vis the prototype of rental housing, from (49a) through (49g). Toward the bottom, the inferences seem to stray rather far from the prototype's core. And what is more, one finds no logical grounds for deciding where the thread of inferences becomes remote, feeble, too far fetched. In principle, it seems, any token entity in the universe, or its type, can be found **relevant** to -- and can thus evoke -- any other token entity, or its type. The only question is -- **how** relevant, **how** obvious, **how** prototypical is the evocation to be.

The case is even more vexing with co-reference relations that evoke the *type*. Thus, consider examples (50a-j), below:

(50) Mary was looking for *a house* to rent;
    (a) ...but *no landlord* would accept her references.
    (b) ...but she had *no money* to pay *the rent*.
    (c) ...but there was *no bus* to the University.
    (d) ...she is used to *being comfortable*.
    (e) ...she is *a big girl* now, so...
    (f) ...being *a single woman* is no picnic, so...
    (g) ...she's *been on welfare* for months, but...
    (h) ... *cream-cheese* has never been *her* favorite dish.
    (i) ... *enchiladas rancheras* have always been *my* favorite dish.
    (j) ... *enchiladas rancheras* have always been *Joe's* favorite dish.

23 'Houses are in neighborhoods', 'one pays rent for a rental house','rental houses have landlords', 'a house may have a yard', 'one may share a house with a roommate', 'one may have a rose-garden in the house's yard', 'one may keep a boa constrictor as a house-pet', respectively.

In principle, it seems, any type can evoke any other type, provided some **relevance relations** can be established, by some inference, however indirect and remote from the prototype. It is all a matter of **degree**.

5.6.3. Coreference and a non-Platonic theory of types

The moral of all this for a logical theory of reference is reasonably clear: The general case -- or common denominator -- in all coreference relations is **relevance**; coreference is ultimately an open-ended, context-mediated relation of **evocation**. A sub-set of evocation relations may also abide by a stricter condition, that of **type coreference** with the antecedent (i.e., either type-token, token-type or type-type co-reference). Finally, a smaller sub-set of type coreference may also abide by a stricter condition yet, that of **token coreference**.

Finally, note that **type coreference** may be considered a mere sub-species of **token coreference** in a Russellian Theory of Types, with the types taken to be merely tokens of the higher a higher meta-type.[24] This pattern of concentric inclusion of evocation sub-types can be represented as a one-way implicational hierarchy:

(51)   a. token coreference ⊃ type coreference
        b. type coreference ⊃ pragmatic evocation

Pragmatic evocation is thus the general case. **Type evocation** is a restricted sub-case, requiring a logical, Russellian Theory of Type. And **token evocation**, in the traditional logical sense of 'having the same denotation', is the most restricted special sub-case of the latter.

The semantic tradition of reference and coreference can handle (51a,) above. But it seems, somewhat surprisingly, that what keeps the door of denotational logic forever slightly open to pragmatics, is the fact that the human mind's concept of **type** does not necessarily abide by Russell's (1919) platonic strictures. Rather, the mind seems to insist on the more flexible -- norm-, stereotype- or prototype-based -- system of categorization, where membership in a category is mediated through a **cluster** of features; where features may be **more** or **less relevant** to the prototype; and where tokens may exhibit **graded similarities**.

---

24 See discussion of the arbitrariness of *taxonomy* in Chapter 1.

In order to account for the evocative -- pragmatic -- reference pervasive in human language, a more flexible, Wittgensteinean Theory of Types must be adopted. Such a theory would not only recognize *central* (*highly* necessary, *mostly* sufficient) features that characterize the type in the main. It must also take account of the more peripheral, inferred, increasingly context-bound features. Centrality to the definition of a prototype is a matter of degree, it is also context-mediated. Therefore, one cannot draw a sharp line to divide type-reference from the pragmatics evocation. Within a non-Platonic theory of categories, i.e. of types, these two are one and the same.

CHAPTER 6

THE PRAGMATICS OF ANAPHORIC REFERENCE: DEFINITENESS AND TOPICALITY

6.1. Introduction: Definiteness, presupposition and knowing other minds *

That definite description is inherently a pragmatic notion, one which depends on context-derived assumption the speaker makes about what the hearer is likely to know, was not by any means always taken for granted in the logical-philosophical tradition. Thus Russell (1905, 1919) treats definite description as somehow a **semantic** matter of **unique identification**. And it is far from clear how such a notion differs from mere semantic reference. When other philosophers departed from such a tradition, as in Strawson (1950),[1] they resorted to the notion of **presupposition**, i.e. the celebrated **three-valued logic**. In such a logic, a proposition could be asserted as either *True* or *False*; or else it can be *Presupposed*, meaning that it is taken for granted to be true, as precondition for other expressions to be either true or false (see Keenan, 1969, 1971). Within such a framework, the contrast between indefinite and definite reference is still ascribed to speaker-related features such as **unique reference**, more specifically to whether that unique reference is asserted (for indefinites) or presupposed (for definites). Thus consider:

---

*I am indebted to Tim Shopen, Morti Gernsbacher, Frank Lichtenberk, Hartmut Haberland and Paul Otto for many helpful comments on an earlier version of this chapter.

1   See also discussion in Hertzberger (1971).

(1) a. **Indefinite reference:**
       A man died
       Asserted:
          (i) 'There exists a man'
          (ii) 'That man died'
     b. **Definite reference:**
       The man died
       Presupposed:
          (i) 'There exists a man'
       Asserted:
          (ii) 'That man died'

Treating definite description as a *semantic* presupposition, as in (1b) above, represents an obvious advance over the two-value logical treatment. It is, for one thing, already *crypto-pragmatic*. Nonetheless, it remains an attempt to handle the pragmatics of definiteness entirely within the confines of a **speaker oriented** logic. As such, this approach resists the rather obvious pragmatic feature of definiteness (and of presupposition in general), namely that it involves assumptions the speaker makes about what the **hearer** knows, believes in, is familiar with or can identify. In other words, definite description is inherently about **knowledge by one mind of the knowledge of another mind**. And thus also, as it turns out, about the **grounds** for one mind making assumptions about what another mind may know, also about **how securely** they may know it. And this feature is anathema to any well-constrained logic. It is indeed strictly disallowed, at least implicitly, in Russell's (1919) Theory of Types.

6.2. Sources of definiteness:
Grounds for knowing other minds

Linguists have resigned themselves for a long time to the fact that definiteness involves the speaker's assumptions about the hearer's beliefs. One reason -- among others -- why it is exceedingly hard to account for such an obvious fact within a logical system is that the **grounds** on which the speaker makes assumption about what the hearer knows, believes, is familiar with, etc. may be rather diverse. These grounds can be described in terms of **sources of shared knowledge** in human discourse; or, alternatively, in terms of the contextual **files** (as was noted in our earlier discussions of **grounds for presupposition**).[2] These grounds may be divided into three major sources, a division that follows broadly our earlier discussion of the major categories of **context**:[3]

(i) **The Generic File**: Knowledge held in common by all members of the language-culture group, including knowledge of the world, culture, and thus shared lexicon;

(ii) **The Deictic File**: Knowledge shared by the speaker and hearer due to being present together at the speech situation;

(iii) **The Text File**: Knowledge shared by the speaker and hearer because of what was said earlier in the discourse, or in prior text

To illustrate these different source-files of definiteness, consider:

(2) **Sources of definiteness**

example	file-source
a. '...I got up this morning and *the sun* was shining...'	generic
b. '...So I turned *the TV* on and *the President*..."	generic
c. '...I sat on the chair, but *the seat* was broken...'	generic plus text
d. '...*his father* was an honest man...'	generic plus text
e. '...Take *this chair* and put it *there*...'	deictic
f. '...We went to the bank and *the cashier* cashed my check...'	generic plus text
g. '...He saw a man and a woman. *The woman* was tall...'	text

As can be seen from these rather rudimentary examples, some definiteness arises from the interaction of two source-files. Thus in (2c) above, *the seat* is definite because (a) the chair whose part it is has been mentioned in the previous discourse, and (b) it is general knowledge that chairs have seats. Similar interactions hold for (2d) and (2f).

The three sources of definiteness illustrated above are only the major ones, in terms of prevalence in human discourse. But as noted earlier above,[4] the source of speaker's knowledge about the hearer's mind is

---

2 See Ch. 4, above. For various formulations of 'files' see Chafe (1976, 1987), DuBois (1980) or Givón (1985b). In the context of an experimental study of discourse processing, see Givón *et al* (1985).

3 See Ch. 3, section 3.2.2.; Ch. 4, section 4.3.3.

4 Ch. 3, section 3.2.2.; Ch. 4, section 4.3.3.; Ch. 5, section 5.5.

essentially unconstrained. That is, any direct or circuitous inference, intuition or inspiration, be it deductive, inductive or abductive, may -- in principle -- serve as legitimate grounds for knowing other minds. Such inferences, intuitions or revelations form the **context** in which speakers consider themselves entitled to use a definite description, whereby they assume hearers will go along. In the next section we will discuss a contextual notion closely associated with definiteness, that of **topic** and/or **theme**.

6.3. Definiteness and topicality

6.3.1. Topic and theme

The more contemporary preoccupation with **topic** dates back to the Prague School's discussion of **theme** and **rheme**, which in turn presumably harkens back all the way to Aristotle. As noted earlier above,[5] propositions -- or sentences -- in discourse tend to contain some presupposed ('old', 'given') and some asserted ('new') information. The Prague School[6] and related formulations,[7] at least under one possible interpretation, would call the first theme and the second rheme. This interpretation thus associates the theme/rheme contrast with the presence vs. absence of an **anaphoric** ('prior-discourse') context.

Later formulations in the 1970s translated this reading of the contrast into **topic** vs. **comment**, respectively. The Praguean formulation already allowed for a number of distinct senses of 'theme'. Thus, consider the following attempts from Firbas (1974):

(3) "...according to *one*... [of the definitions; TG]... the theme expresses *something that is spoken about*; according to the *other* it expresses *something that is known or at least obvious in the given situation*..." (p. 23)

One could easily show instances in which the two definitions are incompatible. Thus, both the indefinite and definite subjects in (1) above are equally 'spoken about'.[8] But while the definite subject in (1b) is 'known' or 'obvious in the given situation', the indefinite subject in (1a) is not.

---

5   See Ch. 4, section 4.6.
6   See for example Firbas (1966, 1974).
7   As in Bolinger (1952, 1954) or Halliday (1967), *inter alia*.
8   And in very much the same sense as the Aristotelian *thema* and *rhema*, which according to most reasonable interpretations stand for the grammatical notions of *subject* and *predicate*, respectively. I am indebted to Hartmut Haberland (in personal communication) for a discussion of Aristotle's distinction and its scope.

Other Praguean attempts to define the contrast between theme and rheme are downright obfuscating. Thus consider (Firbas, 1974):

(4) "...the theme-transition-rheme sequence renders the word-order non-emotive, unmarked, whereas the rheme-transition-theme sequence renders it emotive, marked..." (p. 13)

An attempt to improve the definition by reference to the scalar notion of **communicative dynamism** remains equally impenetrable. Thus consider (Firbas, 1974):

(5) "...By degree of *communicative dynamism* carried by a linguistic element, I mean the extent to which the element contributes toward the development of communication..." (p. 19)

Of the various Praguean senses of 'theme', the two which most commonly carried over to the revived discussion in the mid-1970s were those of **old information** and **that which is talked about.**

6.3.2. In search of the elusive topic

6.3.2.1. Preamble

Beginning with the early 1970s, much of the linguistic work in discourse-pragmatics hinged on the discrete, binary, functional opposition **topic** vs. **comment**, the inheritor of at least one of the Praguean contrast of theme-rheme. This tradition is still on-going, and has been quite beneficial in launching linguistics upon a vigorous search for the functional-pragmatic correlates of grammar. There are, however, a number of indications that the topic-comment tradition has outgrown its usefulness. In the following sections I will attempt to sketch out why this is so, and why this important tradition in discourse-pragmatics must be replaced with a much more complex, cognitively-based notion **discourse function.** I will open the discussion by citing some of the facts that our discrete, unitary notion of 'topic' was supposed -- but failed -- to account for.

6.3.2.2. Definite, pronoun, agreement and zero-anaphora

The topic literature of the 1970s[9] noted that grammatical categories

---

9 See for example Hawkinson and Hyman (1974) or Givón (1976a), *inter alia*.

such as **definiteness** and **pronouns** were somehow associated with topicality, an association widely expressed through the topic hierarchies:

(6) a. DEFINITE > INDEFINITE
     b. PRONOUN > NOUN
     c. SUBJECT > OBJECT

It soon became apparent, however, that given the definition of *topic* as *old* ('presupposed', 'given') information, the following grammatical categories all marked *the* topic equally well:

(7) a. DEF NOUN: *The man* came into the house

     b. INDEPENDENT PRONOUN: ... (she stayed outside, but)
                                   he came into the house

     c. GRAMMATICAL AGREEMENT: ...luego entró en la casa
                                   ...then entered-*he* in the house
                                   '...then he entered the house...'

     d. ZERO-ANAPHORA: ...(he came,) ø looked around,...

If all four grammatical categories in (7) equally mark *topic*, then at the very least the notion requires further elaboration. And if they differ from each other in *degree* of topicality, then what is the substantive value underlying that graded dimension?

6.3.2.3. Dislocated vs. neutral subject and object topics

Grammatical constructions such as *left-dislocation, right-dislocation* and *Y-movement* have all been called, at one time or another, 'topicalization'. Constituents subject to these 'movement rules' were considered, in the topic-comment tradition, to be 'more topical' than their corresponding neutral-ordered counterparts. They were all said to be old information, either definite or generic but seldom REF-indefinite. These constructions are, for example:

(8) a. *The man*, she saw him   (L-Dislocation, OBJ)
     b. *The woman*, she came yesterday   (L-Dislocation, SUBJ)
     c. She saw him, *the man*   (R-dislocation, OBJ)
     d. She came yesterday, *the woman*   (R-dislocation, SUBJ)
     c. *John* she saw right away   (Y-movement, OBJ)
     d. *Mary saw him*   (Y-movement, SUBJ)

Now, if all these 'moved' subjects or objects are topics, surely further elaboration must be required in order to distinguish between them. And again, if they differ in 'degree of topicality' -- what is the substantive dimension involved?

6.3.2.4. Subject and topic

The topic-comment tradition of the 1970's noted that subjects were *more topical* -- or more likely to be the topic -- than objects (see (6c), above). This was clearly reflected in the much higher text frequency of definite, pronominal and zero subjects. It is not clear, however, how the difference between the following three sentences can be accounted for in terms of "topic":

(9) a. John saw Bill   (SUBJ = topic)
    b. John, he saw Bill   (SUBJ-topic; plus SUBJ = topic?)
    c. Bill, John saw him   (OBJ-topic; plus SUBJ = topic?)

If in (9a) *John,* by virtue of being subject, is also the topic, then the same must be true of *John* in (9b); but, in addition, is *John* in (9b) also in addition a *marked-topic*? And if *Bill* in (9c) is the topic (or *marked topic*), what is the status of *John* there? Grammatically, *John* is marked the same way in (9c) as in (9a), so is it still *the* topic? Or perhaps the unmarked topic? Again, extra distinctions of either kind or degree are required. And the suggestion,[10] that somehow the subject is a *grammaticalized topic*, while diachronically revealing, did not add much to sharpening the functional definition of either *topic* or *subject.*

6.3.2.5. Multi-topic neutral clauses

Consider next the phenomenon of *dative-shifting* in bi-transitive sentences, as in:

(10) a. John gave *the book* to Mary
      b. John gave *Mary* a book
      c. John gave *her* the book
      d. *John gave *the book* her
      e. John gave *it* to Mary
      f. *John gave *Mary* it

In the mid-1970s it was already obvious that there was some 'topicality' a symmetry between the direct and indirect object; that the DO was somehow *more topical* than the indirect object; and that 'promotion to direct object' involved **increased topicality** of the erstwhile indirect ob-

10 See Givón (1976a).

ject.[11] In fact, the following topicality hierarchies were proposed at the time to express the gradation of both semantic and grammatical case-roles:[12]

(11) a. AGENT > DATIVE > PATIENT > OTHERS
      b. SUBJECT > DIRECT - OBJECT > INDIRECT - OBJECT

Such hierarchies, if taken literally, suggest that bi-transitive sentences as in (10) have three topics each; and that those topics are further distinguished by either degree or kind of 'topicality'.

6.3.2.6. The scalarity of 'focus'

A similarly vexing problem concerns the relation between the two atomic notions 'topic' and 'focus', and the seeming scalarity of the latter. Even a cursory look at grammar data already suggests such scalarity. Thus consider:

(12) a. It was to *John* that I gave the book   (cleft-focus)
      b. To *John* I gave the book,...   (Y-movement)
      c. The person I gave the book to was *John*   (pseudo-cleft)
      d. I gave the book to *John*   ('neutral')
      e. I gave *John* a book   (dative-shifted)

There is a clear gradation in the degree of 'focusness' ('emphasis', 'contrast') vested in *John* in (12a,b,c,d,e) above, a gradation that was re-Platonized by in the recent past, by using two or three 'underlying' binary features.[13] But is it a gradation in the degree of 'focus'? Or, as the bottom of the scale (12d,e) seem to suggest, a gradation from 'topic' to 'focus'? The two seems to be, somehow, the extreme points on a single scale. Except that in the case of both cleft-focus (12a) and Y-movement (12b) there are strong indications that the focused constituent is at the same time also topical.[14] For example, it is odd to start a lecture with a cleft-focus construction, thought quite natural to start it with a pseudo-cleft. Thus compare:

---

11 See Shir (1979) or Givón (1979a, Ch. 4).
12 See Hawkinson and Hyman (1974) or Givón (1976a).
13 As in, for example, Chafe, 1976; Prince, 1979; Givón, 1979a, Ch. 2, *inter alia*. Such Platonization of a continuum is reminiscent of the way Generative phonologists used to handle the continuum of points of articulation. A similar Platonism still haunts -- surprisingly -- cognitive psychologists, *viz* Clark and Malt (1984).
14 See discussion in Givón (1979a, Ch. 2).

(13) a. What I'm going to talk about today is *evolution*.
  b. ?It's *evolution* that I'm going to talk about today.

The reason for the oddity of (13b) at discourse-initial is presumably due to the fact that a cleft-focused constituent must have been established as 'topic' in the preceding discourse. A similar observation can be made about Y-moved constituents, which are both contrastive and 'topical'.

6.3.2.7. Degree of presuppositionality

As we noted in Chapter 4, scalarity also seems to crop up in the degree of presuppositionality ('backgroundedness') of clauses. Presuppositionality of clauses is, presumably, closely related to topicality of nominal arguments. The following clause-types are clearly ranked with respect to their degree of presuppositionality:[15]

(14) a. V-complement: It was bad *that she left*
  b. REL-clause: The woman *who left...*
  c. Negative: *She* didn't *leave*
  d. Conditional: If *she leaves,...*
  e. 'Neutral': *She left*

Again, if we are dealing with a scalar dimension, what exactly are its underlying parameters?

6.3.3. Interim summary: Searching for the cognitive base of topicality

The combined weight of all the facts discussed above must force us to re-define 'topic' (thus also 'focus') in a way that would satisfy at least the following requirements:

(a) It must accommodate scalarity;
(b) It must accommodate multi-dimensional space;
(c) It must link that multi-dimensional scalar space to some plausible cognitive dimensions, ones that are not merely functional-sounding labels for grammatical categories.
(d) It must allow for an empirical definition -- and hopefully measurement -- of the proposed functional dimensions.

Requirements (c) and (d) above invite further comment concerning early functionalism in linguistics. Many linguists are in the habit of re-christening structural ('grammatical') categories with functionally-

---

15 See Ch. 4, above, as well as Givón (1979a, Ch.2; 1982a).

sounding names (such as 'topic', 'pivot', 'theme', 'focus' etc.). We then assume, somehow -- by a mysterious leap of faith -- that our description has been transformed from mere structuralism to functionalism.[16] It is of course true that the pervasive iconicity of grammars (see Ch. 3,) indeed entitles one to assume that grammatical categories correspond, at least in the main, to functional categories. Nonetheless, if one is to demonstrate a **correlation** between structure and function, both must be defined independently. Otherwise 'correlation' is mere tautology.

6.4. The measurement of topicality: Predictability, importance and attention

6.4.1. Preliminaries: Anaphoric predictability and cataphoric importance of topics in discourse

Beginning in the late 1970s,[17] I have been looking for some scalar dimension that may correlate with our earlier intuitive notion of topicality. A dimension -- or dimensions -- that can be measured and quantified in discourse. In studying the word-order pragmatics of Biblical Hebrew,[18] the dimension of continuity -- of both the more abstract 'theme' and the more concrete nominal topics ('participants') -- suggested itself. With regard to the latter, referential **continuity** was subsequently equated with **accessibility** or **predictability** of reference.[19] Finally, a text-based quantified methodology was developed[20] to measure some of the more obvious sources of referential predictability.

Reasoning from general considerations, the accessibility of a referent to the hearer (or reader) is likely to be affected by the following four factors concerning the preceding -- i.e. **anaphoric** -- discourse context:[21]

---

16 Some recent examples may be seen in Dik (1978) or Foley and van Valin (1985), *inter alia*. The practice is, however, time-honored, and many of us have indulge in it before learning to recognize its inherent circularity.

17 Givón (1977, 1978a, 1979a).

18 See Givón (1977).

19 See Givón (1978a; 1979a, Ch. 2).

20 See Givón (ed., 1983a).

21 Of the three contextual foci discussed earlier above -- generic-cultural, deictic-situational and discourse-textural -- we deal here primarily with the latter. This is not to say that the first two have no effect on the accessibility of referents in discourse. That effect, however, is not easy to quantify and measure in text. Most particularly, generic-cultural knowledge is indispensible for using thematic information to identify referents in discourse. This is the knowledge of stereotyped 'frames', 'scripts', conventional situations, common likelihoods etc. (see Schank and Abelson, 1977, *inter alia*). For some experimental details see Anderson *et al* (1983).

(15) **Factors affecting referential predictability/accessability:**

factor	cognitive dimension
(a) *Referential distance* from the previous mention in the discourse	memory decay of referent
(b) *Referential complexity* of the preceding discourse context	selective access to several referents
(c) 'Redundant' *semantic information* from inside the clause itself	(same as above)
(d) 'Redundant' *thematic information* from the preceding discourse	(same as above)

Of the four factors, (15a) and (15b) are easiest to quantify and measure in discourse. They are the basis of the text-based measures of **Referential Distance** (RD) and **Potential Interference** (PI), respectively. Factors (15c) and (15d), on the other hand, are much harder to measure in discourse, although experimental psycho-linguistic work has demonstrated their clear effect.[22]

Both the RD and PI measures assess the **anaphoric** predictability of referents ('topics') by looking at the preceding discourse context. But, as noted in Chapter 5, another dimension of topicality is that of referential **importance**. And while the importance of a referent is also reflected in its anaphoric continuity, it is best measured independently in the **cataphoric** -- i.e. following -- context. That is, one can presumably assess a referent's importance in the discourse by measuring how long it persists once it has been introduced. The text-measure of **Topic Persistence** (TP) was devised to do just that.

The most current version of the three text-based measures of topicality is given in (16) below:

---

22 For the effect of semantic priming on the recoverability of pronominal co-referents, see Corbett and Chang (1983). For the effect of thematic priming, see Anderson *et al* (1983) or Tomlin (1987).

(16) **Text-based measures of the topicality:**

measure (operational definition)	discourse dimension	cognitive dimension
(a) **Referential Distance:** "The number of clauses (or elapsed time) [23] from the last occurrence in the preceding discourse"	predictability in anaphoric context	memory decay
(b) **Potential Interference:** "The number of semantically compatible referents within the preceding three clauses"	predictability in anaphoric context	competing referent searches
(c) **Topic Persistence:** "The number of recurrences of the referent in the subsequent ten clauses"	importance in cataphoric context	attention

One must emphasize that these text-based measures do not assay directly the presumed cognitive dimensions suggested in (16) above.[See FN 23] Rather, they measure some of their more likely correlates in the text. Using these measures, one can obtain numerical characterizations, highly replicable both within a language and across languages, of the topicality of nominal referents marked by particular grammatical devices. In the following sections we will survey some of the results of text-based studies employing these measurements.

6.4.2. Predictability and the code-quantity scale

As noted in Chapter 3, there exists a strong *inverse* correlation between the degree of predictability of a referent and the phonological size of the grammatical device used to code it. Thus, for example, the grammatical devices in (17) below -- all of them anaphoric-definite categories used under various discourse conditions -- scale rather consistently on our anaphoric predictability measures of referential distance (RD) (16a).

---

23 Both the mental effort and the amount of attention associated with referential processing can be measured experimentally by a variety of direct and less direct means. For some details see Anderson et al (1983), Dahl and Gundel (1982) or Givón et al (1985), *inter alia*. For some more details, see Chapter 7.

(17) The code-quantity scale of referential predictability [24]

most predictable/accessible referent	typical RD value
a. zero anaphora	1 clause
b. unstressed/clitic pronoun/agreement	1–2 clauses
c. stressed/independent pronoun	2–3 clauses
d. full DEF-noun	10 clauses
e. restrictively modified DEF-noun	15 clauses

least predictable/accessible referent

To further illustrate how dependable the RD measure is in scaling grammatical devices, consider the distribution of the RD values for all *pronouns and anaphoric zeros* (categories (17a,b,c) above) and all *definite nouns* (categories (17d,e) above) in spoken English:

(18) **The distribution of referential distance (RD) for pronouns (including zero anaphores) and definite nouns in spoken English** [25]

RD in # of clauses	pronouns		DEF-nouns	
	n	%	*n*	%
1-2	499	86.2	54	26.7
3-8	31	5.7	36	17.8
9-14	8	1.4	17	8.4
15-19	2	0.3	6	2.9
20+	1	0.1	89	43.9
total:	541	100.0	202	100.0
median RD:	1.0 clauses		12.0 clauses	

The principle underlying the correlation between code quantity and information predictability, already noted earlier above, [26] is reproduced in (19) below:

(19) **The code-quantity principle:**

"The less *predictable/accessible* a referent is the more phonological material will be used to code it".

24 For the initial study see Givón (ed., 1983a).
25 From Givón (1983b).
26 See Ch. 3.

Assuming, as one is surely entitled to, that more -- or stronger -- coding attracts more **attention** and is lodged more firmly in **memory**, principle (19) above may be converted into the general cognitive principle (20):

(20) "Stronger -- more salient -- coding will yield a stronger effect in attending to and memorizing the coded information"

The reason why more predictable information requires less -- or weaker -- coding is transparent: Predictable information is more readily **available** in ('recoverable from') context; or, alternatively, it is more vividly **activated**[27] in the memory, thus more strongly attended to. It does not -- unlike new unpredictable information -- require strong activation by massive coding.

6.4.3. Code quantity and referential confusion

The same group of studies[28] also noted that the difference in RD values between unstressed and stressed-independent pronouns -- while reproducible -- was relatively small (1 vs 2-3 clauses, respectively on a scale from 1 to 20). However, the two types of pronouns are strongly distinguished by the measure of **potential interference** (PI), where on a scale from 1.0 to 2.0 unstressed pronouns score at the very bottom and stressed pronouns at the very top. In other words, unstressed pronouns are typically used when no competing referents occur in the immediate anaphoric environment. While stressed pronouns are typically used when such competing referents exist. A simple example may illustrate the use of stressed pronouns in discourse contexts with unpredictability from a variety of sources:

(21) a.   John came home. Later on *he* left.   (unstressed)
     b.   John talked to Bill. Later on *he* left.   (unstressed)
     c.   John talked to Bill. Later on *HE* left.   (stressed)
     d.   John took Mary to see a movie *he'd*   (unstressed)
          already seen. *SHE* hadn't though.   (stressed)
     e.   John and Mary went to see a movie.
          HE had already seen it,   (stressed)
          though *SHE* hadn't.   (stressed)

In (21a) a single referent is introduced and then continued. It is thus totally predictable, and the pronoun is unstressed. In (21b) two referents are introduced, but the one coded as subject continues as subject. That is

---

27 For a compatible notion of *activation*, see Chafe (1987).
28 Givón (ed., 1983a).

still predictable enough, given the strong tendency in connected narrative to continue the subject (see discussion further below); and so an unstressed pronoun is still used. In (21c), on the other hand, the second referent -- first introduced as object -- is resumed upon continuation as subject. Such continuation is less predictable, and a stressed pronoun must then be used. In (21d) two referents are first introduced, one as subject and the other as object. The first one is then continued as subject; that -- as in (21b) -- is still predictable enough, so an unstressed pronoun is used. Then the second referents takes over as subject. Such a switch is less predictable for two reasons: First, an erstwhile object is unexpectedly made into subject. Second, a thematic expectation is set up, contrasting the fact that *John* had seen the movie with the fact that *Mary* hadn't yet seen it. Two expectations of continuity are thus tampered with, and a stressed pronoun is used. Finally, in (21e) both referents are introduced as subjects. When *John* is then continued as subject *all by himself*, the expectation of subject continuity is broken, and a stressed pronoun is used. The code-quantity principle of grammatical coding is thus sensitive to predictability *whatever its source*. This is further evident from surveying the interaction between code quantity and **thematic** predictability.

6.4.4. Code quantity and thematic predictability

The sensitivity of the code-quantity scale to differences in **thematic** continuity may be further illustrated by contrasting the use of zero anaphora and unstressed pronouns in English. As was apparent in (17) above, the referential distance (RD) values for zero-anaphores and unstressed pronouns are virtually the same (1.0 vs. 1.2, respectively, on a scale from 1 to 20). Similarly, both are equally low on the potential interference (PI) scale, scoring at the very bottom of the scale.[29] Whatever unpredictability controlling the choice between these two grammatical devices in discourse must therefore arise from some other source. To illustrate this, consider:

(22) a. He came into the room,
     b. ø looked around,
     c. ø went to the window
     d. and ø looked out.
     e.   (i) ...*He* was dog tired.
       *(ii) ...ø was dog tired.

The discourse in (22) involves a single participant, and as long as the

---

29 Givón (ed., 1983a)

thematic progression is maximally continuous (thus maximally predict-able), zero anaphora is used to code the single referent (22b-d). The use of the period to end (22d), however, marks a subtle increase in thematic discontinuity. The (still predictable) referent cannot be coded with zero anaphora any more, but must be resumed with the phonologically-larger unstressed pronoun.

A similar phenomenon has been demonstrated experimentally in the use of pronouns vs. definite nouns. As seen in (17) and (18), above, pronouns and definite nouns have strikingly different RD values, with the latter used in discourse contexts of much *lower* referential continuity. They also differ, in the same direction, on the scale of potential inter-ference (PI).[30] However, it has been shown [31] that the use of DEF-nouns rather than pronouns can be triggered, in environments of absolute referential predictability, by introducing strong **thematic** discontinuity.

6.4.5. Subject, object and transitivity: Referential predictability and referential importance

6.4.5.1. Preamble: Referential importance

The second major cognitive component of topicality is **referential im-portance**. We have already discussed this feature in Chapter 5, in con-junction with indefinite reference. This feature also plays a major role in the grammar of definite reference.

6.4.5.2. Subject and object

The same text-based studies[32] that established the code-quantity scale (17) also revealed a striking difference between subjects and objects of clauses in terms of their topical predictability. To illustrate this, consider the topicality properties of agents and patients of semantically-transitive clauses[33] in Chamorro discourse. In this language, the majority of semanti-cally transitive clauses in narrative are coded morphologically as **ergative**. When the topicality of the agent in however, clauses is radically low, the clause is coded as **passive**. When the topicality of the patient is radically low, the clause is coded as **anti-passive**.[34] Grammatically, *passive* clauses are those where the agent has been 'demoted' from the role of subject, and a non-agent (most commonly the patient) has become the subject of the

---

30   Givón (ed., 1983a)
31   Tomlin (1987).
32   Givón (ed., 1983a).
33   Clauses are considered semantically-transitive if their verb requires for its normal sense the participation in the event of both an agent and a patient. For discussion see Givón (1984a, Chapters 4,5).
34   See discussion in Ch. 3, above; see also Givón (1984a, Ch. 5) and Cooreman *et al* (1984).

clause. Conversely, *anti-passive* clauses are those where the patient has been 'demoted' from its role as object. The topicality of both arguments was measured by two of our text-based measures, referential distance (RD) and topic persistence (TP). A summary of the results is given in (23) below.

(23) **Transitivity and the topicality of agent and patient in semantically-transitive clauses in Chamorro narrative discourse** [35]

clause type	average RD in # of clauses		average TP in # of clauses	
	agent	patient	agent	patient
ergative	1.49	4.35	2.45	0.81
in-passive	4.06	1.38	1.31	2.00
ma-passive	6.33	3.33	0.44	1.44
anti-passive	1.86	20.00	1.29	0.00

The results reported above demonstrate rather vividly that the subject of a transitive clause is more topical than the object, both in terms of anaphoric predictability (RD) and cataphoric importance (TP). When the agent is 'demoted' from the subject role (passivization), its referential distance increases and its persistence decreases. The patient, when 'promoted' to the subject role (passivization), shows decreased referential distance and increased persistence. Finally, when the patient is 'demoted' from the object role altogether (anti-passivization), its referential distance increases maximally and its persistence decreases maximally.

6.4.5.3. Direct and indirect object

We have suggested earlier above that direct objects are 'more topical' than indirect objects. The striking difference in topicality is measured both anaphorically, in terms of referential distance, and cataphorically, in terms of topic persistence. To illustrate this, consider the following results from a text-based study of the topicality of direct and indirect objects in Nez Perce.

(24) **Topicality of direct and indirect objects in Nez Perce** [36]

object type	average RD in # of clauses		average TP in # of clauses	
	patient	oblique	patient	oblique
DIRECT OBJECT	1.7	2.2	2.3	1.5
INDIRECT OBJECT	8.3	10.1	0.6	0.4

35 From Cooreman (1982b) and Cooreman et al (1984).
36 From Rude (1985). See also Givón (1984d).

The results demonstrate that direct objects are more topical than indirect objects, both anaphorically -- by the measure of referential distance, and cataphorically -- by the measure of topic persistence. When a patient is 'demoted' from direct-object, its RD measure increases and its TP value decreases. Conversely, when an oblique object is 'promoted' to direct-object, its RD measure decreases and its TP measure increases. Once again, importance -- as measured indirectly through text persistence -- proves to be an intimate ingredient of topicality.

6.4.5.4. Grammatical marking of important definites

As noted in Chapter 5, the unstressed demonstrative *this* in colloquial English marks thematically important indefinites, contrasting with *a* which marked unimportant ones. It may very well be that a similar contrast can be shown between the unstressed *that* and the article *the* in colloquial English, with *that* marking more important definites and *the* less important ones.

A reminiscent contrast has been reported (Lichtenberk, 1986) for To'aba'ita (Oceanic), in the use of two demonstratives in discourse. One of them (the spatially proximant *this*) is used to mark thematically important definites; the other (the spatially remote *that*) is used to mark unimportant ones.

Similarly, in Krio (Givón, 1985a; see also Chapter 5), definite nominals are usually marked with the proximant demonstrative *dis* (English 'this'). Definite nouns that are thematically important, in particular those introduced first into the discourse with the numeral *one*, are most likely to be marked, when re-introduced into the narrative after a gap of absence, by the suffix *ya-so* (English 'here-so'). Processing instructions (via grammatical clues) concerning expected cataphoric importance are thus not given only upon the first introduction of a referent, but also upon re-introduction following a gap of absence.

6.4.6. Word-order and topicality [37]

6.4.6.1. The presumed topic-comment ordering principle

Perhaps the area where the Prague-school tradition had registered its strongest impact on 1970s functionalist work was in the pragmatics of word-order. Indeed, a received Praguean wisdom prevails to this day, namely that *topics precede comments, theme precedes rheme, old information*

---

[37] More detailed discussion and many more cross-language examples may be seen in Givón (1987b), from which these materials are condensed.

precedes new information and *the subject more naturally precedes the verb.* A classical example of this approach at its best may be seen in Bolinger (1954), where the relative position of the subject in Spanish clauses was said to abide by this generalization: [38]

(25) a. Context: Quien canta?
                       'Who's singing?'   (topic = singing)
      b. Response: Canta Juán.   (*VS word-order;*
                       'John is singing'   focus = Juá*n*)
      c. Context: Qué *hace Juán*
                       'What is John doing?'   (*topic = Juán*)
      d. Response: Juán *canta.*   (*SV word-order;*
                       'John is singing'   focus = singing)

As recalcitrant as the topic-before-comment generalization seems to be, detailed -- text-based, quantified -- studies show it to be at best seriously flawed and at worse simply false. In the space below we will survey some of the evidence showing why this turned out to be the case. We will see that the *topic-before-comment* ordering principle holds true only for the topicality feature of **importance**. As to the feature of **predictability**, the facts suggest exactly the opposite generalization: Older, more continuous, more predictable information -- if at all expressed -- consistently *follows* newer, less continuous, less predictable information. In other words, the anaphorically less topical information precedes the more topical.[39]

6.4.6.2. **Word-order flexibility and referential predictability**

In (26) below the results of three text-based studies are summarized, all measuring the *referential distance* of the subject NP when coded by various grammatical devices, including when the subject either precedes or follows the verb (or 'predicate').

---

38 Bolinger was obviously not alone in this regard. Many of us in the 1970s --and to this day -- have taken this for granted, as in Li and Thompson (1976), or Givón (1976a, 1976b, 1979a), *inter alia.*

39 How a false generalization could have been maintained so long and gain such currency is an object lesson in methodology. Not one of the works purporting to demonstrate this generalization was based on text-distribution quantified study. All language examples cited in support of the topic-before-comment principle were either constructed from the linguist's own intuition, or picked out selectively from texts.

(26) **Correlation between referential distance (RD) and relative position of the subject in Written Polish, Biblical Hebrew and spoken Spanish-English Pidgin** [40]

topic-coding device	average RD in # of clauses		
	Spanish-English	Biblical Hebrew	Polish
zero-subject/ verb-agreement	1.0	1.1	/
verb-subject order	3.4	4.8	3.1
subject-verb order	13.0	8.4	6.5
zero-comment/ topic repetition	20.0	/	/

The data tabulated in (26) suggest that the following pragmatic principle control the relationship between linear order and referential predictability:

(27) "A more predictable topic follows the comment; a less-predictable topic precedes the comment"

Or, in more general terms of **informational predictability**:

(28) "Less predictable information is placed earlier in the string"

The results of the Spanish-English Pidgin study, together with data from two more Pidgins [41] and from spoken English,[42] suggest another possible generalization, one that recognizes the following ranking of topic-coding devices according to topic predictability:[43]

---

40 The Polish data is from Rybarkiewicz (1984). The Biblical Hebrew data is from A. Fox (1983); the Spanish-English Pidgin data is from Givón (1984b).
41 See Givón (1984b).
42 See Givón (1983b).
43 First formulated in Givón (1983c).

(29) **Ranking of the most basic topic-coding devices according to degree of topic predictability**

most predictable/accessible/continuous topic

COMMENT	(zero topic)
COMMENT-TOPIC	
TOPIC-COMMENT	
TOPIC	(zero comment)

least predictable/accessible/continuous topic

Scale (29) allows one to integrate, tentatively, principle (28) of linear order and principle (19) of **code quantity** into a single cognitively-based principle of **task urgency**:

(30) **The task-urgency principle:**

"Attend first to the more urgent task"

Zero topic-coding is used when the topic is most predictable, thus the task of expressing it is least urgent. *Zero*-comment (repeated topic) is used when the topic is maximally unpredictable, thus the task of establishing it is maximally urgent. While the two word-order devices -- comment-topic vs. topic-comment -- occupy intermediate points on the scale, consonant with principle (28).

6.4.6.3. Dislocated order and anaphoric predictability

In a closely related study, the referential distance of subject NPs in spoken English was measured. Right-dislocated and Left-dislocated subjects were compared to the neutral SV order, as well as to zero-anaphora and topic repetition. The results are summarized in (31) below.

(31) **Referential distance (RD) of grammatical devices coding subject NPs in spoken English[44]**

topic-coding device	average RD in # of clauses
zero-anaphora	1.0
R-dislocation	1.0
Neutral SV order	10.1
L-dislocation	15.3
topic repetition	17.4

44 From Givón (1983b).

English is a rigid-order language, where SV(O) is the most common, neutral order. But when dislocated ordering is used, the pre-posed order (L-dislocation) displays much higher RD values than the post-posed order (R-dislocation). In other words, *pre*-posing occurs when referents are less predictable, *post*-posing when they are more predictable; and the neutral order displays intermediate values. Principle (28) is again reflected in these results.

6.4.7. Word order and topic importance

6.4.7.1. Preamble

The fact that grammar is sensitive to topic importance has already been noted, for indefinite referents, in Chapter 5. Further, in sections 6.3.5.2. and 6.4.5.4, above, it was noted that the use of various grammatical devices is sensitive to the thematic importance of *definite* referents. In this section we will see how word-order, in addition to being sensitive to referential **predictability**, is also sensitive to the topic's thematic importance.

On rather general grounds, one would predict the following correlation between **topic importance** and communicative **task urgency**:

(32)   "The more important a topic is, the more urgent is the task of communicating it"

Given principle (30) above, correlating task urgency with pre-posed order, above, one would expect more important topics to be *pre-posed*, and less important ones to be *post-posed*. In the space directly below I will summarize the results of some quantified, text-based studies that support this prediction.

6.4.7.2. Definiteness and word-order in Papago

Word-order in Papago is completely flexible for both subjects and objects. In a recent study, a strong correlation was shown between definiteness and word-order in this language, with the pre-verbal position favoring *indefinite* NPs, and the post-verbal position *definite* NPs. These results are summarized in (33) below.

(33) Definiteness, contrastiveness and word-order in Papago [45]

	Pre-Verbal		Post-Verbal		Total	
	N	%	N	%	N	%
Indefinite	143	0.89	17	0.11	160	1.00
Definite	7	0.02	277	0.98	284	1.00
"Prag. Marked"	38	0.95	2	0.05	40	1.00

The results indicate that the vast majority of definite -- *predictable* -- referents are deferred, i.e. they appear *post*-verbally. The vast majority indefinite -- *unpredictable* -- referents are pre-posed. In addition, referents under contrastive focus -- i.e. those involving either high referential unpredictability due to referential clutter or thematic unpredictability[46] -- appear primarily *pre*-verbally. The results so far uphold the correlation between pre-posed order and unpredictability, i.e. principle (28).

Still, the results are a bit skewed: The post-verbal placement of *definite* ('given', 'predictable') referents, is almost categorial (96%). The pre-verbal placement of *indefinites* ('unpredictable', 'new') referents, on the other hand, is less categorial (89%, with 11% going post-verbally). When nouns in this exceptional 11% fraction were compared to those in the predominant pre-verbal category,[47] it was found that the post-posed indefinites were all **thematically unimportant** in the discourse. In other words, we have here a conflict between the two major cognitive dimensions underlying topicality -- predictability and importance. Indefinite referents are by definition highly unpredictable, they are thus expected to be fronted. But the few of them that are of low importance are post-posed. In other words, topic importance here *overrides* referential predictability in controlling word-order.

6.4.7.3. Word-order and topic persistence in Klamath

Klamath is also a flexible-order language, much like Papago. A recent study measured the referential distance (RD) and topic persistence (TP) of pre-verbal and post-verbal subjects and objects in this language. The results are summarized in (34) below.

---

45 From Payne (1985).
46 See further discussion below.
47 Payne (1985).

(34) Referential distance (RD), topic persistence (TP) and word-order in Klamath[48]

	RD and TP in # of clauses			
	Pre-Verbal (SV/OV)		Post-Verbal (VS/VO)	
Category	RD	TP	RD	TP
subject-NP (DEF)	7.82	1.98	3.92	1.36
object-NP				
DEF.	9.97	1.60	6.04	2.80
INDEF.	/	1.22	/	0.27

As one can see, by the measure of referential predictability (RD) pre-verbal referents are more unpredictable, post-verbal ones more predictable, both thus abiding by principle (28). In addition -- at least for subjects and indefinite objects[49] -- pre-verbal referents are also more persistent, thus more **important** in the discourse. Of more interest is, of course, the behavior of indefinite objects, where the pre-verbal ones show a much higher persistence measure than the post-verbal ones. On the basis of referential predictability *alone*, one would expect all indefinite object to be pre-verbal. As in Papago, however, topic importance overrides referential predictability.

6.4.7.4. Direct and indirect object

It has been observed that direct object invariably precede indirect objects, and this behavior transcends word-order type.[50] Now, as shown in section 6.4.5.3., above, the direct object outranks the indirect object in both features of topicality, it is both more predictable and more important. But once again we have a conflict here, in the expected correlation of topicality with word-order: By rule (28), the more predictable direct object should *follow* the indirect object. Once again, however, importance overrides predictability, and the direct object invariably precedes.

6.4.7.5. Contrastive NPs and pre-posed order

The pre-posing of object NPs to mark contrastiveness or emphasis in VO languages is one of the most wide-spread word-order devices (*viz*

---

48 From Sundberg (1985).
49 The exceptional behavior of definite objects is so far unaccounted for.
50 See Givón (1984d).

the Papago distribution in (33), above). As noted earlier, Y-moved NPs used to be considered topical. And indeed, in terms of their referential distance (RD) measure, such pre-posed objects turn out to be more predictable than post-verbal, neutral-ordered objects. By our rule (28) then, they should be *post*-posed. However, in terms of their potential interference (PI) measure, they seem to be used in environments of high **referential complexity** -- i.e. un-predictability.[51]

As an illustrative example of Y-movement in English, consider:

(35) (a) ...So we wound up owing money to both the German and the French.
(b) *to the German* we gave a deferred check,
(b) but *the French* we paid in cash...

A recent quantified text-based study investigated the discourse distribution of pre-verbal objects in two VO languages, Biblical Hebrew and Mandarin Chinese. The results are summarized in (36) below.

(36) **Text frequency, referential distance (RD) and potential interference (TP) of pre- and post-verbal objects in Mandarin Chinese and Biblical Hebrew**[52]

Measure	Written Mandarin VO	Written Mandarin OV	Spoken Mandarin VO	Spoken Mandarin OV	Biblical Hebrew VO	Biblical Hebrew OV
% in text	94	6	92	8	97	3
average RD	10.00	3.00	4.00	2.00	12.10	2.50
average PI	1.09	1.47	1.14	1.80	1.69	2.00

The pre-verbal position of Y-moved objects must be due to either high **referential complexity** or thematic **contrastiveness**, rather than to high referential distance. Referential predictability is a *complex* cognitive dimension, to which a variety of factors can contribute. The grammar of human language, in this case word-order, is sensitive to the degree of predictability *whatever* its source.

---

51 There are, in addition, some grounds for suspecting that pre-verbal (Y-moved) objects may code objects that are more *important* than post-verbal ('neutral-ordered') ones. If that turns out to be the case, then the pre-verbal position of such object may be ascribed to *both* low predictability and high importance.
52 From Sun and Givón (1985).

6.4.7.6. Predictability, importance and pre-posed subject pronouns

The pre-posing of stressed independent subject pronouns in *V-first* languages (VSO, VOS) is another example of how contrastiveness, or referential complexity, overrides referential distance in determining word-order. Stressed independent pronouns are universally used under the following discourse conditions: [53]

(a) Fairly low values of referential distance (RD), usually near the bottom of the scale (2-3 clauses on a scale of 1-to-20). That is, the antecedent has typically been mentioned 2-3 clauses back;

(b) High values of **potential interference** (PI), usually near the top of the scale (2 on a scale of 1.0-2.0). That is, another semantically-compatible (thus often contrasting) referent had been mentioned in the preceding 2-3 clauses;

(c) High incidence of **subject/topic switching** from the preceding clause. That is, the independent pronoun is used to switch the topic back from the preceding -- now contrasting -- referent.

As an illustrative example from English, consider:

(37) (a)   ...So we wound up owing money to both Tom and Sylvia.
     (b)   *HE* agreed to accept a deferred check.
     (c)   *SHE* demanded cash...

As noted above, Early Biblical Hebrew (EBH) is a rigid VO language with flexible subject position. That is, the subject may appear either pre- or post-verbally. In terms of frequency, post-verbal *definite* subject nouns are predominant in the EBH text. On the other hand, independent subject *pronouns* are almost categorially pre-verbal, as seen in the distributional figures in (38) below.

(38) **Distribution of pre- and post-verbal subjects in Early Biblical Hebrew[54]**

category	pre-verbal N	pre-verbal %	post-verbal N	post-verbal %	total N	total %
Def-Noun	128	32.3	269	67.7	397	100.0
Pronoun	25	92.5	2	7.5	27	100.0

The pre-posing of independent pronouns thus represents another in-

---

53   See Givón (1983c).
54   From Givón (1977). The text frequency pertains to the book of Genesis.

stance where referential complexity -- or contrastiveness -- is an important source of unpredictability. In this and many other cases, independent pronouns are also strongly associated with the function of topic switching.

There is, further, strong evidence suggesting that independent subject pronoun also rank higher than definite subject nouns in terms of *topical importance*. Thus, in another study [55] the average *topic persistence* (TP) of post-verbal definite subject *nouns* in Early Biblical Hebrew was found to be 0.93 clauses. The average TP measure for independent subject *pronouns* was 3.26 clauses. The pre-posing of independent pronouns is thus triggered by both features of topicality -- low referential predictability and high topical importance. A similar distribution has been reported for spoken Spanish, another VO language with flexible subject position (Silva-Corvalán 1977).

6.4.7.7. Pre-posed indefinite subjects in verb-first languages: Where predictability and importance coincide[56]

Rigid V-first languages are extremely resistant to **pre-posing** any nominal arguments, i.e. placing them before the verb. This holds true to both subjects and objects. There are three pre-posing grammatical devices that are found even in the most rigid V-first languages: Clefting, WH-movement, and the pre-posing of referential-indefinite subjects, otherwise known as the *existential-presentative* construction.[57]

Referential-indefinite subjects are by definition maximally unpredictable, introducing new referents into the discourse. Not only are they unpredictable, but they are also **important** in the subsequent discourse. Otherwise languages tend to introduce unimportant referents in the *object* position. To illustrate this, consider once again the data from colloquial English (see Chapter 5), concerning the **topic persistence** (TP) of indefinite subjects and objects marked by either *a* or *this*. Indefinite subjects marked by either *this* or *a* tend to appear in existential-presentative construction, as in:

(40) a. *...there was this bear* who lived in a forest...

     b. *...there's a guy* I used to know who...

As noted earlier (Ch. 5), *this* codes more important indefinites than does *a*. The higher persistence -- thus importance -- of indefinite-existential subjects (as against non-subjects) can be seen in (41) below.

---

55 See A. Fox (1983).
56 For a more expanded discussion, see Givón (1987b).
57 See extensive discussion in Hetzron (1971) and Givón (1976a).

persistence (TP > 2) indefinite NPs marked by 'this' and 'a'[58]

	'THIS'						'A'				
	Subject		Non-Subj		Total		Subject		Non-Subj		Total
TP	N	%	N	%	N	%	N	%	N	%	N	%
0–2	4	14.2	10	66.6	14	32.5	10	76.9	89	94.6	99	92.5
2 <	24	85.8	5	33.4	29	67.5	3	23.1	5	5.4	8	7.5
TOT	28	100.0	15	100.0	43	100.0	13	100.0	94	100.0	107	100.0

These results recapitulate our earlier discussion concerning the higher topicality of subjects over objects -- higher in terms of both predictability and importance. In the case of *definite* subjects in V-first languages, predictability overrides importance, and -- given the rigid V-first constraint -- the subject follows the verb. However, in the case of *indefinite* subjects, both features of topicality work *in the same direction,* toward a pre-posed order. The fact that the pre-posing of indefinite subjects is so pervasive even in the most rigid V-first language, can be thus ascribed to the *conflation* of both features of topicality.

6.4.7.8. Cleft-focus constructions: Counter-expectancy and word-order

Another NP-fronting grammatical device that appears even in the most rigid V-first language is that of cleft-focus, as in:

(41)   a.   It's *the book* I'm looking for (not the cup)...
         b.   It's *a book* I'm looking for (not a cup)...

As suggested earlier above, there are grounds for suspecting that the fronted, cleft-focused referent is also topical in the sense of givenness; that is, it had been *made topic,* often quite recently, in the preceding discourse.[59]

The existence of cleft-focus fronting even in the most rigid V-first languages thus represents another case when strong referential and thematic counter-expectancy overrides 'givenness', and is the apparent source of unpredictability.

---

58   From Shroyer (1985); see also Wright and Givón (1987).
59   See section 6.3.2.6., above.

6.4.7.9. Word order and thematic predictability

In the preceding sections we have seen that word-order in human language is sensitive to predictability arising from diverse -- primarily referential -- sources. In this section we will survey some evidence suggesting that word-order is also sensitive, in very much the same fashion, to the level of **thematic** predictability in the discourse.

As is generally known, the paragraph-initial clause in discourse occupies a point of **thematic discontinuity**, as compared to paragraph medial or final clauses. In a recent study, the distribution of pre-verbal vs. post-verbal subjects/agents in Tagalog, a V-first language, was studied, in paragraph-initial and non-initial clauses. The results, found to be statistically significant, are summarized in (42) below.

(42) **Pre-verbal subjects/agents and paragraph boundaries in Tagalog**[60]

	Position in the Paragraph					
	Initial (discontinuous)		Non-Initial (continuous)		Total	
	N	%	N	%	N	%
AGT-V	61	0.27	165	0.73	226	1.00
V-AGT	50	0.13	338	0.87	388	1.00
Total	111		503		614	

As can be seen, paragraph-initial clauses display twice the frequency of pre-posed subjects/agents as non-initial clauses. In other words, environments of high thematic discontinuity ('unpredictability') favor the fronting of nominal referents.

The same effect was also shown, in the same study, in the distribution of pre-verbal subjects/agents in clauses preceded by a *comma* or *zero* punctuation, as against clauses preceded by a *period*. As most literate people are bound to know,[61] commas in written discourse signal higher thematic continuity ('predictability') than periods. In (43) below the distribution of pre-verbal subjects/agents in Tagalog, directly following either a comma or zero, or following a period, is given.

---

60 From B. Fox (1985).
61 Amazingly enough, many linguists, at least in their more guarded professional moments, are blissfully unaware of the rudimentary correlation between thematic continuity and punctuation.

(43) **Pre-verbal subjects/agents and punctuation in Tagalog**[62]

| | Punctuation Type | | | | | |
| | Preceded by Comma/Zero (continuous) | | Preceded by Period (discontinuous) | | Total | |
	N	%	N	%	N	%
AGT-V	83	0.37	143	0.63	226	1.00
V-AGT	263	0.68	125	0.32	388	1.00
Total	346		268		614	

As the figures suggest, pre-verbal subjects/agents are much more prevalent in the more discontinuous ('unpredictable') thematic environment following a period, than in the more continuous environment following a comma.

6.5. Discussion

6.5.1. The pragmatic nature of definite reference

In dealing with pragmatics of definiteness and anaphoric reference, one deals essentially with communicative tasks in discourse. Atomic, Platonic notions such as 'identifiable', 'known', 'referred to earlier' etc. go only a short distance toward accounting for the wealth of structural devices used in the grammar of anaphora and definite reference in human language, let alone for the use of grammar in natural communication. A speaker-hearer based functional-pragmatic account is both more realistic and more far reaching in explaining the facts of structure and function. The profoundly pragmatic, **context-driven** nature of anaphora, definiteness and topicality may be summarized through its following features:

(a) it involves the pragmatically-based notions of **importance** or **relevance**;
(b) it involves the speakers communicative **intent**; and
(c) it involves expectations the speaker makes about what transpires in **another mind** -- the hearer's.

---

62 From B. Fox (1985).

6.5.2. Task urgency, code quantity, linear order and attention

We have noted above that both **code quantity** and **linear order** in human language are sensitive to both major features of topicality -- predictability and importance. Both low predictability and high importance induce an *increase* in the quantity of the code used to mark a constituent. Both can induce the *pre-posing* of a constituent. One may suggest, tentatively, that both dimensions are merely sub-types of **communicative task urgency**. A communicative task in discourse is more urgent if the speaker deems it to be either **less predictable** ('less accessible') to the hearer, or **more important**. As is well documented in cognitive psychology,[63] the initial item in a string of information tends to receive **more attention**, it is **memorized better** and **retrieved faster**, compared to non-initial items. The fronted position must therefore be perceptually **more salient**. The pre-posing of more urgent information -- either less predictable or more important -- must then be a communicative device designed to attract more **attention**, much like assigning a higher code-quantity to the information. Our principle (30), above, may be thus recapitulated as:

(44) "Attend first to -- i.e. **code more saliently** -- the **more urgent** task; that is, the **less predictable** or **more important** task".

That (44) is fully consonant with general cognitive and perceptual principles is only to be expected, since grammar is not likely to have evolved in a complete perceptual and cognitive vacuum.[64]

---

63 For studies showing that initial clauses in the paragraph receive more attention, see Cirilo and Foss (1980), Glazner *et al*, (1984) and Haberlandt (1980). For studies showing a slow-down -- i.e. more attention expended -- in the processing of sentence-initial words, see Aronson and Ferres (1983), Aronson and Scarborough (1976) and Chang (1980), *inter alia*. For studies showing that more mental effort is allocated to sentence-initial words than to non-initial words, see Cairns and Kamerman (1975), Cutler and Foss (1977) and Marslen-Wilson *et al* (1978). The favoring of clause-initial words in comprehension has also been reported by Gernsbacher (1985). Finally, a more recent study by Gernsbacher and Hargreaves (1986) shows that the *relative early position* of a noun within the clause affects favorably its retrieval, as compared with the second-placed noun, regardless of subject-object role, and regardless of whether the first noun was at a clause-initial position.

64 For reasons that sometime belie one's understanding, some linguists persist in viewing the organizational principles of language as being so unique and abstract, so as to be virtually independent of cognitive and perceptual organization. For a fascinating argument in this vein, see Chomsky's various contributions to Piatrelli-Palmarini (Ed., 1980). In Chapter 10, below, we will also suggest that such *modular* separation between grammar and cognition is incompatible with what we know about evolution.

CHAPTER 7

MODES OF KNOWLEDGE AND MODES OF PROCESSING: THE ROUTINIZATION OF BEHAVIOR AND INFORMATION

7.1. Introduction*

This chapter deals with a complex phenomenon, one that may be approached from three distinct entry points. Each entry point corresponds to the traditions of one of the three cognitive disciplines -- philosophy, linguistics, psychology. The latter intersects with a fourth tradition, that of neurology. In spite of extreme diversity in method and frame of reference, these traditions seem to converge at, define -- or at the very least evoke -- a recognizable core phenomenon. Of the three, philosophy's claim to a share in this convergence is a bit more tentative, perhaps only suggestive. This is of course no accident, given the traditional remoteness of the mother discipline from empirical concerns.

From the vantage point of philosophy, the core phenomenon may be given in terms of the three **modes of inference** -- also modes of knowledge: Deduction, induction and abduction. From the vantage point of linguistics, the phenomenon has been described more recently in terms of the process of **grammaticalization**, i.e. the rise of grammatical structure as an instrument of language processing. From the vantage point of psychology, the phenomenon has been investigated in terms of the contrast between **attended vs. automated processing**. This latter approach also links the discussion firmly to neurology and motor behavior, perhaps eventually also to artificial intelligence.

The unifying theme here is the **routinization -- or automation --** of behavior and information processing as it is relevant not only to higher cognitive levels, but also to lower sensory-motor functions. Thus, while

*I am indebted to Morti Gernsbacher, Ray Hyman, Daniel Kahneman, Steve Keele, Mike Posner, Walter Schneider and Harry Whitaker for helpful comments and suggestions. I have also benefited from discussing an earlier version of the chapter at the University of Oregon Symposium on Attended vs. Automated Processing, November, 1986

the discussion at this juncture will focus primarily on the routinization of information processing at higher levels, one must keep in mind the enormous ramifications the subject has for behavior and information processing at all levels of biological organization. We will return to some of those broader ramifications in Chapter 10.

7.2. The philosophical tradition: Modes of inference

7.2.1. Preamble

The philosophical tradition has confined its discussion largely to two modes of inference, or **sources** of knowledge:

(a) **Deduction:** by which one infers specific instances from the general rule;

(b) **Induction:** by which one presumably discovers the general rule from a representative sample of specific instances.

In the non-pragmatic reductionist traditions of Western epistemology, there exists an obvious parallelism between deduction and the rationalist approach on the one hand, induction and the **empiricist** approach on the other. Still, complete symmetry here turns out to be somewhat of an illusion. To begin with, the Godfather of Western empiricism, Aristotle, already defined the third -- **pragmatic** -- mode of inference:

(c) **Abduction:** by which one reasons by hypothesis from instances or general rules to their wider context.

Further, several eminent exponents of inductive reasoning, among them Peirce and the 'early' Wittgenstein, have noted that induction itself depends crucially upon an irreducible element of abduction.

7.2.2. The 'early' Wittgenstein on induction and deduction

7.2.2.1. Preamble

In his *Tractatus Logico Philosophicus*, Wittgenstein makes a number of observations concerning the usefulness of the two traditional modes of inference, deduction and induction. Without explicitly outlining a third mode, he somehow manages to point out the fatal flaws of both induction and deduction, in the process laying the groundwork, perhaps unintentionally, for a pragmatic theory of information.

7.2.2.2. The limits of induction

Wittgenstein treats induction in the *Tractatus* from a fairly conservative **deductivist** point of view,[1] arguing that however many instances support the same general rule, no deductive certainty ('logical justification') can be gained from such empirical support:

"...the procedure of induction consists in accepting as true the *simplest* law that can be reconciled with our experience. This procedure, however, has no logical justification, but only a psychological one..." (1918, p. 143)

In calling the justification of inductive inference *psychological*, Wittgenstein dismisses the possibility of *systematic justification* of inductive reasoning. In that he is not alone: In the deductivist's valhalla, whatever is not 100% certain is not worthy of consideration:

"...It is a hypothesis that the sun will rise tomorrow [based on the inductive observation of repeated instances of sunrise; TG]: and this means that we do not *know* whether it will rise..." (1918, p. 143)

As we shall see in Chapter 8, a systematic justification of inductive reasoning can indeed be achieved, and it is neither *psychological* in Wittgenstein's presumed sense, nor is it *logical* in the only other sense he was willing to consider at the time. It is an open question whether Wittgenstein's *psychological* was intended to correspond to the silent pragmatic partner of inductive inference, hypothetical reasoning or abduction. Certainly, if such correspondence was intended, the term *psychological*, in the context of the *Tractatus*, suggests lowly status, an entity not worthy of serious philosophical attention.

7.2.2.3. The limits of deduction

Having disposed of induction, Wittgenstein proceeds to expose the severe limits of deductive logic as a means of transacting new information. The propositions of logic, he observes, yield either **tautologies** or **contradictions**:

---

1 We return to the same argument in Chapter 8, in the context of Popper's deductivism in the philosophy of science (Popper, 1959).

"...The propositions of logic are tautologies. Therefore the propositions of logic say nothing. (They are the analytic propositions)..." (1918, p. 121)

"...Tautologies and contradictions show that they say nothing. A tautology has no truth conditions, since it is unconditionally true; and a contradiction is true on no condition. Tautologies and contradictions lack sense..." (1918, p. 69)

Wittgenstein now zeroes in on the use of propositions to convey information. The information-theory context within which he is working is obviously the Positivist -- Russellian -- one, whereby information is about *objective reality*:

"... Tautologies and contradictions are not pictures of reality. They do not represent any possible situations. For the former admits *all* possible situations, and the latter *none*..." (1918, p. 69)

Wittgenstein next ties up the discussion of tautology and contradiction to the scale of *three* epistemic modalities (certain, possible, impossible), observing that the information-bearing proposition stands at neither extreme of the scale:

"...a tautology's truth is certain, a proposition's possible, a contradiction's impossible. Certain, possible, impossible: here we have the first indication of the *scale* that we need in the theory of probability..." (1918, pp. 69-71; emphasis is mine; TG)

While Wittgenstein's major preoccupation here is *not* information theory but rather **probability**, the two are intimately connected, as is apparent from his immediate return to semeiology:[2]

"...Tautology and contradiction are the limiting cases -- indeed the disintegration -- of the combination of signs..." (1918, p. 71)

Wittgenstein never translates his discussion from the logical terminology of *tautology vs. contradiction* to the information-theoretical context of **totally old** vs. **totally new** information. Still, one may argue that his discussion implicitly presages just that:

"...Contradiction is that common factor of propositions which *no* proposition has in common with another. Tautology is the common fac-

---

2   Indeed, Wittgenstein proceeds later on (1918, pp. 71-73) to define the range between tautology and contradiction in probabilistic terms.

tor of all propositions that have nothing in common with one another...Contradiction is the outer limit of propositions; tautology is the unsubstantial point at their center..." (1918, p. 79)

Wittgenstein's discussion may be summarized by setting up a four-way parallelism between propositional modalities, modes of inference, epistemic certainty and modes of information. In doing so, one allows for the fact that Wittgenstein collapsed together two of the Aristotelian modes -- *fact* and *possible*.[3]

(1) **Propositional modalities and modes of inference**

propositional modality	mode of inference	epistemic certainty	mode of information
tautology:	deduction	certain	presupposed
proposition:			
fact:	induction	possible (strong)	R-asserted
hypothesis:	abduction	possible (weak)	IRR-asserted
contradiction:	deduction	impossible	NEG-asserted

Wittgenstein's collapsing of the two non-deductive Aristotelian modalities (*fact* and *hypothesis*) is itself an interesting omission. It may simply be the deductivist's refusal to further discriminate between modes that attain less than 100% certainty. It certainly reflects Wittgenstein's lack of familiarity with Peirce's work on abduction. It may also suggest some intuition on Wittgenstein's part about induction containing an irreducible core of abductive reasoning. We will return to this issue further below, as well as in Chapter 8. Be that as it may, modes of inference can be correlate to **informational certainty** in a manner that recalls the discussion in Chapter 4:

(2) **Modes of inference and degree of certainty:**
"Deductive processing of information is associated with **maximum certainty**. Inductive-abductive processing of information is associated with **lower certainty**".

As we shall see further below, this correlation establishes a plausible connection between modes of inference and modes of information processing.

---

3   See Chapter 4.

7.2.3. Peirce and abduction

7.2.3.1. Abduction and hypothesis

The fact that no new knowledge can ever be obtained by deduction has of course been known before Wittgenstein. Kant's **analytic** presumably includes deduced propositions.[4] Peirce begins his discussion by observing -- much like Wittgenstein decades later -- that induction, taken by itself, does not account for the most crucial step in the process of gaining knowledge through experience. This is the step of **correlating** isolated facts, **integrating** them into a **system** of knowledge, a system within which they find their **significance.**

Peirce begins his discussion by probing into the early stages of **hypothesis formation:**

"...The first starting of a hypothesis and the entertaining of it, whether as a simple interrogation or with any degree of confidence, is an inferential step which I propose to call *abduction*... This will include a preference for any one hypothesis over others which would equally well *explain the facts*, so long as this preference is not based upon any *previous knowledge* bearing upon the truth of the hypotheses [hereby ruling out deduction; TG], nor on any *testing* of any of the hypotheses, after having admitted them on probation [hereby ruling out induction; TG]. I call all such inference by the peculiar name, **abduction**, because its legitimacy depends upon altogether different principles from those of other kinds of inference..." (1940, p. 151; emphases are mine; TG)

Peirce then goes on to observe that the hypothesis referred to here is not simply a guess that some individual facts ('propositions') are true, but rather a hypothesized **explanation** of new facts by some other, presumably known, fact(s). In other words, abduction is the necessary inferential reasoning step in explanation:

"...Long before I first classed abduction as an inference it was recognized by logicians that the operation of adopting an explanatory hypothesis -- which is just what abduction is -- was subject to certain conditions. Namely, the hypothesis cannot be admitted, even as a hypothesis, unless it be supposed that it would **account for the facts** or some of them..." (1940, p. 151; emphasis is mine; TG)

---

4   See Chapters 1, 4, above.

Peirce now sets up the abstract general form of abductive inference:

> "...The surprising fact C is observed;
> But if A were true, C would be a matter of course;
> Hence, there is a reason to suspect that A is true..."
> (1940, p. 151)

The accretion of knowledge, which necessarily demands abduction, is thus not a simple addition of isolated facts to an unstructured bin of other known facts. Rather, it involves **correlating** and **integrating** those facts into a more **general** description, i.e. in a **wider context**. The first pragmatic element of abduction is, therefore, a hypothesis concerning the existence -- and **relevance** -- of such **wider context**, within which atomic facts may be explained, receive their meaning, make sense.

Peirce next goes on to outline the intimate connection between abduction and induction. The connection is seen from three separate perspectives, which we will discuss in order.

(a) **The use of induction in hypothesis testing:**

> "...The operation of testing a hypothesis by experiment, which consists in remarking that, if it is true, observations made under certain conditions ought to have certain results, and then causing those conditions to be fulfilled, and noting the results, and, if they are favorable, extending a certain confidence to the hypothesis, I call *induction*..." (1940, p. 152)

(b) **The residual uncertainty of induction:**

> "...All induction whatever may be regarded as the inference that throughout a whole class a ratio will have about the same value that it has in a random sample of the class, provided the nature of the ratio for which the sample is to be examined is specified (or virtually specified) in advance of the examination..." (1940, p. 152)

In arguing from specific cases (partial samples) to general rule (the entire population), one can only *extend a certain confidence* to a hypothesis, but never deductively prove it. The decision when *a certain* confidence is good enough is inherently **pragmatic**, having to do with how much uncertainty one is willing to live with, what the consequences of being found wrong are, etc. This is the level of confidence dismissed by the early Wittgenstein as *psychological* (rather than *logical*).

(c) **The abductive residue of imprecise induction:**

Peirce observes that not all inductions are made in a clean experimental environment, where *units* and their *ratios* can be unambiguously *counted*. In everyday life, many inductions involve estimating the **significance** of observed characteristics, which is an abductive judgement concerning the **context** within which the observed characteristic is either more or less significant:

"...So long as the class sampled consists of units, and the ratio in question is a ratio between counts of occurrences, induction is comparatively a simple affair. But suppose we wish to test the hypothesis that a man is a Catholic priest, that is, has all the characters that are common to Catholic priests and peculiar to them. Now characters are not units, nor do they consist of units, nor can they be counted, in such a sense that one count is right and the other wrong. Characters have to be estimated according to their significance. The consequence is that there will be a certain element of guess-work in such an induction; so that I call it an *abductory induction*..." (1940, p. 152)

Peirce's argument above is rather straight-forward: Since observed properties are often non-Platonic -- non-discrete, scalar, involving similarity judgements -- induction often retains certain abductive ('pragmatic') ingredients.

7.2.3.2. Abduction, causation and teleology

The assignment of cause is simply one sub-type of explanation. A causal relation between facts can never be deduced, nor can it be induced; although certainly the process of induction -- see Peirce's description, above -- plays an important role in determining the **degree of certainty** we attach to hypotheses about causation. The reason why assigning causation involves abductive ('pragmatic') judgement is because, like other species of explanation, causation is a relationship between some facts and their **context**. One sub-species of causality involves the **functional** context of facts, associated with biological and social organisms. We will return to discuss both causal and functional explanation in Chapter 8.

7.2.3.3. Abduction, similarity and relevance

We noted in chapter 2 that a major principle via which natural -- prototype-like -- categories get organized is that of **similarity**. We noted, further, that judgements of similarity -- or **analogy** -- cannot be made on either deductive or inductive grounds. This is so because any judgement of similarity requires a hypothetical leap to determine the **appropriate context** within which two entities are said to be similar. And the determination of such **propriety** -- or **relevance** -- is in principle abductive.

7.2.4. The philosophical tradition and information processing: An interim summary

We are now in the position to summarize the discussion of the three modes of knowledge ('modes of inference') within the philosophical tradition, in a way that would clarify the relevance of this tradition to information processing. This interim summary requires the collapsing together of two of the traditional modes -- induction and abduction; we then contrast two extreme poles of information processing: **deductive** vs. **non-deductive**. We have noted ample precedent (viz Peirce and Wittgenstein) for lumping together induction and abduction. One may still propose that atomic bits of factual knowledge may be accumulated without recourse to abduction.[5] However, such atomic data cannot be integrated into a general **system** of knowledge, cannot display any **coherence** vis-a-vis a body of general knowledge, without resorting to abduction. Coherence and integration are in principle contextual, pragmatic notions. As noted in Chapter 4, the very notion of **information** is context-bound. Information accrues on a certain **background**, vis-a-vis which it receives its coherence.

Deductive and pragmatic information processing may be now contrasted as follows:

(3) **Deductive vs. pragmatic information processing**

feature	deductive mode	pragmatic mode
categories:	rigid, Platonic	flexible, Prototype
space:	discrete, uni-dimensional	continuum, multi-dimensional
context-dependence:	context-free	context-sensitive
informational certainty:	high	low
automation:	algorithmic	non-algorithmic

5   Whether such 'bits' of knowledge are at all *meaningful* remains in doubt. Their *appropriate* filing, in the right *contextual slots* of the existing knowledge-base, clearly requires *abductive* judgement. We will return to discuss this, within the context of philosophy of science, in Chapter 8.

7.3. The linguistic tradition: Grammar and modes of information processing

7.3.1. Grammatical vs. pre-grammatical speech

Quite independently of the philosophical tradition, the existence of two extreme modes of organization of natural discourse has been observed, in the context of studying the role of grammatical clues -- grammatical **morphology** and syntactic **structures** -- in language processing. It was first noted that there exists one communicative mode that seems to dispense altogether with these grammatical devices. That mode can be found most clearly in the early stages of **language acquisition**, both first and second. It had been referred to as the **simplified**, **Pidgin** or **pre-grammatical** mode. In addition to early stages of language acquisition, one may also detect some of the features of this mode in informal, colloquial, unplanned speech genres. These genres contrast, in this respect, with more formal, planned, written genres, which tend -- on a scale -- to display more reliance on grammar.[6]

In order to impart, informally, the flavor of the difference between the **grammatical** and **pre-grammatical** linguistic modes, consider the following three simulated passages, all telling the same story. The first tells it in the top-of-the-scale grammatical mode; the second renders it in the mid-scale, conversational-informal mode; the third imparts it in the rock-bottom, pre-grammatical Pidgin mode.

(3) Grammatical vs. pre-grammatical language processing modes

   a. **Fully grammaticalized ('planned') mode:**
       "...After we parted company I realized that the man you told me about was the one who stopped me on my way to work two days before and said that he thought my tie was on backwards..."

   b. **Informal-colloquial ('unplanned') mode:**
       "...Well so we part company, right? Well so right away I realize, I say to myself, why, that man, I say... well you told me about him, right? Well, it was him alright, I say, well he's the one, stopped me on my way to work, it must've been two days ago, maybe, and he told me, he said, I think your tie is on backwards..."

---

6 See initial discussion in Ochs (1979c) and Givón (1979a, ch.5); see also recapitulation in Givón (1984b).

  c. **Pre-grammatical ('pidgin') mode:**
    "...We go, right... time after, time after, you-me go, that
    time, right... me see, say me, say, hey, man, that man,
    man... you know, man, you tell me man, right... same
    man, right, same man... well same man, same, stop, way
    go work, man stop, me stop... say, say me, say... maybe
    two day, maybe one day more, same man... man stop,
    me stop, say, hey, you tie, right there, you tie man, say...
    say you tie, me tie, no good on... no good on, crook, tie
    crook, me tie, crook..."

As one can see, the pre-grammatical Pidgin mode involves the use of almost only lexical words with no morphology, few pronouns, no complex syntactic constructions, much repetition and pausing. The message
eventually comes across, halting, fractured, rudimentary. The **gradation**
implied in having an intermediate step between grammatical and pre-
grammatical modes arises from the fact that grammar has many features of morphology and syntax, and seemingly intermediate speech
modes may use -- on a graduated scale -- some of those features but not
others, in many specific combinations or overall densities.

7.3.2. Pre-grammatical rules

It would be somewhat misleading to say that the Pidgin mode follows
no grammatical rules. Rather, the rules it follows are probably the most
basic, universal, ontogenetically and phylogenetically older and, above
all, the most **iconic** in human grammar.[7] For example, in the grammar of
referent tracking,[8] the Pidgin mode adheres rather closely to both the
quantity principle and **word-order principle** correlating with referential predictability and thematic importance, discussed earlier:[9]

(5) Referential predictability and code-quantity

      <u>**most predictable referent**</u>
      zero anaphora
      pronoun
      full noun
      <u>repeated full noun</u>
      least predictable referent

---

7 See Chapter 3.
8 See Chapter 6.
9 See Chapter 6. For early second-language Pidgins see also Givón (1984b).

(6) **Referential predictability, importance, and word-order:**

"Less predictable or more important referents are pre-posed".

7.3.3. Grammar and automated processing

The pre-grammatical mode of language processing may be contrasted with the grammatical ('syntactic') mode in a number of formal as well as substantive properties:

(7) **Grammatical vs. pre-grammatical linguistic modes:**

properties	grammatical mode	pre-grammatical mode
a. **grammatical morphology**	abundant	absent
b. **syntactic constructions**	complex/ embedded	simple/ conjoined
c. **use of word-order**	grammatical (subj/obj)	pragmatic (topicality)
d. **processing speed**	fast	slow
e. **processing mode**	automated/ routinized	analytic/ attended
f. **context dependence**	lower	higher
g. **informational certainty**	high	low

Grammatical **morphology** (7a) involves, most typically, articles, gender/classifiers, case markers, pronouns/agreement, speech-act markers, tense-aspect-modality, complementizers and subordinators. Embedded syntactic **constructions** (7b) are most typically relative clauses, verb and noun complements, subordinate adverbial clauses, or transitivizing and de-transitivizing constructions. Grammatical **word-order** (7c) most typically refers to the relative position of subject, object and verb. One may refer to all these elements of grammar as **automatization clues** (7e) used in information processing via language. Processing in the absence of such clues (i.e. in the pre-grammatical mode) is relatively **slow** (7d). It is more **analytic**, demanding more **attention** (7e). When information processing is closely attended, one presumably monitors more carefully the fine shades and gradations of the **context** (7f). One may thus say that the grammatical mode is relatively more **feedback-free**, while the pre-grammatical mode is relatively more **feed-back-dependent** (7f). Finally, the more automated, grammatical mode is used in informational contexts of **high certainty**, where the applicability of the linguistic code ('rules') is **less ambiguous** (7g).

7.3.4. Routinized processing and context

One must note that biological -- and thus linguistic -- automated processing is not *entirely* context free. Rather, the dependence of automated processing upon contextual scanning is vastly reduced and **routinized**. Rather than scanning the entire contextual range for shades, degrees and fine detail, the scanner is programmed for only a few, major **processing clues**. Such clues are highly distinct, **salient**, discrete, categorial. They are located at **fixed points** of the contextual range. The scanner is sensitive to those ranges only, disregarding the rest of the range. It is also particularly sensitive to the **coding frequencies** ('modalities') of those clues, disregarding all other frequencies.

7.3.5. Interim summary

In spite of the difference in tradition and source, one can note that certain broad similarities exist between the philosophical distinction of deductive vs. pragmatic inference, and the linguistic contrast of grammatical vs. pre-grammatical information processing. These similarities can be summarized as in (8) below:

(8) **Processing modes: Interim summary**

	deductive/automated processing	pragmatic/analytic processing
a.	fast	slow
b.	algorithmic/automated	non-algorithmic/analytic
c.	depends on rigid categories/ structures	dispenses with rigid categories/structures
d.	context-free	context- dependent
e.	high certainty	low certainty

In the following section we will see how a substantially similar distinction emerges from the empirical study of information processing in perception, cognition, motor behavior and neurology.

7.4. The psychological tradition: Attended vs. automated processing

7.4.1. Preamble

A general summary of the contrast between attended and automated processing, a contrast that crops up in widely differing performance domains of perception, cognition, motor control and neurology, is given in Schneider (1985):

"...Consider, for example, the changes that occur while learning to type. At first, effort and attention are devoted to the smaller movement or minor decision, and performance is **slow** and **error-prone**. After extensive training, long sequences of movements or cognitive processes are carried out with little attention... *Controlled processing* is characterized as a slow, generally serial, effortful, capacity-limited, subject-controlled processing mode that must be used to deal with **novel** or **inconsistent** information... *Automatic processing* is a fast, parallel, fairly effortless process that is not limited by short-term memory capacity, is not under direct subject control, and performs well-developed skilled behavior..." (pp. 475-476; emphases are mine; TG)

In this section we will briefly survey the literature on this contrast in cognitive psychology, kinesiology and neurology.

7.4.2. Cognitive psychology: Perception, Memory and attention

7.4.2.1. Consciousness vs. automation

In their review on the role of attention (or 'consciousness') in perception, memory and retrieval, Posner and Warren (1972)[10] recapitulate the experimental psychological literature that led to positing the contrast between **automated encoding** and **conscious processing**. They write:

"...How can we study automatic processes as distinguished from those that involve conscious search? Even the definition of "automatic" is a difficult matter... Our effort to analyze this problem has involve the notion of a **single limited-capacity central processing system** that integrates signals from all modalities. When this system is occupied by any signal, its capacity is reduced for dealing with any other signals or mental operations that require its use... Many complex mental operations that are learned and that require time can be performed **outside** this system... For our purpose, the use of this system becomes the central definition of a "conscious process", and its non-use defines what is meant by "automatic"..." (1972, p. 34)

The following general features seem to distinguish automated from conscious/attended processing:

(9) **Properties of automated processing:**

    (a) **Informational certainty:**
        Automate processing is associated with **repeated, rehearsed** tasks, or with **expert skills** acquired through **habitual** performance. It thus involves the processing of highly **routinized, conventionalized** activities. In terms of information theory, the automation of processing occurs when information is more **predictable, certain, consistent.**

---

10 Other studies involved in motivating and elucidating the distinction between automated/unattended and conscious/attended processing in experimental psychology include: Attneave (1957), Bartlett (1932), Broadbent (1958), Frost (1971a,b), Hawkins (1969), Hintzman (1970), Keele (1969, 1972), Posner (1969), Posner and Boies (1971), Posner and Keele (1968), Posner and Klein (1971), Posner and Marin (eds, 1985), Posner and Snyder (1974), Schneider (1985), Schneider and Fisk (1983), Schneider and Shiffrin (1977), *inter alia.*

(b)   **Processing speed and error:**
Automated processing is more **rapid** and **error** free. Conscious processing is **slow** and more **error-prone.**

(c)   **Memory file:**
Automated processing tends to be associated with **short term memory.** Conscious processing tends to be associated with **long term memory.**

(d)   **Categories and structures:**
Automated processing relies heavily on the presence of rigid **structures** or **schemata,** thus implicitly on rigid, discrete **categories.**

(e)   **Limiting capacity:**
Several automated tasks can be processed **in parallel.** In contrast, conscious processing seems to be **linear,** relying on a **limiting capacity** that occupies the central processor for a particular slot of time.

Concerning the critical role of **certainty** or **conventionalization** (9a), Posner and Warren (1972) cite studies showing that memory is distorted systematically toward habituated, conventionalized knowledge:

"...memory is often distorted in the direction of convention... Frost (1971a) found recognition errors to be in the direction of orientation most *frequent* or *conventional*... (p. 30; emphases are mine; TG)

7.4.2.2. **Levels of consciousness and automaticity**

The discussion thus far distinguished only between two levels of processing, attended ('conscious') vs. automated. Several recent studies suggest that this extreme dichotomy must be revised, perhaps yielding a scale of **degree of conscious processing,** thus also it converse, **degree of automaticity.** Thus, for example, Posner (1985) cites experimental evidence that points toward the existence of more than one level of visual attention. The modality-independent *highest* ('central') level may simply occupy the very top of a **hierarchic network** of progressively less conscious, less central and more task-specific levels of effortful processing.

In another recent study by Nissen and Bullemer (1986),[11] the performance of aphasic and normal subjects in memorizing random vs. struc-

---

11 See also Cohen and Squire (1980), Squire and Cohen (1984), Mishkin et al (1984), *inter alia.*

tured digit sequences was compared. The results suggested a similar hierarchic array of **levels of attention**. Learning tasks that clearly involved automation nonetheless required some **type** of attention; this was shown by the fact that such learning tasks were interfered with by attention-demanding secondary probe tasks. Further, the level of attention that was involved in these routinized-learning tasks was shown to be distinct from the 'highest' level of conscious attention. Aphasic subjects, who could neither remember learning the primary task nor consciously report its regularities, nevertheless displayed -- qualitatively -- the same repetition-induced learning curve as normal subjects. We will return to this issue further below.

7.4.3. **Kinesiology and motor skills**

A very similar picture emerges in the study of the acquisition of motor skills. In reviewing the literature within the context of **schema theory**, Shapiro and Schmidt (1980)[12] note the role of **repetition** in facilitating the acquisition of motor skills. The routinization of motor skills involves, accordingly, the creation of rigid, complex **generalized schemata** that guide performance along habituated pathways. Skilled, routinized ('schematized') performance is **less conscious** and **non-analytic**; it proceeds **faster**, and allows **parallel processing** of other tasks.

An interesting parallel with the development of language is the existence of some **critical period** in the development of motor schemata:

"...schema development occurs much more easily in children than it does in adults..." (Shapiro & Schmidt, 1980, p. 17 of ms).

It is certainly true that the acquisition of grammar proceeds faster and more completely in children than in adults. There is, thus, some critical period phenomenon in the acquisition of routinized language processing.[13]

Shapiro and Schmidt also note that some components in the acquisition of motor skills, specifically the learning of **novel tasks**, are not schema-governed. Rather, they require consciousness, analysis and decision:

---

12 See there for a general review of the literature; see also discussion in Denier and Thuring (1965), Grillner (1975), Herman *et al* (eds, 1976), Schmidt (1975), Shapiro *et al* (1980), Whiting *et al* (1980), *inter alia*. The literature on the routinization ('automation') of motor behavior covers a wide range of acquired physical skills, including locomotion, piano playing, dance, writing and typing, athletics, etc. It also covers a large range of human, mammal, vertebrate and invertebrate subjects.
13 See for example Ascher and Garcia (1969), Curtiss (1977), Ervin-Tripp (1974), Krashen (1972), Krashen *et al* (1979), *inter alia*.

"...the learning in the motor-learning experiment can be regarded as the discovery of the size of the value to be added to the parameters [of the schema; TG] in order to make the program "work" *in this particular situation*. That learning should, however, be *situation-specific* as opposed to the schema learning which should be general across all uses of the generalized motor program..." (1980, p. 45 of ms).

The issue of conscious ('feedback-dependent') vs. programmed ('feedback-free') learning, is also tackled in two studies by Shapiro (1977, 1978). Schmidt (1980) summarizes those as follows:

"...There is some evidence that if the movement is very long in duration (i.e. 1-2 sec), one could control the action with a *program* set up in advance, or alternatively by *processing the feedback* from each sub-action and making corrective steps..." (p. 125; emphases are mine; TG)

7.4.4. Neurological aspects of automated processing

7.4.4.1. Routinization learning

In a recent review, Schneider (1985) discusses the neurological coding correlates of the contrast between attended ('controlled') and automated processing. He first describes the neurology of information transmission:

"...Cortical information transmission occurs when a population of neurons (e.g. a hyper-column) sends a set of *firing rates* (e.g. a vector of activation) to another population. This set of the firing rates of the output neurons can be *modulated* as a set ... (Szentagothai, 1977)... Learning in the physical system occurs after this set of firing rates *comes into a population* and a *second burst* is output (Levy and Steward, 1983)..." (p. 477; emphases are mine; TG)

Schneider next outlines an information-flow model that integrates the neurological and the performance findings:

"...Communication theory provides optimality considerations regarding how best to allocate transmission time in a network of vector transmission units (see van der Meulen, 1977). Communication theory theorems indicate that if the brain optimally processes information, there should be two modes of transmission: a *serial*, time-sharing, control-process-type mode, and a *parallel*, automatic-process-type mode..." (1985, p. 477; emphases are mine; TG)

A formal model is now described:

"...In the model, controlled processing is conceived of as a *limited central-processing* mechanism that *gates* the transmission of messages between units and compares the received messages. The development of automatic processing is the result of two types of learning. The first, *associative learning*, is the mechanism by which one message is associatively translated to another message. The second type of learning, *priority learning*, is the mechanism by which a unit determines how strongly to transmit a message. The unit-specific message priority determines the *strength* of the automatic message transmission. Automatic processing occurs when priority and associative learning are sufficiently advanced to allow a sequence of transmissions without any controlled-process gating the information..." (1985, p. 477)

If one may attempt a paraphrase, the *gating* function of consciousness is a higher **traffic-control** function; it allocates information-flow priorities at branching nodes where ambiguities -- i.e. potential flow-conflicts -- are possible. The *associative* component of routinization is presumably the process by which repetition of 'similar' information in a 'similar' context creates an association between the information and its context (say, in the most minimal term, the preceding or following chunks of information). Finally, the *priority* component of routinization is an automatized replacement of the 'gating' function of the erstwhile conscious processing. Once processing is automated, all the competing branches at a (potentially-ambiguous) node are assigned fixed **firing strengths**, in effect thus ranking them in terms of relative **priority**, perhaps also in **fixed transmission order**.

The learning process that gives rise to routinized processing presumably thus involves the creation of firmed-up, relatively rigid neural pathways. They are created through experience during the lifetime of the organism, and they may persist for the duration of that lifetime.

7.4.4.2. Genetically determined routinization

There are some indications that some of the routinization that occurs during the lifetime of the organism is not wholly experience-triggered, but at least in part **wired in**, thus presumably triggered automatically by the process of neurological maturation. Thus, reflexive, uncontrolled, clearly routinized early ambulation movement of human neonates is reported[14] to first display a *four-legged* movement pattern, long before any crawling experience has taken place. Later on, a pattern of *bi-pedal* movement is manifest, again prior to any actual walking experience.

14 See Thelen (1984), also Fossberg's (1985) interpretation of Thelen's findings. Similar findings in other mammals are summarized in Smith (1980).

One must note that information flow in many major *lower* physiological functions of organisms, including the control of the digestive, eliminatory, cardio-vascular and pulmonary functions, as well as in many *reflexive* sensory and motor functions, is automated from birth, i.e. genetically pre-programmed.[15] A major feature of such reflexive systems is that the tasks they perform are highly **repetitive, predictable;** thus, the degree of informational **certainty** in these processing systems is very high. It is reasonable to assume that such automation of processing -- which I propose to call **phylogenetic learning** -- evolved biologically under the same adaptive constraint that motivate routinization-learning during the life-time of the organism -- i.e. **ontogenetic learning.** More specifically, one may suggest that:[16]

(a) The general correlation between automation and repetition ('predictability') of information holds for both the ontogenetic and phylogenetic routinization-learning; and

(b) There is an obvious -- tough yet to be elucidated -- correlation between the ontogenetic and phylogenetic processes of routinization-learning.

We will return to discuss these suggestions in section 7.5.3., as well as in Chapter 10.

7.5. The rise and function of automated processing

7.5.1. Properties of automated processing: Interim summary

As we have seen in the preceding sections, a number of identifiable common threads emerge from the comparative study of the automation of processing in language, cognition, perception, motor behavior and neurology. One may summarize these common threads as follows:

(9) **Properties of automated processing:**

(a) **Conscious control:** Automated processing is less monitored, thus less controlled, by analytic consciousness.
(b) **Channel properties:** Automated processing allows non-interfering, multi-channel, parallel processing.

15 See more recent summaries in Smith (1980), Grillner (1975), Gurfinkel & Shik (1977), Stein (1978), as well as older reviews in Paillard (1960) or Galambov & Morgan (1960), *inter alia.*
16 Mishkin *et al* (1984) raise a superficially similar suggestion that turns, on close inspection, to presuppose a very different evolutionary mechanism. See further discussion in section 7.5.3., below.

(c) **Modal specificity**: Automated processing tends to involve more specialized, modality-specific sub-systems.
(d) **Processing speed**: Automated processing is faster.
(e) **Categorial structure**: Automated processing subsumes the development of rigid, discrete categories, as well as structures (i.e. configurations of categories), which presumably act as the automated processing clues.
(f) **Context dependence**: Automated processing is less context dependent; it is thus, relatively, a feedback-independent, non-monitoring mode of information processing.
(g) **Informational predictability**: Automated processing arises under conditions of repetition, habituation, conventionality, routine; it thus involves higher informational predictability.

7.5.2. The functional motivation for automated processing

7.5.2.1. The adaptive tradeoff

The functional context within which automated processing develops, either ontogenetically or phylogenetically, can be described as an **adaptive tradeoff** between three of the properties listed in (9) above:
  (a) conscious control
  (d) processing speed; and
  (g) informational predictability
The other dimensions, and their mode of involvement, are to quite an extent predictable within the context of this tradeoff:

  (i) **Automated processing**:

  Repeated, **predictable** tasks are the only ones that *can* be routinized. Routinization is the *means* for increasing processing speed. Structurally, routinization is achieved via the buildup of discrete, **categorial structures** that act as a network of automated **flow-control cues**. Such automation procedure may be also called an **algorithm**. (Deductive logic is an extreme case of the latter). When central, conscious monitoring is *not* required, **parallel processing** of several automated tasks, each of them **modal-specific**, can take place. Parallel processing is another contributor to increasing processing speed, i.e. an increase in the **economy** of the overall processing system.

(ii) **Attended processing:**

> Conversely, attended processing is reserved for tasks that are **novel**, less repetitive, less predictable. Such tasks require analytic monitoring of shades and gradations of the **context**. Rigid categorial structure *cannot* be built up in such a processing system, since it would sacrifice context-dependent flexibility. Processing speed cannot be built up either, presumably because it would create an unacceptable increase in **error** in monitoring the context. Detailed, non-discrete monitoring is necessarily slow.

In sum, the **adaptive tradeoff** is between conscious, detailed contextual scan and processing speed. The controlling feature is the degree of predictability of the task.

7.5.2.2. Task urgency, predictability and economy

One may describe the pivotal role of predictability in determining processing tasks that will eventually be automated as a manifestation of a biological principle of **economy**. Routinization itself incurs certain costs, associated with the building of the requisite rigid structures. These costs are not justified unless the processing system is used relatively frequently. But under certain adaptive condition this principle of economy can be, and often is, suspended. Thus, for example, hair-trigger response to potential predators is presumably an automated, speedy process, *regardless* of the level informational certainty. In processing such **urgent** survival tasks, the organism presumably biases the automated cues toward a greater **margin of safety**, while sacrificing economy. When survival is less of an issue, normal economy considerations -- manifest in the routinization of frequent, repetitive, predictable tasks -- presumably govern more directly the tradeoff between speed and consciousness.

7.5.2.3. The automaticity continuum

Whenever the processing of some repeated, predictable tasks is automated, consciousness retains higher **governing functions**: Overall flow control, context-dependent monitoring, subtle contingent choices, goal-governed priority assignment. As suggested earlier, however, the contrast between conscious and automated processing is not a single discrete division, but rather a hierarchic, multi-level, scale. The allocation of monitoring consciousness works through this hierarchy in a bottom-up fashion. That is, the *highest* level of attention is assigned to the highest node in the hierarchy. Such a node governs tasks that are *least* automated, being least predictable. Relatively lower levels of attention are assigned to more predictable, thus more automated, task-nodes. Schneider's (1985) gradualistic model of the **process** of routinization-learning is, I believe, rather compatible with this hierarchic, bottom-up model.[17]

7.5.3. Evolutionary aspects of automated processing

7.5.3.1. Rise of consciousness vs. rise of automation

As suggested earlier above, both the ontogenetic and comparative-distributional facts of automated vs. attended processes fairly beg for an integrated behavioral-evolutionary-developmental approach. A stab at this was made by Mishkin *et al* (1984), suggesting that automated processing is phylogenetically *prior* to consciousness, i.e. that the rise of conscious, attended processing is a later evolutionary step. There are a number of reasons why I think this proposal is rather unattractive:

(a) Such an approach implies that information processing in lower organisms is *not* subject to the same adaptive constraints that seem to govern the rise of automated processing elsewhere (i.e. the adaptive tradeoff between consciousness, predictability and speed). This would create an **evolutionary discontinuity** between information processing in pre-conscious vs. conscious organisms, a rather implausible state of affairs.[18]

(b) Such an approach would dissociated the **ontogenesis** of routinization-learning (i.e. automation during the lifetime of individual organisms) from the **evolutionary** process. The latter is described by Mishkin *et al* (1984) as proceeding in exactly the *opposite* direction of the former. Given the high degree of shared directionality between ontogenesis and phylogenesis in general, perhaps even downright partial **recapitulation**,[19] such dissociation is highly unlikely.

---

17 See in particular Schneider's (1985) discussion of *optimization*. In its general outline, this from-the-bottom-up formulation is compatible with the one suggested by Broadbent (1977), whereby the bottom-up development of automaticity is said to involve the gradual adjustment of parameters to the values that were first determined by conscious monitoring. McLeod *et al* (1985) envision a similar gradual process, which they call *encapsulation* of information.
18 See discussion in Chapter 10.
19 See Gould (1977), as well as Chapter 10.

7.5.3.2. **Pre-conditions for routinization:** **Taxonomy and frequency of experience**

An alternative approach to the evolution of automaticity would insist that the earliest mode of information processing at whatever level is -- and has always been -- the attended, conscious mode. This is so because at the very beginning of the organization -- or processing -- of experience, all input is by definition **novel** (with the obvious exception of genetically-coded automated processes that are themselves the product of earlier phylogenetic evolution). **Repetition** of experience in turn instigates in the organism two separate but related processes, the first an absolute *pre-condition* for the second, and both pre-conditions for routinization:

(a) **Taxonomic categorization:**
The organism must classify, by whatever means, individual data ('instances') of experience as to whether they will count as different tokens of **the same type,** or tokens of **a different type,** of experience. As noted in Chapters 1, 2, such taxonomic decisions are made, in principle, on pragmatic, context-dependent grounds.

(b) **Frequency determination:**
Once individual tokens of experience are classified into types, it is possible to determine which **types** of experience are more repetitive, predictable, thus candidates for routinization, and which ones are novel and unpredictable, thus to be processed under conscious control.

A taxonomy of experience (a) and a frequency determination applied to the resulting taxa (b) are two key preconditions for the automation of information processing.

7.5.3.3. **Bottom-up routinization**

As the taxonomic-hierarchic organization of repeated experience proceeds gradually **from the bottom up,** so does routinization. In this fashion, today's higher node that require conscious monitoring may in time becomes tomorrow's repeating, predictable, newly-routinized node -- but a node at a **higher level,** representing **more complex** experience. The role of conscious monitoring is, in this fashion, **pushed upward** progressively. As this upward move proceeds, the nature of consciousness -- thus of *mind* -- becomes increasingly more complex. Yet all along, consciousness retains essentially the same functions:

(a) Monitoring experience types that are least repetitive, least predictable, least categorizable;
(b) monitoring shades and gradations of **context;**
(c) monitoring the **higher controlling nodes** ('gates') of parallel-processed information, whose bulk is handled more routinely at lower, task-specific (or 'modality-specific') nodes; and thus
(d) allocating **purpose-mediated** priorities among lower processing channels.

Hierarchically-lower levels of attention, however many of those there might be,[20] perform the same monitoring functions **downward.**

7.5.3.4. The biological unity of automation

The bottom-up developmental model should be equally valid for describing the rise of automated processing at all three levels of its development:

(a) **Routinized-learning** during the life-time of individuals;
(b) The **ontogenetic sequence** routinization during the embryo's maturation;
(c) The **phylogenetic evolution** of routinized processing.

The tantalizing possibility of a causal interaction among these three levels remained a key issue of evolutionary thinking. First, a possible interaction between levels (a) and (c) is at the crux of the old **Lamarckian** argument. Second, a connection between (b) and (c) is at the crux of **recapitulationism.** We will return to both issues in chapter 10, below.

7.5.3.5. Linguistic parallelisms

It is, lastly, of interest to note that the parallelism between the three biological levels -- individual behavior, ontogenesis and phylogenesis -- is also suggested for the development of **grammatical processing** in human language. It has been suggested[21] that the process of **grammaticalization,** via which grammatical morphology and syntactic constructions evolve, follows substantially the same route in four domains:

(a) language behavior by individuals
(b) historical change of the communal language
(c) the child's acquisition of grammar
(c) the evolution of grammar in the human species

20 See section 7.4.2.2., above, as well as footnote 17.
21 See Givón (1979a, chs 5,7) as well as Bickerton (forthcoming).

If this parallelism is valid, it may reinforce the view that the development of grammar, as a mode of information processing, is another instance of the bottom-up shift from attended to automated processing.

7.6. Some experimental evidence on grammar as an automated language processing mode

We return now to discuss grammar as an automated system of language processing, as outlined in section 7.3., above. The validity of this view of grammar is supported strongly, if indirectly, by the striking parallelism between the parameters that govern grammaticalized vs. pre-grammatical speech, on the one hand, and automated vs. attended processing, on the other. In this section we will survey the results of a series of experiments dealing with referential tracking in discourse, more specifically with the use of anaphoric pronouns vs. definite nouns. As noted in Chapter 6, anaphoric pronouns (and zero anaphora) are used in discourse contexts of **high predictability**. In contrast, definite nouns are used in discourse context of lower predictability. We may illustrate this by reproducing here the text-distribution of the **referential distance** measure (RD; the gap between the last previous mention of the antecedent in discourse) for anaphoric pronoun and definite nouns:[22]

(10) **Distribution of referential distance (RD) of anaphoric pronouns and definite nouns in spoken English narrative (from Givón, 1983b)**

RD in # of clauses	pronouns		DEF-nouns	
	n	%	n	%
1-2	499	86.2	54	26.7
3-8	31	5.7	36	17.8
9-14	8	1.4	17	8.4
15-19	2	0.3	6	2.9
20+	1	0.1	89	43.9
total:	541	100.0	202	100.0
median RD	1.0		12.0	

The median RD value for pronouns is 1.0 clauses to the left. What is more, this median value is highly stereotypical of the pronoun population: 86% of the population conforms to that stereotype. In contrast, the median RD value for definite nouns is 12.0 clauses to the left; and the

22 See discussion in Ch. 6.

population is widely scattered over the scale, with 43.9% not even showing antecedent in the preceding discourse (RD = 20+). This is a much less stereotyped population, so far as both *distance* and *source* of coreference are concerned.

In a series of experiments, the effect of referential distance on the amount of attention (or 'mental effort') expended during the processing of anaphoric pronouns and definite nouns was investigated.[23] Written passages were presented visually on a computer screen, with the subjects releasing successive words at their own reading pace, by pressing a lever. A secondary visual-probe task was flashed on the screen, above the primary text, during the presentation of anaphoric pronouns and definite nouns. The subjects were asked to react to that secondary probe by pushing a second key. Both anaphoric expressions occurred at referential distances of 1-clause and 12-clause from their antecedents in the text. The *probe reaction times* (probe RT) and *word-release times* (key-press time) -- both in the presence of the secondary probe -- were measured. Typical text-frames used in this experiment were, for example:

(11)   a.   **1-clause RD opening:**
           "**THE WOMAN** waited patiently near the counter. The shop was almost empty, nobody seemed to notice her."

       b.   **12-clause RD filler:**
           "[(10a) above, plus:]...It was a large store with many departments spread along the cavernous floor space of three main levels. The time was early in the afternoon on a Monday in late spring, and nobody seemed to be moving around. On weekends the store was always packed with hoards of bargain hunters milling in the aisles, holding sale coupons in hand, and craning their necks in search of the special deal that was somehow always two counters away, or so it seemed."

       c.   **Ending:**
           "...**SHE/THE WOMAN** took out her compact and touched up her hair."

From purely general consideration of memory decay, one would expect a *direct* correlation between referential distance and measured probe RTs. But in fact, the correlation turned out to be direct only for pronouns, but *inverse* for definite nouns, as can be seen from the results, summarized in (12) below:

---

23 Givón, Kellogg, Posner and Yee (1985).

(11) **Probe reaction time as function of referential distance for anaphoric pronouns and DEF-noun** (from Givón, Kellogg, Posner & Yee, 1985)

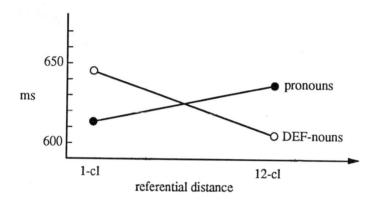

The results suggest a grammar-specific effect: Anaphoric pronouns are processed more efficiently at the minimal referential distance (RD = 1), the one that corresponds to their median, stereotypical value. They lose processing efficacy -- i.e. require more attention to process -- at the higher RD. In contrast, definite nouns are processed less efficiently at the minimal RD value, but gain processing efficacy -- i.e. require less mental effort -- at the higher RD value, the one that corresponds more closely to their median (though not stereotypical) value (RD = 12). One may propose that anaphoric pronouns as grammatical cues automate the speech perceiver's reaction toward expecting a **short-distance memory search** for co-reference. Definite nouns, on the other hand, automate the perceiver's reaction toward a rather different search.

In a related experiment, the word-release ('key-press') times for pronouns and definite nouns were compared (all in the presence of the secondary probe), at both 1-clause and 5-clause RD values. The results are presented below. The key-press values for the probed word (pronoun or DEF-noun), as well as for the two words preceding and following it in the text, are given in (12) on the following page.

(12) **Mean key-press times for anaphoric pronouns and DEF-nouns at 1 and 5-clause RD** (from Givón, Kellogg, Posner and Yee, 1985)

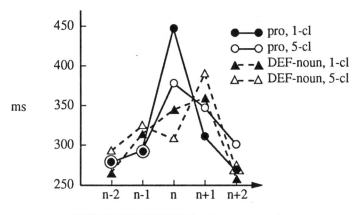

WORD MEASURED (probe target = n)

The results for pronouns, at both RDs, reveal the presence of a processing peak ('processing slow-down') on the probed word. In contrast, for definite nouns that processing peak was *delayed* until the next word (n+1).

Since the results can be merely due to the phonological length difference between nouns and pronouns, another experiment was designed to compare the key-press times, at 1-clause RD, for *indefinite* nouns and two types of DEF-nouns: (a) *anaphoric* DEF-nouns (as in (11) above; i.e. with explicit discourse antecedent); and (b) *thematic* DEF-nouns (i.e. ones without explicit discourse antecedence). The latter share a feature with indefinites: They appears *in the text* for the first time. To illustrate these categories, consider the following alternative ending to the department-store frame in (11) above, where (13) below represents the two new optional endings (in addition to (11c)):

(13) **Indefinite and Thematic-definite endings:**
"A/THE SALESMAN" finally came over and asked her what
she was looking for".

'The Salesman' in (13) is thematically predictable from the conventionalized department-store frame ('script').[24] The results of the last experiment are given in (14) below.

(14) **Mean key-press times for INDEF, anaphoric-DEF and thematic-DEF nouns at 1-clause RD** (from Givón, Kellogg, Posner and Yee, 1985)

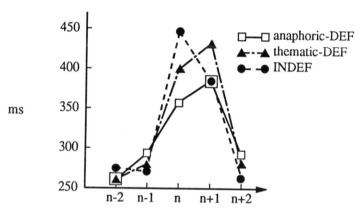

WORD MEASURED (probe target = n)

The results may be summed up as follows:
(i) The *delayed processing-peak* effect observed first in (12) is not a function of the larger phonological size of nouns, since indefinite nouns do not display this effect.
(ii) Definite nouns display the delayed processing-peak effect regardless of whether their source is *anaphoric* or *thematic*.

24 See discussion in Chapter 6, above.

The explanation tentatively suggested in the original study makes use of the notion of grammar as an automated processing device. It runs as follows:

(a) Pronouns are an unambiguous processing clue, instructing the speech perceiver to search for a co-referent within a highly **stereotyped** memory range -- 1 clause back;

(b) Indefinite nouns are equally unambiguous, instructing the perceiver to proceed and[25]
   (i) Open a new referent file; and
   (ii) Not search memory files for coreference.

(c) In contrast, definite nouns are a highly **ambiguous** clue as to the **source** of shared knowledge. As noted in Chapter 6, definiteness may arise **anaphorically** (i.e. the presence of an antecedent co-referent within the prior text); it may arise from **discourse-thematic** knowledge (which usually displays some generic elements); or it may arise from **generic** shared knowledge. The one-word delay in the processing-peak observed in our experiments may represent the processing time allotted for a decision about the **source** ('file') of the definiteness of the noun. Once that determination is made, the appropriate memory-file is then searched, resulting in the characteristic slow-down effect of processing.

The experimental study of grammar as an automated language-processing device is still in its infancy. The results of experiments such as the ones cited above are preliminary and tentative. The general properties of grammatical vs. pre-grammatical speech, and the study of the contexts under which they occur, strongly suggest that grammar is indeed a *partly* automated processing system.[26]

---

25 As noted in Chapter 5, above, the grammar of indefinites presents another set of grammatical clues that automate referential processing. Those clues flag a new referent in the discourse by a special marker when it demands **more attention**. An experimental study of the processing of indefinites is now under way.

26 For a similar approach to grammar, with extensive neurological and evolutionary support, see Lieberman (1984).

CHAPTER 8

FACT, LOGIC AND METHOD: THE PRAGMATICS OF SCIENCE

8.1. Introduction*

8.1.1. Epistemology and organized science

In this chapter we return to consider the role of the three modes of inference -- deduction, induction and abduction -- in the acquisition, integration and interpretation of new knowledge. This time, however what is at issue is not information processing by the biological organism (i.e. the mind), but rather information processing by the scientist. In the course of our survey, we will make two -- essentially empirical -- observations concerning some striking parallels. The first is *epistemological:*

(a) The information-processing behavior of organized science strongly parallels that of the organism ('mind').

The second parallel, itself peculiarly isomorphic to the first, is *historical*:

(b) The array of traditional philosophical positions in the philosophy of science essentially recapitulates the array of traditional positions in epistemology.

In terms of parallel (a), **abductive-contextual reasoning** is the key to the scientist's extension of aggregate cultural knowledge, much like it was shown to be the key to the organism's ability to process new information. In terms of parallel (b), the discrete cleavage between the two extreme reductionist schools in epistemology -- rationalism and empiricism -- is echoed faithfully in the split between rigid **deductivism** and rigid **inductivism**, respectively, in the philosophy of science. And, in both epistemol-

*I am indebted to Henning Andersen, T.K. Bikson, Robert Nola, Paul Otto, Frank Schroeck and Martin Tweedale for many helpful comments on an early version of this chapter. I have also benefitted from the opportunity to present earlier versions at the Cognitive Science Colloquium, University of Oregon (November 1986), the Pragmatics Workshop, Roskilde University (May 1987), and the Colloquium of the Institute for Theoretical Physics, University of Köln (June 1987).

ogy and science, it appears, untenable reductionist positions resolve towards the **pragmatic middle ground**; that is, through understanding the role of abductive-contextual reasoning in information processing.

8.1.2. The legacy of reductionism

In his *Logic of Scientific Discovery*, Karl Popper makes the following observation concerning the polarization of the philosophy of science, an observation prompted in large measure by Wittgenstein's *Tractatus*:

> "...The positivist dislikes the idea that there should be meaningful problems outside the field of 'positive' empirical science -- problems to be dealt with by genuine philosophical theory. He dislikes the idea that there should be a genuine theory of knowledge, an epistemology or a methodology*...
>
> *In the two years before the first publication of this book, it was the standing criticism raised by members of the Vienna Circle against my idea that a theory of method which was neither an empirical science nor pure logic was impossible: What was outside of these two fields was sheer nonsense..."
>
> (1959, p. 51; emphases are mine; TG)

Popper's complaint, while directed explicitly at the *positivists*, can be read nonetheless as a broader objection to the reductionist view of truth and knowledge. That view conceded legitimacy to only two of Kant's modes of truth (analytic and synthetic), arrived at via only two modes of inference (deduction and induction, respectively).

Reductionism, as attractive as it may seem to the purist, turns out to be both philosophically bankrupt and methodologically unrealistic. Extremists of both philosophical stripes, as Popper demonstrates repeatedly in his own corner of the field, are quite capable of debunking each others' folly. They do so with insight, eloquence and, above all, with remarkable gusto. What remains to be done then, once the dust has cleared, is to constructively identify the many points in the complex process of empirical science where pragmatic reasoning is relevant, indeed indispensable.

8.1.3. What is an apt paradigm-metaphor for behavioral and cognitive science?

One of the most persistent legacies of earlier discussions in the philosophy of science is a strong preference for physics as the paradigm discipline. Given the relatively clean, formal, law-like nature of generalizations in physics (as compared to the rather messy study of biology and behavior), such early preference may have been historically justified. In large measure, however, it also bears some historical -- though not necessarily logical -- responsibility for the persistence of extreme reductionism in the philosophy of science. It is only in a science as abstract and formalizable as physics that the role of non-deductive, non-inductive methods could ever be ignored. The methods of the more 'messy' sciences, such as biology, psychology or linguistics, are much harder to reduce into a clean deductive-inductive dichotomy. In such empirical disciplines, generalizations are less law-like; they often involve complex multi-variable interactions; 'laws' are almost always mediated by protracted evolution, ontogenetic development or historical change, all of which tend to exhibit some **off-equilibrium transition phases.** During such phases, the connectivity between individual facts -- even when those facts would ultimately prove to possess strong causal links -- is less than perfect, often less than obvious. Such evolutionary, developmental or historical process are, in turn, governed by the **functional-adaptive** behavior of an entire population. And such behavior is in turn the product of the **teleology** of individual organisms. Thus, while the argument for the indispensability of pragmatics as method applies to science in general, it applies in spades to the bio-behavioral disciplines.

8.2. Reductionism in the philosophy of science

8.2.1. Theory vs. practice in science

"...I think there is a moral to this story, namely, that it is more important to have beauty in one's equations than to have them fit experiment..."

> P.A.M. Dirac (commenting on the history of Schrodinger's wave equations; cited in Bach, 1965, pp. 113-114)

"...the best and safest method of philosophizing [doing science]...seems to be, first to inquire diligently into the properties of things, and of establishing these properties by experiment, and then to proceed more slowly to hypotheses [theories] for the explanation of them..."

> Isaac Newton (commenting on his own work; cited in Andrade, 1954, p. 64)

It is much easier to find clear-cut examples of either extreme deductivism or extreme inductivism in the pronouncements of philosophers of science, than in the work of practicing scientists. The two quotations above, from eminent physicists, represent reflective positions rather than empirical practice. So-called **naturalistic** accounts of science may yet succeed in untangling the two. Such accounts seem to emanate from two distinct sources. First, the positivists suggested a 'naturalistic' account, in an attempt to make the study of methodology itself *empirical*. Here is how Popper (1959) views their endeavor:

"...only two kinds of statements exist for them: logical tautologies and empirical statements. If methodology is not logic, then, they will conclude, it must be a branch of some science -- the science, say, of *the behavior of scientists at work*..." (1959, p. 52; emphases are mine; TG)

Second, Kuhn's (1962) *socio-historical* account is also 'naturalistic' in Popper's sense. Popper is considerably more benign in his comments here, at least implicitly:

"...I am quite ready to admit that there is a need for a purely logical analysis of theories, for an analysis which takes no account of how they *change* and *develop*. But this kind of analysis does not elucidate those aspects of empirical science which I, for one, so highly prize..." (1959, p. 50; emphases are mine; TG).

Nola (1986) has recently pointed out that Popper himself has advocated at various times either an **apriori-conventionalist** (Nola's 'rule-conventionalist')[1] approach to methodology, or an **empirically-based** (Popper's 'naturalistic') approach. The first is of course embedded in Popper's (1959) central argument: Methodology is a set of *conventions*

---

1   Popper also identifies another *conventionalist* approach, one he ascribes variously to Poincaré and Duhem, H. Dingler, Cornelius, Ajdukiewicz and Carnap. Nola (1986) calls this 'methodological conventionalism'. Popper opposes it vigorously as an attempt to solve the problem of induction, an attempt to debunk his falsificationist approach to methodology, as well as a stratagem: "...I regard conventionalism as a system which is self-contained and defensible. Attempts to detect inconsistencies in it are not likely to succeed. Yet in spite of all this I find it quite unacceptable. Underlying it is an idea of science, of its aims and purpose, which are entirely different from mine. I do not demand any final certainty from science (and consequently do not get it); the conventionalist seeks in science 'a system of knowledge based on ultimate grounds', to use a phrase of Dingler. This goal is attainable; for it is possible to interpret any given scientific system as a system of implicit definitions..." (1959, p. 80). A similar, formal conventionalist argument is attributed by Popper to Carnap, presumably referring to Carnap's attempt to get away from the indeterminacy inherent in Popper's *falsificationist* approach: "...For there is always a possibility of '...attaining, for any chosen axiomatic system, what is called its "correspondence with reality"'..." (*ibid*, p. 81; the quotation is from Carnap (1923)). Popper goes on to suggest that conventionalist stratagems are particularly useful in times of scientific crisis, in defense of the established 'classic' system, as means of explaining away its inconsistencies: "...Whenever the 'classical' system of the day is threatened by the results of new experiments which might be interpreted as falsification according to my point of view, the system will appear unshaken to the conventionalist. He will explain away the inaccuracies which may have arisen; perhaps by blaming our inadequate mastery of the system. Or he will eliminate them by suggesting *ad hoc* the adoption of certain auxiliary hypotheses, or perhaps certain corrections to our measuring instruments..." (1959, p. 80).

whose status is *presupposed*, in advance of undertaking a scientific investigations. The second is found in Popper's later appeal (1974) to typical **exemplars** of 'true science', in whose work one may find the workings of scientific methodology. As Nola (1986) notes, this is an appeal to some intuitive yet still inherently empirical criteria for deciding what is 'true science'. Such criteria may take into account either the judgement of history, or the collective opinion of certified scientists.

It is doubtful that either extreme deductivism or extreme inductivism is ever practiced in a truly empirical science. Even in philosophy they are on occasion mitigated by a measure of eclecticism.[2] Still, it is of some use to explore, however briefly, the philosophical positions of extreme inductivists and deductivists.

8.2.2. Inductivism

8.2.2.1. Extreme inductivism in philosophy

8.2.2.1.1. Induction and the discovery of 'laws'

In the intellectual climate of the 1920s and 1930s, when Popper first elucidated his approach to the method of science, the dominant dogma in the philosophy of science was an extreme variant of empiricism -- **logical positivism**. That dogma held that empirical science, and implicitly also the organism, proceeded to acquire knowledge via **the method of induction**. To cite Popper:

"...According to this view, the logic of scientific discovery would be identical with inductive logic... It is usual to call an inference 'inductive' if it passes from *singular statements* (sometime called 'particular statements'), such as accounts of the results of observations or experiments, to *universal statements*, such as hypotheses or theories..." (1959, p. 27)

Popper ascribes these views to Carnap, Russell, Reichenbach and the 'early' Wittgenstein, *inter alia*, observing that whatever role induction must play in the acquisition of knowledge, it could not possibly be the role suggested by the inductivists. Scientific generalizations -- laws, hypotheses, theories -- cannot be arrived at *solely*, or even *primarily*, via induction. Nor can they be proven by induction.

---

2   As I suggest further below, there is an important pragmatic element underlying Popper's conventionalism, one arising from his concepts of **goals**, **aims** or **purposes**.

8.2.2.1.2. Induction and the 'leap of faith'

In arguing against the feasibility of an *inductive method* in science, Popper uses a variant of the argument of the **incompleteness of facts**. He first points out, following Hume, that the so-called *principle of induction* upon which inductivist methodology is founded has no *logical* status whatever, it is merely a **leap of faith** that asserts (quoting Hume):

"...that those instances...of which we have had no experience [are likely to] resemble those of which we have had experience..." (1959, appendix *vii, p. 369)[3]

And further, again quoting Hume:

"...All probable arguments are built on the supposition that there is conformity betwixt the future and the past..." (*ibid*)

As we have seen earlier above,[4] the same observation was made by Wittgenstein in the *Tractatus*:

"...the procedure of induction consists in accepting as true the *simplest* law that can be reconciled with our experience. This procedure, however, has no logical justification, but only a *psychological* one..." (1918, p. 143; emphases are mine; TG)

A similar, even more explicit, observation was made earlier by Peirce,[5] who in addition also suggested that induction is a means for raising the investigator's **confidence** in a generalization:

"...The operation of testing a hypothesis by experiment, which consists in remarking that certain conditions ought to have certain results, and then causing those conditions to be fulfilled, and noting the results, and, if they are favorable, *extending a certain confidence* to the hypothesis, I call induction..." (1940, p. 152; emphasis is mine; TG)[6]

8.2.2.1.3. Vindicating induction's 'leap of faith'

There are a number of arguments that can be raised against the surprising consensus of Wittgenstein and Popper, both of whom dis-

---

3 Popper is quoting here from Hume's (1739-1740) *Treatise of Human Nature*.
4 See Chapter 7.
5 See Chapter 7, as well as Peirce (1940, p. 152)
6 Peirce seems to be here at extreme variance from Popper's contention that the mode of reasoning involved in such experimental procedure is deductive -- by *modus tolens* -- rather than inductive. As I we see further below, the discrepancy is only apparent. Each refers to a different phase of testing.

miss the 'leap of faith' associated with induction as a mere *psychological* phenomenon.

(a) **Epistemology and 'grounds for belief':**

It is indeed true, though somewhat trivial, that induction endows the investigator with a certain **degree of confidence,** and thus ultimately involves **grounds for belief.** But dismissing grounds for belief as 'psychological' -- thus outside the purview of philosophy -- may be an overly rigid stricture. After all, one respectable epistemological interpretation of the three modes of inference -- deduction, induction and abduction -- is that they specify three different **grounds for belief** in the truth or falsity of propositions (see discussion in Chapters 4 and 7).

(b) **Epistemology and abduction:**

Popper is indeed right that induction does not serve as the *sole* logical tool for arriving at generalization via experience. Nonetheless, *some* inductive reasoning is involved, somewhere, in such a process. However, the crucial 'leap of faith' associated with induction, via which one proceeds from individual cases to general statements, demands a third mode of inference -- **abduction.** And since abductive reasoning falls within the legitimate domain of epistemology, the rejection of induction merely because it subsumes abduction would be surely an unnecessary stricture.

(c) **Real-world constraints on generalizing from experience:**

More substantively, the expectation that *the untested members of the population approximate the behavior of those members tested in the limited sample* is, on purely logical grounds, indeed a leap of faith. It is, nonetheless, a very tenable **working hypothesis** for biological organisms. Such a hypothesis must lie at the very heart of the organism's -- and the scientist's -- ability to generalize. In generalizing from experience, both the organism and the scientist must abide by realistic constraints on time, space and means. They hardly have a choice in this matter.

(d) **Induction and natural categories:**

The 'leap of faith' that underlies induction rests upon one fundamental, indeed crucial (though often ignored), tenet of a pragmatic **theory of natural categories.**[7] One may give this tenet as (1a) below, from which the **inductive-abductive hypothesis** (1b) follows:

(1) **Inference from clustering of categorial properties:**
- (a) "Individual members of a natural category do not share only a single criterial property. Rather, they most often share many properties, which are thus the *definitional core* of their categorial membership".
- (b) "Therefore, if known members of a group exhibit properties A, B, C etc., and if a sample sub-group also exhibits property Z (to a statistically-significant degree), then it is *highly likely* that the rest -- untested -- members also exhibit property Z".

(e) **Induction and survival imperatives:**
The suggestion, by the deductivist Popper and the inductivist 'early' Wittgenstein, that induction was somehow tainted by its admittedly *psychological* element, is a bit short-sighted on other grounds as well. These grounds involve the **functional-adaptive** imperatives associated with category-governed behavior in a real-world bio-adaptive environment. Consider, for example, the categorizing behavior of a herbivorous animal engaged in an inductive extension of the range of the category *tiger*. Suppose it already knows tigers by a thick cluster of their prototypical traits, such as shape, color, size, speed, sound, habitat, nocturnality etc. Suppose now it has just observed the *life-threatening, predatory* behavior of one or two individual tigers. Prior experience that tigers share a great number of **clustered** properties (1a), is precisely the kind of solid foundation that allows -- indeed impels -- the organism to take an inductive-abductive 'leap of faith' of the type (1b), and conclude that other tigers, yet to be encountered in the future, are **very likely** to match the behavior of the observed minuscule sample. Such conclusions, however logically fallacious, are essential for the organism's survival.

8.2.2.1.4. The level of generalization in induction

With all that was said above to justify the 'leap of faith' of induction, one must concede Popper's main anti-inductivist argument: Induction

---

7   See discussion of prototype categorization in Chapter 2. Within such a framework, the fewer properties are shared by members, the fewer induction-based prediction can be made about the behavior of members in various contexts.

is indeed *not* the way one arrives at hypotheses -- neither in science nor elsewhere. As noted above, even the most innocuous hypothesis of generalization already depended crucially upon the third mode of inference, abduction. This is all the more true with more profound **explanatory hypotheses**, those that concern relevance, connectivity and coherence, causality, and function. We will return to discuss those further below.

8.2.2.2. **Extreme inductivism in the behavioral sciences**

That extreme inductivism did indeed hold sway in early 20th Century philosophy is amply documented. Equally well documented is the strong impact logical positivism had upon two nascent behavioral-cognitive disciplines, psychology and linguistics. In psychology, this impact was expressed in the long tenure of the American **behaviorist** movement, associated with illustrious names such as Watson and Skinner.[8] The latter's stimulus-response paradigm is a straight-forward attempt to interpret behavior and cognition as cummulation of experience-derived inductive generalization. In linguistics, the same approach was embodied in the equally long tenure of the **American Structuralist** (or 'Bloomfieldian') movement.[9] The conscious philosophical pronouncements of Leonard Bloomfield, whose conversion to empiricism was prompted by exposure to behaviorist psychology, follow a straight and narrow inductivist line:

"...the only useful generalizations about language are inductive generalizations..." (1933, p. 20)

The Bloomfieldians ridiculed all attempts to make universal hypotheses that did not relate directly to observable facts. In fact, they rejected the making of any general statements beyond the somewhat trivial first-level generalization. In his review of Sapir's *Language*, Bloomfield writes:

"...we must study people's habits of language -- the way they talk -- without bothering about mental processes that we may conceive to underlie or accompany habits. We must dodge this issue by a fundamental assumption, leaving it to a separate investigation, in which our results will figure as data along the results of other social sciences..." (1922, p. 142)

---

8   See Skinner (1938, 1957) as well as Chomsky's (1959) review of the latter.
9   See for example Bloomfield (1922, 1926, 1933), as well as discussion in Bach (1965) or Givón (1966).

In rejecting the **mentalism** associated with the 19th Century German Romanticist Herman Paul, Bloomfield writes:

"...The other great weakness of Paul's 'Principles' is in his insistence upon "psychological" interpretation... [and on] mental processes which the speakers are supposed to have undergone... The only evidence for these mental processes is the linguistic process; they add nothing to the discussion but only obscure it..." (1933, p. 17)

Bloomfield's extreme inductivism forced him, in turn, to interpret meaning purely extensionally, much like the positivists. Consequently, he had no recourse but to exclude the study of meaning from the realm of linguistics:

"...In order to give a scientifically accurate definition of meaning for every form of the language, one should have to have a scientifically accurate knowledge of everything in the speakers' world... In practice, we define the meaning of a linguistic form, whenever we can, in terms of some other science..." (1933, pp. 139-140)

Finally, in rejecting Paul's and Sapir's 'mentalistic' approach to meaning, Bloomfield describes it as an 'untenable delusion':

"...The *mentalistic* theory... supposes that the variability of human conduct is due to the interference of some non-physical factors, a *spirit* or *will* or *mind*...that is present in every human being...[and] is entirely different from material things and accordingly follows some other kind of causation or perhaps non at all..." (1933, pp. 32-33)

Fortunately, Bloomfield the descriptive linguist consistently neglected to follow the dictates of Bloomfield the inductivist philosopher, producing linguistic descriptions that abounded in higher-level generalization, postulated meanings and invisible mental constructs. Historically, Bloomfield's extremism was partially prompted by the excesses of a previous wave of deductivist language philosophy,[10] and was in turn the foil for a subsequent wave of extreme deductivism.

---

10 Most specifically the German romanticist Herman Paul, whose disciple Bloomfield was prior to his conversion to behaviorism.

8.2.3. **Extreme deductivism**

8.2.3.1. **Popper and the Hypothetico-Deductive (HD) method**

"...The game of science is, in principle, without end..."

> K. Popper, *The Logic of Scientific Discovery,* (1959, p. 53)

8.2.3.1.1. **The reduction of science**

In his *Logic of Scientific Discovery,* Karl Popper advances a number of extreme deductivist positions, later coopted by more rigid exponents. Still, Popper's position remains somewhat problematic. Given the prevailing intellectual climate of reductionism, Popper's cogent arguments against inductivism have been often interpreted as a plea for the opposite extreme. What is more, in making a deliberate choice to focus his attention on the phase of **hypothesis testing,** Popper almost invites extreme interpretations. After all, hypothesis testing is the phase where the role of deduction is most obvious. Nonetheless, a number of aspects of Popper's approach to methodology can be interpreted as *pragmatic.* Or, put another way, extreme deductivism is not the only alternative to extreme inductivism.

Popper's **deductive-falsificatory** approach to the testing of scientific hypotheses rests on a curious separation between **grounds for knowledge** and **truth:**

"...I propose to look at science in a way which is slightly different from that favored by the various **psychologistic** schools: I wish to distinguish sharply between *objective science,* on the one hand, and *'our knowledge'* on the other. I readily admit that only observation can give us 'knowledge concerning the facts', and that we can (as Hahn says) 'become aware of facts only by observation'. But this awareness, this **knowledge** of ours, does not justify or establish the **truth** of any statement. I do not believe, therefore, that the question which epistemology must ask is '...on what does our *knowledge* rest?...' or more exactly, how can I, having had the *experience* S, justify my description of it, and defend it, against doubt... In my view, what epistemology has to ask is, rather: How do we **test** scientific statements by their **deductive consequences?**...." (1959, pp. 97–98; boldfacing is mine; TG)

Both epistemology and science are thus reduced to one dimension, **hypothesis testing;** and this is indeed a rather extreme philosophical stricture, one that relegates all other phases of science (observation, induction, abduction) to the realm of *disinterest.*

Popper does not in fact deny that non-deductive mental processes play a role in science. He only asserts -- by fiat -- that those other mental processes are *merely psychologistic;* they *have no logical status,* and are therefore *of no interest* to a 'true' epistemology. Popper's argument seems to rest on the following three value-laden assertions:

(i)   Induction (and abduction) are unsystematic, unpredictable psychologically-motivated processes;
(ii)   Only deductive logic has epistemological status;
(iii) The phases of science (and epistemology) that are of interest to the philosopher are those that involve deduction, thus truth.

8.2.3.1.2. The falsification method of testing

Having argued that induction is not a useful method for **confirming** the truth of scientific statements, and thus that there is no **positive proof** in science, Popper proceeds to outline the deductivist alternative -- the method of testing by **falsification.** This method requires first dividing the statements of science into two classes -- **singular** statements of 'individual facts', and **general** statements of rules, laws, hypotheses, theories etc. A general statement is tested deductively via **modus tolens** in the following way:[11]

(2) **Testing hypotheses through falsifiability:**
    (a) Take a general statement -- hypothesis -- G;
    (b) Derive from it deductively a hitherto unobserved singular statement P;
    (c) Creates an **experiment** which bring about the condition under which the facts of P should -- so G predicts -- be observed;
    (d) If statement P turns out to be false, then -- via **modus tolens** -- general statement G must also be false.

8.2.3.1.3. Falsification vs. verification

It is certainly fascinating how two great minds, Peirce and Popper, could describe the very same process, the experimental testing of a hypothesis, in such diametrically opposed terms -- Peirce as **verification by induction,**[12] Popper as **falsification by deduction.** Recall Peirce's version:

---

11 Following Popper (1959, p. 76).
12 Henning Andersen (in personal communication) suggests that Peirce was a confirmed *falsificationist* in his philosophy of science. If true, the following passage certainly sounds like a *verificationist's* credo. But see also fn. 6, above.

"...The operation of testing a hypothesis by experiment, which consists in remarking that, if it is true, observations made under certain conditions ought to have certain results, and then causing those conditions to be fulfilled, and noting the results, and, if they are favorable, *extending a certain confidence* to a hypothesis, I call *induction*..." (1940, p. 152)

In fact, Popper and Peirce are both right. They merely describe two different phases of the process of testing. Popper describes the **deductive consequences** of discovering a counter-example: Once a factual prediction of the hypothesis is shown by experiment to be false, the entire hypothesis is rejected. Peirce deals with the cumulative **inductive effect** of the **repeated failure to falsify** a hypothesis. Since, as Popper concedes, the game of science is endless, recurrent failure to falsify indeed increases the scientist's confidence in it. And that confidence may indeed be based upon firm inductive-abductive grounds.

Indeed, Popper concedes Peirce's position implicitly, when observing that the deductive-falsificatory method may have a severe drawback. That drawback indeed echoes some of the reasons for rejecting **verification** as a mode of hypothesis testing: Both processes are potentially endless. In the case of falsification, this is so because if one fails to reject a prediction via one experiment, the hypothesis from which the prediction had been derived is *not* verified. Rather, it is simply *not yet* proven false, given *one* experimental procedure. But:

(a) Other experimental procedures may yet prove it false; and
(b) The number of specific predictions that can be deduced from a hypothesis, especially from a rich and complex hypothesis, may be *potentially infinite*.

It is precisely within the context of such repeated attempts to falsify a hypothesis that inductive-abductive reasoning comes into play.

8.2.3.2. Pragmatic elements in Popper's method

In this section we will briefly note a number of areas in Popper's writings that may be interpreted as pragmatically inclined.

8.2.3.2.1. Hypothesis formation

Popper (1959) considers the process of **hypothesis formation** capricious, unpredictable, and thus of no epistemological interest. By doing so, he certainly ignores a major point where abductive inference comes into play in science. Nevertheless, he does not reject the importance of the process of discovery *per se*. He only asserts that it is not a *logical* process. To illustrate his position, consider:

"...there is no such thing as a logical method for having new ideas, or a logical reconstruction of this process. My view may be expressed by saying that every discovery contains 'an irrational element' or 'a creative intuition', in Bergson's sense. In a similar way Einstein speaks of the 'search for those highly universal laws...from which a picture of the world can be obtained by pure deduction. There is no logical path', he says, 'leading to these...laws. They can only be reached by intuition, based upon something like an intellectual love ('Einfühlung') of the objects of experience..." (1959, p. 32; quoting from Einstein, 1934, p. 125 of English translation)

8.2.3.2.2. The conventional nature of methodology

A number of steps in Popper's proposed methodology are pragmatically justified. As Nola (1986) points out, Popper's *aprioristic* approach takes the methodology of science to be a **presupposed** set of **conventions**, adopted by **agreement, decision** or **choice**, among people sharing the same **goals**:

"...My criterion of demarcation will accordingly have to be regarded as *a proposal for an agreement or convention*. As to the suitability of such conventions opinions differ; and a reasonable discussion of these questions is only possible between parties having **some purpose in common**. The choice of that purpose must, of course, be ultimately a matter of **decision** going beyond rational argument..." (1959, p. 37; boldfacing is mine; TG

A number of Popper's proposed conventions elaborate the falsificatory method of testing of hypotheses. One meta-convention seems to possess a more profound status. It involves the 'principle of **causation**', which Popper interprets as a claim that 'for every event there is a causal explanation'.[13] As a methodological rule of **explanation**, Popper renders it as follows:

"...It is the simple rule that we are not to abandon the search for universal laws and for a coherent theoretical system, nor ever give up our attempts to explain causally any kind of event we can describe..." (1959, p. 61)

Since, as noted earlier above,[14] overall coherence and explanation -- be it causal or otherwise -- are context-dependent notions, Popper here implicitly concede an important role to pragmatic reasoning.

---

13 Nola goes on to comment: "...this turns out to be unfalsifiable but a respectable piece of metaphysics..." (1986, p. 18)
14 See Chapter 7.

8.2.3.2.3. Utility and results

Next, Popper contends that his proposed apriori conventions for scientific methodology can be best judged by their **utility** in producing good science:

"...My only reason for proposing my criterion of demarcation is that it is *fruitful*: That a great many points can be clarified with its help... It is only from the *consequences* of my definition of empirical science, and from the methodological decisions that depend upon this definition, that the scientist will be able to see how far it conforms to his intuitive idea of the goal of his endeavors. The philosopher too will accept my definition as *useful* only if he can accept its *consequences*. We must satisfy him that these consequences enable us to detect inconsistencies and inadequacies in older theories of knowledge..." (1959, p. 55; emphases are mine; TG)

Since usefulness of results can only be judged in the context of **goals**, this is one more pragmatics element in Popper's approach to method.

8.2.3.2.4. The sociology of science

As pointed out by Nola (1986), Popper's (1974) invocation of *exemplars of great science* is a retreat from his earlier 'apriorism' toward a version of 'naive empirical conventionalism'. Such an approach is in some respects reminiscent of Kuhn's (1962). To the extent that Popper regards science as a convention-bound, socially-mediate **activity**, his approach is once again pragmatic.

8.2.3.3. Deductivism in a social science[15]

It is perhaps not an accident that a nascent would-be science, such as linguistics, become so fatally attracted to recurrent waves of extreme philosophical reductionism. As elsewhere in the history of ideas, one extreme tends to beget -- as violent reaction -- its opposite. And so, the strict empiricism of Bloomfield was in turn supplanted by the equally rigid rationalist deductivism of Chomsky. The view of the scientific method as demanding a choice between only two reductionist poles may be illustrated by the following passage from Bach (1965), where methodological inductivism and deductivism are labeled 'Baconian' and 'Keplerian', respectively:

---

15 I have benefitted here from the erudite discussion found in Derwing (1973) particularly chapter 7.

"...Whereas the Baconian stresses caution and 'sticking to facts' with a distrust of theory and hypotheses... the Keplerian emphasizes the creative nature of scientific discovery, the *leap to general hypotheses* -- often mathematical in form, whose value is judged in terms of fruitfulness, simplicity and elegance...The prevailing assumptions of American linguistics prior to 1957 were essentially Baconian in character... [Chomsky's approach, on the other hand is a] deductively formulated method..." (1965, pp. 113-114)

In the same vein, Lees (1957) observes:

"...Once it has developed beyond the *prescientific* stage of collection and classification of interesting facts, a scientific discipline is characterized *essentially* by the introduction of *abstract constructs* and theories and the validation of those theories by testing their predictive power..." (1957, p. 376; emphases are mine; TG)

Aside from the invocation of the potentially pragmatic 'fruitfulness',[16] and apart from the glaring departure from Popper's insistence on falsification (thus subscribing to the inductivist's confirmatory bias), deductivist linguistics closely recapitulates the salient features of extreme deductivism in philosophy:

(a) **Disinterest in discovery:**
Rejecting the naive notion of discovery by induction, deductivist linguists -- in spite of lip service to 'creativity' -- have tended to consider the process of discovery unconstrained, unsystematic, not meriting serious attention. The early generative attacks on the bogey-man of *Discovery Procedure*[17] were also clear reflection of this.

(b) **Formalization:**
Since deduction requires an explicit notation, deductivist methodology is often obsessed with formalism. In linguistics, this most commonly leads to interpreting language as a formal rule-system -- closed, complete, consistent. The pervasive structuralism that tends to accompany this approach, and its relative detachment from the study of function and

---

16 See discussion of the pragmatic elements in Popper's approach, above. 'Fruitfulness' in the Chomskian tradition turns out to be inseparable from **simplicity/economy**. This is a consequence of the notion of 'competence' that pervades the generative approach to data. See discussion in Derwing (1973, ch. 7,8) or Givón (1979a, ch. 1), *inter alia*.

17 Longacre's innocent field manual, *Grammar Discovery Procedures* (1964), came in for an inordinate share of critical abuse, since it dared to suggest that some procedures are more efficient than others in discovering rules of grammar.

functional explanation, are not surprising. Much like extreme deductivists elsewhere,[18] 'explanation' within this approach has tended to be system-internal, deductive and circular.

(c) **The neglect of primary facts:**
In general, deductivist linguistics has tended to downgrade the value of facts, to suggest that 'facts are cheap'.[19] Chomsky's notion of *linguistic competence* played an important role in circumventing deductive-falsificatory testing. Observable facts can be dismissed as mere *performance*. What matters above all is the elucidation of abstract theoretical constructs.[20]

(d) **Simplicity, economy, elegance:**
In the absence of firm empirical criteria, the role of formal ones -- simplicity, economy, elegance -- becomes paramount. This again constitutes a retreat from Popper's falsificatory testing method. To illustrate the ascendance of 'simplicity' over facts in deductivist linguistics, and the subsequent dilution of 'empirical validation', consider the following quotation from some of the more empirical proponents of this approach:

"...We have argued that there is strong *empirical support* for the claim that declaratives have abstract underlying structures and that this support derives *primarily* from considerations of the *simplicity* and *generality of grammatical rules*..." (Bever *et al*, 1965, p. 289; emphases are mine; TG)

The two historical episodes of extreme reductionism in linguistics, both equally structuralist, managed between them to present a caricature of a science: You may either practice dogmatic inductivism and forego making any but the most shallow generalization; or you may practice rigid deductivism and give up on the vital connection between data and theoretical constructs. The middle ground -- pragmatic-analogical reasoning, induction-abduction, or even methodological pluralism -- was never contemplated.

---

18 See the discussion of Hempel and Oppenheim (1948), further below.
19 See discussion in Derwing (1973, pp. 229-230).
20 See discussion in Givón (1979a, Ch. 1). In a recent BBC radio interview, Chomsky observed (I quote from memory): "...We have enough facts on human language, perhaps too many. What we really lack are the right kind of abstract constructs with which to build a theory..."

8.3. Pragmatic accounts of the scientific method

8.3.1. Preamble

Until a few decades ago, Peirce's pioneering work on abduction and abductive-induction stood out as the sole non-reductionist alternative in the philosophy of science. This picture has been slowly changing. Perhaps the single most forceful exponent of a pragmatic approach in the philosophy of science was the late R.N. Hanson. As he noted, deductive and inductive methods need not be conceived of as exclusive opposites:

"...the two accounts are not alternatives: They are compatible..." (1958, p. 70)

In this section we will survey some of the major tenets of a pragmatic philosophy of science.

8.3.2. The fact-driven nature of hypothesis formation

"...The particular facts are not merely brought together, but there is a new element added to the combination by the very act of thought by which they are combined...The pearls are there, but they will not hang together until someone provides the string..."

Aristotle, *Posterior Analytic*
(vol. II, p. 19)

As Hanson (1958, 1961) points out, hypothesis formation proceeds by a systematic type of reasoning, one that is perhaps more elusive than deduction and induction, yet nonetheless distinct: **abductive-analogical reasoning**. Further, this type of reasoning in science proceeds indeed in the direction suggested by inductivists -- **from data to hypothesis:**

"...The critical moment comes when the physicist perceives that one *might reason about the data* in such and such a way. One *might explain* this welter of phenomena P, throw it all into an intelligible *pattern*, by *supposing* H to obtain. But P controls H, not vice versa. The reasoning is *from data to hypotheses and theories*, not the reverse..." (1958, p. 88; emphases are mine; TG)

In discussing a celebrated example from physics, Hanson observes that it represented (a) reasoning from facts that demand explanation to an explanatory hypothesis; but (b) neither deduction nor induction:

"...Was Kepler's struggle up from Tycho's data to the proposal of elliptical orbit hypothesis really inferential at all? He wrote *De Mortibus Stelae Martis* in order to set out his reasons for suggesting the ellipse. These were not deductive reasons; he was working from *explicanda* to *explicans*. But neither were they inductive -- not, at least, in any form advocated by the empiricists, statisticians and probability theorists..." (1958, p. 85)

As to the deductivist account of hypothesis formation, Hanson observes:

"...Disciples of the H-D account often dismiss the dawning of an hypothesis as being of psychological interest only, or else claim it to be the province solely of genius and not of logic. They are wrong. If establishing an hypothesis through its predictions has a logic, so has the conceiving of an hypothesis..." (1958, p. 71)

Hanson is equally critical of rigid inductivists:

"...So the inductivist rightly suggests that laws are somehow related to **inference from data**. He wrongly suggests that the resultant law is but a summary of these data...Yet the original suggestion of hypothesis type is often a reasonable affair. It is not as dependent on intuition, hunches and other imponderables as historians and philosophers suppose when they make it the province of genius but not of logic. H-D accounts all agree that physical laws explain data, but they obscure the *initial connection between data and laws...*" (1958, p. 71; emphases are mine; TG)

And again about extreme deductivists:

"...H-D accounts begin with the hypothesis as given, as cooking recipes begin with the trout. Recipes, however, sometimes suggest 'first catch your trout'. The H-D account is a recipe physicists often use after catching hypotheses. However, the conceptual boldness that marks the history of physics shows more in the ways in which scientists *caught* their hypotheses than in the ways in which they elaborated these once caught. To study only the verification of hypotheses leaves a vital part of the story untold..." (1958, pp. 30-31)

And further:

"...Physicists do not start from hypotheses; they start from data. By the time a law has been fixed into an H-D system, really original physical thinking is over. The pedestrian process of deducing observation statements from hypotheses comes only after the physicist sees that *the hypothesis will at least explain the initial data requiring explanation*. [The] H-D account is helpful only when discussing the argument of a finished research report... the analysis leaves undiscussed the reasoning..." (1958, p. 71; emphases are mine; TG)

Relying extensively on Peirce's work on abductive inference, Hanson (1958) quotes Peirce:

"...[induction] sets out with a theory and it measures the degree of concordance of that theory with fact. It never can originate any idea whatever. No more can deduction. All ideas of science come to it by way of abduction. Abduction consists in *studying the facts* and *devising theories to explain them*. Its only justification is that if we are ever to understand things at all, it *must be*[21] in that way. Abductive and inductive reasoning are utterly irreducible, either to the other or to deduction, or deduction to either of them..." (C.S. Peirce, *Collected Writings* (1934), vol. V, p. 146)

And again quoting from Peirce:

"...Deduction proves that something *must* be; Induction shows that something *actually* is operative; Abduction merely suggests that something *may be*..." (*ibid*, p. 171)

Following Peirce, Hanson recapitulates the general schema for hypothesis formation via abduction:

(3) **Hanson's account of hypothesis formation:**
   "... 1. Some surprising phenomenon P is observed.
   2.   P would be explicable as a matter of course
         if H were true.
   3.   Hence there is *reason to think* that H is true. H cannot be
         retroductively [i.e. *abductively*; TG] inferred until its contents is present in 2. Inductive accounts expect H to emerge from repetition of P. H-D accounts make P emerge from some unaccounted-for creation of H as a 'high-level hypothesis'..." (1958, p. 86; emphases are mine; TG)

---

21 'Must be' here is the mode of *hypothesis*, not *deductive necessity*. See directly below.

8.3.3. The status of 'observable' facts

"...Facts are not picturable, observable entities..."

R.N. Hanson, *Patterns of Discovery*
(1958, p. 31)

As one may recall, Popper -- in describing the process of deductive falsification -- set up a sharp dichotomy between *singular statements* ('facts'), and *universal statements* ('generalization'), be those latter ones rules, laws, hypotheses or theories. Both inductivists and deductivists have accepted this traditional division, taking for granted the objective, given, atomic status of 'facts'. *The fact* vs. *generality* distinction presupposes, in turn, a distinction in *vocabulary*, between terms referring to **observable entities** ('non-theoretical terms', see Achinstein, 1965) and those referring to **theoretical constructs**. Popper (1959, p. 64) refers to the latter distinction as 'individual concepts' vs. 'universal concepts'. Carnap, an inductivist, sets up a somewhat similar distinction between "...terms designating observable properties and relations..." and "...terms which may refer to unobservable events, unobservable features of events...", a distinction that is, up to a point, the same as the one between **theoretical** and **non-theoretical** terms.[22]

Within a pragmatic approach, the objective 'givenness' of facts is, rather, a problematic matter. Feyerabend (1970), for example, casts doubt on the theory-independent status of clean facts, noting that they are conceptualized within the **context** ('framework') of a particular theory, on whose vocabulary they are at least partially dependent. This is, partly, a late-Wittgensteinean argument, similar to the one advanced by Hanson.[23] Similarly, Achinstein (1965) points out that between purely theoretical and purely observable terms, a **continuum** of intermediates exists. Generalization is thus taken to be a graded process. To illustrate this with a simple example, consider the following empirically-supported 'fact' of classical astronomy:

---

22 See discussion in Achinstein (1965, p. 234). In another place, however, Carnap argues that a distinction between 'individual' and 'universal' terms is **context dependent**: "...this distinction is not justified...every concept can be regarded as an individual or universal concept according to the *point of view* adopted..." (1934, p. 313; English Translation supplied by Popper (1959, p. 67)). Needless to say, Popper disagrees strongly with this pragmatist lapse of Carnap's, although he finds part of the argument correct as it stands (though irrelevant). For this reason alone, a full parallel between Popper's division of *statements* and Carnap division of *terms* cannot be drawn, as much as Achinstein's discussion may suggest otherwise.

23 See Hanson (1958, Ch. 2, pp. 31-34); the following Wittgensteinean quotable is found there: "...If a distinction cannot be made in language it cannot be made conceptually..." (p. 34).

(4) "The orbit of Mars is elliptical"

Statement (4) is obviously already a generalization, inducted-abducted from *more particular* observable facts that conform more closely to Popper's standards, such as for example:

(5)   a.   "On a certain date, at a certain hour, minute, second (etc.), the location of Mars relative to the sun was at certain distance and/or at coordinates *xyz, etc.*"
      b.   "On another date, etc.... the location of Mars was at.... (etc.)"
      c.   etc.

But are statements (4a,b,c) etc. really about the *ultimate* observable facts? How finely must their time-axis be established (day, hour, minute, second?) before such facts are transformed from 'general' to 'particular'? The answer is, of course, that a sharp boundary cannot be drawn as a matter of principle; rather, the boundary is pragmatically determined, it depends on either **perceptual calibration,** or on the **frame/context** -- be that frame perceptual-cognitive (for the organism) or theoretical (for the scientist) -- within which the observation was made.

The objective status of the 'particular facts' in (5) is further undermined by the total relativity of the spatial coordinates from which the observations were made (i.e. Earth's position), and via which the position of both planets vis-a-vis the sun was expressed. These 'facts' are observed -- or constructed -- in a **frame-dependent** fashion, they have no firm existence outside that frame.

In Chapter 3, above, we noted that in epistemology likewise the status of 'events' is equally frame-dependent, and for similar reason. The argument there revolved, first, on the spatial **framing** of events, i.e. what physical components may be judged as parts of it, which ones should be excluded, and on what grounds. As we pointed out there, the grounds for inclusion in the event frame were **pragmatic** at various levels, having little to do with either hard fact or deductive logic. The continuum of space, and of the entities within it, allows no firmer, more principled grounds.

It is easy to show that the time-specificity of so-called observable facts dissolves in the same way. Consider the following examples, all presumably statements of particular, facts:

(6)   a.   Joe saw the mule.
      b.   Joe kicked the mule.
      c.   Joe fed the mule.
      d.   Joe chased the mule.
      e.   Joe rode the mule.
      f.   Joe trained the mule.
      g.   Joe loved the mule.

The time-span that is normative or characteristic of the events depicted in (6a-g) varies gradually. Normatively, *seeing* is instantaneous. Normatively, *loving* is protracted. The progression between them is gradual. Further, (6b) through (6f) are transparently complex, composite activities, having many sub-parts. And if anything is likely to have been 'observed fact', it was those sub-parts. And how about the sub-parts of those sub-parts? *Ad infinitum?* A similar argument can be made concerning *see* (6a), whose instantaneous status is after all only relative to the perceptual calibration of our sensory apparatus. Finally, *feed, chase, ride, train* and *love* are **frame-dependent, culture-mediated** notions, as Wittgenstein (1953) would have surely pointed out. Being assembled constructs, their status as observables is only as firm as the cultural conventions -- world-views, theories, hypotheses -- within which they are embedded.

Hanson (1958) illustrates the frame-dependence of observed facts with the following example from Biology:

"...Imagine these two [scientists] observing a Protozoon --*Amoeba*. One sees a one-celled animal, the other a non-celled animal. The first sees *Amoeba* in all its **analogies** with different types of single cells: liver cells, nerve cells, epithelium cells. These have a wall, nucleus, cytoplasm, etc. Within this class *Amoeba* is distinguished only by its independence. The other, however, sees *Amoeba's* **homology** not with single cells, but with whole animals. Like all animals *Amoeba* ingests its food, digests and as-similates it. It excretes, reproduces and is mobile -- more like a complete animal than an individual tissue cell..." (1958, p. 4)

To sum up, then, facts may be graded **on a scale,** from those closer to observation to those most theory-dependent. But the scale itself is con-text-dependent, as are the criteria by which facts are placed at particular points on the scale. In the philosophy of science, such context-depend-ence has come to be referred to, in Hanson's term, as **the theory laden status of facts.**

One must note, lastly, that in adopting Hanson's notion of theory laden facts one merely recapitulates the Kantian middle-ground com-promise between Platonic and Aristotelian epistemology; whereby one may read for 'facts' Kant's *percepts,* and for 'theories' Kant's *concepts.*

8.3.4. The relevance of data

We have noted above that 'fact' is a loaded, context-determined, theory-dependent notion. In this section we will briefly discuss another aspect of the pragmatic nature of facts, one that has an immense practi-cal impact on the conduct of empirical investigations. It involves the choice of facts for which one wants to account via hypotheses. That is:

(7) "Of all the innumerable facts of the world, how does one know which ones are **relevant** to:
   (a) The general empirical *domain?*
   (b) This particular empirical *cycle* within the domain?
       or
   (c) The particular *hypothesis?* "

The decisions one needs to make in order to answer (7) are all, in principle, **pre-empirical** and **abductive**. One makes them without recourse to either deduction or induction. Innumerable facts about the universe may be -- ultimately -- related, connected or relevant to the subject matter ('domain', 'cycle', 'hypothesis'). Their relevance is a matter of **degree**; one uses **common sense** in ruling out the more remote relations; one concentrates one's meager resources on those facts that are **more likely** to be **relevant**, whose connection to the domain, cycle or specific hypothesis is **more intimate**. For example, if one is puzzled by some facts in the Swahili verb system (see section 8.3.5., directly below), then various verbal prefixes or suffixes may be relevant at various phases of the investigation. But one must rank tense-aspect prefixes as **more relevant** than derivational suffixes, or more than subject/object agreement prefixes; and verbal suffixes would be more relevant than nominal suffixes. But by what criteria?

Consider next a biologist investigating some puzzling facts about the human cardiac structure. This biologist would surely judge it **more likely** that relevant facts may come from the circulatory, pulmonary or autonomous-nervous domains, than from, say, the reproductive, skeletal or olfactory sub-domains. But his decisions in this matter are made **prior to** having made an overall theory of the domain; they are **prerequisites** for the eventual construction of such a theory. They are **abductions** about the **likely** connectivity within a **yet to be elaborated** higher context. As Hanson (1958) concludes regarding the **Amoeba** example cited earlier:

"...This is not an experimental issue, yet it can affect experiment. What either man regards as significant questions or **relevant data** can be determined by whether he stresses the first or the last term of 'unicellular animal'..." (1958, pp. 4-5).

As Hanson further observes, not only is the relevance of the data an abductive-pragmatic matter, but also the choice of what would constitute a **significant question**. These two issues are intimately connected, since the choice of particular *puzzling facts* is inseparable from the choice of *significant questions* concerning those puzzling facts. The puzzlement is indeed, itself, the question. As Bromberger (1966, pp. 79-81) points out, 'why' questions are only appropriate if the facts questioned are somehow surprising. And one's surprise depends, in turn, on one's **presuppositions** about the domain, i.e. on one's **prior context**.

8.3.5. The impetus for an empirical cycle: Puzzling facts

At the beginning of a typical empirical cycle there stands a **puzzle**. The puzzle may be referred to as a **distortion**, an **inconsistency** between some newly observed (or newly noticed) facts and the bulk of current knowledge. These facts simply are **incompatible** with current knowledge, with the existing organized ('theoretical') **framework** of the domain. Somehow, these puzzling facts are deemed **relevant** to the particular domain. Still, they **don't make sense** within the existing framework, they **do not cohere** with it.

This distortion, puzzle, incompatibility of facts, constitute the **impetus** for a typical empirical cycle. They **demand explanation**, i.e. demand the construction of a new hypothesis within which they will cohere. Bromberger (1966) has aptly characterized this impetus as a **'why' question** which demands a **'because' answer**. And that 'because' answer is the emerging hypothesis about how some surprising facts might cohere.

The puzzle is not inductive, and is only marginally deductive, in the sense that the incompatibility may -- at least theoretically -- have been **detected** through the deductive-falsificatory method. But just as plausibly the newly acknowledged facts may have fallen out of other phases, other procedures, other experiments, or other investigations. The puzzle precipitates the need to construct -- by abduction -- a new hypothesis, explanation, theory. The impetus to formulate a hypothesis that will re-impose coherence, however fragile and temporary, is described evocatively by Popper, as a pre-empirical imperative that is part of the methodological conventions of science:

"...It is the simple rule that we are not to abandon the search for universal laws and for a coherent theoretical system, nor ever give up our attempts to causally explain any kind of event we can describe..." (1959, p. 61)[24]

8.3.6. Intermezzo: A case-study of an empirical cycle

To illustrate how puzzling facts serve as impetus to the abduction of new explanatory hypotheses, consider the following run-of-the-mill example from historical grammatical reconstruction. In this sub-field of

---

24 Popper attributes this imperative to H. Gompertz' (1907) *Das Problem der Willensfreiheit*.

linguistics, the method of **internal reconstruction** is a standard tool for hypothesis building. This method relies heavily and conspicuously on abductive-analogical reasoning.

Internal reconstruction is said to be triggered by an **irregularity in the paradigm**, i.e. 'distortion' or 'incompatibility' within the extant body of knowledge. Consider the following case of the Swahili verbal system. The bulk of 'regular' verbs in Swahili are bi- or poly-syllabic. In finite verb paradigms, the verb stem must be preceded by a tense-aspect marker, which is in turn preceded by a subject-agreement marker:

(8) a. a-li-*sóma*   *'He read'*
     b. a-me-*sóma*   *'He has read*
     c. a-na-*sóma*   *'He is reading'*
     d. a-ta-*sóma*   *'He will read'*
     e. a-ø-sóma   *'He reads'*

This system looks rather neat, until the following distortions are noticed: First, a small group of verbs are monosyllabic, and the paradigm for these verbs contains an added element **-ku-**, tucked in between the tense-aspect marker and the verb stem:

(9) a. a-li-kú-*la*   *'He ate'*
     b. a-me-kú-*la*   *'He has eaten'*
     c. a-na-kú-*la*   *'He is eating'*
     d. a-ta-kú-*la*   *'He will eat'*
     e. á-ø-*la*   *'He eats'*

Second, an added irregularity involves the fact that -ku- does not appear in the habitual (*zero*) tense (9e).

The first distortion demands explanation of two sub-questions:

(10) a. "What is the reason for having -ku- in monosyllabic verbs but dispensing with it in bi- or poly-syllabic ones?"
      b. "Why -ku- rather than any other phonological sequence?"

The answer to (10a) turns to be relatively transparent, once one recalls that the Swahili word-stress is overwhelmingly penultimate; that the lexical stress must fall on the verb stem; and that mono-syllabic verb stems cannot carry this stress without violating the penultimate stress rule. One makes the interim, tentative, functional-explanatory hypothesis (11), through which the hitherto disparate facts of -ku- and the Swahili stress rules are linked in a single general pattern:

(11) "The function of -ku- *must be* to augment the monosyllabic verb stem so that it may carry the prescribed penultimate stress"

But why -ku-? In historical linguistics, given what we know about the process of **grammaticalization** via which lexical stems give rise to grammatical morphology, this question may be re-cast as:

(12) "What is the **source** of -ku-?"

One now casts around to see where other instances of a -ku- may be found, not just mere instances, but ones whose syntactic and functional distribution may tag them as *plausible candidates* for being the source of the -ku- in short-verb paradigms. In short, plausible, **relevant** candidates. The first relevant observation is that **ku-** also marks the infinitive of verbs, as in:

(13) ku-*sóma*   *'to read'*
      kú-*la*   *'to eat'*

The next relevant observation is that -ku-marked infinitival verbs appear in complements of modality verbs such as:

(14) a. a-na-taka   **ku-*sóma***   *'He wants to read'*
          he-PRES-want INF-read

      b. a-li-kwisha   **kú-*la***   *'He finished eating'*
          he-PAST-finish INF-eat

At this point an abduction-wise investigator possesses just about enough facts to attempt an abductive leap to an explanatory hypothesis. But before considering the hypothesis, let us consider some additional puzzling facts, this time concerning the relative-clause form of Swahili verbs.

In their REL-clause form, verbs in three of the tenses -- excepting the 'perfect' and 'habitual' ('zero') -- may take an *infix relative pronoun* between the tense marker and the verb stem. For long-stem verbs, the pattern is as follows:

(15) a. mtoto a-li-ye-*sóma*   *'The child who read'*
          child   he-PAST-REL-read

      b. mtoto a-na-ye-*sóma*   *'The child who's reading'*
          child he-PRES-REL-read

      c. mtoto a-taka-ye-*sóma*   *'The child who'll read'*
          child   he-FUT-REL-read

In (15c) we now spot one additional puzzle: The future marker -ta- has somehow acquires an additional syllable in this REL-pattern, appearing now as -taka-. As we shall see below, this puzzling fact eventually falls into place, and in fact contributes an important clue for resolving the initial puzzle. This salutary role of an erstwhile puzzle may be re-cast as a well-known general principle of empirical work:

(16) "What constitutes an inexplicable puzzle within an existing context, often turns out to both lead to and be explained by an expanded, more comprehensive context".

More puzzling yet, the 'perfect' -me- tense, which earlier followed the pattern of the other three tense-aspects in (15), now joins the 'habitual' (zero) tense in displaying an idiosyncratic REL-clause form:

(17) a. mtoto amba-ye a-me-sóma   'The child who has read'
          child say-REL   he-PERF-read

      b. mtoto a-somá-ye   'A/the child who reads'
          child he-HAB-read-REL

As different as the relativization patterns (17a,b) are, they nonetheless supply us with an added clue, one that turns out to be crucial for constructing a comprehensive hypothesis: In both, the REL-pronoun is a *verb suffix*. In (17a) it is suffixed to a 'relative subordinating verb' -amba 'say'. In (17b) it is attached to the relativized verb itself.

Another piece of evidence is the fact that the four tense-aspects in (15a,b,c) and (17b) may all follow, optionally, the 'REL-auxiliary' pattern that is obligatory for the 'perfect' (17a).

At this point the hypothesis fairly leaps out of the page at you,[25] especially if you know something about the most common diachronic source of tense-aspect markers: They tend to arise, overwhelmingly, from a small group of verbs in the complement construction of modality verbs (as in (12) above), via the process of **grammaticalization**.[26] The verbs that most commonly contribute to this process are *have, be, want, go, come,* and *finish*. Further, each of these verbs gives rise, most commonly, to a highly specific tense-aspect:

(18) a. 'be'   ⇒ 'progressive'
      b. 'want', 'go'   ⇒ 'future'
      c. 'have', 'finish', 'come' ⇒ 'perfect'

25 This is, roughly, the point where the abductive hypothesis occurred to me, in writing Givón (1972a, ch. 4).
26 For grammaticalization in general, with many illustrations from the rise of tense-aspect markers from verbs, see Givón (1973a, 1979a, ch. 5, 1982a, 1984a, ch. 6).

The assorted facts surveyed thus far now fall into a tentative but unmistakably **coherent** pattern. This pattern leaves a number of facts still hanging loose, puzzling, yet to be integrated into the overall coherence. Nonetheless, the pattern is there, a full-fledged **abductive, explanatory hypothesis**:

(19) a. "The four tense-aspects that involve some phonological material (unlike the 'habitual'/'zero') *must have* all arose from erstwhile verbs.

      b. Further, their grammaticalization into tense-aspect markers *must have* proceeded from the modal-verb constructions as in (14). In such constructions, the current main verb *must have* still been the complement of the modal verb".

Hypothesis (19) immediately explains two major pieces of our puzzle, first the shape and verb-prefix position of -ku- when it appears in front of short-stem verbs; and second, the position of the relative pronoun -- following the tense-aspect marker --in the 'infix' constructions (14):

(19) c. "The shape and position of -ku- *must be* both frozen relics, reflecting the syntax at the pre-grammaticalization phase of the construction, as complementizer".

      d. "The 'infix' REL-pronoun *must be* also a frozen relic reflecting the syntactic stage of the time when the tense-aspect was the main verb and thus carried the REL-pronoun as suffix".

Hypothesis (19a-d) must be further augmented, however, with:

(19) e. "The verb-suffix position of the REL-pronoun, as in (17), *must have been* the older, original position in Swahili relativization. It is the process of grammaticalization from verb to tense-aspect that created the 'infix' REL-pattern in (15)".

As satisfying as hypothesis (19a-e) is, it still leaves the exceptional behavior of both the 'habitual' and 'perfect' tense outside the new coherence system. The first, it turns out, poses no problem, since it displays neither verb-related characteristics (infinitive on the following verb, infixed REL-pronoun), nor any phonological material. It may be thus dispatched summarily by the further elaborating our hypothesis:

(19) f. "The ø tense did not arise from a verb; it *must have* been
          simply a morphologically-unmarked form. The relativi-
          zation of verb-stems in the habitual thus follows the
          older -- suffixal -- pattern (cf. (19e))".

The perfect -**me**- is a bit more problematic, since it shows one verb-related feature (-**ku**- before short stems) but not the other (the 'infix' REL-
pronoun). As it turned out, however, the answer to the next important
question indirectly also resolves the problem of the 'perfect'.
    As hypothesis (19a-f) stands now, it predicts one absolutely vital set
of facts, namely that:

(20) "Each one of the four supposedly verb-derived tense-aspect
      markers in Swahili -- **li, na, ta,** and **me** -- *must have had* a spe-
      cific verbal origin".

One may consider the testing of this prediction as Popper's deductive-
falsificatory step. That is, if (20) were not the case, hypothesis (19) must
be rejected, by *modus tolens.*
    Of the four marked tenses in Swahili, the first three -- with least ir-
regularities in their pattern -- readily yield verbal etymologies, traceable
to 'be', 'have' and 'want', respectively:

(21) a. a-**li**   mu-ngaanda (from Bemba)
          he-be   in-house
          'He is in the house'

      b. a-**na**   chakula
          he-have food
          'He has food'

      c. a-na-**taka**   ku-la
          he-PRES-want INF-eat
          'He wants to eat'

The perfect -**me**- turns out to be related to Swahili -mal-*iza* 'finish'
(Bemba -mal- 'finish'). Its current shape in Swahili is derived historically from the so-called *modified base* form (Bemba -meel-e) by predictable
phonological reduction.
    We have then *plausible* etymological sources; but these sources are not
free of problems:

(22) a. Normally 'be' tends to grammaticalized into the 'progressive' aspect (as in English); but the Bantu -li- became 'past' in Swahili;

b. Normally 'have' tends to grammaticalize into the 'perfect' aspect (as in English); but Swahili -na- became the 'present-progressive'.

The answer to these two puzzles, it turns out, has to do with more idiosyncratic historical developments in Swahili, where -na- indeed became first the 'perfect', then later changed into the 'present', which was in turn re-interpreted as 'present-progressive'. And -li- was indeed first a 'past-progressive' tense-aspect, and only later was re-interpreted as 'simple past'.[27]

Lastly, we still have the functional-explanatory hypothesis (11) concerning the appearance of -ku- only before short verb-stems. Given the added facts we have unearthed since first abducting (11), and the current shape of hypothesis (19a-f) that has emerged gradually as a result, we must now modify (11) slightly, in order that it **fit into the coherence pattern** of (19). That is, it must be now expressed in coherent historical-developmental terms:

(19) g. "The reason why -ku- was retained before short verb stems even after grammaticalization of the preceding verb into tense-aspect, *must have been* because it carried the verb's lexical stress and thus behaved like part of the verbal stem".

Our sub-hypothesis (19g) of course takes advantage of other general knowledge, concerning phonological reduction ('erosion') that occurs during grammaticalization, and how it impacts primarily de-stressed syllables.

We wind up, at the end of a protracted process that involved many diverse steps, with a *general theory* of the phenomenon (Swahili tense-aspect morphology). Within this general theory, the *distortion* that gave us impetus for launching the cycle of investigation found its resolution, coherence, context. The whole process involved the gathering of additional *relevant facts*, the successive fitting of those facts into a *unified overall pattern*, the gradual construction and refinement -- via successive *abductions* -- of *explanatory hypotheses*. The process even involved one crucial *falsificatory test*. The theory we have constructed explains the original puzzle, but it also explains other puzzles along the way. It explains them all within a single -- albeit complex -- hypothesis. And it ex-

---

27 See details in Wald (1973).

plains them all in conformity with a number of well-known *general principles* observed independently in human language. Whether our hypothesis will last further falsificatory testing only time will tell.[28]

8.4. The pragmatics of explanation

8.4.1. Preamble

"...What is scientific explanation? It is a **topically unified** communication, the contents of which imparts **understanding** of some scientific phenomenon. And the better it is, the more efficiently and reliably it does this, i.e., with less redundancy and higher *over-all* probability. What is understanding? Understanding is, roughly, **organized knowledge,** i.e., knowledge of the relations between various facts and/or laws. These relations are many kinds -- deductive, inductive, analogical, etc. (Understanding is deeper, more thorough, the greater the span of this relational knowledge)..."

M. Scriven (1962, p. 102)

The single most crucial notion in science, the one that transforms the enterprise from a mere gathering of disparate facts to a meaningful activity of expanding our understanding, is the notion of explanation. As only fitting, it is also the most controversial in the philosophy of science. The traditional philosophical positions display here a certain *asymmetry:* Induction, being a progression from facts to general rule, is in principle irrelevant to explanation; explanation is not part of induction's domain. The few avowed inductivists ever to actually practice empirical science -- most conspicuously in psychology and linguistics -- have either disavowed interest in explanation *(viz* Bloomfield), or else indulged in postulating 'inductively transparent' general principles which somehow

---

28 Several other 'distortions' in the Swahili verbal paradigms also fit into the general pattern of hypothesis (19). The presence of -**ku-** following REL-pronoun infixes of short-stem verbs augments its plausibility. The appearance of -**ku-** with the negative of the -**me-** aspect (-**ja-ku-**) turns out to cohere with (19) as well; -**ja-** is identified as the verb 'come'. Irregularities in the negative form of the 1st person singular (ni- turning into si-) turn out to reinforce our reconstruction of -**li-** as 'be'; the same is true of the form **ndi-yo** 'yes' (historically ***n-li-yo** 'it-be-REL') vs. **si-yo** 'no'. Historically
    it-be-REL
the negative form was ***n-li-yo,** where the old negative
    it-be-NEG-REL
suffix followed the verb "be". (Nasal prefixes regularly zero out in Swahili before voiceless consonants). The post-verbal negation pattern is still found in some tense-aspects in Swahili.

purported to explain *(viz* Skinner). Such principles turned out, on closer examination, to be mere *labels* for the facts, extending not an inch beyond those facts.

Extreme deductivists, on the other hand, have laid explicit claim to a rather formal notion of explanation: **deduction from the general rule.** While formally legitimate, this is nonetheless the most impoverished species of explanation. Still, it does manage to identify, correctly if implicitly, one important **pragmatic** aspect of the enterprise:

(23) **Explanation as contextualization:**
"Explanation, at its most general, is indeed the viewing of the facts to be explained **in a wider context**; it fits facts **in a larger pattern**".

As noted throughout, pragmatics is the method of **contextualizing** hitherto isolated chunks of knowledge, of **abducting** their likely **connectivity**, of discovering how they fit in a wider **pattern**. Since general rules, or explanatory hypotheses, are not discovered by deduction, the most deduction can achieve is the **testing** of the relationship between a general rule and the instances it purports to generalize.

8.4.2. **Deductivism: Generalization as explanation**

As unsatisfactory as it may be as explanation, deduction from a general rule must be viewed as a weak instance -- abstract schema -- of explanation. It is weak, indeed impoverished, since by citing the rule as part of the explanation one merely acknowledges that the instance belongs to a class, whose members all abide by the same rule. That leaves open the more interesting question, namely why is the rule the way it is?

The most extreme deductivist approach to explanation may be found in either Popper's (1959, p. 59) or Hempel and Oppenheim's (1948, p. 11) schema of **causal explanation**, within which a puzzling fact, yet to be explained, is -- causally or otherwise -- linked to another fact (called *antecedent condition*), via some general rule. The *antecedent condition* itself requires no explanation, since it is already understood (i.e. contextualized) within the prevailing general pattern. The *explanandum* is said to be deduced from the *explanans;* the latter combines the 'antecedent condition' plus the general rule:[29]

---

29 Simplified from Hempel and Oppenheim (1948, p. 11).

(24) **Schema of deductive explanation:**

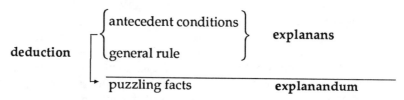

The potential poverty of deductive explanation of the type (24) becomes obvious when one notes that from the general rule *All Greeks are bald* and the antecedent condition *Socrates is Greek*, one may 'deductively explain' the newly noticed fact that *Socrates is bald*. This 'explanation' indeed contextualizes -- or connects -- the fact of Socrates' baldness with the fact of his being Greek. But as to contributing much to our **understanding** -- causal or otherwise -- of Socrates' baldness (or, for that matter, of the baldness of all Greeks), this deductive 'explanation' is more than a trifle disappointing. In a real science, this mode of 'explanation' is only a preliminary step, indicating a certain -- hopefully temporary -- conceptual poverty, not to mention a measure of downright circularity.[30]

One may as well note that a species of deductive explanation in fact crops up occasionally in avowed inductivists' feeble attempts to 'explain'. Thus consider:

(25)

$$\text{deduction} \left[\begin{array}{l} \left\{ \begin{array}{l} \text{individual X is fittest} \\ \text{only the fittest survive} \end{array} \right\} \quad \textbf{explanans} \\ \hline \text{individual X survived} \qquad \textbf{explanandum} \end{array} \right.$$

The circularity in (25) arises from the fact that the 'cause' and 'effect' are not independent facts, but merely two names for the same fact.

A somewhat similar conceptual poverty crops up in the behavioral psychologist's causal explanation of rote-learning: [31]

---

30 For discussion of such circularity in deductivist linguistics, see Derwing (1973, Part III), or Givón (1979a, ch. 1).

31 As noted by Chomsky (1959) in his review of Skinner (1957).

(26)

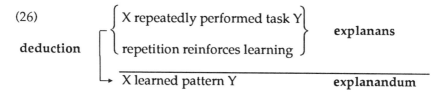

deduction

$\left\{\begin{array}{l}\text{X repeatedly performed task Y} \\ \text{repetition reinforces learning}\end{array}\right\}$ **explanans**

X learned pattern Y   **explanandum**

In the same vein, the generative grammarian may claim to explain some facts of language by citing the general formal rule of which they were an instance, as in:[32]

(27)

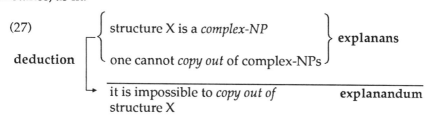

deduction

$\left\{\begin{array}{l}\text{structure X is a }\textit{complex-NP} \\ \text{one cannot }\textit{copy out}\text{ of complex-NPs}\end{array}\right\}$ **explanans**

it is impossible to *copy out of*   **explanandum**
structure X

In summing up the difficulty raised by assuming that deduction from general rule is much of an explanation, Scriven (1962) says:

"...Hempel and Oppenheim's first mistake, then, lies in the supposition that by subsumption under a generalization one has automatically explained *something*, and that queries about this "explanation" represent a request for *further* and *different* explanation..." (1962, p. 97)

A more serious criticism of the deductivist's explanation-via-rule is of course that it mis-represents both the **directionality** and **mode** of explanation in much the same way as it misrepresented the directionality and mode of scientific discovery: In real science, explanations are constructed **abductively,** in the *absence* of a general rule. Indeed, explanation is the process of hypothesizing the general rule, thus making a **necessary connection** (the 'rule') between some puzzling facts (the 'effect') and some old facts (the 'cause'), facts that until then were considered unrelated. The deduction schema in (23) is in fact the **testing stage** of an explanatory hypothesis, not its discovery.

---

32 This type of argument remains common in deductivist linguistics. For discussion, see Givón (1979a, ch. 1) or Derwing (1973, Part III).

8.4.3. Causal explanation: Co-occurrence, dependency and complex patterns

"...The belief in causality is metaphysical. It is nothing but a typical metaphysical hypothesization of a well-justified methodological rule -- the scientist's decision never to abandon his search for laws..."

> K. Popper *The Logic of Scientific Discovery* (1959, p. 248)

8.4.3.1. Preamble

Traditional deductive-inductive philosophy of science, with its heavy reliance on classical physics for examples of scientific practice, naturally selected simple, chain-like mechanical causation as its paradigm case of explanation. Here is how Russell (1948) describes it:

"...Inference from experience to the physical world can...be justified by the assumption that there are causal chains, each member of which is a complex structure ordered by the spatio-temporal of *com-presence*...All members of such a [causation] chain are similar in structure..." (1948, p. 244; emphasis is mine; TG)

The key term in justifying the inference of a causal relation between events is Russell's spatial and/or temporal *com-presence*, which one might as well re-christen **co-occurrence.** But as simple as that may seem at first, causation turns out to be a theory-laden notion, a construct that is inferred, often in complex and indirect ways, from various co-occurrences and, in particular, from their **asymmetries.**

8.4.3.2. The context-dependent, theory-laden nature of 'cause'

As Hanson notes, members of a 'simple causation chain' are all, presumably, "...discrete events bound to neighbouring events very much like themselves..." (1958, p. 50). In an eloquent dissection of the ontology of causation, Hanson shows why this simple chain-type model of causation is a caricature of science, either in physics or in the more complex biological and behavioral sciences:

"...what we refer to as 'causes' are *theory-loaded* from beginning to end. They are not simple, tangible links in the chain of sense experience, but rather details in an *intricate pattern of concepts...*" (1958, p. 54; emphases are mine; TG)

Further:

"...This is the whole story about necessary connection. 'Effect' and 'cause', so far from naming links in a queue of events, gesture towards *webs of criss-crossed theoretical notions,* information, and patterns of experiment...The notions behind 'the cause x' and 'the effect y' are intelligible only against a *pattern of theory,* namely one which puts guarantees on inferences from x to y..." (1958, p. 64; emphases are mine; TG)

8.4.3.3. The multi-variable empirical environment

At the bottom of adopting the simple causal chain as explanation lies the assumption that events are **mono-causal**, and that the coherence structure of **complex, multi-factored** domains can be reduced to the simple mechanics of cause-and-effect. But even in the relatively simple mechanical domain of billiard games, Hanson points out, "...causal-chain accounts of their performance are oversimplified..." (1958, p. 53).

The idea that a simple causal relation can always be established is an over-simplification in complex, multi-variable science. In such a science, often many factors link onto each other in a 'criss-cross pattern' whereby identifying any one -- or any group -- as *the* cause of any other fact or group, simply doesn't reflect the complexity of the pattern. Further, as Hanson (1958) notes, the only reason why a complex science can sometime give the misleading impression of indulging in simple causal-chain explanation is because of the practice of **controlled experiments.**

Controlled experiments are the typical fare of complex, multi-variable science, where causal connections and other dependencies cannot be determined without extreme abstraction from real-world conditions. In a controlled experiment, all factors except two are held constant, effectively removed from consideration. One of the remaining two factors is then manipulated (i.e. its value varied), and the effect of the manipulation on the value of other variable is recorded. If the results are *asymmetrical* in a way that manipulating x registers an effect on y, but not vice versa, one is justified in calling x the **independent variable** ('cause') and y the **dependent variable** ('effect').

In the next experiment, the procedure is repeated, but at least one of the variables is replaced by a hitherto untested one. Hanson further notes:

"...To characterize such an enterprise as 'this happens, then that, then those things take place, which results in...', is a bad caricature..." (1958, p. 67)

Consider, lastly, the complex problem of the Swahili verb paradigms (section 8.3.6., above). In what sense is any one of the facts unearthed in the course of trying to explain the initial 'puzzling fact', the 'cause' of that initial fact? The answer is that the dependency relations among all those facts are much too rich and complex to be expressed as a simple causal chain. This is not to say that we did not make a number of causal hypotheses within the general pattern. But the general pattern did not consist of a single chain of causal relations.

8.4.3.4. The bio-ontology of causal reasoning

As noted above, there appears a curious agreement across the philosophical spectrum concerning the supposed **metaphysical** status of the notion 'cause'. All philosophical schools seem to agree that 'cause' is neither inductively nor deductively supported. In this section I would like to outline briefly why the belief in causation is neither irrational, nor merely a convenient 'psychological' metaphor. Rather, it is a complex bio-adaptive **abduction** that organisms must make, in their attempt to **predict the behavior** of animate and inanimate entities in the environment, entities whose behavior bears crucially on the organism's survival. Much like the scientist's search for cause, as given in Popper's methodological imperative, the organism's causal reasoning is a **survival imperative**, a necessary component in an **empirical** interpretation of information. Much like the scientist, the organism's causal reasoning displays an eclectic mix of inductive, deductive and abductive ingredients.

The irreducible **inductive** core of causal reasoning is the observation concerning a recurring pattern of **temporal-sequential order** of types of events (or entities stereotypically associated with them). This is indeed Russell's (1948) *com-presence*, except that is rather pre-presence.

(28) **Temporal precedence:**
  "In order for event-type A to be the 'cause' of event-type B, tokens of event-type A always precede those of event-type B".

Sequentiality is, however, a necessary but not sufficient ingredient. The next necessary ingredient in causal reasoning is the observation of a certain **logical dependency** relation between the occurrences of tokens of A and B. This involves the **asymmetrical conditional** distribution in the temporal relationship between the tokens of event-types A and B:

(29) **Skewed conditional distribution:**
  " In order for event-type A to be the 'cause' of event-type B, it must be the case that whenever a token of B occurs, a token of A has always preceded it; but sometimes a token of A occurs and no token of B follows".

The two event-types now display the **deductive**-logical relationship of **dependency**, whereby B is dependent on A, but A is independent of B.

But causal reasoning carries added, complex, abductive-inductive analytic ingredients, whose survival-based motivation is readily apparent. Most central is the division of entities in the environment into **animate-agents** and **inanimates**. The latter are bound by the (essentially Newtonian) laws of **inertia**. The former are not. The next ingredient is an abduction concerning internal vs. external **motivation** for events (i.e. observed changes in the environment) that involve both types of entities:

(30) **Agency and motion under own power:**

    (a) "All entities that move -- i.e. are involved in salient events/changes -- without any external 'cause' to motivate their motion, must be **agents**, capable of acting/moving **under their own power**".

    (b) "Otherwise entities are **inanimate**, i.e. incapable of initiating their own motion/action. When such entities are involved in events/changes, an **external cause** must be postulated".

Von Wright (1971) notes that our notion of the 'cause' of behavior rests upon **introspection**. This is, strictly speaking, a more appropriate observation about our notion 'agent': It is unlikely that 'intent', the central ingredient of 'agent', could ever be induced from external observations. But the interplay between this introspection and an inductive-abductive Newtonian notion of **inertia** is a crucial analytic step:

(31) **Inertia vs. motion: Norm and counter norm:**

    (a) "The majority of entities are **inanimate** and obey the law of inertia. They are the normative **ground**. When they move, an external cause must be sought to **explain** their motion".

    (b) "Only a relative minority are **agents**, capable of counter-inertia behavior. They are the counter-normative **figures**. When they move, no external cause need be sought".

A philosopher may of course wish to argue that there is no logical motivation for such observations. For the bio-organism, however, the adaptive, survival value of this progressive abductive-inductive analysis is rather obvious:

(32) **Agency, counter-inert motion and survival:**

    (a) "Animates-agents are either potential predators or prey. One must be **on one's guard** whenever agents are around, since their behavior ('motion', 'action') **cannot be predicted** from the observable environment".

    (b) "Inanimates are safer, they tend to stay put, or else their limited motion is **predictable** through normative inertia considerations, and from more visible environmental clues".

The introspective judgement concerning **intended acts**, the division of events into **externally motivated** and **intended** events, and the division of entities into agents and non-agents, are all motivated by survival imperatives of the biological organism. The scientist's information-processing behavior merely recapitulates analytic patterns grounded in the very dawn of biological evolution.

8.5. Functional explanation

"...if a piece of wood is to be split with an axe, the axe must of necessity be hard; and, if hard, must of necessity be made of bronze or iron. Now exactly in the same way the body, which like the axe is an *instrument* -- for both the body as a whole and its several parts individually have definite operations *for which they are made;* just in the same way, I say, the body if it is to do its work, must of necessity be of such and such character..."

                         Aristotle, *De Partibus Animalium* (in McKeon, ed., 1941; emphases are mine;TG)

8.5.1. Preamble

The process of constructing an explanation -- even when partially masked by the deductivist's strictures -- is a profoundly pragmatic enterprise. It depends crucially on abducting the proper **context** within which facts fit, fall into pattern, make sense. Seeking the proper context for hitherto isolated facts is, in principle, an enterprise that cannot depend on either deductive or inductive logic. It demands abducting connections *outside* the extant **organized domain,** across **uncharted regions,** or into other sub-systems whose relevance to the domain is yet to be shown. The contextual-pragmatic nature of explanation becomes even more obvious when one transcends the pristine realms of physics and chemistry, with their relatively simple causality, and moves on into the messier study of bio-behavior.

The special challenge of functional explanation in biology and behavior has not gone unnoticed by deductivists. In non-biological science, the deductivists take it for granted, *why X?* questions could only mean *what was the cause of x?* In the biological domain, however, explanations that cannot be so easily reduced to simple causation have been considered meaningful, as a matter of course, for two millennia. Here is how Hempel (1959) describes, as neutrally as possible, the view advocating the uniqueness of functional explanation in bio-behavioral science:

"...In the exact physical sciences, according to this view, all explanation is achieved ultimately by reference to causal or correlational antecedents; whereas in psychology and the social and historical disciplines -- and, according to some, even in biology -- the establishment of causal or correlational connections, while desirable and important, is not sufficient. Proper understanding of the phenomena studied in these fields is held to require other types of explanation. Perhaps the most important of the alternative methods that have been developed for this purpose is the method of *functional analysis,* which has found extensive use in biology, psychology, sociology and anthropology..." (1959, p. 121; emphasis is mine; TG)

The description of the 'method' of functional explanation offered by Hempel is loaded in one crucial respect: It implies that somehow functional explanation is itself a different *species* of explanation from 'the establishment of causal or correlational connections'. A biologist or behavioral scientist may as well counter as follows:

(33) **Species of explanations:**

   (a) *Causal connection* are just one species of connection obtaining between phenomena and their wider context;

   (b) *Correlation* is merely the *heuristic* from which the scientist proceeds to abduct an explanatory connection; it is another name for Russell's observed *spatio-temporal compresence;*

   (c) *Functional explanations* are different from causal ones merely in that the context to which a phenomenon is linked via such explanations is some biological or behavioral **function.**

8.5.2. Structure and function in biology

Since, as Aristotle observed in rejecting structuralist interpretation of biology, the notions *function* and *instrumentality* are peculiar to the bio-behavioral domain, a few words of introduction to that domain are in order. In physics or chemistry, the notion of a **complex system**, made up hierarchically out of smaller sub-parts is of course familiar. One strives to elaborate the connectivity within such a system, quite often discovering causal connections among its sub-parts.

Causal explanation of this simple type is also well known in biology, and is practiced extensively at the more mechanical, physico-chemical, *lower levels* of biological organization. In both physics and biology, thus, one may legitimately ask *why X?* with the sense of *what caused X?*. In addition, however, in the biology one may ask *why* questions in yet another sense, one that is without precedence in physics or chemistry. This sense may be given in the least loaded terms as follows:

(34) "Why is organ -- or organism -- X **structured** the way it is?
    That is:
    (a) What **functional requirements** motivate -- i.e. 'correlate to' -- that structure?
    (b) How does in **perform** its function?
    (c) How does its function **constrain** its structure?"

These are the most common questions, standard fare, in the explanatory study of biological design.[33] They go to the heart of the complex relationship between environmental adaptation, individual behavior, population dynamics, and the evolutionary process through which bio-organisms -- and socio-cultures -- are shaped and re-shaped.

The hidden reference buried inside function-oriented questions such as (34), as Hempel and Oppenheim (1948) correctly note, is of course to a certain implicit **teleology**. While inorganic physical facts are simply there, or are there *for causes*, bio-behavioral facts are there *for reasons*. And those reasons may not be dismissed as either 'metaphysical' or 'anthropomorphic imputations', existing only in the interpreter's mind (see section 8.5.4., below). Rather, they are the *theoretical construct* peculiar and appropriate to the phenomenological domain of bio-behavior, *explanatory hypotheses* about the **adaptive behavior** of individual organisms or species.

---

33 And if one substitutes 'socio-cultural pattern' ('culture') or 'grammatical structure' ('grammar') for 'organ' ('organism'), these become immediately the kind of explanatory questions relevant to anthropology or linguistics.

8.5.3. Some features of bio-behavior

8.5.3.1. Adaptive tasks and survival imperatives

The adaptive behavior of organisms must be viewed ultimately within the context of one governing 'meta-goal': The **survival impera-tive.** Organisms, species and socio-cultures seem to behave *as if* they pursue this ultimate **meta-goal.** In pursuing their meta-goal, organisms (and socio-cultures) proceed to create a **complex system.** That is, they break the meta-goal down into a **hierarchy** of sub-tasks. Higher sub-tasks are, for example:

(35) **Higher biological sub-tasks:**
    (a) the survival of the individual (metabolism, defence); and
    (b) the survival of the species (procreation).

These higher sub-tasks in turn are further broken down into their sub-component such as, for example:

(36) **Lower sub-tasks ('functions'):**
    (a) ambulation (defensive, foraging, social)
    (b) feeding (foraging, ingestion, digestion)
    (c) synthesis (energy, growth, maintenance)
    (d) waste elimination (solid, liquid)
    (e) transmission (breathing, circulation)
    (f) information processing (perception, cognition)
    (g) reproduction (sexual, vegetative)
    (h) defense (protective, offensive)
      etc.

Roughly at this level in the hierarchy of functional organization, specific anatomical and histological **structures** -- organs -- begin to display their systematic correlation -- sometimes even **isomorphism** -- to particular **functions** ('sub-tasks').

8.5.3.2. The law-governed behavior of bio-organisms: Uniformity and adaptive choice

A population of inorganic physical entities *of the same kind* -- say molecules of the same chemical compound or balls of the same material, size, weight and shape -- obeys the laws that govern their behavior in a relatively uniform, seemingly exceptionless fashion. Every member of such a population, when put under identical conditions, is expected to 'behave' the same way. This exceptionless obedience to 'laws' also characterizes the workings of the lower levels of complex bio-organization, where similar causes uniformly produce similar effects.

There is a radical gap between this type of mechanical causation and the way organisms -- or their populations -- abide by functional-adaptive 'laws'. They behave *as if* they **make choices.** Sometimes they choose to 'disobey' a functional-adaptive 'law', and consequently 'take the penalties' (become mal-adaptive or extinct). Often, however, there are more than one structure-type that can perform the same function; or more than one behavior-pattern capable of yielding the same adaptive ends. Both structurally and behaviorally, bio-organisms seem to have a certain range of **adaptive options.** Let us illustrate this with a few simple examples.

The sub-task of *reproduction* may be achieved, structurally and behaviorally, either vegetatively ('cloning') or sexually. And within the two major options a great number of minor variations are possible and indeed attested. Some lower-level organisms alternate between the two modes, depending on environmental -- contextual -- considerations. Such choice may be labeled as purely deterministic. But other organisms have 'opted for' either one mode or the other. And while the history of evolution may yet reveal the reasons that affected such a 'choice', a strategic choice among available options was nonetheless made, based upon an evaluation of the options within some environmental context.

The function of *ambulation* outside water may be achieved by either walking, crawling or flying, and each one of those in turn allows a great number of structural-behavioral variants. Did birds 'have to' take to the air? Were snakes 'impelled' to atrophy their limbs and slither? Simple, deterministic 'causal' interpretation cannot quite explain why close relatives have opted for other alternatives.

The function of *self-defence* may be performed in a myriad of structural-behavioral ways, some offensive, other defensive, some active others passive, some strategic others tactical. Closely-related species often chose widely divergent structural or behavioral ways of performing this function.

8.5.3.3. **Bio-organisms as interactive systems:** **Mutual dependencies and cross-constraints**

When an organism 'opts for' a certain structural-behavioral solution for performing one sub-task, other sub-tasks within the organism, even if not *directly* associated with the performance of the same task, seldom remain wholly insulated from that choice. Rather, they tend to **interact** with it, or **constrain** it, in ways that are peculiar to bio-systems. Unlike their non-biological counterparts, be those complex and hierarchic, bio-systems can seldom be described as predictable sums of their parts. Their sub-parts are most often **functionally interactive,** a mode of inter-action that has no exact analog in non-biological systems, however complex, hierarchic or causally-connected they may be. Further, the functional interaction between sub-parts of a bio-system is a matter of degree, depending on the **relevance** relations between the various sub-tasks.

Consider, for example, aviary flight-motion. It is usually correlated with a certain streamlined body surface, aero-dynamic shape, adapted limb design, weight distribution, bone structure, feeding habits, metabolic rate, breathing rate and heart-beat rate, defensive and reproductive behavior. Some of these features are more directly relevant to flight; others are less relevant to flight but more relevant to other sub-tasks. They all interact and constrain each other. And, above all, they are rigidly constrained by their general context -- vertebrate design.

In contrast, other sub-tasks -- say, sugar metabolism or the liver's synthetic function -- are much less relevant to flight, thus much less likely to interact with or constrain it. And when flight-motion is embedded in another bio-design context -- say insects -- different systemic constraints exert their pressure. The insect flight-system and its mutually-constraining contributory parts present at best a weak **analog** to aviary flight, a radically different 'solution' -- functionally as well as structurally -- to the same general task.

8.5.3.4. **Higher-level interaction governing bio-behavior**

What makes bio-behavioral systems even more complex, as a domain for empirical investigation, is the involvement of several pair-wise meta-interactions. Among those are:

(37) **Meta-interactions in bio-behavior:**
   (a) Organism vs. the environment
   (b) Organism vs. the social group
   (c) Organism (or social group) vs. the species
   (d) The metabolic body (*phenome*) vs. its genetic code (*genome*)
   (e) Lifetime learning vs. evolutionary change
   (f) Evolutionary change vs. ontogenetic development
   (f) Physical structure vs. user's program
   (g) Individual behavior vs. the group's culture

All these pair-wise meta-interactions, and the complex multiple inter-actions among them, set the bio-behavioral empirical domain even further apart from the non-biological sciences. They make it impossible to interpret bio-behavior as a variant -- or analog -- of the non-biological physical domain and its simple mechanical causation. S.J. Gould comments on this point in his critique of those who consider adaptive behavior as a matter of mere **genes**:

"...the fascination generated by Dawkins'[34] theory arises from some bad habits of Western scientific thought -- from attitudes (pardon the jargon) that we call *atomism, reductionism,* and *determinism.* The idea that wholes should be understood by decomposing into "basic" units; that properties of microscopic units can generate and explain the behavior of macroscopic results; that all events and objects have definite, predictable, determined causes. These ideas have been successful in our study of simple objects, made of few components, and uninfluenced by prior history.... But organisms are much more than amalgamations of genes. They have a history that matters; their parts interact in complex ways. Organisms are built by genes acting in concert, influenced by environments, translated into parts that selection sees and parts invisible to selection. Molecules that determine the properties of water are poor analogues to genes and bodies. I may not be a master of my fate, but my intuition of wholeness probably reflects biological truth..." (Gould, 1980, pp. 77-78)

In sum, biological adaptation to survival imperatives is a complex, hierarchic, interactive, multi-factored process; the way bio-organisms are said to 'obey' functional 'laws' is much more complex, much less mechanistic, and not as strictly exceptionless, as the way inorganic objects or molecules obey physical or chemical laws. But this difference, and the enormous complexity involved, should not obscure the fact that adaptive motivation and functional explanation are just as legitimate hypotheses in the study of bio-behavior as the laws of physics or chemistry are in their respective domains.

8.5.3.5. **Some examples of law-governed behavior in bio-culture**

To illustrate how function-mediated bio-behavior may abide by general 'laws' without obeying them in the strictest sense, consider the following brief examples from language.

8.5.3.5.1. **Local vs. global adaptive behavior**

In general, grammatical morphology within the word is overwhelmingly *linear* at its historical point of origin. Morphemes precede or fol-

---

34 Gould was criticizing R. Dawkins' (1976) *The Selfish Gene.*

low each other in order, each signalling a single meaning ('function'). This reflects two general functional-adaptive 'laws' of natural communication:

(38)   a. **Code transparency:**
           "One form, one meaning"

       b. **Linear processing channel:**
           "Process one meaning-bearing element at a time"

Both 'laws' are motivated by some basic constraints on the various component of the communication system -- neurological, perceptual, cognitive, linguistic. They are 'obeyed' *in the main*, with numerous exceptions. Some languages, such as Turkish or Swahili, tend to obey these laws rather strictly, as evident in the highly regular Swahili verb paradigm:

(39)   a-li-on-a
       he-PAST-see-INDIC
       'He saw'

Others, such as Hebrew, collapse pronoun, tense and verb stem into a single *portmanteau* morpheme:

(40)   ra'a
       he/see/past
       'He saw'

And when one begins to sift through exceptions to 'laws' (38a,b), one recognizes a certain pattern: The 'violations' of such laws tend to arise over time, as **historical developments** that are motivated by other 'laws'. Those other 'laws' are in turn just as functionally motivated, but by *other* communicative functions. When a communicating organism strives to fulfill those other functions, the end product is often in conflicts with 'laws' (38a,b) above.

Put another way, the organism orients its behavior **locally** when solving particular functional problems, hinged in particular sub-domains of the complex system. But the results eventually reverberate **globally**, where they may also display **counter-adaptive effects** in other parts of the system. At the time of making an adaptive choice in one functional sub-domain, the organism is unaware of potential counter-adaptive ramifications in other sub-domains. But should this make general functional 'laws' such as (38a,b) less valid or less general? Are such 'laws' mere **inductive generalization** with no theoretical, explanatory status? Hardly. Rather, the complex, multi-variant nature of the communicative system, much like elsewhere in the bio-organism, conspires to make generalizations appear less than law-like, as compared to physics.[35]

8.5.3.5.2. Conflicting motivations

Consider next the status of typological generalizations in language. Recall the functionally-motivated generalization discussed in Chapter 6:

(41) "More **important** information **precedes** less important information".

As noted there, this 'law' is motivated by a cognitive principle that governs the allocation of **attention** to string-initial element, a principle backed by a wealth of experimental evidence. 'Law' (41) seems to apply most generally to languages with flexible word-order. But one may show that it is also reflected in rigid-order languages, such as SVO (English), VSO (Mayan) or SOV (Japanese). In all these language types, the subject (S) precedes the object (O); and the subject indeed tends to code the more important ('topical') referent in the clause. But how about the -- admittedly few -- languages that exhibit the rigid orders VOS (Malagasy) or OVS (Hixkaryana) -- where the subject *follows* the object? They surely 'violate' our functionally-motivated 'law' (41). However, these language-types abide by another, equally well motivated, ordering principle, one also discussed in Chapter 6:

(42) "Less **predictable** information **precedes** more predictable information"

Now, since the subject is both *thematically* more important and *anaphorically* more predictable, its relative ordering seems to engender a conflict between 'laws' (41) and (42). SOV, SVO and VSO languages solve this conflict by opting to go with the *importance* principle (41). While OVS and VOS languages solve it by opting to go with the *predictability* principle (42). And the general validity of the two laws need not be diminished as a result.

8.5.3.5.3. Historical change in law-abiding behavior

Consider next a related case, that of Biblical Hebrew. It had flexible ordering of the subject, abiding primarily by principle (42). Thus, for example, definite subjects in early Biblical Hebrew appeared overwhelm-

---

35 For many more examples of this phenomenon in grammar, see Givón (1979a, ch. 6). For its close equivalents in phonology, see Hyman (1973).

ingly *after* the verb, while indefinite subject appeared predominantly *before* it. As a corollary, Biblical Hebrew made use of neither the numeral 'one' nor the existential-presentative construction to mark indefinite subjects. It simply relied on principle (42). In other words, of two structural alternative available to code indefinite subjects -- word-order and morphology -- Biblical Hebrew 'chose' the one over the other.

In the course of history, Modern Hebrew wound up with the rigid word-order SVO -- which now does not allow the coding of indefiniteness by word-order. Instead, the language developed the use of the numeral 'one' -- and an existential-presentative construction -- for this purpose, following the pattern shown for Krio and Mandarin (see Chapter 5). Is principle (42) now less 'law', when Hebrew abides by it no more? Was it more 'law' when Hebrew abided by it earlier? And since, as an SVO language, Hebrew now abides more by principle (41), is that principle now more 'law', and was it less 'law' when Biblical Hebrew did not abide by it?

8.5.4. **The reductionist attack on functional explanation**

8.5.4.1. **Motive as 'cause' in socio-behavior**

The notion of 'function' without the teleology of a willful **agent** has been -- and indeed should be, if one agrees with Gould -- an anathema to reductionist philosophers. In attempting to exorcise the teleological ghost out of functional explanation, Hempel and Oppenheim (1948) chose to split the domain into two parts. The first encompasses the socio-behavioral sciences, and is said to deal with intentional behavior by identifiable **agents**, to which conscious **purpose, motive** or **intent** can be attributed. The agent's motives, it is contended, are simply a subspecies of the *cause* component of the *explanans* in the deductive causal-explanation schema (see (24) above):

"...motivational explanation, if adequately formulated, conforms to the conditions for causal explanation, so that the term "teleological" is a misnomer if it is meant to imply either non-causal character of the explanation or a peculiar determination of the present by the future. If this is borne in mind, however, the term "teleological" may be viewed, in this context, as referring to causal explanations in which some of the antecedent conditions are motives of the agents whose actions are to be explained..." (1948, p. 16)

The problem with this reduction of *function* to *motive* is of course that it excludes from legitimate functional explanation a wide range of cultural, social, and cognitive behavior that is altogether independent of conscious motivation by the behaving agent. Such behavior is clearly functional-adaptive in the most simple biological sense, and one cannot explain it in any but a functional context.

In the vast socio-cultural domain, for example, individuals and cultural groups behave very much like biological species -- *as if* they have purpose. As a scientist, one **abducts** the functional motivation that must underlie observed social structures and cultural behavior patterns. Such abducted functions are unimpeachable scientific hypotheses, dealing with invisible entities that explain visible patterns. Yet there is no evidence to suggest that individuals or socio-cultures are aware of functional considerations that motivate much of their behavior. The patterns evolve historically, as a conflation of myriad small, step-wise, *local* and often sub-conscious decisions. Individual local steps must be explained at a variety of levels within the complex process. The global pattern of such explanations reveals the mechanisms via which complex structure and complex function become matched through protracted evolution ('history'). But complex global functions, however legitimately abducted as explanation, cannot be reduced to conscious motives of the 'agents'.

Further, as noted in Chapter 7, many physiological, sensory-motor and cognitive processes in the behavior of higher organisms -- including humans -- become **automated**, either during phylogenetic evolution, or during the individual's lifetime learning. Such functions are clearly 'performed', by or within the organism, without conscious intent. Two examples from anthropology and linguistics will illustrate this.

Consider first one function that may be performed by at least some kinship systems,[36] the provision for *exogamy* (avoidance of in-breeding). It is indeed a theoretical construct, much like its close analogs in biology. But unlike biology, where purely *physical* structures are often involved in blocking in-breeding,[37] in human socio-culture the task is achieved via 'symbolic' categorization of *kins*, a categorization that guides the mating behavior of individuals. One thus can -- and indeed should -- abduce this functional explanation without necessarily assuming that memebers of the practicing culture are aware of this -- and other -- functions of the kinship system.

There exists an obvious analogy between the abduced function of exogamy of human kinship system, and in particular the way it correlates with social structure, and the match-up of function with structure in

---

36 See discussion of the function of kinship systems and related controversies in chapter 9. It is of course naive to assume that direct biological motivation, such as avoidance of in-breeding, can furnish the entire interpretation of kinship systems.

37 Some of the blocking devices in plants are already 'behavioral' rather than purely 'structural'. Thus, for example, avocado species vary the time of opening their male and female flowers 'in order to' insure cross-pollination.

pre-human biology. Many plant and animal species display remarkably similar correlations between the putative exogamy function, and an array of structural *and* behavioral 'means' 'designed' to 'achieve' it. Much like members of human cultures, these organisms are blissfully ignorant of their 'goal'.

Consider next a simple example from language, where one may legitimately abduce that the function of having a regular consonant-vowel alternation in speech, or more generally, the function of **dissimilatory processes** in phonology, is to facilitate both speech perception and articulation. One could indeed demonstrate experimentally the counter-adaptive effect of vowel-free or consonant-free phonology on speech perception, articulation, and even on lexical memory. One can -- and indeed must (if one is to adhere to Popper's meta-imperative of science) indulge in such explanatory abductions; one can construct experimental procedures to test them. One can and indeed must do all that in the relatively secure knowledge that:

(a) Such functional explanations of dissimilatory processes are legitimate explanatory abductions in a biological-behavioral science; and

(b) The speakers involved in the daily performance -- or historical development -- of such dissimilatory processes are blissfully unaware of their 'motives'.[38]

8.5.4.2. The denial of bio-teleology

In turning to deal with functional explanation in biology, where a conscious willful agent cannot be invoked, Hempel and Oppenheim (1948) dismiss the enterprise as an attempt to ascribe **anthropomorphic behavior** to non-human systems. To this practice they concede, at best, a salutary heuristic value:

"...One of the reasons for the perseverance of teleological considerations in biology probably lies in the fruitfulness of the teleological approach as a *heuristic device*: Biological research which was *psychologically motivated* by a teleological orientation, by an interest in purposes in nature, has frequently led to important results which can be stated in non-teleological terminology and which increase our scientific knowledge of causal connections between biological phenomena...Another aspect that lends appeal to teleological considerations is their *anthropomorphic character*. A teleological explanation tends to make us feel that we really "un-

---

38 As noted in Chapter 7, grammar is also an **automated instrument** of information processing, an instrument whose users are unaware of specific, 'local' communicative sub-goals.

derstand" the phenomenon in question, because it is accounted for in terms of purpose, with which we are *familiar* from our own experience of purposive behavior. But it is important to distinguish between understanding in the *psychological* sense of a feeling of *empathic familiarity* from understanding in the theoretical, or cognitive, sense of exhibiting the phenomenon to be explained as a special case of some general regularity..." (1948, p. 17 emphases are mine; TG)

This condescending rendition of the motivation behind functional explanation in bio-behavior may be summarized as follows:

(a) The hidden motives of the scientist indulging in such explanations are psychological rather than scientific;

(b) Functional hypotheses somehow cannot aspire to the status of 'general regularity' that more mechanical rules or causal explanations have attained;

(c) The only worthy type of explanation -- i.e. of contextualization -- of facts in science is the deductive variety, i.e. the viewing of the *explanandum* 'as a special case of some general regularity'.

What Hempel and Oppenheim seem to be doing is vent their methodological prejudice. They offer no coherent guideline for constructing an empirical methodology for bio-behavioral science.

8.6. Closure: Explanatory domains, ranges of facts and the legacy of structuralism

In choosing -- via abduction' hypothesis and experience-derived common sense -- the likely **explanatory domains** that will serve as context within which one purports to interpret puzzling facts, one automatically also chooses the relevant **data ranges**. This is, one suspects, one more facet of Hanson's (1958) **theory-laden facts**. Suppose, for example, that one aims to explain why the human body is structured -- in its anatomy and histology -- the way it is. One then seeks first the most obvious domains within which those structures *interact*, or are *embedded*:

(42) **Explanatory domains in biology:**
  (a) The external environment
  (b) Survival imperatives
  (c) The *genome*
  (d) Functions performed by the structures
  (e) Phylogenetic evolution
  (f) Ontogenetic growth
  (g) The social group

Of these, domains (a) and (b) turn out not independent of each other, but rather make up a mutually-dependent complex. Domain (c), in biology as in linguistics, tends out to be somewhat of a red herring. It merely bounces the *why* question to its rightful next level -- domains (e) and (f). Domain (d) is the bread-and-butter of understanding biological structures -- within the teleological constraints of (a) and (b). Finally, in many species functional-adaptive physical structures and behavioral patterns (d) -- most conspicuously sexual reproduction, feeding and defense -- have evolved within some social-interactive context (g), and are constrained by it.

Given such decisions on relevant explanatory domains, one now proceeds to seek facts from the very same domains: Ecology (a), global and local function (b, d), genetics (c), evolution (e), embryology (f), and group behavior (g). In this fashion, *pre-empirical, common-sensical*, theory-bound decisions about the relevant explanatory domains automatically define the range of relevant facts, to be gathered, sifted, correlated and eventually used for constructing explanation for the initial puzzle.

But one could also choose, if one is so inclined, an alternative method. One could begin by severely restricting the range of explanatory domains vis-a-vis which the facts are to be analyzed. In so doing, one automatically also restricts the range of facts deemed *relevant*, (a) to the entire domain, (b) to the abduction of specific hypotheses, and (c) to deductive-falsificatory testing. In the physical and biological sciences, the decision to restrict the range of facts is a **methodological convenience**, used in *preliminary, in vitro, controlled* experiments. In the social sciences, this pre-empirical decision has on occasion been invested with a *theoretical* aura, and extended illicitly to the explanatory domains.

Psychology, linguistics and anthropology have all, at one time or another, fallen victim to recurrent waves of **structuralism**. In rejecting functional explanation, structuralists in the social sciences have, at one time or another, adopted the philosophical stance of *either* reductionist school. Inductivist such as Bloomfield or Skinner, in ignoring Popper's meta-imperative, saw nothing to explain. Deductivists, like Lounsbury or Chomsky, saw structure as its own explanation. Since, to recast Kant's dialectic, *data not defined by theory is empty, and theory not driven by data is blind*, structuralism tends to whittle empirical science from both ends.

CHAPTER 9

LANGUAGE, CULTURE AND TRANSLATION

9.1. Introduction*

> "...to imagine a language means to imagine a form of life..."
>
> L. Wittgenstein, *Philosophical Investigations* (1953, p. 8)

Throughout the discussion in various chapters above, we saw how the interpretation ('meaning' or 'function') of linguistic expressions always depends, at least to some extent, on the context within which those expressions are used. This is true even of the most semantic features of grammar. As Ron Langacker has observed, *semantics is conventionalized pragmatics*. The degree to which meaning is conventionalized may vary, and this is true for both lexicon and grammar. But in human language no meaning can be one hundred percent conventionalized, for reasons that have to do with the unpredictability and open endedness of context. Thus, a residue of context dependence in interpreting linguistic expressions always remains, regardless of how conventionalized they may be.

As suggested at various points throughout (but see in particular chapters 3 and 6), the contexts within which human language is interpreted fall roughly into three major divisions:

(a) **The shared deictic context:**
   (i) *Speaker-hearer relations*: goals, speech-act value, social status/power relations, mutual knowledge and recognized mutual obligations;

---

*I am indebted to Dwight Bolinger, Pete Becker, George Grace, Kenneth Pike, Michael Shapiro, Anna Wierzbicka and -- last but not least -- my colleague Phil Young for many helpful comments and suggestions. I have also benefitted from the opportunity to present some of the ideas discussed here to critical audiences at SIL Papua-New Guinea (Ukarumpa, 1985), Auckland University (Auckland, 1986), Australian National University (Canberra, 1986), the University of Texas at Arlington (Dallas, 1987) and Universität zu Köln (Köln, 1987).

(ii)   *Deixis of the speech situation*: you & I, this & that, here & there, now & then.

(b)   **The shared discourse ('text') context:**
The knowledge shared by speaker and hearer due to prior transacted information -- the memory-stored discourse.

(c)   **The shared ('generic') world-view context:**
Shared knowledge of the physical and cultural universe, as coded in:
(i)   *The (encyclopedic) lexicon;*
(ii)   *Shared conventions of behavior & communication.*

In this chapter we will concern ourselves with the third division of context, the shared generic knowledge, implicit in the fact that the speaker and hearer are members of the same speech community -- or culture.

The issue of **translation** -- i.e. the transfer of knowledge across major linguistic-cultural boundaries -- invades the discussion rather naturally. Translation -- or paraphrase -- is indeed one of the best *test cases* we have for understanding linguistic expressions. The argument for an intimate connection between translation, understanding and culture runs roughly as follows:

(1)   **Translation and cultural world-view:**

If understanding a language entails understanding the culture's world-view, then cross-language translation is possible only to the extent that cross-cultural translation is possible.

The inquiry into the possibility of cross-language -- thus cross-culture -- translation opens up an even more vital question, having to do with the **universality** of language and thought:

(2)   **Translation and universality:**

If understanding a language requires understanding the cultural world-view, then cross-linguistic translation is only possible if cross-cultural differences are relatively *shallow*; that is, if the world-view held by different human cultures is largely *universal*.

It is thus not an accident that the discussion of translatability coincides, to quite extent, with the discussion of linguistic and cognitive universals.

In an intellectual climate that fosters extreme reductionism, the question of translation and universality has been approached in stark categorical terms of: Human thought is either universal or not, cultures either overlap in all but their decorative trivia, or diverge unpredictably. Translation is either a totally viable proposition, or an altogether futile mirage. As elsewhere, the pragmatist's position in considerably less than enviable, demanding the recognition of the murky, impure middle ground. We will begin our discussion with a survey of reductionist approaches in philosophy, anthropology and linguistics.

9.2. Modern extreme reductionists

9.2.1. Preamble

A certain measure of isomorphism again obtains between the traditional debate of rationalist vs. empiricist in epistemology, and the debate on translatability and universals. But the isomorphism is far from complete, and the relationships between the protagonists are on occasion not strictly predictable from their proclaimed philosophical roots.

As one may recall, both Plato and Aristotle held unabashed universalist positions concerning the human mind, albeit for radically different reasons. Plato's universalism sprang from his belief in the primacy of a universal set of **innate mental categories**. Aristotle's universalism was founded upon the postulated primacy of a fixed set of underlying **forms of the external world**. Since the human perceptual filter was, for Aristotle, a faithful mirror, universality of world gave rise to universality of mind.

Both Plato and Aristotle, in the best pre-empirical Greek tradition, discoursed upon universals of language (and mind) on the basis of a sample consisting of a single language and culture. Neither was overly concerned with the implications of linguistic or cultural diversity. When such diversity was eventually acknowledged, a considerable reassessment of the notion of universals took place among Plato and Aristotle's spiritual descendants.

9.2.2. The anti-universalism of modern empiricists

> "...The world is all that is the case. The worlds is the totality of facts, not things...*The limits of my language* mean the *limits of my world*..."

> L. Wittgenstein, *Tractatus Logico Philosophicus* (1918, pp. 7, 115.)

Somewhat characteristically, the 'early' Wittgenstein stakes out an enigmatic high grounds, one that remains open to considerable claim-jumping by latter-day interpreters. The identification of *language* with *world* may be interpreted as conservative Aristotelian empiricism, akin to Russell's or Carnap's *referential* approach to meaning. Given such reading, the diversity of the physical habitat would presumably determine -- in a Darwinian fashion -- a diversity of human languages. One could certainly interpret the traditional Sapir-Whorf discussion of the Eskimo's snow vocabulary and the Bedouin's camel terminology as reflecting such an empiricist approach.

One could, however, read Wittgenstein's 'limits' as the flip side of the Sapir-Whorf coin: Language -- or cultural world-view -- imposes the limits on the way one could perceive (or 'coherently interpret') the world. This second interpretation is plausible because of Wittgenstein's insistence that the world is not the totality of things but rather of *facts*:[1] It is a bit easier to demonstrate the relativity -- i.e. context dependence -- of 'fact' than of 'entity'.[2]

The linguistic anthropologists of the early 20th century in fact diverged as to which possible reading of Wittgenstein they were compatible with. In the manner of late 19th Century post-Darwinian social science, they were rather impressed with the seeming correlation between environmental and racial diversity. Further, they were deeply involved in the study of an immense, baffling diversity of human languages and cultures. Both the empiricist among them, such as Bloomfield, and the rationalists, such as Sapir, of necessity diverged from Aristotle and Plato, respectively, on the question of universality.

Bloomfield himself did not couch his comments in terms of culture or mind, but rather in terms of linguistic structure, as is apparent in his inductivist credo:

"...The only useful generalizations about language are inductive generalizations..." [1933, p. 20]

In criticizing the mentalistic universalism of H. Paul and his associates, Bloomfield writes:

"...even the fundamental features of Indo-European grammar, such as, especially, the parts of speech system, are by no means universal in the human speech. Believing these features to be universal, they [H. Paul *et al*; TG] resorted, whenever they dealt with fundamentals, to philosophical and psychological pseudo-explanations..." [1933, p. 17]

In the classical anti-universalist argument from diversity, Bloomfield then observes:

---

1   Popper (1959, p. 35, fn. *1) commended Wittgenstein on this 'slip' of his inductivist habit.
2   See discussion of the 'objectivity' of 'fact' and 'event' in Chapters 3 and 8.

"...North of Mexico alone there are dozens of totally unrelated groups of languages, presenting the most varied types of structure. In the stress of recording utterly strange forms of speech, one soon learns that philosophical presuppositions were only a hinderance..." [1933, p. 19]

9.2.3. The anti-universalism of modern mentalists

Unlike Bloomfield, Benjamin Lee Whorf was an unabashed, dyed-in-the-wool mentalist, and thus, one would presume, a philosophical Rationalist in the Herman Paul (i.e. German Romantic) tradition. Nonetheless, the so-called Sapir-Whorf Hypothesis on language and culture[3] boils down to an extreme **relativist** ('anti-universalist') position. One version of the hypothesis, further, is inherently an empiricist position:

(3)   **Sapir-Whorf I:**

    (a)   *Diversity*:
        (i)   Language reflects culture;
        (ii)   Culture reflects environment;
        (iii)   Environmental diversity accounts for cultural, thus linguistic, diversity.

    (b)   *Translation*:
        (i)   Cross-linguistic translation requires cross-cultural translation;
        (ii)   but cultures -- thus languages -- diverge immensely and unpredictably;
        (iii)   Therefore, neither universality nor translatability is viable.

One may, however, read another -- early Wittgensteinean -- interpretation into the Sapir-Whorf Hypothesis, one that is indeed more compatible with philosophical Rationalism:

(4)   **Sapir-Whorf II:**

    (a)   *Diversity*:
        (i)   Cultural world-views, thus also the languages that codes them, diverge immensely;
        (ii)   Linguistic categories pre-determine the way we perceive/construe the world (a Rationalist or Kantian hedge);

---

3   See Whorf (1950, 1956); Sapir (1949).

(b) *Translation*:
Given the manifest cultural-linguistic diversity, 'real' translation is not possible.

Perhaps the boldest expression of cultural-cum-linguistic relativism can be found in Whorf's discussion of the Hopi Indians' sense of time and space:

"...Just as it is possible to have any number of geometries other than Euclidean which give an equally perfect account of space configurations, so it is possible to have descriptions of the universe, all equally valid, that do not contain our familiar contrasts of time and space..." (1950/1956, p. 58)

The description is startling because it touches upon probably the most universal, evolutionarily oldest, biologically most in-wired features of organismic -- and human -- cognition. These are the very features that Kant recognized as our in-built mental trap, our species-determined point of view.[4] Whorf goes on to explain what prompted him to challenge the universality of our time-space schema:

"...[the Hopi] has no general notion or intuition of **time** as a smooth flowing continuum in which everything in the universe proceeds at an equal rate, out of a future, through a present, into a past; or, in which, to reverse the picture, the observer is being carried in the stream of duration continuously away from the past and into the future.
   After long and careful study and analysis, the Hopi language is seen to contain no words, grammatical forms, constructions or expressions that refer directly to what we call "time", or to past, present, or future, or to enduring or lasting, or to motion as kinematic rather than dynamic (i.e. as continuous translation in space and time rather than an exhibition of dynamic effort in a certain process), or that even refer to space in such a way as to exclude that element of extension or existence that we call "time"...Hence the Hopi language contains no reference to "time", either explicit or implicit..." (1950/1956, pp. 57-58)

We know now that the analysis of Hopi grammar and lexicon upon which this radical assertion is based was woefully superficial and misleading. It depended, in fact, on a rather narrow culture-specific criteria of what could constitute explicit or implicit reference to "time". Nonetheless, mentalistic cultural relativism of this kind has been extremely influential in both linguistics and anthropology.

---

4 See discussion of Kant's Transcendental Schema in Chapter 1.

9.2.4. The universalism of modern Rationalists

The rationalist line of transmission -- from Plato via Descartes to Chomsky and Katz -- is more predictable on the issue of translatability. Modern Rationalists have preserved the Greek-Latin-French tradition of expounding upon linguistic universals on the basis of a woefully restricted sample of the world's linguistic diversity. As far as modern Platonists are concerned, understanding linguistic expressions requires no reference to context. And, in defiance of one hundred years of cross-cultural linguistic anthropology, the cultural context -- thus world view -- is taken as a matter of course to be uniform and unproblematic.

As George Grace (1986) has noted, using terminology adapted from Austin, some modern rationalists adopt a strict **locutionary** approach to translatability, disregarding even *structural* cross-language diversity. An example of this is Katz's *effability* principle:

"...Every proposition is the sense of some sentence in each natural language..." (1976, p. 37)

In an earlier rendition, Katz identifies most succinctly the particular brand of universalist motivation that prompts his interest in translation:

"...Effability makes a very strong claim about natural languages. What is so important about this claim that one should take on its defense? First, there is the fact that without it there is no basis for *an interlinguistic notion of proposition* on which to base hypotheses about *the relation of logic and language*..." (1972, p. 22; see also Katz, 1978, pp. 219-220; emphases are mine; TG)

As Grace (1986) points out, universalists of Katz's stripe assume that grammar is a relatively trivial matter, highly interchangeable across languages, thus posing only a weak barrier to translation. For every 'sentence' in one language one can find some meaning-equivalent 'sentence' in any other language. As we shall see below, it is relatively easy to show that this extreme position is untenable.

Grace (1986) goes on to discuss another universalist approach, that of **perlocutionary** translation. This approach concedes the existence of non-trivial structural differences between languages. It then allows for a sentence of one language to be translated into any 'expression' of another language, be that expression a single sentence of the same structure, a single sentence of a different structure, or a number of sentences assembled together in whatever configuration. Such a position is characterized well in the following quotation from Osgood and Sebeok (eds, 1954):

"...This comes out clearly in statements such as "anything *can* be expressed in any language, but the structure of a given language will favor certain statements and hinder others..." (1954, p. 193)

Edward Sapir's position on the issue, while not crystal clear, imparts a surprisingly universalist flavor, given what one would have inferred from Whorf's extreme relativism:

"...It would be absurd to say that Kant's 'Critique of Pure Reason' could be rendered forthwith into the unfamiliar accents of Eskimo or Hottentot, and yet it would be absurd in but a secondary degree. What is really meant is that the culture of these primitive folks has not yet advanced to the point where it is of *interest* to them to form *abstract conceptions* of a philosophical order. But it is not absurd to say that there is nothing in the *formal peculiarities* of Hottentot or Eskimo which would obscure the clarity or hide the depth of Kant...It is not absurd to say that both Hottentot and Eskimo possess all the formal apparatus that is required to serve as a matrix for the expression of Kant's thought. If their languages have not the requisite Kantian *vocabulary*, it is not the languages that are to blame but the Eskimo and Hottentot themselves..." (1949, p. 154; emphases are mine; TG)

First, Sapir seems to view cross-language differences in grammar -- 'formal peculiarities' -- as relatively trivial, in so far as translatability is concerned. One would presume a **perlocutionary** approach to translatability is what he may have had in mind. Second, Sapir seems to consider the main obstacle to translation, the lexicon-culture complex, as a relatively superficial matter of **technical vocabulary** ('abstract conceptions'), whose paucity can be easily remedied. Finally, Sapir seems to ascribe the cultural barriers to translation to primarily the natives' **motivation**, something that is again presumably easy to remedy, given sufficient incentive.

In the next section I propose to summarily dispense with the stronger -- Grace's *locutionary* -- approach to translation, by showing that cross-language grammatical diversity renders this type of translation untenable.

9.3. Grammar and translation

In this section I will attempt to show that if cross-language translation is possible, it is only possible in Grace's more lax *perlocutionary* sense. That is, it is not always the case that a single sentence in one language can be translated into a single sentence in another language. And in particular, the Western logician's concept of 'proposition' does not always match the structural facts of sentencehood.[5] In attempting to demonstrate this, I will survey, in order, a number of test cases.

9.3.1. Serial verb constructions

The phenomenon of serial-verb constructions involves a certain well-documented diversity in the way languages code unitary 'events'. A 'simple event' that English tends to code with a single verb -- thus presumably single sentences/propositions whose core is that verb -- is coded in other languages by a 'serial construction' of two or more verbs. To illustrate this, consider the following contrast between English and some West African languages:

(5) **Serial verb constructions**[6]

    a. iywi *awa* utsi iku   (Yatye)
        boy *took* door shut
        'The boy shut the door'

    b. mo *fi* ade   ge ñakã   (Yoruba)
        I *took* machete cut wood
        'I cut (the) wood with the machete'

    c. nam utom ẹemi *ni* mi   (Efik)
        do work this *give* me
        'Do this work for me'

    d. ọ gbara *gaa* ahya   (Igbo)
        he ran   *go* market
        'He went to the market'

As far as translatability -- and the universality of the notion 'proposition' -- is concerned, serial-verb constructions may be viewed from two perspectives:

(a) One could consider verb serialization as a relatively trivial matter of **grammatical structure** and **lexicalization**, as suggested in Givón (1975a). The multi-verb serial constructions in (5) will be thus viewed as single sentences, coding single men-

---

5 This is not to suggest that other problems for translation do not arise from the cross-language variability of grammar. Indeed, they often do. For some discussion, see Keenan (1978) or Givón (1978b).
6 From Givón (1975a).

tal propositions; their divergence from their English counterparts is a relatively superficial fact of structure/grammar.
Given this view, Katz-type ('locutionary') translatability is unproblematic.

(b) Alternatively, one may view verb serialization as a profound
cross-cultural **cognitive** difference in event perception, as
suggested in Pawley (1976, 1987), whereby cultures that
practice this type of event coding indeed perceive our unitary event as a *chain of multiple events*. Given this view, 'locutionary' as well as 'perlocutionary' translation are problematic.

Even when one finds general empirical grounds, independent of
grammar, for rejecting interpretation (b) of verb serialization,[7] there remains the fact that serial-verb constructions sometime display the **gram-
matical-structural** trimmings of multi-sentence ('multi-propositional'?)
constructions. Thus, consider the following example from Kalam, a
clause-chaining Papuan language, with a high incidence of verb
serialization.[8] While most serial verbs in this language are stripped bare
of any grammatical morphology, some require typical **medial verb** morphology on both verbs in the construction, thus technically signalling
two consecutive clauses within the thematic clause-chain:

(6)   ...mon *dangiy-ek   yin-ek*   saŋdi-sap...
          fire *light-DS   burn-DS*   leave-PRES
          '...She lights the fire and leaves...'
          (lit.: '...*she* lights the fire (till) *it* burns (and) *she* leaves...'

The subject of the first verb in (6), chain-medial 'light', is 'she', and the
verb is marked by DS ('different-subject', cataphoric switch-reference)
morphology. The subject of the second verb, chain-medial 'burn', is
'fire', and the verb is again marked by DS morphology. The subject of
the third verb, chain-final 'leave', is once again 'she', and this verb is
marked by finite morphology. The grammar treats the first two clauses
as independent. But in text they and their equivalents appeared
predominantly as fixed expressions, semantically **co-lexicalized**, much
like the Mandarin resultative verb compounds that display no verb
morphology (Thompson, 1973).

---

7 See Givón (1987).
8 See Pawley (1966) for a general description of Kalam. The data is from my own field notes,
   with generous help from Lyle Scholz and Andy Pawley.

9.3.2. **Pre-posed adverbial clauses in strict verb-final language**

As noted recently by Thompson (1985) and Ramsay (1987), the discourse function of pre-posed adverbial clauses in English is very different from that of post-posed adverbial clauses. Typical examples of the two ordering types are:

(7) (a) **Pre-posed:**
...To do that, you pull the lever and release the bolt...

(b) **Post-posed:**
...you pull the lever *to release the next bolt*, then...

The functional differences between constructions such as (7a) and (7b) above may be interpreted, among other things,[9] as reflecting the **degree of integration** ('coherence') of the purpose clause vis-a-vis its main clause. What is important for the present discussion is that pre-posed adverbial clauses seem to have stronger referential and thematic connections to the **preceding** discourse, and a much looser referential/thematic connection to their main clause (in spite of their obvious *semantic* relation to the latter). Pre-posed adverbial clauses thus display what Haiman (1978) has termed -- for 'if' clauses -- *topic characteristics*. Further, structurally, pre-posed ADV-clauses tend to be separated from their following main clause by a comma (i.e. pause).

Post-posed adverbial clauses, on the other hand, are much more integrated -- thematically, referentially and semantically -- with their preceding main clause. They are also more integrated with it **structurally**, and usually follow it without a pause. One could thus argue that both thematically and structurally, pre-posed adverbial clauses are 'more independent', while post-posed ones are more 'part of the main clause'.

The cross-linguistic distribution of the ordering of adverbial clauses is skewed in the following way:

(a) All language seem to have *pre-posed* ADV-clauses;
(b) Many strict verb-final languages[10] allow no *post-posed* ADV-clauses.

Thus, the meaning (or 'function') of the more-integrated post-posed

---

9 See for example Ramsay (1987) as well as discussion in Givón (1986a).
10 Such as, for example, the clause-chaining Tibeto-Burman languages of Nepal (Newari, Sherpa), or New Guinea Highlands languages such as Hua (Haiman, 1979) or Chuave (Thurman, 1978), *inter alia*.

ADV-clauses, as in (7b) above, cannot be conveyed in languages of type (b). Their grammar simply makes no provision for it.

9.3.3. Verb complement structure

In English, there is a systematic meaning difference between the complement-taking constructions of 'want' and 'wish', as in:[11]

(8) a.   She *wanted* him to leave

    b.   She *wished* that he would leave

The syntactically more integrated single-clause-like expression in (8a) usually implies some *direct verbal contact* between the subject of 'want' and the subject of the complement clause, thus an *attempted verbal manipulation*. On the other hand, the more loosely-bound two-clause structure in (8b) is more likely to characterize a *private wish*, with no direct contact and no attempted manipulation. In some languages 'want' is a single lexical item that can take only the looser construction type (8b), never the tightly-bound (8a). Spanish and Israeli Hebrew are such languages:

(9) a.   quería   que se-fuera   (Spanish)

           wanted-3s that REFL-go-SUBJUNCT-3s
           'She wished that he would leave'

    b.   *le   quería   (a)   ir
       him   wanted-3s (to)   go/INF

    c.   hi ratsta   she-hu yelex   (Hebrew)
       she wanted-3sf that-he 3sm/FUT/leave
       'She wished that he would leave'

    d.   *hi   ratsta   oto/lo   la-lexet
       she wanted him/DAT-him to-go/INF

Now, even if this restriction in Spanish and Hebrew is only a superficial fact of grammar, and if (9a) and (9c) above are in fact ambiguous and code the meaning of both English (8a) and (8b),[12] still we face a clear-cut situation whereby the single-clause English construction (8a) finds its

---

11 See discussion in Chapter 3, above, as well as Givón (1980a).
12 There are indeed grounds for believing that Spanish and Hebrew simply cannot express the shade of meaning of the English (8a) with the verb 'want', as distinct from 'She *told* him to leave'.

Spanish and Hebrew translation in much looser two-clause constructions. In other words, locutionary translation is not possible.

9.3.4. Co-lexicalized complement-taking verbs

In some languages, modality and manipulative verbs do not appear
as separate words. Rather, they are co-lexicalized together with the complement verb, appearing together as a single word. This represents one
further step of **structural condensation** beyond the English example
(8a), above. As illustration, consider the following from Yaqui (Jelinek,
1986):

(12) a.   inepo siim-*pea*
           I   leave-*wish*
           'I wish to leave'

      b.   aapo Mary-ta   siim-*'i'a*
           he   Mary-OBJ leave-*want*
           'He wants Mary to leave'

      c.   inepo Mary-ta   siim-*sae*-n
           I   Mary-OBJ leave-*tell*-PAST
           'I told Mary to leave'

      d.   apo'ik-ne siim-*tua*-k
           him-I   leave-*make*-PERF
           'I made him leave'

      e.   apo'ik-ne siim-*tua-tevo*-k
           him-I   leave-*make-ask*-PERF
           'I had him leave'

      f.   enči-ne yi'i-*mahta*-k
           you-I dance-*teach*-PERF
           'I taught you to dance'

      g.   inepo 'a-yi'i-*vič a*-k
           I   him-dance-*see*-PERF
           'I saw him dance'

Clearly then, clause-per-clause ('locutionary') translation from either
English, Spanish or Hebrew into Yaqui is not possible.

9.3.5. **Non-embedded background clauses**

In languages such as English, restrictive relative clauses are embedded within the noun phrase whose head noun they modify. Thus, they form a single, complex sentence together with their main clause. In many other languages, restrictive relative clauses cannot be embedded at all. To illustrate this, consider the following examples from Chuave, a New Guinea Highlands language (Thurman, 1978). In this language, restrictive REL-clauses, unreduced verb complements and ADV-clauses are coded structurally the same way, as backgrounded **topic clauses** that must precede the main clause:

(13) a. **REL-clause:**
          gan moi-n-g-u-a,
          child be-he-TOP-him-NONSIM
          'The child (who) is here,

          Gomia tei   awi d-i
          Gomia there send leave-IMPER
          send (him) to Gomia!'

          or: 'Send the child who's here to Gomia!'

      b. **V-complement:**
          kasu di-in-g-a,
          lie   say-they-TOP-NONSIM
          'That they told a lie,

          fai-ke-Ø-m-a
          right-NEG-PAST-it-EMPH
          (it's) not right'.

          or: 'It's not right that they told a lie'.

      c. **ADV-clause:**
          ne iki-num   moi-n-g-i,
          you house-your be-you-TOP-SIM
          'While you are in your house,

          tei   u-na-y-e
          there come-FUT-I-DECLAR
          I will come there'.

          or: 'I'll come over when you're at home'.

d. **Topic clause:**
    koma du-pun-g-a-rai,
    before say-we-TOP-NONSIMULT-that
    'Concerning that talk we had before,

    niki do-∅-m-e
    bad be-PAST-it-DECLAR
    it was no good'.

Clearly, a single though complex sentence of English in (13a,b,c) must be rendered into Chuave as two separate sentences.

9.3.6. The grammatical coding of evidentiality

In a recent paper, Thompson (1987) shows that the marking of evidentiality (see discussion in Chapter 4) in English is often achieved via main clauses containing cognition verbs, as in expressions such as:

(14)   a.   *I think* she did it
       b.   She was there, *I hear*
       c.   *They say* it was a disaster
       d.   It was a disaster, *I understand*

But in many languages the very same distinction are coded by grammatical particles, most commonly attached to the verb (Nichols and Chafe, eds, 1986). Thus, consider the following example from Turkish (Slobin and Aksu, 1982):

(15)   a.   Kemal gel-di
            Kemal come-PAST/direct experience
            'Kemal came' (I have direct evidence)

       b.   Kemal gel-miš
            Kemal come-PAST/indirect experience
            'Kemal came' (I heard, or I infer)

The choice of evidential status is obligatory in the use of the past tense in Turkish. Locutionary -- clause-per-clause -- translation between English and Turkish is not possible here. If the evidential force of Turkish propositions is to be rendered into English, it must be coded there by a separate verbal clause.

9.3.7. Manipulative speech acts in Korean

In English, weak manipulative speech acts involving obligation or permission are rendered as a single clause with a modal verb, as in:

(16) a. You *must* do this.
      b. You *may* leave.
      c. You *should* listen more carefully.
          etc.

In Korean, on the other hand, such speech acts may only be rendered by a concatenation of two clauses, the first of which is a pre-posed *conditional* clause, followed by a main clause that expresses an *evaluative* judgement. Thus consider the following examples (Kim, 1986):

(17)
  a. i   ch'aek-un an   ilk-o-myon,   an   twe-n-ta
      this book-TOP NEG read-MOD-if NEG become-   PRES-PRT
      'You must read this book'
      (Lit.: 'If you don't read this book, it won't be OK')

  b. i   ch'aek-un an ilk-o-to,   twe-n-ta
      this book-TOP NEG read-MOD-even/if become-   PRES-PRT
      'You may not-read this book'
      'You don't have to read this book'
      (Lit.: 'Even if you don't read this book, it'll be OK')

  c. i   chaek-un an ilk-o-ya,   twe-n-ta
      this book-TOP NEG read-MOD-only/if become-   PRES-PRT
      'You must/should/may not read this book'
      (Lit.: 'If you only not read this book, it'll be OK')

  d. i   chaek-un ilk-o-myon, an   twe-n-ta
      this book-TOP read-MOD-if NEG become-   PRES-PRT
      'You must not read this book'
      (Lit.: 'If you read this book, it won't be OK')

Once again, single-clause expressions in one language can only be rendered as two-clause expressions in another language.[13]

---

13 There are grounds for suspecting that the difference between Korean and English here is not merely in grammar, but also in culture. As Brown and Levinson (1978) have observed, more polite, deferent manipulative speech acts tend to be coded by longer, more circuitous, multi-clausal linguistic expressions. The fact that Korean cannot code these manipulative expressions as single-clause expressions may be one indication of the level of deference that must involve their use.

9.4. Meaning, culture and translation

9.4.1. **Preamble: Meaning, understanding and context**

"...Understanding is, roughly, *organized knowledge*, i.e. knowledge of the *relations* between various facts..."

> M. Scriven, *Explanations, predictions and laws* (1962, p. 102)

Until now we dealt with the easier problem of translation, the one that centered on the cross-language differences in grammatical structure. As we have seen, such differences render the more extreme doctrine of clause-for-clause *locutionary* translation, untenable. In the course of the discussion we touched relatively little upon meaning or culture. This is not because grammatical organization never reflects cultural-semantic perspective, but rather because the bulk of cross-cultural differences are reflected in the organization of **lexical meaning**.

As one may recall, in the lax sense of translation, Grace's *perlocutionary*, identity of form may be dispensed with but identity of meaning is preserved. In this section I will attempt to show why even this weaker option is not viable, leastwise not in a form that would preserve Katz's *effability* hypothesis – and especially its theoretical presuppositions – intact.

We will consider two alternative versions of a universalist translatability hypothesis, subject both to the empirical weight of specific case studies, and show how they crumble under that weight. In the process, we will note than attempts to develop *missing vocabulary* for a *target language*, with which to translate concepts from a *source language*, may yield three possible results:

(18)   **Options of cross-cultural translation:**

    (a)   Failure of cross-cultural translation;

    (b)   Profound readjustment in the target populations' cultural world-view; or

    (c)   The maintenance, in the mind of the target population, of two -- well segregated but conflicting -- cultural world views.

Paradoxically -- but in keeping with the pragmatic middle ground -- we will then suggest that these results do not necessarily militate for extreme cultural relativism. Rather, the balance between cultural universality and cultural specificity -- the possible **overlap** of world-views -- is a matter of *degree*. It may vary from one source:target dyad to the next; and within each dyad, from one cultural sub-domain to the next. And, like similar issues in the typological comparison of language *structure*, the matter must be resolved empirically.

It is, I believe, relatively safe to concede that the major impediment to cross-language -- thus cross-culture -- translation is meaning, as coded primarily in the lexicon. This is so because 'missing vocabulary' does not entail trivial, accidental gaps in a lexicon construed, as deductivists have construed it all along, as a mere *list* of atomic concepts. Rather, the vocabulary of a language -- that massive repository of the cultural world view of a speech community -- is a highly structured **network**. Within such a network, individual words ('concepts') are not defined purely **componentially**, i.e. by the mere inclusion of some universal, Platonic 'semantic features'.[14] Rather, they are defined, in large part, **relationally**, relative to other concepts partaking in the network. Meaning, as noted in Chapter 2, and thus *understanding*, is at least in part **contextual** and **relational**. (As Scriven notes, following Wittgenstein, understanding must pertain to *relations* rather than merely to items and their sub-components). And it is this fundamental feature of meaning -- thus of understanding -- that conspires to make cross-cultural translation such a thorny issue. And this is true even for those of us who find it meaningful talk about universals of language, mind and culture.

9.4.2. Translating across lexical gaps: Case studies

In this section we will consider a number of test cases in the translation of vocabulary. In each case, vocabulary items will be revealed to project deeply into the cultural-semantic network of world-view. In each case, either cross-cultural translatability is impossible, or some *degree of* non-trivial change of the target culture must first occur, before meaningful translation can take place.

9.4.2.1. The red herring of technological vocabulary

Consider the following passage from Carroll (1953), where the problem of cultural differences is (a) identified as the main barrier to translation, (b) correctly lumped together with the problem of technology, but (c) at the same breath trivialized:

"...In general (that is, *aside from differences arising from culture and technology*) contrary to the popularly held misconception, anything that can be said in one language can be said in any other language..." (1953, p. 47; emphases are mine; TG)

---

14 As in Katz and Fodor (1964).

One seems to discern a similar trivialization in Sapir's discussion of how one may translate Kant into Eskimo or Hottentot:

"...it is not absurd to say that both Hottentot and Eskimo possess all the formal apparatus that is required to serve as a matrix for the expression of Kant's thought. If their languages have not the requisite Kantian *vocabulary*, it is not the languages themselves that are to be blamed but the Eskimo and Hottentot themselves..." (1949, p. 154; emphasis is mine; TG)

Sapir seems to consider vocabulary gaps as *accidents* that can be easily remedied by the speakers, given sufficient incentive. The target language -- the *system* -- is not to blame, its formal structure is no impediment to translation, it is inherently just as capable as the source language of producing fresh technical vocabulary -- new atomic slots of meaning -- upon demand.

There are, of course, perfectly good cases where new technology -- thus new technical vocabulary -- may be introduced into the culture without creating profound conceptual dislocation. But when this occurs, one usually finds that the *functions* performed by the new technology are already extant in the culture; they have been recognized within the cultural word-view. What takes place is simply a **substitution** of one manner of performing those functions by another. To illustrate this, consider the acquisition of firearms -- technology and vocabulary -- by the Ute indians of Colorado. A missive-shooting weapon, the bow-and-arrow, had already been in existence. The new weapon, initially the flint gun, was named *tɨpɨ́y*, literally 'rock', 'flint'. Gunpowder was then named *tɨpɨ́y-kuca-ti-pu̧*, literally 'that which makes the gun start' (i.e. 'gun-starter'). The verb 'shoot' is currently *kukwí-* , most likely related to *kukwí-vi* 'charcoal'; this suggests a likely connection with black powder. Finally, the newly introduced ammunition, 'bullet', was referred to as either *'úu-* 'arrow' or its derivative *'úu-aĝa-tu̧*, lit. 'that which has arrow'. Up to this point, the new technology fitted into pre-existing slots, roughly as follows:[15]

(19) **Borrowing into an existing technological structure:**

slot	pre-existing	new adaptation
instrument	bow	'flint' (=gun)
missile	arrow	'arrow' (=bullet)
propellant	string	'gun-starter' (=powder)
act	pull/release	'charcoal' (=shooting)

15 For the Ute vocabulary see Givón (1979b).

Beyond a certain point, however, there are clear limits to this seemingly successful technological borrowing, and its concomitant lexical adaptation: The conceptual apparatus -- or context -- needed to elucidate *what precisely causes the missive to propel* is simply not there. This limit is apparent from naming powder *gun-starter*, then deriving the act of shooting from *charcoal*. Both derivation are accurate observation on the causal chain involved -- accurate as far as they go. From that point on, they also reveal the limits of the borrowing, namely the failure to borrow the conceptual apparatus which may explain the actual *chemical process* involved in the new technology. This crucial correlate of the new technology was not borrowed into Ute culture of that time. And rightly so, since that is precisely the part that would have required a considerable, far-from-trivial restructuring of the cultural world view. And Ute culture at the time of borrowing firearms had no pressing need to engage in such conceptual restructuring. And when the chemical concepts underlying gunpowder are finally borrowed into a bow-and-arrow civilization, their incorporation into the culture's world view demands massive re-structuring and non-trivial cultural change.[16]

9.4.2.2. Cosmology and the physical universe

Consider a pre-Copernican speech community X, such as many, in which the concept 'sun' entails, among other things, a physical phenomenon of a certain size, luminescence, warmth, east-to-west trajectory, daily and yearly cycle, etc. In addition, it is also the major deity, male in gender (as contrasted with the female moon), the creator, to be thanked for the gift of life, to be propitiated against all manner of misfortune and natural calamity. Culture X has a distinct word for the sun (also meaning 'day', 'light' and 'God'). That word carries with it an intense **affective** and **spiritual** load, even when 'merely referring' to the physical phenomenon. The question now is -- in what sense is the word 'sun' in culture X translatable into present-day English, and vice versa?

---

16 While the concepts of modern chemistry did not find their way into Ute culture with the borrowing of fire-arms, the advent of warfare with an invading culture did not leave the Ute world-view unscathed. Traditional Ute warfare was seldom aimed at total extermination of the enemy -- either warrior or home population. Ute warfare -- much like in pre-Napoleonic time (see Rapoport, 1968) -- was aimed at demonstrating one's superiority, then extracting from the enemy maximal benefits. Within this framework, war often took a somewhat symbolic guise, with the warrior's *power* ('Medicine') being overwhelmingly spiritual. The advent of firearms, their exterminatory potential, and the martial practices of their white bearers, exerted a profoundly depressing effect on the Utes' concept of 'Medicine Power' (*puwáv*). Tried and true methods of making oneself powerful ceased to work, rendered inexplicably useless in the face of thick volleys of cavalry bullets. The cultural-spiritual ramifications for this -- to the Utes inexplicable -- failure were enormous, resulting in withdrawal, despair and recourse to a rapid succession of non-native religious modes (see Jorgensen, 1972).

In attempting to answer this question, we will set up three alternative hypotheses, beginning with:

(20) TRANSLATABILITY I: **The referential hypothesis**

"(As a strict logical positivist may argue:) Whatever extra semantic-cultural baggage the two cultures may load upon 'sun', the word still refers, in both cultures, to the same **physical object**, thus presumably to the same **experience**. The rest is frills, obfuscation or prejudice".

Hypothesis (20) is admittedly somewhat of a straw-man. Meaning is indeed a matter of experience,[17] but experience is in principle *not* a mere matter of 'objective' reference. Consider, for example, the following three references to 'the sun', uttered at the winter solstice:

(21) a.   The sun is not very hot today.
       b.   The sun is angry today.
       c.   The sun's rays are least dense today.

Of these three references to 'sun', only (21a) is translatable both ways. (21b) is comprehensible in X but senseless in English. And (21c) is comprehensible in a sub-culture of today's English but senseless in X.[18]

One may of course proceed to learn *about* culture X, then understand (21b) to mean:

(22) a.   The speaker believes the sun is a powerful deity,
       b.   and asserts it is angry today.

Has successful translation from X to English then taken place? Perhaps, but a number of provisos must be considered.

First, the meanings -- in terms of truth conditions -- of (21b) and (22) are not the same. The speaker of X, felicitously uttering (21b), believes that 'The sun is a deity'. But the speaker of English felicitously uttering (22) does not; he/she only believes (22a) -- i.e. that 'The speaker of X believes that the sun is a deity'. Further, the speaker of X asserts (21b) -- 'The sun is angry'. But the speaker of English asserts (22b) -- i.e. 'The speaker of X asserts that the sun is angry'.

---

17 As one of Anthony Powell's characters observes in *Books do Furnish a Room*: "...It is not what happens to people that is significant, it is what they think happens to them..." (1971, p. 145)
18 Phil Young (in personal communication) notes that an adjustment in an individual's world-view does not necessarily change the culture. Still, all cultural change must begin with the world-view of *some* individual member(s).

Second, the cultural context -- belief, world-view -- was supplied as a necessary ingredient in order for even the less-than-adequate (22) to serve as translation of (21b) into English. Without such context no translation was possible at all. Understanding someone else's cultural world-view is akin to having one's own enlarged. This is so because the exclusive world views of either X or English, before they came to grapple with how to translate (21b,c), *precluded* the existence of any other world view. Admitting that another world view exists, even without granting it legitimacy, already carries with it the germ of profound cultural change.[19]

Third, does the admission of existence of another world view, i.e. granting (22a), really guarantee an English speaker an understanding of (21b)? Consider: Anger has consequences in terms of other beliefs held by the speakers of X, of certain expectations, fears and concomitant behavior. These other beliefs, expectations, fears and normative behavior are part of the meaning of what it means for a speaker of X to understand (21b). What is at issue is a whole range of cognitive and affective habitual associations of 'sun'. And these associations are not accessible to speakers of English, unless they themselves come to regard the sun as a deity. Sharing 'the same meaning' thus lasts only as long as the state of 'sharing the same beliefs' can be maintained. In other words, meaningful cross-culture translation may require **bi-culturalism**. And bi-culturalism, in turn, entails holding simultaneously two sets of **incompatible beliefs**. And, switching back and forth between two sets of incompatible beliefs may be a prerequisite for understanding meanings in another culture.

Logicians and deductivist linguists tend to take for granted that people do not hold contradictory beliefs. This presupposes that the entire body of knowledge stored in the human mind is always accessible for weeding out contradictions. But as noted in Chapter 7, massive evidence from cognitive psychology suggest that only a tiny proportion of a person's knowledge-base is accessible -- or placed in the focus of attention -- at any given time. Holding two cultural world-views that can be accessed selectively, in the appropriate context, is probably the norm for (at least) complex, fractionated cultures such as ours. Equally massive experimental evidence also suggests that the semantic organization -- i.e. knowledge structure or **world view** -- of technical experts is qualitatively different, usually much more elaborate and detailed with a **different pattern of inter-connections**, than the world-view of naive members of the culture.[20]

---

19 It is by no means clear that the majority of speakers of American English embrace a model of the universe that even remotely approximates the scientists'. See further discussion of this in section 9.4.2.4., below.

20 See extensive review in Ericsson (1985), as well as the earlier work by Chase and Simon (1973) and Chase and Ericsson (1981, 1982), *inter alia*.

Let us consider now an alternative hypothesis, a slight modification of (20) above:

(24)   TRANSLATABILITY II: **The 'universal core' hypothesis**

"(As a more reasonable universalist may wish to argue:) The concept 'sun' in the two cultures -- X and English -- overlaps partially. That overlap may be termed the *core* ('universal') element of 'sun'. That element, at the very least, is translatable from X to English and vice-versa".

Hypothesis (24) concedes the arguments against hypothesis (20), contending itself with only partial translation whenever there is sufficient overlap. This certainly sounds reasonable, and presumably the degree and actual identity of the overlapping 'universal' elements can be determined empirically. Still, a number of arguments against hypothesis (24) remain.

First, perhaps somewhat trivially, the world-view overlap between X and English may not be the same as between X and other languages, or English and other languages. The question of universality may turn out to involve a considerable muddle.

Second, for hypothesis (24) to be a viable doctrine of universality and translation, a strictly Platonic view of meaning must be entertained, one in which atomic units of meaning may be found in different languages and have *the same semantic value* in all languages, regardless of the divergent networks/contexts within which they are embedded. As we have argued throughout, the plausibility of such a state of affairs is indeed low.

9.4.2.3. Spatial orientation in Guugu Yimidhirr

Miller and Johnson-Laird (1976) have claimed that some features of spatial organization -- or space perception -- such as *front-back* and *left-right* distinctions, are cognitive human-universals. And that in contrast, cardinal compass points (North, South, East, West) orientation is a relatively late derivative of industrial-scientific cultures. In the cultures/languages of Aborigine Australia, the opposite seems to be true. For example, Haviland (1986) observes that in one such culture, Guugu Yimidhirr, no right-left or front-back designations are ever used to indicate the position of objects in geographical space, relative to the speaker, hearer, or any other reference point. Rather, the cardinal compass points are invariably used whenever objects are identified in space. Near obligatory reference to those absolute compass points is made whenever locative post-positions are used. Further, when entities are referred to as subjects or objects of clauses designating states or events, a frequent use of the relatively few deictic markers of the language can be seen, and these markers are nearly always further marked by the compass-points markers. Even the gestures accompanying the descriptions of physical entities within geographic space are oriented toward the absolute compass points. To illustrate the grammar of these distinctions briefly, consider the following text-derived examples from Haviland (1986):

(25)

   a.   ...yarra *dyiba*-rra   waguur ganbarr-in...
        yonder *south/to*-FOC outside jump-PAST
        '...then (they) went inland yonder to the South...'

   b.   ...coconut nhyayun *dyiba*-almun galmba dagaarrgarr-in...
        coconut that/from *south*-FOC also grow/REDUP-PAST
        '...coconuts used to grow there on the South side
        (coming from an unspecified distance to the South)...'

   c.   ...nyundu nhila nhaamaalman Bala yarrba *gunggaalu*...
        you now see/REDUP/ASP Bala this/way *north/from/*FOC
        '...if you look nowadays this way North from Bala...'

   d.   ...*guwa*-alu mission-bi gaday...
        west-FOC mission-to come/PAST
        ...they came to the mission (station) to the West...'

   e.   ...ngayu gurray nyundu yarrba ganbarra *ngaal*-nguurr...
        I   say/PAST you this/way jump/IMPER *east*-FOC
        '...I said: "You jump in there on the East side...'

It can be shown, further, that Guugu Yimidhirr speakers who learn English have no trouble manipulating correctly left-right and front-back spatial references. But would the introduction of such distinctions into the Aborigine language be a purely trivial matter? Haviland (1986) and others who have studied Aborigine cultures think not.[21] The ever-present coding of physical space in terms of compass points has profound

---

21 Ken Liberman (in personal communication).

ramifications in Aborigine culture. A competent member of the culture is compelled to be forever *oriented* vis-a-vis those points in navigation, movement and the conceptual organization of the habitat. The survival value of the system is rather transparent. It also has considerable bearing upon the people's emotional and spiritual life, their **connected, contextualized self-image.**[22] Right-left and front-back distinction would accomplish nothing in conveying these multiple network connections.

Conversely, the mere translation of the Aborigine compass-point expressions into English would convey little if any of the immense cultural significance they carry for the Aborigine. The references would be dead, comprehensible only in the most limited sense. This is because in our present culture the cardinal compass points are not embedded within the same context -- network -- as they are for the Aborigine.

Haviland (1986) notes another case of translation difficulty. A three-way grammar-coded distinction is made in the use of the compass-point makers in expressions depicting directionality or motion, one that has to do with the **deictic focus** of the event:[23]

(26)   aboriginal feature   English rendition

    a.   Focus on the departure point   ("near")
    b.   Focus on the goal point   ("remote")
    c.   Lack of clear point focus
       (or focus on the ongoing process)   ("intermediate")

Such an array is quite familiar in the analysis of the deixis of verbs, in English and elsewhere. Thus, for example, the verbs 'go', 'come' and 'be' in their spatial use tend to pattern the same lines as (26a,b,c) above,

---

22 John Haviland (in private communication) has noted the extreme anxiety and confusion produced in traditional Aborigines when they are brought into an environment where their compass-point orientation is confused or contradicted. Other land-based cultures have been known to display similar geographical-spiritual attitudes. Thus, in his evocative account of the Kaluli *gisaro* ceremony, Edward Schieffelin (1976) points out that the subject matter of the performance by the visitors' troupe in the ceremony, a performance that moves the Kaluli audience to tears -- indeed to cathartic frenzy -- often consists of 'mere' detailed description of the well-known topography of the host audience's country.

23 The distinction is superficially similar to Langacker's "profile" (see Langacker, 1987). However, one could separate it from "profile" in view of the following facts. Bemba (Givón, 1972a) has two verbs "come" and two verbs "go", thus creating both "profile" and "deictic focus" contrasts:

verb		'profile'	'deictic focus'
-isha	'come to'	to	toward
-fuma	'come from'	from	toward
-ya	'go to'	to	away
-shya	'go from'	from	away

respectively.[24] Further, when these three verbs are re-interpreted in terms of temporal-aspectual space, the spatial-to-temporal reanalysis retains the deictic pattern:[25]

(27) a. 'go' $\Rightarrow$ FUTURE = clear initiation point (but hazy termination point)

 b. 'come' $\Rightarrow$ PERFECT(IVE) = clear termination point (but hazy initiation point)

 c. 'be' $\Rightarrow$ PROGRESSIVE = clear ongoing process (but hazy initiation & termination points)

In spite of this highly universal potential, when English-speaking Aborigines try to explain the distinctions in (26), they invariably convert them into a three-way *distance* gradation: near, intermediate, remote. The reason why they choose this particular pattern of substitution is itself transparent: In the more normative case, when the speaker is at the reference point (Haviland's 'anchor' of the compass points), (26a) indeed tends to also involve proximity, (26b) remoteness and (25c) intermediate distance. But the English-speaking Aborigines insist on their 'mis-translation' even when clear inconsistencies are pointed out to them. This is, presumably, because for them the deictic focus distinctions are **contextualized** within the network, in relation to the compass-point orientation system. In English the distinction is available either in the tense-aspect system ('gonna' vs. 'have' vs. 'be') or in the verb lexicon ('go' vs. 'come' vs. 'be'). Still, this seemingly universal distinction does not seem to transfer well into a target language, when the new context is sufficiently **dissimilar** from that of the source language.

The subtlety of both the compass-point and the focus grammar is immense, given that the point of reference ('anchor') can be here-and-now, or moved to other reference points in space/time. Again, conceptual space in one language is not made of atomic slots that can be filled in during translation. English speaking Aborigine cannot reproduce these 'slots' readily in a new cultural context. Neither our Hypothesis I (20) nor Hypothesis II (24) can handle this. Let us entertain one more alternative:

(28) TRANSLATABILITY III: **The split-view hypothesis:**

 (a) Translating from one language to another can only be done by a **bilingual** individual;

 (b) Therefore, translation from one culture to another can only be done by a **bi-cultural** individual;

---

24 See DeLancey (1983).
25 See Givón (1973a).

(c) Being bi-cultural means holding **two incompatible world-views;**

(d) In translating words from one world view into another, one changes their meaning by embedding them in a different context.

Guugu Yimidhirr speakers may be fully bilingual/bicultural; but their two world-views are kept apart, they remain segregated, considerable portions of the two do not overlap.[26]

9.4.2.4. Science and popular culture: Righteous food

One need not go to Australia to find examples of coexisting multiple world-views. Our own culture, in its split between the scientific and the traditional perspective, affords us many examples of this phenomenon. As one instance, consider people's food beliefs.

There is a surprisingly large segment of the American population currently disposed to believe -- and not necessarily on religious grounds -- that, in Victor Lindlahr's words,[27] *you are what you eat.* This belief flies in the face of all we know, through science, about the biochemistry of digestion and metabolism, and the synthesis of bodily substances. Nonetheless the belief persists, indeed in a variety of versions. For example, the Zen Macrobiotic diet fad of the 1960s strove to eliminate mucous substances from the body by restricting their ingestion. Dieters who feed on an exclusive protein diet actually expect their body to produce no fat. And people who eat unrefined sugar somehow believe in thus escaping the harmful effects of carbohydrates. In a recent study, Sadalla and Burroughs (1981) show that Americans' food preferences are intimately associated with social and personal value projections. These value projections have relatively little to do with what educated Americans know in their capacity as members of a science-oriented culture. It is indeed true that the major split in popular food values closely parallels the educated vs. non-educated socio-economic dichotomy. But groups on the opposite sides of this major cleavage display, equally, irrational food-value projections that have little to do with the biochemistry of nutrition and metabolism. Now, in holding, in addition to the scientific world-view, another system of food-beliefs that is incom-

---

26 The idea that humans -- even mono-cultural ones -- are routinely capable of holding several incompatible world-views is rather respectable in the psychological study of self-deception. For several discussions, see J. Elster (ed., 1985) *The Multiple Self,* whose title is of course somewhat of a giveaway.

27 Lindlahr's (1940) summary of his food beliefs somehow manages to transform the logical relation between 'food' and 'self' from *causal* connection to *identity*: "...As far as nutrition is concerned, you are the result of your deeds. In other words, *"you are what you eat!"*..." (p. 74).

patible with science, educated secular Americans closely resemble educated devout Catholics who partake in the communion sacrament. In
both cases, two incompatible belief systems dwell in a person's mind
without necessarily causing any destructive consequences. The reason
this is possible -- and in fact characteristic -- of the human mind, is because the two system are compartmentalized, i.e. **contextually segregated**; they are never deployed -- accessed -- in the same context. Still
-- is translation from the one context into the other possible? This question is better re-phrased as:

"Are the contexts interchangeable?"

9.4.2.5. Sin, taboo and Christianity

Smalley (1959) discusses the pitfalls facing Christian missionaries in
preaching the Gospel to the Senoufo people in West Africa. What he perceives as particularly problematic is the fact that in English one can distinguish between 'taboo' (or 'forbidden') and 'sin'. In the Bambara-
based contact language used in the region, one can apparently make the
same distinction. But in Senoufo itself there is only one word that
covers, rather inadequately, part of the range of the two infractions --
kapini 'taboo'. As Smalley observes:

"...Taboos among the Senoufos are innumerable. It is taboo for a man
to see his wife sewing, or to hear her sing the "marriage song". It is taboo
for a man to whistle in a field except when he is resting, or for a woman
to whistle except to make a little wind when trying to blow the chaff off
the grain on a still day. It is taboo for women to see a certain fetish, or
for anyone to watch the old women when they go out to perform a certain ceremony..." (1959, p. 62)

While the emotional attitude toward breaking taboos roughly evokes
the Christian attitude toward serious sin, the actual behaviors covered
under *kapini* are rather different from those covered under 'sin'. Smalley
continues:

"...When we inquired of the Senoufos about things commonly considered sinful by us, we found that before they ever saw the white man
those who habitually practiced adultery, lying and stealing were called
silegebafeebi, or 'without-shame-people'..." (1959, p. 62)

But using *silegebafeebi* for 'sin' does not quite carry the requisite emotional weight. After weighing a number of other translations of 'sin', including *kapini* itself, Smalley winds up rejecting all solutions that

involve identifying 'appropriate vocabulary'. What is left at the end is the following admission:

"...The solution to intercultural communication is not so much to translate as to *re-express* in another language and cultural system..." (1959, p. 64)

The strong inference is that only by imposing **cultural change** on the Senoufo can the Christian concept of 'sin' be taught:

"...What do we want to say to the Senoufo? Do we want to tell them that they should not steal? Then let's say it..." (1959, p. 64)

In an equally frank treatment, Reyburn (1958) shows how among the Kaka people in the Camerouns, some forms of adultery are built into the kinship system, while others are strongly embedded into the social fabric, together with pre-marital sex and polygamy:

"...This is in essence how a Kaka philosopher might state the case. Consequently, pre-marital relations, extra-marital relations, extreme sexual indulgence, plurality of wives and many children are all aspects of the good life..." (1958, p. 96)

The inescapable conclusion is, again, that there is no translation possible without profound, intrusive cultural change.

9.4.2.6. Ute leadership

The concept of 'leader' or 'chief' is a notorious problem for cross-cultural translation, depending upon the elucidation of an entire system of social organization. The fortunes of many pre-Western cultures have foundered upon this harmless theoretical predicament. The Utes of Colorado and Utah are a case in point. Hunters-gatherers till herded into reservations in the late 1800s, the Utes made do traditionally with a rather loose social organization, flexible bands whose leadership structure and decision-making tradition were radically different from our own. Two types of leadership positions were recognized and lexically coded:

(29) a. *ta'wá-vi*   'chief' (from *ta'wá-ci* 'man')
      b. *puwá-ĝatụ*   'medicine-man' (lit.: 'he who has Power').

Neither designation was hereditary, nor were they self-selected, nor elective, nor temporally defined. Rather, both designations were contingent upon circumstances, and upon recognition by the community. Authority -- and decision -- was never binding. In particular, the more 'secular'[28] authority of the *ta'wá-vi*, was purely consensual. Decision making was collective, ponderous, and above all spiritual rather than programmatic. Deliberation may last for days, speeches might drag on interminably, competition for the floor was minimal. The orator's goal was never to 'convince' others of the 'rightness' of his argument, but rather to establish his **spiritual bona fide**. The latter amounted to a demonstration, by circuitous rather than direct verbal means, that the speaker was *of the same spirit* with the group. Collective action was only taken under such conditions of **spiritual consensus**. To this day Ute deliberations, carried out in strict adherence to Roberts' Rules of Order, reflect, rather transparently, this deliberative style.

With all the above in mind, how is one to translate into Ute:

(30) a. 'Take me to your leader!'; or
      b. 'Who is your chief?'

In its rightful context, the question was far from academic. In the late 1800s, U.S. authorities sought to negotiate territorial concessions with the Utes. Repeated efforts to identify the proper leadership were invariably frustrated, and eventually 'Chief' Ouray was appointed. Ouray, half Apache himself, proceeded to negotiate and sign treaties on behalf of the entire Ute nation (all seven bands), eventually ceding the bulk of the traditional Ute habitat, roughly half of Colorado and half of Utah. Were those treaties binding? According to the U.S. government (who soon proceeded to break them), they were indeed. Ute opinion on the subject was not solicited. It was taken for granted that a 'chief' may speak for his people, that 'binding' instruments -- 'treaties' -- may be 'signed', and then be somehow invested with 'legal' authority, instruments whose consequences extended onto 'perpetuity', and among the consequences of which land was 'ceded'. The Ute nation came to substantial grief on the simple matter of the cross-cultural intranslatability of 'leader', 'chief' and the attendant conceptual baggage.

9.4.2.7. You 'owe', I 'pay': Obligation and exchange in Melanesia

Most languages have lexically-coded notions such as 'give', 'receive', 'trade' or 'exchange'. In addition, some such as English also have lexically-coded notions for 'loan', 'lend', 'borrow', 'owe' or 'debt'. In our culture, 'owing' is intricately associated with the semantic field of

---

28 The separation of 'secular' from 'spiritual' authority is another cross-cultural translation problem, since a Ute leader's authority was always spiritual, even when the domains were he was called upon to perform would have seemed to us 'secular'.

'promise' and 'obligation'. A promise may be sealed as a legal 'contract', it may be a verbal 'assurance' or 'word of honor'. In addition, owing may be due to other culturally-recognized sources of **obligation**, ones that do not require any specific act of exchange. Thus, for example, what middle-class American parents feel they owe their children quite often involves little if any expectation of **reciprocity**.

In the Trobriand culture described by Malinowski (1935), the semantic field of 'owing' is organized rather differently. An institutionalized instrument, the *urigubu*, binds members of the society in intricate ways. The directionality of giving and receiving *urigubu* changes during the lifetime of a male member of Trobriand society. As a child, he benefits -- as resident of his father's hamlet -- from gifts paid by his mother's brothers. As an adult, he gives *urigubu* -- as a resident of his maternal uncles' hamlet -- to his own father, as well as to the husbands of his sisters. Leach (1958) summarizes the institution of *urigubu* as follows:

"...All the affines [i.e. relations by marriage; T.G.]...are potentially hostile 'aliens' whose relationship is modified into a kind of treaty of friendship by the fact of marriage and *urigubu* gift giving..." [p. 136]

Translating expressions such 'owe' or 'pay' between English and Trobriand would require the elucidation of an entire social structure which supports -- and is supported by -- such customs. The mere observation that 'owing' is a matter of 'obligation' (leaving the social sources of 'obligation' unspecified) is clearly not much of a cross-cultural translation. The social configurations and activities that produce an acknowledged obligation are radically different in the two cultures. The institution of *urigubu* in the Trobriands is the main venue of obligations that result in exchange of material gifts. Its **connections** are highly specific to Trobriand culture,[29] it evokes highly specific nodes within the cultural-semantic network. And those nodes in turn evoke other nodes.

Perhaps the best testimony to the profound social specificity of cultures such as the Trobriand may be seen when such cultures come into contact with -- or, most commonly, are massively impacted by -- our own urban, nuclear-family oriented social system. Extremely destructive conflicts of values arise under such conditions, most conspicuously in the areas where the two cultures have radically different interpretations of -- i.e. *semantic field* or *cultural contexts* for -- 'owing', 'obligation' and 'exchange'.[30]

---

29 The institution is broadly similar to the exchange system in the Melanesian basin. For a more typical non-Austronesian Papua-New Guinea variant, see Schieffelin's (1976) description of exchange relations among the Kaluli.

30 Such conflicts are currently raging in the contact interface in Papua-New Guinea, due to partial education and urbanization.

9.4.2.8. Culture and grammar: Deference

One may as well note, albeit briefly, that lexicon is not the only place where culture-specific notions are coded in language. Some culture-dependent domains are occasionally also coded in grammar. A prime example of this may be found in the grammar of speech acts, inter-personal relations and deference.[31] As a quick illustrative example we may re-examine the case of the Korean manipulative speech acts cited in section 9.3.7., above. We said that Korean codes such expressions with two clauses, while English codes them with one, as in:

(31)   'You must read this book'

While we earlier considered this difference between English and Korean to be trivially structural, there is good evidence that it goes beyond structure, and is culturally motivated. Briefly, Korean culture is much more inclined to code grammatically social functions such as deference.
The systematic lengthening of manipulative speech acts in a well-known device for 'softening', 'toning down', or deference. In addition to such indirection, Korean has an extensive use of grammatical markers that code deference to both the **hearer** and the **referent**. As an example consider (from Kim, 1987):

(32)   Yi-kyosu-nim-i   si-rul
      Yi-professor-HON/R-SUBJ   poetry-OBJ

      karuchi-si-oss-o-yo
      teach-HON/R-PAST-ASSERT-HON/H

      'Professor Yi teaches poetry'

The referent honorific (HON/R) is coded both on the subject and on the verb. The addressee honorific (HON/H) is coded on the verb. But, like many European languages, it may also be coded on the *second person pronoun*, as in:

(33)   Yi-kyosu-nim,   kkeso-n-un   si-rul
      Yi-Pressor-HON/R   you/HON/H-TOP-SUBJ   poetry-OBJ

      karuchi-si-oss-mni-kka?
      teach-HON/R-PAST-HON/H-Q

      'Prof. Yi, did you teach poetry?"

---

31 See some discussion in Chapter 4, as well as extensive discussion in Brown and Levinson (1978).

One might of course argue that languages simply have the universal category 'deference', and the cultural world-view then dictates the context where it is applicable. However, in languages such as Korean the choice of various honorific markers varies with the specific status relations between the speaker and hearer, and between the speaker and referent. In order to appropriately control the choice of the honorific grammatical particles, speakers must be conscious at all times of an intricate, hierarchic, often subtle network of social relations. Thus, translation between English and Korean requires not only finding appropriate 'equivalent' deference expressions, but also understanding the different networks of social organization.

9.5. The kinship controversy: An old battlefield revisited

9.5.1. Preamble

The debate between extreme -- 'cognitive' or 'biological' -- universalists and extreme -- 'cultural' -- relativists has been waged most bitterly and most revealingly, at least in Anthropology, upon the old battlefield of *kinship* terms. In the course of the various skirmishes dating back almost to the turn of the century, two other issues have been commonly invoked. Both concern the interpretation of human cultures, and the basis for cultural universals, if such universals are to be found:

(a) The contrast between **functionalism** and **structuralism**
(b) The role of **biology** in determining cultural universals

In the following sections we will attempt to probe into the controversy's core.

9.5.2. Kroeber's incipient structuralism

In a pioneering work that laid down the foundations for a comparative study of kinship systems, Kroeber (1909) outlined the universal parameters that underlie kinship terminology. Those were, in an implicit order of generality:

(34)   a.   generational stratification
        b.   the blood vs. marriage distinction
        c.   the lineal vs. collateral distinction
        d.   sex:
            (i)   of the kin person
            (ii)   of the mediating kin
            (iii)   of the speaker
        e.   age stratification (within a generation)
        f.   the life condition of a mediating link

In a manner remarkably prescient of the **typological-universalist** approach in current linguistics, Kroeber pointed out how cross-cultural differences in kinship systems may be seen as differences in the degree of *completeness, elaboration* and *consistency* of applying the universal parameters in (34) to the various kin categories of the language. Illustrating his point with Amerindian data, he shows a descending implicational hierarchy from (34a) down, one that is again reminiscent of typological universals of language. The point where Kroeber's realistic -- rather than extremist -- universalist approach inexplicably crumbles, is where he endeavors to explain the observed balance between universality and specificity. At that point, Kroeber rejects out of hand any appeal to sociofunctional explanation:

"...The causes which determine the formation, choice and similarities of terms of relationship are *primarily linguistic*. Whenever it is desired to regard terms of relationship as due to *sociological causes* as indicative of *social conditions*, the burden of proof must be entirely with the propounder of such views..." (1909, p. 26; emphases are mine; TG)

The term 'linguistic' apparently meant for Kroeber a structural-cognitive parameter wholly *independent* of socio-cultural function. He proceeds to argue, somewhat circularly, that the perceived 'similarity' among kins grouped together via a common kin term is merely a function **sharing a larger number of underlying features** from the list in (34):

"...A woman and her sister are more alike than a woman and her brother, but the difference is conceptual, in other words linguistic, as well as sociological. It is true that a woman's sister can take her place in innumerable functions and relations in which a brother cannot; and yet a woman and her sister, being of the same sex, *agree in one more category of relationship* than the same woman and her brother, and are therefore more similar in relationship and more naturally denoted by the same term..." (1909, p. 26; emphases are mine; TG)

If such a cognitive-universalist approach is to be adopted, then one wonders how cultures that group 'mother' with 'mother's brother' together under the same kinship term can be interpreted: As demonstrating another linguistic-psychological organization? But why?

The equation of 'linguistic' with 'psychological' remains problematic when it merely serves to close the search for further explanation. In the absence of socio-cultural -- i.e. *functional* -- explanation, one must conclude that the 'similarities' invoked by Keroeber are vacuously **structural**, perhaps accidents of neural organization, perhaps **bio-perceptual** in motivation. Kroeber goes on to reiterate his anti-functional universalism as follows:

"...It has been an unfortunate characteristic of the anthropology of recent years to seek in a great measure specific causes for specific events, connections between which can be established only through evidence that is subjectively selected... Terms of relationship reflect *psychology, not sociology*. They are determined primarily by *language* and can be utilized for sociological inference only with extreme caution..." (1909, p. 27; emphases are mine; TG)

One senses here an underlying current of empiricist, inductivist, positivist dogma, reminiscent of Bloomfield's methodological strictures of 15 years later.

9.5.3. Malinowski and Leach: Naive ('biological') vs. complex ('socio-cultural') functionalism

The position of B. Malinowski in the kinship controversy is somewhat paradoxical. On the one hand, he was, together with Radcliffe-Brown, an early exponent of functionalism in Anthropology. This is evident in:

"...To explain any item of culture, material or moral, means to indicate its functional place within an institution..." (1926, p. 139)

On the other hand, in searching for functional explanations, Malinowski often invoked naive **bio-survival** explanations. This is apparent when he ascribes 'an immense biological value' to magic rituals, which enable a man:

"...to maintain his poise and his mental integrity in fits of anger, in the throes of hate, of unrequited love, of despair and anxiety. The function of magic is to ritualize man's optimism, to enhance his faith in the victory of hope over fear..." (1954, p. 90)

Malinowski's propensity for seeking transparent biologically-based explanations for cultural phenomena is nowhere more evident than in his treatment of the Trobriand kinship system. As Leach (1958) points out in his celebrated re-analysis, Malinowski (1932, 1935) chose to ignore his own data concerning the social structure, residency distribution, and the directionality of the *urigubu* exchange system of the Trobriands, electing instead to interpret the kinship system as one based essentially on **biological descent** and **mating restrictions**. The use of the term *tama* for both the biological 'father' and 'other males of father's clan' is ascribed by Malinowski to linguistic **extension by similarity**. The Trobriand social structure, residency pattern and the *urigubu* exchange system are thus largely incidental to Malinowski's analysis. Leach demonstrated, I think rather brilliantly, how the kin term *tama* is motivated by the interaction of all these cultural factors, with *tama* grouping together 'males domiciled at ego's father's hamlet'. This analysis also accommodates the relational changes ensuing from the male child's maturation, change of residency, and marriage.

The crux of Leach's re-analysis of Trobriand kinship involved Malinowski's inexplicable category *tabu*, a conjunctive grab-bag at the 'core' of which Malinowski detects 'lawful (marriageable) woman'. Malinowski was forced to invoke either **homonymy**, or **polysemy** and **metaphoric extension** in order to explain away facts that did not fit. Leach's re-analysis is much more systemic and general. Perhaps most attractively, it offers an integrated socio-cultural motivation. In seeking to understand why Malinowski adhered to his analysis in the face of numerous discrepancies, Leach writes:

"...Why should Malinowski have been so keen to insist that various meanings of the word *tabu* are wholly unrelated? Why, when he himself laid such stress on the taboo between a man and his sister, should he repudiate the logic by which a boy regards his father's sister as *tabu*? The answer seems to be that it was because he took over uncritically from his predecessors the bland assumption that the key to the understanding of any system of kinship terminology must always be sought in *rules of preferred marriage*..." (1958, p. 144; emphasis is mine; TG).

In recapitulating the social dynamics of *tabu*, Leach concludes:

"...How could it possibly be that the term which thus describes 'lawful woman' should also mean 'forbidden', 'dangerous,' 'sacred'? The only possible explanation for Malinowski was that we are here dealing with two or more entirely different words [i.e. homonyms; TG]. What he failed to notice was that when a man does marry a *tabu* relative either close or remote, she and her immediate kinsmen forthwith cease to be *tabu,* and come into the much more closely bonded categories of *lubou* and *yawa.* In other words, marriage is a device whereby the dangers of *tabu* are for the time being exorcised..." (1958, pp. 144-145).

A closely related discussion may be found in Hocart's (1937) comparison of *genealogical* and *classificatory* kinship systems. Hocart begins by challenging the significance of the distinction. Biology-bent functional universalists, after Malinowski, had been seeking to interpret the so-called 'classificatory' kinship systems of Austronesia, Amerindia, Africa as an **extension via similarity** of the biologically-based, supposedly human-universal 'genealogical' system. Hocart turns the argument upside down, suggesting that non-genealogical systems may in fact be older, and that specific changes in social organization have motivated later evolution of seemingly biologically-based kin systems.

9.5.4. Structural universalism: The kinship semantics of Scheffler and Lounsbury

It did not take long for deductive universalists in anthropology to go on the counter attack, seeking Leach's intellectual hide. Armed to the teeth with the newly assembled tools of Generative linguistics, most particularly the Katz-Fodor brand of discrete, context-free Platonic categories, structural Anthropologists such as Lounsbury (1965), Scheffler and Lounsbury (1971) or Scheffler (1972) strove to resurrect Malinowski's biology-based -- or *nuclear-family-based* -- analysis of Trobriand kinship. At first glance, the grafting of Malinowski's functionalism onto an extreme school of linguistic structuralism appears somewhat bizarre. The secret of their underlying compatibility lies, I think, in two related points:

(a) Resurrecting Malinowski automatically knocks down Leach's socio-cultural functionalism; and
(b) Malinowski's functional analysis, being more clearly biology-based, is also more transparently universalist.

Beyond mere logic, a similar blend has been negotiated more recently, in the grafting of Bickerton's (1981) 'bio-program' onto Chomsky's structural innatism (see section 9.6, below).

It was inevitable that a distinct brand of linguistics -- either one of the two successive schools of American structuralism -- would be enlisted in the service of anthropological structuralism. The tools of structuralist linguistics indeed fit the occasion well:

(a) Katz-Fodor type discrete categorial analysis
(b) accidental homonymy in the Saussurean tradition of 'arbitrary code'
(c) primary vs. extended reference
(d) conjunctive vs. disjunctive definitions
(e) deep underlying abstract rules.

Lounsbury (1965) summarizes as follows the facets of Leach's analysis he finds most objectionable:

> Kinship terms are 'category terms'...
> (2) Kinship terms, so-called, do not necessarily have anything to do with relationships defined by genealogical connections...
> (3) ...The nuclear family...is not universal; or at least not universally relevant as an element in social organization of kinship..." (1965, p. 143)

Of the three points in contention, (1) has always been a mere semantic quibble, a red herring. The gist of the argument is indeed (2) and (3). In challenging Leach's analysis, Lounsbury suggests that:

> "...there is a perfectly comprehensible *underlying logic* to the terms and their referents as reported by Malinowski... I will take the opportunity to express my scepticism about this whole view of primitive kinship... this mystique about a pre-bilateral mentality, as it were, that cannot see *the individual family* as a significant legal institution in such societies, that denies therefore the roles of its unique constituents as furnishing the basis for *calculus* of legally and socially significant relationships, and that consequently cannot see the difference between *kinship* and *social structure*..." (1965, p. 146; emphases are mine; TG)

Lounsbury's apriori preoccupation with the biological nuclear family as the human-universal basis for all kinship system is openly acknowledged:

> "...the real issue, which is that of the precise nature of the jural rules of society, and the role that family relationships have in formulating these..." (1965, p. 147)

Finally, in keeping with the structuralist tradition of being more interested in formalization than in explanation, Lounsbury observes:

> "...I have not given a *sociological* explanation of the Trobriand kinship terms as Leach has attempted to do. All that has been given here is a *formal analysis* stated in terms of *semantic rules*. But these semantic rules

must have certain clear implications of a sociological nature. Their discovery and statement, moreover, constitute a necessary preparation for a proper sociological explanation; for it is these semantic rules that have to be accounted for. When these fundamental principles are explained, then the whole terminological structure that results from them is explained..." (1965, p. 175; emphases are mine; TG)

There is nothing methodologically outrageous about the insistence that description precedes explanation. The problem with Lounsbury's approach arises, rather, from the conflation of four other pre-empirical predilections:

(a) The apriori assumption that the *core* of kin terms must be found in nuclear-family blood relations;
(b) The apriori insistence that semantic description look like a *calculus*, i.e. a deductive logic;
(c) The belief -- rather Chomskian -- in *deep underlying abstract rules* that govern the behavior of surface forms;
(d) The cleaning up of data that do not fit either assumption (a) or (b) by invoking the 'linguistic' notions of polysemy or analogic extension.

These methodological assumptions bear a transparent kinship to deductive-rationalist linguistics. The ensuing universalism is a necessary by-product of the methodology.

9.5.5. The crux of the matter: Kinship terms and translation

It ought to be obvious why the analysis of kinship terms is so crucial for a theory of language universals and translatability. If Lounsbury and Scheffler are right, and if kin terms 'at the core' are based on transparent **bio-functional** universals, then the cross-cultural diversity of kinship terminology is relatively superficial, merely an 'extension by similarity' from common 'core meanings'. In that case, Translatability Hypothesis II (24) can then be resurrected; cross-cultural translation is relatively easy, at least in the most important 'core areas'. In the case of the Trobriand *tama* and English 'father', *tama*'s 'extended' connections are mere superficial embellishments; its 'core' remains identical with that of 'father'. If, on the other hand, one adopts Leach's **socio-cultural** functionalism, translatability between *tama* and 'father' in either direction is problematic in the extreme. The overlap of cultural contexts is much smaller; the connections *within* the two networks are strikingly different. Consequently, the *core vs. periphery* universalist hypothesis (24) is much less useful as a model for successful cross-cultural translation.

9.6. The methodological conundrum: Navigating between untenable extremes

Cultural universalism has come down to us in two main strands. The oldest, philosophical variety, dates back the traditional Platonic concerns with absolute, immutable, context-free categories of **The Human Mind** (or Aristotle's equally immutable 'forms' of **External Reality**). Whether in the guise of **mentalism** (á la Von Humboldt, H. Paul or Sapir), or of **structuralism** (á la Kroeber, Levy-Strauss, Lounsbury or Chomsky), this extremist strain of universalism is well entrenched today in Philosophy, Linguistics and Cognitive Psychology.[32]

A second, equally extreme variety of more recent universalism, can be traced down from Darwin through Malinowski's 'naive' functionalism, all the way to an updated version, so-called **Socio-biology**. What is taken to be universal under this version is not Human Mind, but rather **Human Nature**.[33] This bio-functional universalism tends to assume, in Geertz's (1984) inimitable words:

"...that culture is [the] icing, biology [the] cake; that we have no choice as to what we shall hate... that differences are shallow, likenesses [are] deep..." (1984, p. 269)

The inherent circularity of this raw bio-functional 'explanation' of cultures, and its cavalier dismissal of cultural diversity, is aptly noted by Geertz:

"...The issue is not whether human beings are biological organisms with intrinsic characteristics. Men can't fly and pigeons can't talk. Nor is it whether they show commonality in mental functioning wherever we find them. Papuans envy, Aborigines dream. The issue is, what are we to make of these undisputed facts as we go about explicating rituals, analyzing ecosystems, interpreting fossil sequences, or comparing languages..." (1984, p. 268)

When one rejects both versions of extreme universalism, however, one must recognize that extreme *Whorfian relativism* won't do either. This extremism would mean, in essence, suspending the study of anthropology -- and thus linguistics -- as a *systematic* discipline.

Is there a middle ground? Let us consider the words of two scholars

---

32 In addition to Katz and Fodor's various works, and its 'cognitive' counterparts such as Miller and Johnson-Laird (1976), see more recent examples in Hollis and Lukes (eds, 1982), particular Gellner (1982), Horton (1982), or Sperber (1982).

33 See Midgeley (1978), Edgerton (1978), Baggish (1983), Spiro (1978) or Salkever (1983), *inter alia*. For other attacks on cultural relativism from a moral perspective, see Johnson (1983) or Thomas (1983).

who have wrestled with this issue. First, Wierzbicka's reflection on cross-cultural translation:

"...Does language reflect culture? In many ways, it undoubtedly does, although it is not always easy to determine which aspects of the culture reflected in a given language pertain to the present and which to the past... The dangers of subjectivism and arbitrariness involved in a search for such correlations are no doubt real enough. But to abandon the search because of these dangers is, to my mind, analogous to saying, as Bloomfield did, that linguistics should stay clear of meaning because all attempts to study meaning are fraught with dangers of subjectivism and arbitrariness.

As I see it, the important thing is to try to sharpen our analytic tools, and to develop safeguards for the study of "dangerous areas". A *semantic metalanguage for a cross-cultural comparison of meaning* seems to me, in this respect, a requirement of the first priority..." (1986, p. 368; emphases are mine; TG)

The crux of the matter is -- what exactly does one mean by 'meta-language'? If it turns out to be a throwback to rigid, Platonic inventory of discrete universal categories, then one is bound to admit we have not advanced far. If, on the other hand, one takes 'metalanguage' to mean a *methodological* exhortation to strive gradually toward developing a *tentative, flexible, phenomenological vocabulary*, then Wierzbicka's point seems rather well taken.

Consider next the following observations made by C. Geertz:

"...The besetting sin of interpretive approaches to anything -- literature, dreams, symptoms, culture -- is that they tend to resist, or to be permitted to resist, conceptual articulation and thus to escape *a systematic mode of assessment*. You either grasp an interpretation or you do not, see the point of it or you do not, accept it or you do not. Imprisoned in the immediacy of its own detail, it is presented as self-validating, or, worse, as validated by the supposedly developed sensitivities of the person who presents it; any attempt to cast what it says *in terms other than its own* is regarded as a travesty -- as, the anthropologist's severest term of moral abuse, ethnocentric.

For a field of study which, however timidly (though I, myself, am not timid about the matter at all), asserts itself to be a science, this just will not do. There is no reason why the conceptual structure of a cultural interpretation should be any less formulable, and thus less susceptible to *explicit canons of appraisal*, than that of, say, a biological observation or a physical experiment..." (1973, p. 24; emphases are mine; TG)

The middle path, as Lao Tse observed, is often murky, dull, unattractive. It so obviously lacks the captivating brilliance of the clean extremes. But the siren call of ingenious extremist is seldom good science, however good rhetoric it may be.

9.7. A pragmatic approach to translation

> "...Translation, as every translator learns quickly, is not just a matter of imitation, or finding our words to imitate their words, but it is also the recreation of the context of the foreign text..."

> A.L. Becker, "Communication across Diversity" (1979, p. 2)

9.7.1. The mirage of reductionism

The first admission one must make concerning cross-cultural translation, is that it should have never been formulated as a question of *either or*. Such formulation is the sad legacy of our Western reductionist tradition. Rather, translation is a matter of *more or less*. Cultural experience -- hence context -- is always different, however 'trivial' the differences may be judged. Therefore, perfect Katzian translation of Platonic concepts and propositions, whether locutionary or per-locutionary, is in principle an anti-empirical mirage. But equally destructive is the extreme doctrine of total relativism. Aside from being empirically premature, it also deprives us of binding methodology, or in Geertz's words, of 'explicit canons of appraisal'.

9.7.2. The illusion of perfect communication

Is there anything particularly earthshaking about admitting that cross-culture translation is a matter of degree? Consider for a minute the normal process of communication within the same culture, the same sub-culture, the same sub-dialect: Is it ever anything but a rough approximation? Have two minds ever shared an identical point of view, the very same context? Hardly. Has this ever been considered an insurmountable barrier to communication? Hardly. Communication proceeds as a matter of course in a **noisy channel**, with relative success and, on occasion, spectacular failures. Indeed one of the main functions of declarative discourse is to bridge over -- temporarily, contingently, and for limited tactical goals -- the yawning gaps in 'shared' knowledge and 'common' point-of-view among members of the 'same' culture, so that a specific communicative transaction may take place. In elaborating his view of culture as **organized diversity,** Wallace (1961) notes:

"...Culture...is characterized internally not by uniformity, but by diversity of both individuals and groups, many of whom are in continuous and overt conflict in one sub-system and in active cooperation in another..." (1961, p. 28)

9.7.3. The negotiation of 'shared' context

A large portion of grammar as a communicative device serves for the **negotiation of common grounds** between speaker and hearer. The negotiation of context, being a prerequisite to a reasonable degree of successful communication, is a direct consequence of *intra*-culture diversity. The process of context-negotiation never arrives at establishing an *absolute* identity of point of view. A lifetime would not suffice to achieve that. But the lack of total understanding does not necessarily entail a total lack of understanding. What the negotiation of context aims for is a **reasonable degree of overlap** in points of view, a relative, temporary, contingent commonality, one that will 'do the job', more or less. The same goes for cross-cultural communication. The Platonic quest for 'exact', *complete* translation remains a mirage. But *partial* sharing of experience -- and the enlargement of one's context through contact with other points of view -- has always been the norm, within as well as across cultures. In fact, the ability to learn -- and learn from -- the experience of other members of the social unit is probably at the very core of the notion 'culture'.

9.7.4. Relative overlap of contexts

The degree of overlap between two points of view, be they of two persons or of two cultures, is an *empirical* matter and a matter of *degree*. One can well imagine an extreme condition whereby the contexts -- for a concept to be translated -- overlap so little, that only a few connections in the network are shared. Under such conditions, translation is a hopeless task. One may render this Diagrammatically as:

(35) **Minimal overlap of contexts**

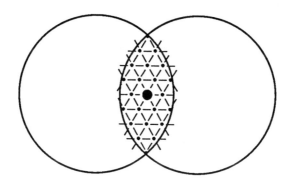

One may also imagine a situation whereby two points of view may overlap considerably, share many connections within the network of surrounding the concept, not only the immediate connections but also their respective connections, and their respective connections, and so on. Diagrammatically this may be rendered as:

(36) **Large overlap of contexts**

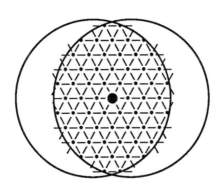

The more deeply -- and richly -- the two contexts overlap, the more successful is a translation likely to be.

However difficult the task is of determining what cultures share and how exactly they differ, it is nonetheless an empirical issue, to be faced, agonized, wrestled with. Practicing either anthropology or linguistics as a science is often frustrating. But that is not a cogent reason for giving it up. Or, as Geertz puts it:

"...The objection to anti-relativism is not that it rejects an it's-all-how-you-look-at-it approach to knowledge or a when-in-Rome approach to morality, but that it imagines that they can only be defeated by placing morality beyond culture and knowledge beyond both. This, speaking of things which must needs be so, is no longer possible. If we wanted home truths, we should have stayed at home..." (1984, p. 276)

CHAPTER 10

ADAPTIVE BEHAVIOR, GROUP VARIABILITY AND THE GENETIC CODE: THE PRAGMATICS OF EVOLUTIONARY CHANGE

10.1. Prospectus*

This chapter constitutes an attempt to resurrect, in a modified form and hopefully with some lasting impact, one of the most persistent themes in the history of biology: Lamarck's phoenix-like Second Law of biological evolution. To be more precise, I will attempt to vindicate some of the underlying intuitions of the Lamarckian position. In undertaking this, one must concede from the start that the actual mechanism proposed by Lamarck to account for -- as he saw it -- the inheritance of acquired traits, has been shown to be empirically untenable. Here is how Lamarck (1809) expressed his Second Law:

"...All the acquisitions or losses wrought by nature on individuals... are preserved by reproduction to the new individuals which arise, provided that the acquired modifications are common to both sexes, or at least to the individuals which produce the young..." (1809, p. 113; see also Mayr, 1972)

With many other astute biologists (Darwin included), Lamarck could not help observing the correlation between the use and disuse of organs, on the one hand, and their evolutionary fate, on the other. The Western propensity for reductionism, however, has backed us into the usual choice between two uncomfortable extremes: A rigid *mutationist* stance, or equally rigid *Lamarckist* rendition of the interplay between individual behavior and genetic substance in determining the course of evolution. Mayr (1982) sums up this reductionism as follows:

* I am greatly indebted to Prof. Ernst Mayr for many valuable suggestions and comments on an earlier draft of the manuscript.

"...Behavior was for Lamarck an important evolutionary mechanism. The physiological process initiated by behavioral activity ("use versus disuse"), combined with an inheritance of acquired characters, were for him the cause of evolutionary change...the mutationists went to the other extreme. According to them, major mutations generate new structures, and these "go in search of appropriate function"..." (1982, p. 611)

In the last one-hundred years, non-reductionist reassessment of the role of the individual's lifetime adaptive behavior in shaping the evolution of gene-coded traits has indeed taken place. Mayr's articulation of such a non-extremist position closely parallel's Kant's **interactionist** -- pragmatic -- position in epistemology:

"...The modern evolutionist rejects both interpretations. To him, **changes in behavior** are indeed considered important **pacemakers in evolutionary change**..." (*ibid*; emphases are mine; TG)

In a similar non-reductionist formulation of the interaction between 'habit' and 'structure', Mayr (1960) observes:

"...It is now quite evident that every habit has some structural basis but that the evolutionary changes that results from adaptive shifts are often initiated by a change in behavior, to be followed secondarily by a change in structure...The new habit often serves as the pacemaker that sets up **selection pressures** that shifts the mean of the **curve of structural variation** [within the population; TG]..." (1960, p. 106; emphases are mine; TG)

In combining the role of genetic variability within the population, on the one hand, and natural selection, on the other, the mechanism by which behavior affects evolution has been *de-Lamarckized*, with the original intuition preserved intact:

"...Many if not most acquisitions of new structures in the course of evolution can be ascribed to selection forces exerted by newly acquired behavior..." (Mayr, 1982, p. 612).

The mechanism I will discuss below, of how adaptive (thus to my mind also *purposive*) behavior guides evolution, is in a clear sense a further elaboration of Mayr's non-reductionist position. It involves two closely related features of biological information processing, discussed in two earlier chapters. The first pertains to the organization of **knowledge structure**; the second to the mode of **information processing**. Expressed as developmental processes, the two are:

(a) The rise of categorization schemata (ch. 2)
(b) The rise of automated processing (ch. 7)

While the argument itself is relatively simple, the background required for appreciating it is indeed complex. It spans the protracted struggle between the Platonic and pragmatic interpretation of the biological universe, and the position of human life and mind within it.

10.2. Pre-evolutionary biology

The nature of biological organisms, their uniqueness vis-a-vis the inorganic universe, and why they happen to display their particular structural design, have been recurrent themes in the history of Western thought. With the advent of evolutionary thinking, three related questions joined -- and eventually almost superseded -- the old biological agenda:

(a) How did biological organisms get to be -- over time -- the way they are?
(b) How does biological evolution connect to the phenomenon of mind?
(c) How do biological evolution, and the evolution of mind, connect to the phenomenon of culture?

As noted earlier above,[1] Western biology got an early start as a functionalist discipline when Aristotle disposed of the early Greek structuralist schools. In so doing, Aristotle inadvertently also set the stage for the major cleavage in the Western approach to biological design. On the one hand stood the Platonic -- or philosophical Rationalist -- tradition, treating biological design the way it treated mental categories (or, for that matter, the structure of the universe itself): They were all there, perfect and immutable, since the very beginning and for all times, pre-ordained by some higher intelligence.[2]

---

1 See the discussion of Aristotle's biological functionalism in Ch. 1, as well the general discussion of functionalism as a pragmatic approach to the bio-behavioral sciences in Ch. 8.
2 Mayr (1959a), following Popper (1950), characterizes the Platonic position variably as "essentialist" and "typological", in the sense that members of a Platonic 'type' exhibit the same identical 'essence' (*eidos*) and no intra-population variability. Mayr contrasts this with "population" or "variationist" thinking (essentially similar to our pragmatic alternative to Platonic categorization; see Ch. 2, above), whereby 'types' show a distributional curve of their characteristic ('prototypical') properties. For extensive discussion of the inherent variability of biological species, its origins and its role in evolution, see Futuyma (1979, ch. 8,9,10,11 and 16). It is a somewhat amusing historical curiosity that 'typological' in modern linguistics has come to mean more-or-less the opposite of what it means for Mayr, i.e. the recognition of the inherent variability within the type 'human language'.

Perfection of design, however, may be interpreted differently for the biological organisms than for the inorganic (or mental) universe. Aristotle, while sharing Plato's belief in a stable, perfect universe, nonetheless pointed out that the perfection of biological design must be interpreted in functional -- i.e. pragmatic -- terms:

(a) The design is there to serve some function.
(b) Biological structure is **motivated** by considerations that are not merely formal or aesthetic.
(c) The motivation involves an **interaction** between the organism and its **environment** -- i.e. its **context**.

From here, the road toward an adaptive, behavioral -- and eventually evolutionary -- brand of functionalism is *in principle* short:

(d) That interaction between organism and environment involves the organism's **adaptive behavior**.
(e) Adaptive behavior is governed by the organism's **perceived adaptive tasks** (or '**purpose**'), given perceived environmental challenge.
(f) Biological adaptation occurs **over time**, it involves the organism's modification of its structures in order to better perform various functions.[3]

It would be misleading to suggest that an evolutionary, bio-adaptive interpretation was the only logical conclusion that could be drawn from the transparent function-adapted nature of biological structure. Indeed, Aristotle himself interpreted the instrument's seemingly perfect fitness to its task in strictly Platonic terms: Biological structure has been so created at the beginning, it is part and parcel of the immutable **Grand Design**.

Biological science under the Church and through the Middle Ages perpetuated, as a matter of theological necessity, this Platonic version of Aristotelian functionalism. Thus, for example, St. Thomas Aquinas' fifth teleological argument for the existence of God, in *Summa Theologicae*, hinges in part on the perfect, task-adapted, functional design of bio-organisms. As we shall see below, a similar Platonic stance was retained by the early exponents of both embryonic ('ontogenetic') and speciated

3 Anti-functionalist linguists often cite the existence of *excess structure*, some of which has no obvious functional motivation, as an argument against functionalism. The same argument was raised in biology against adaptive natural selection. As Mayr (1962) points out, the argument is against *naive* functionalism, rather than against adaptive selection *per se*. The extremely complex nature of genetic structure, the complex interactive relationship among genes -- and between *genotype* and *phenotype* -- are largely responsible for 'excess structure' (see also Futuyma, 1979, ch. 3).

('phylogenetic') evolution. Indeed, the conversion of Aristotelian functionalism into modern bio-adaptive evolutionary thinking waited upon the eventual conflation of three ranges of facts that were either not available, or in one case available only scantily, to pre-scientific biologists.

10.3. The rise of evolutionary thinking: Biological diversity, embryology and the fossil record [4]

10.3.1. Preamble

Perhaps one of the best arguments for the fact-driven nature of hypothesis formation[5] concerns the three ranges of facts that eventually motivated -- i.e. allowed the abduction of -- an evolutionary interpretation of biological design. The three are:

(a) Biological diversity
(b) Embryonic development
(c) The fossil record

We will discuss the three in order.

10.3.2. Biological diversity

Biological diversity had been well documented since Aristotle.[6] However, extensive geographic exploration and the flowering of medical investigation from the Renaissance onward, contributed to an exponential growth in the available information on extant flora and fauna species. With the advent of the microscope, van Leeuwenhoek's discovery of mono-cellular **micro-organisms,** on the one hand, and Malpigi's pioneering of **histology,** on the other, added a vital new dimension to the study of biological diversity: Micro-diversity, the diversity of cell and tissue types. The explosion of documented diversity soon created the need for the first level of processing the facts, i.e. **classification.** Linnaeus' taxonomy,[7] a natural response to that pressing need, was accomplished -- like all taxonomies -- through the contemplation of **similarities** and their **gradation.** Similarities, and in particular fine

---

4   In my perusal through the history of evolutionary thinking, as well as in other matters concerning biology, I have relied repeatedly on the works of two profound scholars, Ernst Mayr (in particular Mayr, 1976, 1982) and Stephen J. Gould (in particular Gould 1977, 1980).
5   See Ch. 8.
6   Aristotle, *De Generatione Animalium.*
7   Linnaeus (1753, 1758)

gradations, in turn demand some cogent interpretation. One possible interpretation of graded similarities among species was evolution.

10.3.3. Embryonic development

The history of embryology -- the study of ontogenetic evolution -- goes all the way back to Aristotle. Its importance for the eventual emergence of evolutionary thinking springs from two sources:

(a) The development of embryos -- **ontogenesis** -- is itself an evolutionary process.
(b) From the very start, ontogenesis was viewed as proceeding by **analogy** with the external ('macrocosmic') diversity of the biological world.

Thus Aristotle, in *De Generatione Animalium*, already viewed ontogenesis as a clear **recapitulation** of the ranking of the extant speciated diversity:[8]

"...We must observe how rightly nature orders generation in regular gradation. The more perfect and hotter animals [mammals; TG] produce their young perfect... The third class [birds; TG] do not produce a perfect animal, but an egg and this egg is perfect. Those whose nature is still colder than these produce an egg, but an imperfect one, which is perfected outside the body..." (*De Generatione Animalium*, 733b, lines 1-10)

Aristotle's ranked *taxa* were not evolutionarily ordered, but rather ordered in terms of increased perfection. Ontogenesis was thought to recapitulate this static ranking in its temporal sequence, through which the embryo gradually acquired the three types of 'souls' used to rank the biological *taxa*:

"...For nobody would put down the unfertilized embryo as soulless or in every sense bereft of life... That they possess the *nutritive soul* is plain. As they develop they also acquire the *sensitive soul* in virtue of which an animal is an animal..." (*ibid.*, 736a, lines 33-38)

The last -- *rational* -- soul was reserved, as a matter of course, for mankind. Similarly:

---

8 Aristotle's 5 classes, in order of perfection, were: (1) mammals, (2) ovoviparous sharks; (3) birds and reptiles; (4) fish, cephalopods, and crustaceans; and (5) insects.

"...At first all such embryos seem to live the life of a plant..." (*ibid.*, 736b, lines 13-14) "...Since the embryo is already potentially an animal but an imperfect one, it must obtain its nourishment from elsewhere: accordingly it makes use of the uterus and the mother, as a plant does of the earth, to get nourishment, until it is perfected to the point of being now an animal potentially locomotive..." (*ibid.*, 740a, lines 24-28)

The great embryologists of the 17th, 18th and early 19th Centuries simply reaffirmed this Aristotelian recapitulationist creed as their database increased in size and diversity.[9] But again, their interpretation was not initially evolutionary. Indeed, two pre-evolutionary schools endeavored to interpret the embryological sequence. The first believed in **epigenesis**, whereby some 'vital force' powered ontogenesis. The second, more literally inclined, believed in **preformation**, whereby the entire sequence of ontogenetic development was germinally present, 'encapsulated' in (to render Bonnet's *emboitment*), or 'rolled into' the embryo from the start, then merely 'un-rolled' during ontogeny.[10] Both schools thus endeavored to preserve a measure of Platonic stability in the biological universe. And all pre-evolutionary schools tended toward a liberal measure of what Mayr (1982) calls *Natural Theology*, whereby the perfect progression observed in both the ranked species and ontogenesis reflected God's perfect scheme of Creation.[11] Only the eventual evolutionary interpretation of Aristotle's ranking dispatched this persistent view.

10.3.4. The fossil record

The third range of facts that contributed crucially to the rise of evolutionary thinking was the -- relatively late -- discovery of the fossil record

9　See for example, Sir Thomas Browne, in *Religio Medici* (1642): "...For first we are rude mass, in the rank of creatures which onely are, and have a dull kind of being, not yet privileged with life... next we live the life of Plants, the life of Animals, the life of Men..." (quoted from Gould, 1977, p. 16). Or, consider the following from the writings of John Hunter (published posthumously by Richard Owen, 1841): "...If we were capable of following the progress of increase of the number of the parts of the most perfect animal, as they first formed in succession, from the very first to its state of full perfection, we should probably be able to compare it with some one of the incomplete animals themselves, of every order of animals in Creation, being at no stage different from some of the inferior orders..." (1841, p. 14)

10　The term 'evolution' was first used to characterize this ontogenetic process of 'unrolling'. Both postulated causes of ontogenesis -- the epigenesist 'vital force' and the preformationist 'encapsulation' -- found their eventual translation as the **genetic code**. See extensive discussion in Gould (1977, pp. 16-28).

11　John Ray's (1691) *The Wisdom of God Manifested in the Works of Creation* may be cited as a typical example. But as Mayr (1982) points out, eminences such as Leibniz, Linnaeus and Herder were inclined toward similar views.

in the late 18th Century.[12] The intellectual impact of this discovery on biological thinking could not be over-estimated. To begin with, it confronted contemporary thinking -- static, Platonic, creationist -- with incontrovertible evidence of hundreds of perfectly well-formed species that used to exists but didn't any more. In that connection, it destroyed the prevailing notion of a single *scala naturae* of species, gradually ascending toward perfection: Many of the extinct fossils represented separate, unique branches that somehow petered out. What is more, in the profile of rock strata, the **graduated similarities** between the fossil inhabitants of adjacent strata are often striking. The temptation to interpreted such gradation developmentally, thus in analogy with ontogenesis, is indeed strong.

With the fossil record in place, an evolutionary interpretation of the three ranges of fact became feasible, indeed almost necessary. Such new interpretation was an *abduction* that would relate all three factual domains within a single wider context. It required two crucial intellectual adjustments:

(a) Extending the developmental, temporal concept of 'evolution' from **ontogenesis** (where is originated) to **phylogenesis**, which then displaced the abstract scalar ranking of extant species.

(b) Reinterpreting the old Aristotelian recapitulation not as an analogical relation between ontogenesis and the abstract *scala* of the species, but as a much more powerful analogy between two developmental process, ontogenesis and phylogenesis.

10.4. **Rear-guard defense of Platonism**

10.4.1. **Preamble**

As noted above, it was always possible for devout Platonists, religious and otherwise, to interpret both the implicit scale of biological diversity and the developmental course of embryology as controlled by a resident universal principle of *divine guidance toward perfection*. Charles Bonnet expresses this most succinctly in terms of the familiar **Great Chain of Being**:

---

12 Associated initially with Cuvier (1769-1832) in Paris.

"...Between the lowest and the highest degree of spiritual and corporal perfection, there is an almost infinite number of intermediate degrees. The succession of degrees comprises the *Universal Chain*. It unites all beings, ties together all worlds, embraces all the spheres. One *single being* is outside this chain, and this is *He* who made it..." (1764, p. 27)

While evolutionary thinking increasingly permeated the intellectual climate of the late 18th and early 19th Centuries, Platonic interpretations of the biological order persisted. These interpretations retained their non-pragmatic character even -- rather paradoxically -- when pragmatic notions such as *context* and *function* were invoked. In the following two sections we will consider briefly two historical high-points that constituted the immediate precursors to Darwin.

10.4.2. Naturphilosophie

Associated initially and most strongly with German Romanticism, and with illustrious names such as Goethe, Herder and Schelling, this school endeavored to describe one fundamental universal order, of metaphysics, the physical world, biology and Man. The Romantic agenda sought to demonstrate:[13]

 a. The ever-present universal order
 b. The superiority of Man
 c. The scalar contiguity of all life; and, thus,
 d. Mankind's affinity to the other divisions of Nature

The biological agenda of Naturphilosophie was profoundly developmentalist, evolutionist and -- because of its overriding commitment to a single underlying principle -- also profoundly *recapitulationist*:

(i)   All developmental processes in nature abide by a single tendency and a single developmental course.
(ii) The same laws govern embryonic development (ontogenesis) and the evolution of species (phylogenesis).
(iii) The animal kingdom must itself be considered a single organism, evolving from lower to higher stages.

In Tiedemann's words:

"...Even as each individual organism transforms itself, so the whole animal kingdom is to be thought of as an organism in the course of metamorphosis..." (1808, cited in Russell, 1916, p. 215)

---

13 For the discussion in this section I relied heavily on Gould (1977, pp. 35-50). For the general agenda of German Romanticism see also Goede von Aesch (1941).

Or in the words of the French transcendentalist Serrés:

"...The entire animal kingdom can, in some measure, be considered ideally as a single animal which, in the course of formation and metamorphosis of its diverse organisms, stops its development, here earlier and there later..." (1860, p. 834)

What had continued to elude this profoundly developmentalist vision were the two inter-dependent pragmatic, contextual ingredients, whose interaction would eventually extract evolutionary thinking from its residual Platonism: The ecological context of the **environment**, on the one hand; and the functional context of the organism's **adaptive behavior**, on the other.

10.4.3. Lamarck's adaptive functionalism

In the transformation of biological thinking -- and of evolutionary theory -- from a Platonic to a pragmatic approach, and thus in the protracted transition from Aristotle to Darwin, Jean-Baptiste Lamarck (1744-1829) occupies a pivotal, if paradoxical, position. Following Cuvier, and at a relatively advanced age, Lamarck was quick to recognize the devastating implications of the fossil record for the single, idealized Aristotelian *Scala Naturae*. Both the details of separate branches and the extinction of terminal species within branches forced a hierarchic, tree-like reformulation of the old scale. Further, by analogy with the fossil record, the scale could at last be re-interpreted in evolutionary terms.

The fossil record also brought with it the second -- perhaps most revolutionary -- element in Lamarck's evolutionary thinking: The recognition of **environmental change** as the context that motivated biological change. The nascent study of geology increasingly pointed to a recurrent coincidence of the two developmental processes: Biological species residing in the contiguous geological strata seemed to change *together* with their environment. The impact of this recognition on Lamarck's thinking -- and through it on the history of Biology -- could not be over-emphasized.

Still, Lamarck, in keeping with the religious climate of his time, strove to retain as large a residue of Platonism as could be compatible with the newly discovered facts. He accomplished this by recognizing two separate, indeed conflicting, *mechanisms* that may causally drive -- i.e. explain -- evolution. The first one is transparently Platonic:[14]

---

14 For the discussion of Lamarck, I relied heavily on Mayr (1982, pp. 343-362), as well as on Mayr (1972).

(a) An **innate, God-given** capacity -- or drive -- for progress toward **perfection** (with the latter defined in purely formal terms of *structural complexity*):

"...Nature, in successively producing all species of animals, beginning with the most imperfect or the simplest, and ending her work with the most perfect, has caused their organization gradually to become more complex... [And, the cause of this progress toward increasing perfection derives] from powers conferred by the Supreme Author of all things..." (1809, pp. 60, 130, resp.)

Lamarck's second mechanism, in spite of a Platonic residue ('perfect harmony'), is context-dependent, thus pragmatic:

(b) An **interactive** process of constant **adaptation** to the ever-changing **environment** (so as to maintain as much as possible **perfect harmony** with the environment).

A third element in Lamarck approach is even more transparently pragmatic. It pertains to the putative role the adaptive behavior of individuals plays, given perceived environmental-adaptive tasks, in the evolution of species. Lamarck's position on this issue has remained deservedly controversial in evolutionary biology. In essence, he proposed a mechanism by which the individual's life-time adaptive change is incremented into the species' genetic pool, Lamarck's *Second Law*:

"...Everything which nature has caused individuals to acquire or lose as a result of the influence of environmental conditions to which their race has been exposed over a long period of time -- and consequently, as a result of the effects caused by either the extended use (or disuse) of a particular organ -- is conveyed by generation to new individuals descending therefrom..." (1809, p. 113)

We shall return to discuss this position of Lamarck's further below.

10.4.4. Darwin

The transformation of evolutionary thinking was completed by Darwin, whose position -- with important refinements -- has remained dominant to this day. Darwin's re-interpretation of the three bodies of biological data -- diversity, embryology and the fossil record -- hinged upon two processes, one in-built into the organism and thus incipiently Platonic, the other contextual-interactive and thus pragmatic:

(a) Species have a certain characteristic range of **variability** in both their genotype and phenotype. That variability is now known to be the product of two forces:
  (i) The incidence of random **mutation**; and
  (ii) The massive reshuffling of genetic material due to **recombination** through sexual reproduction.[15]

(b) The interaction with the environment weeds out the less well-adapted variants by the process of **natural selection**.

The translation of (a) into molecular-genetic terms was only a natural step, once Mendel's pioneering work had been re-discovered. The modern field of **population genetics** has also filled in the blanks about the genetic variability within populations and its interaction with natural selection.

As pragmatic as (b) seems, it nonetheless misses one crucial component of evolution -- the role played by the **adaptive behavior**, indeed **adaptive experimentation**, of individuals. The missing ingredient is Mayr's "pacemaker of evolution". Stripped of the actual erroneous mechanism, this was the essence of Lamarck's grand vision.

10.5. **The siren-call of Lamarckism**

There has been, from the very start, one seductive aspect to in Lamarck's *Second Law*. And while we know now that the actual transfer mechanism proposed by Lamarck has no factual support, the attraction of that one element persists. It is worth noting, for example, that Darwin himself was far from opposed to Lamarck's position on the inheritance of acquired traits. Thus, we find the following words in *The Descent of Man*, under the heading of *The effect of the increased use and disuse of parts*:[16]

"...it is well known that use strengthens the muscles in the individual, and complete disuse, or the destruction of the proper nerve, weakens them. When the eye is destroyed, the optic nerve often becomes atrophied. When an artery is tied, the lateral channels increase not only in diameter but in

---

15 This element in Darwinian thinking, given the current emphasis on populations genetics, intra-species variability and non-Platonic distribution of genetic traits within the species, is as close as Darwinians ever get to the old Platonic (Mayr's "essentialist") view of fixed genetic types.

16 Mayr (1972) notes that Darwin referred to use and disuse, as a mechanism for transfer of acquired traits, on 13 separate pages in *The origin of Species*, the same number of references found in Lamarck's *Philosophie Zoologique*. Mayr (in personal communication) also notes that the general thesis of Lamarck's Second Law, the inheritance of acquired traits, had been the received wisdom in biology since the Greeks.

thickness and strength of their coats. When one of the kidneys ceases to act, the other increases in size, and does double work....Whether the several foregoing modifications would become hereditary, if the same habits of life were followed during many generations, is not known, *but it is probable...*" (1861, pp. 24-25; emphasis is mine; TG)

Darwin follows this observation with many examples in support of Lamarck's Second Law, concluding with the following remarks concerning its applicability to human evolution:

"...Although man may not have been much modified during the latter stages of his existence through the increase or decrease use of parts, the facts now given show that his liability in this respect has not been lost; and we positively know that the same law holds good with the lower animals. Consequently we may infer that when at a remote epoch[17] the progenitors of man were in a transitional state, and were changing from quadrupeds into bipeds, *natural selection would probably have been greatly aided by the inherited effects of increased or diminished use of different parts of the body...*" (1861, p. 27; emphasis is mine; TG)

What is so attractive about Lamarck's **interactive** view of evolution, a process whereby the efforts invested by individuals in survival strategies during a life-time of learning, of searching for adaptive solutions to environmental dilemmas, somehow contributes to the long-term adaptive history of the species? What has continued to beckon to thinkers as diverse as the sedately empirical Charles Darwin, the Stalinist stooge Trofim Lysenko,[18] the mercurial dilettante Arthur Koestler[19] and the prophetic Gregory Bateson?[20] One may speculate on this briefly.

For Darwin, the attraction was simple: The facts seem to point in that direction; increased use, increased development and eventual inheritance of the increased trait seemed to correlate, go hand in hand.

Lysenko's motives were the most suspect, if not necessarily the most transparent. Scientific conviction and naked ambition aside,[21] the

---

17 Darwin here displays, inadvertently and to be sure only by the weakest of implications, the fatal tendency of separating the early -- 'physical' -- epoch of human evolution from the more recent -- 'cognitive' -- phase. As we shall see shortly, he is in illustrious company there.

18 Lysenko is considered such an unworthy scientist that neither Mayr (1982) nor Gould (1977, 1980) dignify his work with a bibliographic citation.

19 As in Koestler (1967, 1972). For the former, see in particular Ch. XI: "Acting before reacting -- Once more Darwin and Lamarck".

20 As in Bateson (1979).

21 Gould (1980) is surprisingly charitable in referring to Lysenko: "...Lysenko's debate with the Russian Mendelians was, at the outset, a legitimate scientific argument. Later, he held on through fraud, deception, manipulation, and murder..." (p. 67)

ideological context whereby an anti-Mendelian dogma became *de rigueur* in Soviet biology owes much to Marxist resentment of inherited social privilege. The transmutation of acquired protoplasmic experience into inherited traits was viewed by the Stalinists as a clear *analog* to the proletariat bettering its social lot through life-long struggle. The analogy concerns the relationship between the cell's relatively large, hard-working protoplasm, saddled with all the day-to-day metabolic chores, governed by the small, metabolically inactive nucleus that controls and transmits inheritance.

Koestler arrived at the necessity of Lamarckian evolution with a distinct spiritual agenda. In adopting a neo-Lamarckian view, he seems to have not been bound by the need to elucidate a coherent alternative to Lamarck's defunct transfer *mechanism*. Rather, Koestler's Lamarckian forays seem to spring from his Romantic preoccupation with the **creative spirit** of all sentient beings.[22] His actual argument boils down to roughly this: If organisms *seem to behave as if* they creatively seek an adaptive solution, they *must therefore in fact be doing* just that. However sympathetic one may be to Koestler's spiritual presuppositions, the empirical merit of his argument -- except perhaps as a heuristic -- is questionable.

Bateson, whatever his initial motivation,[23] came a considerable dis-

---

22 See discussion of the German Romantic movement in section 10.4.2., above.

23 The title of Bateson (1979), "Mind and Nature, A Necessary Unity", is of course suggestive of Bateson's intellectual agenda, which -- among other things -- demanded the abolition of the old Cartesian dualism, i.e. the cleavage between the evolution of mind and the evolution of body. As we shall see further below, this dualism has persisted in 20th Century philosophy and linguistics. It was also taken for granted by many of Darwin's great evolutionist contemporaries. In his Introduction, Bateson takes pains to distinguish his proposal from the traditional *Great Chain of Being*. His meta-observations on his own agenda are a rare model of empirical accountability: "...In what is offered in this book, the hierarchic structure of thought, which Bertrand Russell called *logical typing*, will take place of the hierarchic structure of the Great Chain of Being and an attempt will be made to propose *a sacred unity of the biosphere* [emphasis is mine; TG] that will contain fewer epistemological errors than the versions of that sacred unity which the various religions of history have offered. What is important is that, right or wrong, the epistemology shall be *explicit*. Equally explicit criticism will be then possible..." (1979, p. 21)

tance toward resolving the puzzle of the transfer mechanism. He seems to have identified a number of the necessary ingredients: (a) The role of a **hierarchic categorization** of the phenomenological domain ('perceived task environment');[24] and (b) the process of **practiced, skilled learning**.[25] In rejecting the old Lamarckian mechanism, Bateson also seems to have adopted a version of modern **population thinking**:

"...The reader is reminded here of what was said about the fallacy of Lamarckism...Lamarck proposed that environmental impact could directly affect the genes of the *single individual* (emphasis is mine; TG). That is untrue. What is true is a proposition of next-higher logical type: that the environment does have direct impact on the gene pool of the *population*..." (1979, p. 131),

Lamarck's Second Law may now be re-considered in light of the interaction among three factors:[26]

(a) The adaptive behavior of individuals
(b) The genetic *and* behavioral variability within the population
(c) The genetic evolution of the species

24 Here Bateson (1979, pp. 21, 127-139, and elsewhere) credits Russell's Theory of Types (see discussion in Ch. 1). Bateson makes use of Russell's idea of 'types' to argue for the hierarchic relation between individuals and populations. While the argument is important in its own realm, it is not connected to the second ingredient of the mechanism, automated processing.
25 See Bateson (1979, pp. 216-217). Bateson did not tie the two together as necessary components of a unified mechanism by which life-long learning is transferred into the population's genetic pool.
26 Bateson has rightly viewed the progression from (a) to (b) as a progression up the hierarchy of types. In some yet-to-be elucidated sense, perhaps the progression from (b) to (c) is also an instance of meta-level shifting. Bateson's position on this second possibility is not clear. The phenomenology of human language is replete with examples of close interaction between the *group* and the *type*. Consider, for example, the use of plurality in pronominal reference, as in: 'If *anybody* comes late, *they* better...' (type reference) 'I talked to the *team* and *they*...' (group reference) In English (as well as in Spanish, Hebrew and many other languages), impersonal-'passive' semi-referring or non-referring subjects are coded as plurals, as in: '*They* found him drunk on the beach'. For a recent discussion, see Gernsbacher (1987). The process of generalization of experience also displays a progression from plurality to generality. Thus, the progression: 'I saw a *mule* there yesterday' (single instance) 'I saw *mules* there regularly' (plural instances) 'One sees *mules* there regularly' (generalized experience). For further discussion of this, see Givón (1984f, section 8). While the actual solution to the Lamarckian puzzle seems to have eluded him, Bateson came close. His last book (1979) was written as he waged a losing battle with cancer.

10.6. The transfer mechanism: Adaptive behavior, population dynamics and species evolution

> "...Learning alters the shape of the search space in which evolution operates and thereby provides good evolutionary paths toward sets of co-adapted alleles. We demonstrate that this effect allows learning organisms to evolve *much* faster than their non-learning equivalents, even though the characteristics acquired by the phenotype are not communicated to the genotype..."
>
> Hinton and Nowlan, "How learning can guide evolution" (1987)

10.6.1. Preamble

In the years since Darwin, the Lamarckian intuition of "behavior guiding evolution" did not die out. Rather, it persisted as the middle ground between the two reductionist extreme, naive Lamarckism and mechanistic mutationism. The interaction between learning behavior and evolution was suggested by both Baldwin (1896) and Lloyd Morgan (1896). It was pursued by Waddington (1942, 1953) under the label of **canalization** or **genetic assimilation**, and has by now become a respectable mainstream idea among Darwinians.[27] The element of this 'guidance' that has been left under-elaborated will be the focus of the discussion below.

10.6.2. The software of adaptive behavior: Skilled user strategies

In this section I will sketch out an explicit mechanism by which the acquired life-time adaptive learning by individuals may be transmitted into the species' genetic pool. This mechanism does not attempt to replicate Lamarck's naive notion of direct, mechanistic causal link between increased use, somatic ('protoplasmic') growth and inheritance. Further, the mechanism I propose takes for granted both random mutation and recombination, thus incorporating Darwin's idea of 'spontaneous' variation as interpreted by current molecular and population genetics. Lastly, the mechanism also takes for granted Darwin's notion of **natural selection**. I will propose, however, a crucial shift of emphasis concerning the idea of **adaptive traits**. Both Lamarck and Darwin, and indeed

---

27 See e.g. Futuyma (1979, pp. 376-378) and Mayr (1982, pp. 611-612). Elsewhere Mayr (in personal communication) notes: "...As the Darwinians say: "Behavior is the pacemaker of evolution"..."

many contemporary evolutionary biologists, persist in interpreting 'trait' to mean purely **physical** trait -- i.e. a particular organ, its detailed shape and physical design. In other words, they interpret evolution to mean primarily the evolution of adaptive **hardware**. The hardware, however, like all instruments and organs, is totally useless -- indeed meaningless -- without its concomitant **software**: The cognitive-behavioral strategies and habits that govern the hardware's **use**.

It has been convenient for biologists, particularly in the study of so-called *lower organisms*, to downgrade the role of adaptive 'user strategies' and 'behavioral habits' in task-driven evolution. This has been done, quite routinely, by assuming that together with physical modification of an organ, new genetic combinations also bring with them -- automatically -- the appropriate **behavioral habits**, the necessary **strategies of use**. And, further, that from the very start these software concomitants of structural-genetic modification are **instinctual** and **wired-in**.[28] But hardware use is not always 100% predicted from hardware structure. More often than not, the hardware entails -- leaves open -- a range of behavioral options, among which individuals make **deliberate adaptive choices**.[29] This is, presumably, what Mayr (1974) had in mind in coining the term 'open behavioral program'.

Persisting in a mechanistic, deterministic approach to the relationship between hardware and software is both empirically risky and theoretically impoverished. This is certainly the case in the study of evolutionary change in 'higher species',[30] those that possess:

(a) a complex neurology,
(b) complex cognitive skills, and
(c) complex socio-cultural behavior and communication.

A complex neurology, and its entailed range of complex cognitive skills, evolves **interactively**, with the neurology often modified during the

---

28 Concerning such behavioral, strategic *software*, Mayr (in personal communication) comments: "...But this is a non-inheritable product of the hardware..." However see discussion directly below of Mayr's (1974) distinction between 'open' and 'closed' behavior programs. His 'open' program is an evolutionary strategy that leaves important adaptive choices open to the individual, thus not fully determined by gene-coded structure.

29 Gregory Bateson's view of evolution involves a similar cyclic **interaction** between the hardware and software of adaptive behavior. He writes: "...the hierarchy is not only a list of classes, classes of classes, and classes of classes of classes, but has also become *a zigzag ladder of dialectics between form and process*..." (1979, p. 215; emphases are mine; TG) Bateson applies this interactive/dialectic -- pragmatic -- model to a wide range of phenomena. His approach is strikingly similar, in general outline, to Kant's pragmatic middle ground in epistemology, i.e. the interaction between percept and concept (see Ch. 1).

30 There is, to my mind, no compelling reason for assuming that the same argument does not hold true for our study of the evolution of 'lower' organisms. It is our recalcitrant Cartesian dualism that leads us to persist in assuming otherwise. See discussion further below.

life-time of the individual. That interactive modification has been studied in great detail at both the behavioral-cognitive and neurological levels. It comes under the heading of **automated processing**, or **skilled learning**, as discussed in Chapter 7. In the next section I will sketch out the relevance of skilled, automated learning to the way behavior guides evolution.

10.6.3. The adaptive advantage of skilled learning and automated processing

Within each population ('social group'), all members of the same species, biologists acknowledge a range of genetic variation that governs the distribution of phenotype traits, both physical and neurological. But the use individuals make of their genetically-based traits is not completely predictable. Rather, in many important areas, in particular the areas of the most complex adaptive behavior,[31] the hardware leaves individuals a range of options. As a result, each individual, however genetically defined, has a certain range of **lifetime learning** ('experience') that is unpredictable and potentially unique.

The life experience of an individual includes **preferred strategies** or **routinized behavior patterns**; these are the individual's particular solutions to adaptive tasks, the way that individual perceives them. Let us consider a simple example. Gould (1980) described the evolution of the Panda's prehensile "thumb", a 'sixth toe' that in other five-toed mammals has nothing to do with toes or their prehensile use, from the *radial sesamoid* bone. The concomitant musculature evolved, in parallel fashion, from the accompanying *abductor muscle*. The development -- now genetically coded -- was presumably gradual. At the very beginning, presumably, the tool -- bone & muscle -- was not obviously suited to its new use. A newly-recombined genetic pattern, resulting in a slightly divergent phenotype, may have facilitated recognition of the potential for a new, prehensile, use of the *radial sesamoid*. But is it really necessary to assume that a new genetic pattern *must have preceded* the discovery of the new use? As Mayr (1982) notes, such extreme mutationism is unnecessary.[32] Suppose instead:

---

31 See discussion in Ch. 7, concerning the retention of non-automated processing in higher monitoring functions. This is another instance where the life-time behavior of the organism, in partly automating those higher functions through skilled learning, pioneers the eventual transformation of those function into genetically-determined "closed programs".

32 Recall Mayr's (1982) rejection of extreme mutationism: "...Many if not most acquisitions of new structures in the course of evolution can be ascribed to selection forces exerted by newly acquired behavior..." (p. 612; see Also Mayr, 1960).

(i) Some member(s) of the Panda population discovered, through their own process of adaptive trial-and-error and analysis, the potential of the *radial sesamoid* for prehensile use;

(ii) Those individuals perfect their behavioral pattern of use of the new instrument. In the best tradition of routinized, automated skilled learning, they become **experts** in the use of the instrument. Their behavior becomes **automated, skilled, a habit.**

(iii) As is well established, routinized processing involves a certain **rigidified patterning** of the neurological pathways -- 'connections' -- that govern the behavior.

(iv) Presumably, the physical instrument itself also develops in size and appropriate design during this protracted, expert life-time use.

So far, *none* of the developmental changes catalogued above could be transmitted to subsequent generations. Nothing has penetrated the genotype, yet. All we have yet, within the population, is one or more, certainly a small minority of individuals who answer to the following description:

(a) They have adapted the old organ to an unconventional use, as a new tool;

(b) Their behavior pattern -- including attended neurology -- has become highly automated vis-a-vis the new use.

(c) The organ itself has adopted physically, at least to some degree, the shape appropriate for the new use.

Presumably, other individuals within the population have made other behavioral adaptation during their lifetime. Some of those adaptations pertains to either:

(a) Different physical-behavioral solutions to the **same task;** or
(b) Different task interpretations of the **same organ.**

In the case of the Panda's thumb, adaptation type (a) may be, for example, the use of the 'true' thumb as a prehensile instrument. Adaptation type (b) may be, fort example, a weapon-like use of the *radial sesamoid*. All these individuals, with their routinized behavior patterns, now live together within the same population, interacting and inter-breeding.

Enter classical Darwinian new genetic combination. Among the many types of new genetic variants, only a few are relevant either to the task ('prehensile control') or the organ (*radial sesamoid* or the true thumb). Let us consider specifically what may happen when the new genetic variant that enters the population makes the *radial sesamoid* more amenable to prehensile use. Via interbreeding it soon begins to distribute gradually through a wider range of the population. Suppose, further, that four individuals -- A,B,C,D -- who possess this new gene now proceed to develop the following life-long strategic experience:

A routinizes the prehensile use of the *radial sesamoid*;
B routinizes the prehensile use of the true thumb;
C routinizes the defensive use of the *radial sesamoid*;
D routinizes none of the above.

The new genetic pattern favors them -- in classical Darwinian selection terms -- **differentially**. It favors most individual A who has routinized -- on his/her own -- the behavior pattern (i.e. 'software') that goes with the use of the new physical equipment (i.e, 'hardware'). That individual will be more successful in spreading the new genetic trait in to the gene pool.

Consider next a slightly modified scenario: Suppose that two new variations entered the genetic pool at the same time: variation (i) with an enlarged real thumb, and variation (ii) with an enlarged *radial sesamoid*. Suppose also that individual A above was the unaware but lucky repository of variation (ii), and individual D above was also a receptor of variation (ii). Further, no such individuals as B or C above existed within the population; so that whatever individual received variation (i) resembles C in being *behaviorally unskilled* vis-a-vis either (ii) or (i). In terms of the endowed genetic **hardware**, individuals A and D are equally competitive. However, in terms of the **use** of the hardware -- the life-time acquired, routinized behavioral **software** -- individual A has a clear adaptive advantage.

Consider, finally, the survival chances of the two genetic **variations**. Variation (ii) has a higher probability of spreading in the gene pool, since an individual exists who has the habituated skills to **take advantage of it**, who can **appreciate its adaptive edge**. In contrast, variation (i) has a lower probability of spreading: No individual has bothered to acquire and automate the behavioral software that would take advantage of its potential. Behavior, especially routinized skilled learning, is indeed *the pacemaker of evolution*.[33]

---

33 In a recent computer simulation study, Hinton and Nowlan (1987) have demonstrated the viability of the mechanism outlined above. An earlier oral report of their finding was given in Hinton (1986). While my own thinking on the subject goes back at least to Givón (1982a), I am delighted to see this convergence.

10.7. Socio-cultural, transmitted learning and evolutionary continuity

10.7.1. Background

In advocating rejection of Lamarck's old transfer mechanism in favor of a neo-Darwinian combination of genetic variation and natural selection, Gould (1980) makes the following observation concerning one developmental domain, uniquely human, where Lamarckism seems to have at long last triumphed:

"...Lamarckism, so far as we can judge, is false in the domain it has always occupied -- as a biological theory of genetic inheritance. Yet, by analogy only, it is the model of the "inheritance" for another and very different kind of "evolution" -- human cultural evolution. *Homo sapiens* arose at least 50,000 years ago, and we have not a shred of evidence for any genetic improvement since then...All that we have accomplished [since then; TG], for better or worse, is a result of cultural evolution. And we have done it at rates unmatched by orders of magnitude in all the previous history of life....Cultural evolution has progressed at rates that Darwinian processes cannot begin to approach. Darwinian evolution continues in *Homo sapiens*, but at rates so slow that it no longer has much impact on our history. This crux in the earth's history has been reached because Lamarckian processes have finally been unleashed upon it. Human cultural evolution, in strong opposition to our biological history, is Lamarckian in character. What we learn in one generation, we transmit directly by teaching and writing. Acquired characters are inherited in technology and culture..." (1980, pp. 70-71)

There's much that one would like to agree with, indeed applaud, in Gould's formulation. Our cultural evolution is indeed supremely Lamarckian. But there are also some disturbingly sweeping attitudes that cry for careful challenge.

(a) **The lack of genetic change in *Homo sapiens*:**

The reason why there is no evidence for significant genetic modification since 50,000 years ago is due to the nature of the evidence and the likely nature of more recent adaptive change: The evidence for change has hinged traditionally on **skeletal structure**, the only surviving remains of earlier man. Profound progressive changes in neurological organizations that may have been responsible for the evolution of higher cognitive capacities, reasoning, planning, strategic judgement and language may have taken place since then without any trace on cranial remains, and in particular on cranial shape and overall capacity. But such changes may have been quite crucial for our cognitive and cultural development during that period. *Homo sapiens*, as Gould himself suggests, has evolved toward increasing adaptive dependency on the **software** of cognitive strategies and socio-cultural behavior patterns. But the genetic modification supporting those may go completely undetected from cranial hardware alone.

(b) The uniqueness and non-contiguity of human culture

In making culture to be a totally novel phenomenon, a human-specific evolutionary departure, Gould departs -- I confess somewhat to my own disappointment -- from his exemplary attempts elsewhere[34] to resist, indeed debunk, the sharp demarcation between pre-human and human evolution. The truth of the matter is that socio-cultural organization, and the dependence for survival on socio-behavioral strategies, precedes *Homo sapiens* by a wide evolutionary margin. It is of course true that the pace has markedly accelerated in our most recent evolution. But the precursors for that process had evolved long before the advent of man. Some of our close relatives, such as the Chimpanzee or the Japanese Macaque, are known for transmitting to the social group behavioral traits that were discovered by solution-seeking, task-driven individual members.[35] But many perfectly serious biologists have traced the evolution of socio-culture much further back.[36] And the difference between 'simple imitation' and 'deliberate teaching' -- the latter the hallmark of cultural transmission, turns out to be a matter of gradation (Bonner, 1980, ch. 6). So that there is no reason to assume that other social mammals (such as wild dogs, wolves, or horses), as well as lower social species, are incapable of acquiring adaptive behavior by observing the behavior of an enterprising, inventive, adventuresome member of their social group.[37]

It is of course perfectly true that the **rate** of transmission of information is vastly faster in cultural than in 'purely genetic' transmission (Bonner, 1980, ch. 2). Further, the rate of cultural transmission itself has been vastly accelerated with the advent of human language, and again accelerated exponentially with the development of writing. Nonetheless, socio-cultural transmission of the individual's adaptive skilled learning predate *Homo sapiens* by a wide margin.

---

34 See in particular Part 2, "Darwiniana" in Gould (1980), where the theme recurs both in discussing Wallace and in discussing the extremist positions of *socio-altruism* and *socio-biology*. We will return to this subject further below.

35 See, for example, discussion in Goodall (1965), Simonds (1974) or de Waal (1982) *inter alia*.

36 See Bonner (1980) for an extensive discussion and literature review.

37 See, for example, discussion of wild dog social behavior in van Lawick-Goodall and van Lawick (1971). For a general discussion, see again Bonner (1980).

10.7.2. The interaction between individual learning and group transmission in evolution

It is easy to see now why socio-cultural development did not introduce the Lamarckian pattern into evolution. Rather, it served to vastly *accelerate* an *already established* evolutionary pattern. To argue this, we will first recapitulate the discussion in section 10.6.3. above in a simplified form.

10.7.2.1. Role of the individual's routinized behavior in gaining adaptive-selectional advantage

(i) Suppose one random mutation "M" is introduced into a population, a mutation favorable to gaining a certain adaptive advantage;

(ii) Next, suppose there are two groups of individuals in the population:
    Group A = routinizes an adaptive strategy compatible
        with mutation M;
    Group B = does not routinize that strategy;

(iii) Suppose also that the distribution of individuals displaying mutation M and those that don't is equal within groups A and B.

(iv) In consequence, the following four sub-groups are now present in the population:
    Group A-M = has both mutation M and its appropriate,
        routinized use-strategy;
    Group A-∅ = doesn't have mutation M but has the
        appropriate routinized use-strategy;
    Group B-M = has mutation M but doesn't have the
        appropriate routinized use-strategy;
    Group B-∅ = has neither mutation M nor the
        appropriate routinized use-strategy;

(v) In terms of chances for survival during their life-time, the four groups are ranked as follows:
    A-M = highest survival chances
    A-∅ = intermediate survival chances
    B-M and B-∅ = lowest survival chances

(vi) Consequently, the gene carrying mutation M has the highest probability of spreading through the population through the progeny of sub-group A-M.

So far we have reckoned without any socio-cultural transmission of behavior strategies. That is, within our putative population, individuals experiment strictly on their own and do not imitate the behavior of proximate members of their social group. But even before the rise of communication and explicit teaching,[38] imitation of successful adaptive behavior is likely. Socio-cultural transmission must therefore predate deliberate, explicit communication.

10.7.2.2. The role of socio-cultural transmission in accelerating the spread of favorable genetic traits

It is easy to see now how socio-cultural transmission of acquired be-havior patterns, whether by implicit imitation or explicit instruction, could vastly accelerate the adaptive advantage that the individuals of Group A, above, possess. Many individuals of group B-M – i.e. those who had the appropriate genetic trait but did not develop the appropriate use-strategy on their own -- may acquired that behavior strategy by contact with members of group A-M. In a population with little socio-cultural communication, their survival chances remain low. Cultural transmission now increases those chances in the direction of the most favored group, A-M. Indeed, the ranks of group A-M will now swell by those erstwhile B-M members. And as a result, the spread of mutation-M within the popula-tion will increase more rapidly, since more survivors carry it.[39]

10.7.3. Summary

To paraphrase Hinton (1986) on the course of **directed evolution**: In-dividuals within a population act as **advanced scouts** for evolution. Their life-time experience, in experimenting and testing the range of likely survival strategies available to the species, and the resultant skilled learning and routinized neuro-behavioral patterns, have profound consequences for the eventual course of the genetic evolution of the species. These genetic consequences can be postulated even without the introduction of socio-cultural transmission. The latter vast-ly amplifies them; it gives a new advantageous genetic variant a tremen-dous boost, by accelerating the rate of its spread within the population.

---

38 Explicit instruction is well-documented in primates and carnivores (see footnotes 35, 36, 37, above). Implicit transmission via imitation undoubtedly pre-dates it. And, as Bonner (1980) has noted, the difference between imitation and explicit teaching is not sharp, but rather is a matter of degree.

39 Hinton and Nowlan's (1987) simulation study disregard this possibility, thus supplying a formal elucidation of our earlier -- pre-cultural -- scenario (section 10.6.3, above).

10.8. The difference of mind and the difference it makes[40]

10.8.1. The difference of Man

Our historical survey (see sections 10.2. and 10.3., above) makes it clear that the idea of the **uniqueness of Man** -- the apex of perfection-seeking biological evolution -- had permeated biological thinking all the way to Darwin and even beyond. Thus Aristotle, in setting up his three-step progression of 'soul' up *scala naturae* -- from *nutritive* (metabolic) to *sensible* (sensory-motor) to *rational* (cognitive) -- explicitly singled out the **rational mind** as the criterial trait by which to differentiate human from pre-human. This tradition has persisted, via Descartes and others, into 20th Century philosophy and linguistics. It is a tradition that insists on a sharp cleavage in the continuity of the evolutionary ladder, a cleavage that is invariably placed between mankind and its immediate ancestors.

One of the hallmarks of the sharp cleavage tradition is the Platonic rigidity of its criteria. It strives to define various cognitive faculties and cultural traits from a discrete, anthropo-centric perspective. Pre-human precursors of any alleged human-specific trait are thus excluded from consideration by being pronounced 'different in kind', rather than 'different in degree'. Chomsky's (1968) view of the sharp break between pre-human and human communication is an example of this conceptual trick.[41] The updated Cartesian checklist of Man's unique attributes is given by Mortimer Adler as:[42]

---

40 The title of this section owes an obvious debt to Mortimer Adler's (1967) *The Difference of Man and the Difference it Makes*; the position for which I argue is the exact opposite of Adler's.
41 See extensive discussion of this issue in Ch. 3, in particularly as related to the distinction between symbolic vs. iconic signs. In addition, by branding the inventory of animal signs "closed", Chomsky implicitly likens it to an *instinctive* behavioral program, reminiscent of Mayr's (1974) 'closed program'.
42 Summarized from Adler (1967, p. 91).

1. *Language*: Propositions, sentences, verbal symbols
2. *Tools*: Useful artifacts, technology
3. *Organization*: Social, political and legal structure
4. *Culture*: Transmitted traditions, history
5. *Religion*: Magic, ritual, spiritual belief
6. *Ethics*: Morality, conscience, sense of right and wrong
7. *Aesthetics*: Adornment, entertainment, art

With the exception of the last three traits, which Adler himself concedes to be 'interpreted behavior', the sharp break between human and pre-human behavior hinges primarily on definitional games. In each one of traits (1) through (4) above, extensive pre-adaptations can be shown to have existed prior to the evolution of man.[43] We will touch upon the neurological basis for such pre-adaptations further below.

10.8.2. Darwin, Wallace and evolutionary contiguity

One of the great signs of intellectual courage that characterized Darwin's work was that he did go ahead and write *The Descent of Man*, where he insisted on straight-forward evolution continuity and no ex-emption for 'the top rung of the ladder'. As Gould[44] points out, Alfred Wallace and Charles Darwin arrived at the explanatory principle of *natural selection* independently, and roughly at the same time. Unlike Darwin, Wallace chose to exempt the evolution of *mind* from the normal adaptive, selectional constraints on physical bio-evolution. A religious

---

43 See extensive discussion in Lamendella (1975, 1976), de Waal (1982), Simonds (1974) or Lieberman (1984), among many others. A wonderful example of the transformation of an iconic into symbolic sign is described in de Waal (1982), where the Chimpanzee's gesture of extending the arm-and-hand for the purpose of grasping has transformed gradually into the conventionalized signs for: (a) 'I want it'; (b) 'give it to me'; (c) 'I need your support against my enemy'; (d) 'I need love and comfort'. The chain of gradual symbolic transfor-mation bears striking resemblance to normal *metaphoric extension* in human language (see Ch. 2). Serious main-stream evolutionary biologists have also recognized the early pre-human roots of both consciousness and culture. For representative examples, see Bonner (1980) or Griffin (1976, 1984).

44 Gould (1980, part 2, chapter 4).

motivation for this exemption may be taken for granted. But Wallace also produced cogent theoretical arguments in support of retaining the Cartesian dichotomy. His argument turns out to have been an extreme super-selectionist extension of Darwin's position: *All* evolving traits must have some selectional advantage. Darwin never espoused such extremism, writing:

"...I am convinced that natural selection has been the main but not the exclusive means of modification..." (*The Origin of Species*, 1872 edition)[45]

Rather, Darwin believed that "adaptive change in one part can lead to non-adaptive modifications of other features".[46]

Wallace, in surveying the brain-size of non-Western 'savages', which together with Darwin and all their contemporaries he considered both *intellectually inferior* and *evolutionarily prior*,[47] observed:

"...In the brain of the lowest savages, and, as far as we know, of the prehistoric races, we have an organ...little inferior in size and complexity to that of the higher type..." (1890)[48]

Thus concluding that the brain may be vastly over-designed, i.e. an instance of *excess structure*, Wallace argues that the evolution of mind is not governed by the same principle -- adaptive selection -- as the evolution of the body:

---

45 Quoted in Gould (1980, p. 45)
46 See Gould (1980, p. 45)
47 A pervasive sense of racism is virtually taken for granted in the discussion of 'savage human races' by Darwin and his contemporaries, for whom these races exhibited clear signs of lower evolutionary characteristic, somewhat intermediate between ape and man. Indeed, part of Darwin's argument for an evolutionary descent of man hinged, at least by implication, on the intermediate evolutionary status of the non-Caucasian races. Thus, in discussing the importance of the olfactory sense in pre-human mammals, Darwin writes: "... The sense of smell is of the highest importance to the greater number of mammals...But [it is] of extremely slight service, if any, even to the dark-coloured races of man, in whom it is much more highly developed than in the white and civilized races..." (*The Descent of Man*, 1871, p. 12) And further: "...It appears as if the posterior molar or wisdom teeth were tending to become rudimentary in the more civilized races of man...In the Melanian races, on the other hand, the wisdom teeth are usually furnished with three separate fangs, and are generally sound; they also differ from the other molars in size, less than in the Caucasian races..." (*ibid.*, p. 14) And further: "...In man, the canine teeth are perfectly efficient instruments for mastication. But their true canine character, as Owen remarks, "is indicated by the conical form of the crown...The conical form is best expressed in the Melanian races, especially the Australian..."" [*ibid.*, pp. 30-31)
48 Quoted from Gould (1980, p. 48).

"...Natural selection could only have endowed savage man with a brain a few degrees superior to that of an ape, whereas he actually possesses one very little inferior to that of a philosopher...The habits of savages give no indication of how this faculty could have been developed by natural selection, because it is never required or used by them. The singing of savages is more or less monotonous howling, and the female seldom sings at all. Savages certainly never chose their wives for fine voices, but for rude health, and strength, and physical beauty..." (1890)[49]

We will return to the question of evolutionary contiguity directly below.

10.8.3. More rear guard skirmishes of Platonism: The abduction of Gould's punctuated equilibrium

"...Both Darwin and Agassiz, then, denied the "biological reality" of species, but for diametrically opposed reasons. Darwin denied it because he considered species an arbitrary segment in a continuous stream of individuals. Agassiz denied it because to him not the physical species as such had reality but only the category of thought that we call "species"..."

E. Mayr, "Agassiz, Darwin and Evolution" (1959c, p. 261)

As the idea of evolution becomes more widely accepted in the social and human sciences, Platonic-Cartesian biases for the 'uniqueness of man' undergo strange metamorphoses. Often, the ensuing conceptual stance is eerily reminiscent Wallace's. Thus Chomsky, for example, has more recently taken to citing Gould's position on gapped evolution -- *punctuated equilibrium* -- [50] in support of the uniqueness and evolutionary non-contiguity of the human language faculty. Chomsky's agenda is two-fold, and Gould is pressed into service in support of its first firmament: The process of evolution seems to alternate between periods of gradual ('quantitative') and abrupt ('qualitative') change, with the latter most characteristic of rapid speciation. The evolution of human language, Chomsky asserts, must have been of that second type.

The idea of **gradual change** has been *anathema* to Platonists from the very start, running smack against their notion of discrete *ideal types*. We

---

49 Quoted from Gould (1980, pp. 49-50).
50 See Eldredge and Gould (1972) and Gould and Eldredge (1977).

have already noted (Ch. 1) how Aristotle wrestled with the implications of gradual change by positing an added level of reality, the *sinolon*, where change could register in the graduated space between the *forms*, while the *forms* themselves remain discrete and immutable. By a coincidental inverse analogy, early evolutionists used the evident **graduated similarities** among biological species as an argument for evolutionary change and against abrupt creationism. Thus, Lamarck (1809) observed:

"...With regard to living bodies, it is no longer possible to doubt that nature has done everything little by little and successively..." (1809, p. 11) and "...These changes only take place with an extreme slowness, which makes them always imperceptible..." (*ibid.*, p. 30)

Gould's notion of **punctuated equilibria**,[51] and in particular the way Chomskians have made use of it to support the alleged evolutionary discontinuity (thus Cartesian uniqueness) of man, mind and language, is open to a number of factual and theoretical objections.

(a) **Generality:**
Gould himself cautions against too general applicability of 'punctuated' change:

"...I emphatically do not assert the general "truth" of this philosophy of punctuational change. Any attempt to support the exclusive validity of such a grandiose notion would border on the nonsensical. Gradualism sometimes works well..." (1980, p. 153).

(b) **Speciation and accelerated change:**
It is generally accepted now (see e.g. Mayr, 1959b, 1970) that abrupt evolutionary gaps are associated most typically with **speciation** -- the emergence of new species. And further, that the primary impetus for this abruptness is the combination of:

(i)   The isolation of a small population;
(ii)   Consequently, lack of dilution ('neutralization') of new genetic traits; and thus
(iii) The accelerated spread of innovation across the isolated population.

Futuyma (1979) sums up the seeming contradiction between gapped speciation and gradual genetic change as follows:

---

51 See Gould (1980, part 5, ch. 17) as well as Eldredge and Gould (1972) and Gould and Eldredge (1977).

"...Thus the theory of punctuated equilibria suggests that major changes can happen very rapidly, but it still does not tell us whether they occur through *intermediate morphological steps*..." (1979, p. 163; emphasis is mine; TG)

Gould himself puts it as follows:

"...A new species can arise when a small segment of the ancestral population is isolated at the periphery of the ancestral range..." (1980, p. 152)

And:

"...Large, stable central populations exert a strong homogenizing influence. New and favorable mutations are diluted by the sheer bulk of the population through which they spread. They may build slowly in frequency, but changing environments usually cancel their selective value long before they reach fixation..." (*ibid.*)

But the bulk of the non-variant population could only dilute the new genetic variant if it is *inter-breedable* with it. Or, in other words, if the new variant has not diverged across an **inter-species gap**. The *process* of speciation must therefore be a **graduated** -- though possibly quite rapid -- cumulation of **successive small steps**. It is only its ultimate *product* that is guaranteed to seem gapped. This is so because of the interaction of several factors, all already noted above:

(i)   The geographic **isolation** of the small sub-population, within which selectively-favored innovations spread without dilution;

(ii) The acceleration of the rate of spread of the mutation due to **automated, skilled-learning** by individual members. That is, the "guidance of evolution by behavior";

(iii) The further acceleration of spread of the new favorable variation due to **socio-cultural** transmission.[52]

None of these factors militates for the evolutionary non-contiguity of higher cognitive faculties. Rather, they suggest that pre-human biological evolution must have already been guided by purposive behavior, de-

---

52 One must note, lastly, that pre-adaptation via automated behavior and skilled learning favors not only the first mutation in the appropriate adaptive direction, but also *the entire chain* of compatible mutations. Thus, the first panda who routinized the prehensile use of the *radial sesamoid* created a favorable survival chance not only for the first genetic variant leading to the re-shaping of that bone as a 'thumb', but for the entire chain of convergent variations leading in the same direction.

pendent on population dynamics, and quick to take advantage of socio-cultural transmission.

10.8.4. Modularity and the Platonization of mental faculties

The Chomskians' rear-guard struggle to salvage the Cartesian agenda apparently also requires that human language be discontinuous with so-called 'general cognitive capacities',[53] perhaps because such capacities -- or their unmistakable pre-adaptive precursors -- can be shown to exist in pre-human mammals. To this end, latter-day Platonists press into service the notion of neurological modularity,[54] whereby the human language-processing capacity is alleged to be a separate neurological module, quite independent of the neurological regions that support the other, 'lower' cognitive functions.

The neurological evidence concerning the left-hemisphere specialization -- lateralization -- of language, as well as the seeming grammar-specificity of Broca's region, has often been used to prop the argument for a human-specific language-module. But as Lieberman (1984) points out, a number of other complex faculties are also controlled from the same brain region. In particular, that region seems to specialize in **automated rhythmic-hierarchic** skills, including complex motion, music and hierarchically-organized visual patterns.[55]

The claims of separate neurological module for language also fly in the face of what is known in biological evolution in general as the process of **homoplasy**, whereby old organs are adapted to perform novel (but initially similar and thus compatible) functions (Futuyma, 1979, p. 140). As Gould (1980) points out, "nature is a tinkerer", taking advantage of existing structures whenever they are extendable, rather than inventing new ones. The extension of bio-design thus proceeds in a *Rube Goldberg fashion*. And the extension of both bio-design and bio-function is in a sense rather analogous to metaphoric ('Wittgensteinean') extension of meaning:[56] Small steps of novel contextual adaptation proceed along **gradients of similarity** of both structure and function.

---

53 See Chomsky (1968), as well as more recent formulations in Chomsky's various contribution in Piattelli-Palmarini (ed., 1980).

54 See Fodor (1983).

55 See some discussion in Ch. 7. The neurological literature supporting the alternative approach, that of **shared modules**, is quite extensive (e.g. Bradshaw and Nettleton, 1981; Greenfield and Schneider 1977; Grossman, 1980; Ibbotson and Morton, 1981; Lieberman, 1984; Kimura, 1979; Martin 1972; Poeck and Huber 1977; Robinson, 1977; Robinson and Solomon, 1974; Whitaker, 1983; *inter alia*. More recently the same approached to module sharing has been demonstrated in the study of rhythmic motor skills (Keel, 1986; Keel and Ivry, 1986; Keel *et al*, 1985, 1986).

56 See discussion in Ch. 2.

10.9. Closure: The language parallels

10.9.1. Variation and change

> "...Every characteristic of organisms *has a frequency distribution*...Evolution in a broad sense may be considered any change in the form of the frequency distribution of one or more characteristics..."

> D. Futuyma, *Evolutionary Biology*
> (1979, pp. 19-21)

As noted above, biological evolution proceeds through the interaction of three factors:

(a) The inherent variability within the species ('type')
(b) The adaptive-purposive behavior of individuals
(c) The adaptive selection pressure of the environment

The parallels between biology and linguistics here are indeed striking. In Ch. 2 we noted how the only approach to mental categories that is compatible with behavioral facts is a **variationist** approach, akin to Mayr's *population thinking*. Bill Labov's pioneering work on variation (see e.g. Labov, 1975b) has shown the applicability of this thinking to populations of *speakers*, as well as to population of *utterances*. Further, Labov's work has also pointed out another pervasive parallelism between linguistics and biology: The intimate connection between **synchronic variation** and **diachronic change**. So that " today's variants are tomorrow's main-stream behavior". Much as in bio-evolution, linguistic diachrony can be characterized as a **shift in the frequency distributions** that characterizes the population.

In its much shorter history as a separate empirical discipline, linguistics has experienced the same damaging pressures from Platonic idealization -- Mayr's "essentialism" -- as had biology. In both disciplines, the advent of **contextual-pragmatic thinking** is marked by the very same features:

(i)   Population-variationist thinking
(ii) Graduated-scalar definition of 'types'
(iii) Functionalist-adaptive approach to both behavior and structure
(iv) Ecological-environmental framing
(v)   Historical-evolutionary explanation of stasis

The fact that Aristotle turns out to have been the spiritual father of pragmatic thinking in both disciplines may of course be an accident, but surely a happy one.

10.9.2. History, diachrony and recapitulation

"...Every biological phenomenon, every structure, every function, indeed everything in biology, has a history. And the study of this history, the reconstruction of the selection pressures that have been responsible for the biological world of today, is as much a part of the causal explanation of the world of organisms as physiological or embryological explanations. A purely physiological-ontogenetic explanation that omits the historical side is only half an explanation..."

E. Mayr, *Evolution and the Diversity of
Life* (1976, p. 16)

In arguing against Dawkins' non-behavioral, non-functional approach to biological evolution, an approach that reduces 'adaptation' to a mere lottery of *genotypes*, and would thus effectively ignore the interaction between the *phenotype* -- task-oriented organs -- and the environment, Gould (1980) makes a plea for a **historical** interpretation of bio-organisms:

"...[Dawkins' reductionist] ideas have been successful in our study of simple objects, made of few components, and uninfluenced by prior history...But organisms are much more than amalgamations of genes. They have *a history that matters*..." (1980, p. 77; emphasis is mine; TG)

One of the most salient features of bio-evolution as a historical process is the parallelism, noted in one guise or another ever since Aristotle, between the evolutionary sequence ('phylogenesis') and the embryonic sequence ('ontogenesis'). How this parallelism -- usually referred to as **recapitulation** -- actually comes into being is a complex, absorbing story that is not within the immediate scope of our discussion.[57] As noted in Chapter 8, both language and socio-culture are adaptive, functional-pragmatic, historically-derived structures. They are historical in very much the same sense as Mayr and Gould consider bio-organization to be historical:

---

57 See Gould (1977). The most vigorous exponent of classical recapitulationism was Haeckel (1866). A comprehensive overview may be also found in de Beer (1930).

(a) They bear the traces of their evolutionary history; and
(b) that evolution is itself task-driven.

The possibility that in language -- as in biology -- ontogenesis recapitulates phylogenetic evolution has been discussed in some detail elsewhere.[58] What human language and socio-culture add to the recapitulation paradigm is a third component -- **socially-transmitted history**. As Gould (1980, Part 2, ch. 7) notes, the historical transmission of language and socio-culture is a clear instance of Lamarckian evolution. The fact that Lamarckian principles may also be involved in pre-human bio-evolution detracts little from Gould's observation.

The striking parallels between child language development (ontogenesis) and language history (phylogenesis) have been noted earlier.[59] As suggested in chapter 7, the rise of grammatical morphology and syntactic constructions involves the -- at least partial -- **automatization** of language processing. The course of child language acquisition shows striking parallels to the historical rise of grammar. Mayr's notion of **behavior-guided evolution** applies well to the three developmental domains of language: Ontogenesis, phylogenesis and diachronic ('historical') change. In the phylogenetic evolution of language, the three interact as follows:

(a) **Ontogenesis**: The adaptive behavioral experimentation by the young of the species constitutes an important component of 'directed' evolution. The young are characterized - neurologically and otherwise -- by more flexible, less differentiated structures. Such 'immature' structures are still capable of life-time skilled, automated learning in new adaptive directions.

(b) **History**: Linguistic and socio-cultural history constitute an **intermediate selection process**, through which the lifetime behavioral innovation of both young and adult is subjected to the test of adaptive, task-driven socio-cultural selection, within the variant pool of the population.

(c) **Phylogenesis**: Finally, the adaptive experimentation by individuals, transmitted via the filter of socio-cultural history, is the **behavioral precursor** of eventual genetic evolution.

---

58 See Lamendella (1976), Givón (1979a, chapters 5 & 7) and Lieberman (1984, ch. 11)
59 See Slobin (1977) or Givón (1979a, chapters 5,6,7), *inter alia.*

10.9.3. The evolution of communicative context

As noted in a number of chapter above (see in particular Ch. 3), human language at its present stage of evolution makes systematic communicative use of three main divisions of context:

(a) The **generic** culturally-shared context
(b) The **deictic** situation-shared context
(c) The **textual** shared-discourse context

Given the reasonable certainly that culture organization and its concomitant, shared cognitive world-view, predate *homo sapiens* (Bonner, 1980; Griffin, 1976, 1984); and given the clear evidence of animal deictic 'pointing' behavior (see Ch. 3, above), it is most likely that the use of the first two categories of context had already become well-established in pre-human communication. The evolution of human communication can be viewed, from one perspective, as a systematic shifting of the balance among the three, toward increased reliance on the third division of context: the stored shared text.

That the notion 'shared text' is itself contiguous to both 'generic' and 'situational' shared knowledge is also likely. Higher mammals' pointing behavior suggests just that. Its amplitude can escalate gradually if:[60]

(i)   the interlocutor fails to respond; or
(ii)   the pointed object is more surprising; or
(iii) The communication is more urgent

Human anaphoric reference shows a similar *strategic escalation* under the very same conditions. But in pre-human communication, the 'text' that one relies on (or 'refers to') remains largely what one mind *assumes* the other knows. The rise of propositional-declarative language may be viewed as an attempt to make 'shared information', a *sine qua non* for biologically-based communication, more explicit.

---

60 See discussion in Chapters 3 and 6.

CHAPTER 11

THE MYSTIC AS PRAGMATIST: LAO TSE AND TAOISM

11.1. Introduction*

In this chapter we survey one pre-Western pragmatic tradition. We could have just as easily selected one of the pre-Socratic Greeks, such as Anaximander, Heraclitus or Protagoras. However, their teachings survive mostly in fragments or incidental references in the works of others. In electing to go instead with a non-Western dialectician, Lao Tse, one has the advantage of at least one coherent, if short and sometimes enigmatic, text of Philosophical Taoism (the *Tao Teh Ching*), together with the more earthy writings of its second major exponent, Chuang Tse.

I must confess to another motivation for favoring Lao Tse's pragmatism over the pre-Socratic Greeks. Many pragmatic traditions seem to reveal a stubborn streak of mysticism. In rational, post-Socratic Western philosophy, this streak got stamped out vigorously -- together with the pragmatic middle ground. I have often wondered (i) why the mystic streak was such a persistent, natural concomitant of the pragmatic tradition; and (ii) why reductionist philosophy found it so necessary to stamp out both. My tentative answer to (i) is that the **open-endedness** that is tolerated by the pragmatic method, and in particular the **non-closure** of knowledge and description, leaves ample room for the possibility that some metaphysical entity may lurk beyond the reach of our limited point of view. My tentative answer to (ii) is that open-endedness and non-closure have been anathema to Platonism from the very start.

The Western rational tradition is reasonably consistent in its attempt to deal separately with the three major branches of philosophy:

(i)   Metaphysics (cosmology; theory of origins)
(ii)   Epistemology (theory of knowledge or method)
(iii) Ethics (theory of human conduct)

Whether by logical necessity or by cultural drift, the separation has eventually lead to a massive narrowing of the horizons in 'respectable' 20th Century

*I am indebted to T.K. Bikson, Pete Becker, Haj Ross and Martin Tweedale for comments on an early precursor of this chapter.

philosophy, where a brand of inquiry has evolved that preoccupies itself almost exclusively with the *method* itself, or worse, with the *meta-language*.

The *Tao Teh Ching*, in its own peculiar way, displays the converse of the narrow preoccupation of major contemporary figures such as Russell, Carnap or Wittgenstein. It deals with metaphysics, epistemology and ethics not only within the same slim volume or the same short sutra, but often in the same breath. One may of course ascribe this to the mystic's fabled lack of analytic rigor. But one then risks missing an important point: This seeming disregard for sub-disciplinary boundaries is the product of deliberate choice; it reflects the unitary, integrative vision of Taoism, whereby all three sub-fields of inquiry flow from a single source, the metaphysics of *Tao*. When tracing out the separate philosophical strands running through Lao Tse's intellectual tapestry, one must bear in mind that the endeavor is to some extent futile, it does violence to the strong undercurrent of **oneness** that is so pervasive in Taoist thinking. Thus, in dissecting Taoist dialectics with Western analytic tools, a measure of pragmatic -- context-mediated -- *double vision* is sometimes useful and occasionally indispensible.

11.2. Taoist metaphysics: Unity in diversity

11.2.1. The One

> "...The world was so brand new, that many things had not yet been named, so that to refer to them one had to point with the finger..."
>
> G. García-Marquez, *Cien Años de*
> *Soledad* (1975, p. 9)

At the core of Taoist metaphysics rests the notion of *Tao*. Variously rendered as 'The Way', 'The Power', 'Nature', 'God', or 'Entropy', it defies translation. From a synchronic perspective, it is the **unifying principle**, as well as the **ultimate reality** behind the phenomenological universe. It is the law of nature, the flow of gravity, the inherent **directional bias** of the universe. From a diachronic perspective, it is the mystery before the beginning, the primal source. It is pre-sensory, pre-cognitive, non-verbalizable. Or, as the *Tao Teh Ching* puts it:[1]

> The Tao that can be told of in not the real Tao,
> Names that can be given are not real names

$$(1)$$

---

1 All citations from the *Tao Teh Ching* are taken from my own unpublished translation, (Copyright © 1976 by the Shaolin-West Foundation) for which much thank is due to Jia-Hsi Wu (in personal communication). Numbers refer to traditionally-numbered sutras in the book. The attribution of authorship of the book to Lao Tse is traditional, with the most likely codification occurring in the 5th or 6th Century B.C. (see Welch, 1957).

The first fundamental dichotomy set up by Lao Tse is between*Tao*, the unnameable, and the phenomenological world of forms. In the latter, entities are individuated, distinctions can be made, names may be given. The world of forms flows from *Tao* ('The Father'), once a **Principle of Differentiation** ('The Mother') is introduced:

> Nameless is the Father of heaven and earth,
> Named is the Mother of all things

$$(1)$$

The undifferentiated, pre-formed *Tao* is likened to a piece of uncarved wood (*Pu*), in which the world of forms is latent but not yet manifest:

> Tao is absolute, nameless,
> Like a piece of uncarved wood

$$(32)$$

The dichotomy between the pre-formed world of *Tao* and the phenomenological universe of forms is made relevant, from the very start, to the realm of human conduct. This is done through depicting *Tao* as equally irrelevant to human *emotions* as it is to human cognition:

> Seek the hidden core without passion,
> Revel in its myriad forms with passion

$$(1)$$

In spite of the dichotomy, Taoist mysticism insists that *Tao* ('the hidden core'), while impenetrable to human distinction making, is nonetheless the source of the phenomenological world ('the myriad forms'):

> The two flow from the same source
> But get different names [2]

$$(1)$$

This theme, of the inaccessibility of *Tao*, is indeed recurrent:

> Looked at, it cannot be seen,
> It is the invisible.
> Listened to, it cannot be heard,
> It is the inaudible.
> Reached for, it cannot be touched,
> It is the intangible...
> ...Without beginning, without end,
> It cannot be defined,
> And so it reverts to the realm of no thing

$$(14)$$

---

2 In Taoist epistemology, 'names' stand equally for 'sensory distinction' and 'cognitive categories'. As noted in Chapter 1, the historical cleavage between the Aristotelian and Platonic, about the primacy of concepts or percepts, was resolved in the Western tradition by Kant. This chicken-egg quibble never arose in Taoism, which in a sense has always been Kantian.

From a diachronic perspective, within Taoist cosmology, *Tao* is the **primal source**:

> Before heaven and earth
> There was a mystery,
> Silent, boundless, alone,
> Changing yet always the same,
> Mother of all things

(25)

All things in the formed world arose from that primal 'no thing':

> All things arise from being,
> Being arises from non-being

(40)

11.2.2. The Two

> "...What keeps the Yin and the Yang together,
> The circle around them
> Or the line inbetween?..."
>
> S. Buker

In the Western rational inquiry, the existence of discrete categories is founded upon the *Law of the Excluded Middle*. Taoist dialectics remains squarely outside this tradition. Within the unifying principle of *Tao*, contraries do not clash, but rather find their resolution:

> In it sharp edges are blunted,
> Tangles resolve,
> Bright lights are tempered,
> Conflicts submerge

(4)

What makes this contradictory doctrine coherent is its belief in the non-contradictory nature of apparent dichotomies. In the more analytic terms of Western pragmatics, the Taoist position exploits two complementary features of pragmatics:

(a) The Wittgensteinean **scalarity** of conceptual space; and
(b) The **context-dependent** nature of perceived opposites; i.e. the fact that they are irreconcilable only from a certain **perspective**.

The major symbolic representation of the Taoist doctrine of complementarity of opposites is the emblem of the Supreme Ultimate (*Tai Chi*), made out of the *Yin* and *Yang*:

(1)

Traditionally, *Yin* stands for the dark, female, curving, passive; while *Yang* stands for the light, male, angular, active. But as the emblem suggests, there is a speck of *Yin* within the *Yang* and a speck of *Yang* within the *Yin*. Their contrariness is thus only relative, a matter of degree or perspective.

The mystic union of *Yin* and *Yang* within the circle of *Tao* represents the very essence of Taoist metaphysics -- **unity in diversity**. This metaphysics may be interpreted both diachronically and synchronically:

> From Tao one is born,
> From one, two,
> From two, three,
> From three, all.
>
> Yin is the back of all,
> And Yang its face,
> From the union of the two
> The world attains its balance

(42)

The latency of one opposite within its contrary is of course familiar to students of the semantics of *antonyms*[3] and the pragmatics of negation.[4] The *Tao Teh Ching* expounds this dialectics as follows:

> What shrinks must first be large,
> What weakens must first be strong,
> What falls must first be high,
> What loses must first possess

(36)

---

3 See discussion of the semantics of paired adjectives in Bierwisch (1967) or Givón (1970), *inter alia*.
4 See discussion in Chapter 4.

The same dialectics characterizes, by analogy, the relationship between life and death:

>Thirteen organs accompany life,
>Thirteen organs usher in death,
>Thirteen organs move a man
>Through life to death.
>Why is this so?
>Because living tips the scale toward death

(50)

While *Yin-Yang* is *per se* a binary distinction, it is reasonably clear from the *Tao Teh Ching* context that duality is a mere stand-in for **diversity** or **multiplicity**. That is, once the first dichotomy has been provided for, in departing from the pre-formed *Tao*, one has opened the Pandora Box of the world of forms. The Taoist approach to this post-*Tao* universe is reminiscent of the Buddhist notion of *Samsara* -- the world of illusion. Yet a subtle difference persists, and is indeed the hallmark of Taoist pragmatism. Lao Tse never denies the reality ('usefulness') of the world of forms. While exhorting us to not lose sight of the forest (Ultimate Reality) for the trees (worldly forms), the latter is conceded its rightful context:

>Thirteen spokes unite at the hub,
>But the wheel hinges on its empty hole.
>Clay is molded into a cup,
>But the space within is what is filled.
>Walls and a roof make a house,
>But the hollow inside is where you live.
>Thus, while the tangibles have their place,
>It is the intangible that is used

(11)

As we shall see further below, the dialectic unity-in-diversity of *Yin* and *Yang* is equally central to Taoist epistemology and ethics.

Lastly, Lao Tse sensibly emphasizes the **pre-rational**, indeed mind-boggling nature of *Tao* as ultimate reality.[5] Human attempts to rationalize it are bound to yield logically contradictory results:

> Tao is an empty bowl,
> Drawn from, it remains full,
> Fathomless, it is the source of all things
>
>   (4)

And further:

> The thing called Tao
> Is elusive, evasive.
> Evasive, elusive,
> Yet full of latent forms,
> Elusive, evasive,
> Yet full of latent objects
>
>   (21)

And again:

> Thus, it is said of Tao:
> Whoever understands it seems duller,
> Whoever follows it seems to retreat,
> Its even path seems crooked
>
>   (41)

---

5   One may wish to compare Lao Tse's terseness and common sense with Heidegger's (1959) belabored discussion of 'being' and 'non-being', and heavy-handed rationalization of the irrational: "...The question "How is it with being?" is included as a preliminary question in our central question "Why are there essents rather than nothing?" If we now begin to look into that which is questioned in our preliminary question, namely being, the full truth of Nietzsche's dictum is at once apparent. For if we look closely, what more is "being" to us than a mere word?..." (1959, p. 32) It has been noted (see e.g. Popper, 1950) that the marriage of Platonic reductionism and obfuscatory mysticism tends to produce virulent results. Here is how Heidegger motivates his metaphysical quest: "...We ask the questions "How does it stand with being?" "What is the meaning of being?" *not* in order to set up an ontology of the traditional style, much less to criticize the past mistakes of ontology. We are concerned with something totally different: to resolve man's historical being-there -- and that always includes our own future being-there in the totality of the history allotted us -- to the domain of being, which it was originally incumbent upon man to open up for himself..." (*ibid.*, p. 34) Heidegger's grand design slowly unfolds with a Nitzschean Jeremiad: "...The spiritual decline of the earth is so far advanced that the nations are in danger of losing the last bit of *spiritual energy*..." (*ibid.*, p. 31; emphasis is mine; TG) Now the juxtaposition begins to sound familiar: "...What philosophy essentially can and must do is this: a thinking that breaks the path and opens the perspectives of knowledge that sets the norms and hierarchies, of the knowledge in which and by which *a people fulfills itself historically and culturally*...the challenge is one of the essential prerequisites for the *birth of all greatness*, and in speaking of greatness we are referring primarily to the *works and destinies of nations*..." (*ibid.*, p. 9; emphases are mine; TG) The original version of this text was delivered as Heidegger's inaugural lecture, on the occasion of his elevation to the post of Rector of the University of Freiburg in 1935.

11.2.3. The circle: Tao as drift

The Supreme Ultimate, by whatever name, is taken by all mystic traditions to hold sway over the world of forms. The capricious pique of Zeus, the jealous fury of Jehovah, are both reflections -- somewhat crude, to be sure -- of this power. In contrast, *Tao* is said to be a gentle, non-coercive force. It prevails not by brute exertion, but through its **non-arbitrariness**. This aspect of *Tao* is an essential ingredient in Taoist metaphysics (as well as epistemology and ethics):

> Tao acts by returning,
> Its function is soft, gentle

(40)

It is this non-coercive yet ultimately prevailing force that is likened to the uncarved wood (*Pu*):

> Tao is absolute, nameless,
> Like a piece of uncarved wood,
> Useless, harmless

(32)

And again:

> Tao is everywhere,
> Left, right, source of all,
> Nothing is rejected.
> It gets involved but lets be,
> Provides but lays no claim,
> Mild and even-tempered,
> It seems small

(43)

And, in a metaphor reminiscent of the proverbial fisherman:

> Tao's net is loose, wide,
> Its mesh is large,
> Yet nothing slips through

(73)

The concept of 'power' that emerges here is akin to **gravity** or **entropy**. *Tao* does not prevail by force, nor by arbitrary choice, nor by the exercise of will, but through being the **inherent directionality** of the universe. The symbolic expression of this mode of power, the circle in which the *Yin* and the *Yang* both clash and unite, is again a metaphor for Taoist cosmology as well as epistemology. In the latter, it stands for the two core pragmatic features:

(i)   The **graduality** of the transition along semantic space;[6] and

(ii)   the contextual **relativity** of polar distinctions.

The *Yin-Yang* emblem assumes, in Taoism, the broad scope and significance that similar pictorial metaphors carry in other great mystic traditions.[7]

11.3. Taoist epistemology

11.3.1. Two realities, two modes of knowledge

Western epistemology, whether empiricist or rationalist, shares the fundamental assumption concerning the *separateness* of mind and world. Taoist epistemology concedes such separateness as one half of the truth -- in the context of the world of forms. In this world, percepts and concepts are relevant and necessary. Lao Tse's intuition in this matter is surprisingly Kantian, taking it for granted that perceptual-conceptual knowledge will never penetrate the *Ding am Sich*:

> The Tao that can be told of is not the real Tao,
> Names that can be given are not real name
>
> (1)

Behind the reality of the world of forms lies another reality, that of *Tao*. Since the two are not apprehended by the same mode, human knowledge remains fundamentally paradoxical:

> In accumulating knowledge,
> Can you renounce the mind?
>
> (1)

Scholarly knowledge gets the short end of the stick in Taoist writings, a fact that is perhaps motivated by the contemporary context of Confucian scholarship:

> Banish wisdom, discard knowledge,
> And people will know a hundred-fold more
>
> (19)

---

6   This aspect of the circle serves, in Taoist pragmatics, the same role as Aristotle's *synolon*, which made possible the change from one discrete 'form' to another.

7   The Buddhist *Mandala* to name one, the Plains Indians' *Medicine Shield* to name another, the Navajo-Hopi *Four-Corners* emblem, or the Indo-European *Wheel of Fortune*.

Nature has only few words,
How many fewer should man have?

(23)

The distinctions that the intellect can make are relevant only within their narrow domain:

You break up nature to make tools and artifacts,
In the hands of the sage, tools are means to an end.
The master carver never carves

(28)

As Lao Tse suggests, perceptual-conceptual knowledge can easily become a trap, enticing one to carve up the ultimate unity into irrelevant detail:

Civilization breeds names,
Names have their limit

(32)

Scholars aim to know,
The sage aims to loose knowledge

(48)

Taoist epistemology thus takes for granted two types of reality, each with its own -- contextually appropriate -- mode of knowledge. Mundane reality can be apprehended through perceptual and conceptual distinctions. In the ultimate reality, all such distinctions dissolve. Or, in the words of Chuang Tse:[8]

Great knowledge sees all in One,
Small knowledge breaks One into many

(ii, 2)

Having thus dispensed with rationalism, Lao Tse proceeds to dismiss empiricism with equal vigor:

The five colors blind the eye,
The five notes deafen the ear,
The five tastes dull the palate

(12)

8   From Merton's (1965) translation.

The supreme ultimate, *Tao*, is in principle inaccessible to distinction-making:

> Looked for, it cannot be seen,
> Listened to, it cannot be heard
>
> (35)

Is *Tao* then knowable? Lao Tse, like other mystics before and since, proffers somewhat contradictory advice. First, he suggests that through knowing the ultimate one may know the mundane:

> The source of the universe
> May be likened to its mother,[9]
> From knowing the mother
> One may know the sons
>
> (52)

Second, he suggests that the ultimate can be known through self-contemplation:

> How do I know this of the world?
> Through myself
>
> (54)
>
> He who knows others is wise,
> He who knows himself is wisest
>
> (33)

11.3.2. Yin and Yang: The context-dependence of categories

As we have noted on several occasions above, post-Socratic Western epistemology is founded upon the Law of the Excluded Middle, thus upon categories that are discrete and mutually exclusive. The Taoist approach to categories, on the other hand, recognizes the relativity of binary distinctions, the fact that they are polar only within a limited context. The best expression of this doctrine, below, is indeed reminiscent of Socrates' pragmatic line in *Hippias Major* (itself attributed to Heraclitus; see Chapter 1):

---

9 'Mother' in this particular sutra stands for the pre-formed world of *Tao*. In another instance (cf. sutra 1 of the *Tao Teh Ching*), the same term is used for the first stage of the post-*Tao* universe, i.e. the yet-to-be-divided-but-already-divisible universe.

When the world sees beauty, it knows ugliness,
When it perceives good, it recognizes evil.
Thus,
The dark and the light reflect each other,
The hard and the soft explain each other,
The long and the short reveal each other,
The high and the low define each other,
The loud and the silent expose each other,
The front and the back outline each other

(2)

Taoist epistemology may be summed up as follows:

(a) Discrete categories and binary distinctions are arbitrary divisions of the continuum;
(b) Reality is context-bound and multiple; therefore
(c) Paradoxes are inherent; and
(d) Each mode of knowledge is applicable only within its rightful domain.

11.4. Taoist ethics

11.4.1. The ethics of entropy

Ethics, the branch of philosophy dealing with social conduct and motivation, has remained a problematic link in the chain of argument in most philosophical traditions, East and West. Rational Western philosophers have striven, for the most part in vain, to make ethics a logical derivative of their epistemology or metaphysics.[10] Western religions have derived ethics, somewhat arbitrarily, from the Supreme Deity's commandments, with an elaborate reward-and-punishment scheme to secure compliance.[11] In this tradition, the absolute, discrete -- Platonic -- categories *good* and *evil* somehow contrive to emerge -- *Deus ex machina* --

---

10 One of the least satisfactory aspects of Kant's philosophy is his muddled attempt to integrate his ethics into the grand schema of his metaphysics and epistemology.
11 Modern utilitarians, such has Mill, have not fared much better, substituting the vagaries of the social covenant for the wrathful Deity.

as the product of the deity's arbitrary will and infinite power to mete reward and punishment.

Taoist ethics, like all else, springs from *Tao* as the natural flow, the inherent directionality, the **grain** against which the carver finds the going rough and unrewarding. The doctrine of *Wu-Wei* ('no do'), the cornerstone of Taoist ethics, is rooted in this aspect of *Tao*. Taoist ethics, unlike the Western right/wrong, the Buddhist *Karma*[12] or the Confucian Canon (in opposition to which Lao Tse fashioned his approach), makes no reference to absolute 'right' or 'wrong'. And although Lao Tse extols the utilitarian virtues of *Wu-Wei*, utility and the common good do not play a central role in motivating Taoist ethics. The core dichotomy is rather that of **natural** vs. **unnatural**, that which conforms with *Tao* vs. that which goes against the flow. The latter is not evil or immoral, but only unwise and self-destructive.

11.4.2. Wu-Wei and Tao: The water metaphor

Wu-Wei is variously translated as 'no do', 'inaction', 'passivity', 'serenity', 'gentleness' or even 'peace'. The most persistent metaphor used by Lao Tse to expose this principle of human conduct is that of gravity-bound water:

> Be like water,
> It quenches all thirst yet lays no claim,
> It flows to the lowest place
> And thus rejoins Tao
>
> (8)
>
> Nothing is weaker than water,
> Yet nothing like it wears down the strong,
> Nothing is quite like it.
> The weak wears down the strong,
> The soft overcomes the hard
>
> (78)

The interplay between *Wu-Wei* and *Tao* is made explicit from the very start:

---

12 One may argue that *Karma* entails no moral imperatives, but only the factual observation concerning the cause-and-effect relationship between one's personal conduct and eventual destiny. It is nevertheless true that in both main-line *Mahayana* and *Theravada* Buddhism, the long path of Karmic accretion has become identified, at least in practice, with a rigid system of good-and-evil, reward-and-punishment ethics. Both branches of *Vajrayana* (Tibetan Tantrism and Zen) assert this to be the case. For some more discussion, see Blofeld (1958).

Tao never acts,
Yet through it all is done.
If rulers did likewise,
The world will turn of its own accord

(37)

And further:

Those who aim to win the world
And bend it in their image
Will fail.
The world is God's vessel,
It cannot be re-made.
To tamper is to spoil,
To grab is to lose hold.
Some things go fast while others lag,
Some things glow hot while others freeze,
Some things grow strong while others wilt,
Some break, some mend,
The sage never interferes

(29)

The follower of *Tao*, the would-be sage, is exhorted to abide by the paradoxical 'no do':

Yield and you shall become whole,
Bend and you shall remain strait,
Be empty and you shall be filled,
Wear out and you shall be renewed,
Have nothing and you shall have all

(22)

Attain the utmost by being passive,
Follow the peaceful road.
When things burst around,
I contemplate their immobility,
Like lush growth
Forever returning to earth.
To return is to regain peace,
Peace is regaining one's destiny,
To regain one's destiny
Is to know the Eternal One

(16)

The most common misinterpretation of *Wu-Wei* is to equate it with inaction. Rather, *Wu-Wei* may be viewed as an exhortation to shun **arbitrary, unmotivated action**, shun going against the grain, swimming up-river, opposing Tao. In the Western ethical tradition, action is motivated through *will*, that hallmark of the purposive *agent*. Taoist ethics elects to emphasize instead **recognition** or **perception** of the natural drift. Action, when undertaken, best **accommodate** to such perception. Much like knowledge, action remains a paradox:

> The master carver never carves
>
> (28)

But *never carving* does not mean 'not carving', much like *Wu-Wei* does not mean 'inaction'. Rather, one is exhorted to not carve *against the grain*, not act *against the drift*.

11.4.3. **Wu-Wei as a utilitarian creed**

Above all, Lao Tse says, going with the flow is **practical**:

> To strive is to oppose Tao,
> Whoever opposes Tao dies young
>
> (55)

As noted earlier above, Taoist ethics is not founded upon utilitarian considerations. Nonetheless, its practicality is never ignored. The follower of *Tao* is said to possess the quality of *Teh*, another term that defies translation, standing for the 'essence of the sage'.[13] Thus:

> Whoever has Teh is like a child,
> Snakes won't bite him,
> Beasts won't attack him,
> Birds won't prey on him.
> His bones are soft, his flesh tender,
> Yet his grasp is firm
>
> (55)

The dangers of over-doing receive particular attention in the pragmatic ethics of Lao Tse:

---

13 The common rendition of *Teh* as either 'virtue' or 'power' (cf. Waley, 1934) is both restricted and misleading, pulling *Teh* toward the Confucian *Li*.

> Pull the bow-string too hard
> And you wish you'd stopped in time.
> Temper a sword too sharp
> And the edge will soon wear out.
> Fill your house with jade
> And it cannot be guarded

(9)

Arbitrary striving is disparaged in the following words:

> He who stands on his tip-toes will soon tire,
> He who hurries his step will not walk far,
> He who burns bright will not shine for long

(24)

In contrast:

> A good traveller leaves no tracks,
> A good speaker is seldom heckled,
> A good merchant needs no scales,
> A well-shut door requires no bolt

(27)

11.4.4. The Code: Li vs. natural kinship

The natural ethics of *Wu-Wei* evolved in the context of the prevailing Confucian Canon. Rigid and prescriptive, the Canon rested upon the notion of *Li*, variously translated as 'morals', 'standards', 'etiquette', 'propriety', 'ritual' or 'ceremony'. To this social-based standard, Lao Tse contrasted his *natural morality*, in which the only imperative -- if imperative it indeed is -- is to recognize the flow of *Tao* and refrain from opposing it. Like Rousseau, Lao Tse was a firm believer in the inherent decency of unspoiled humanity *au naturel*. That natural state is often likened to the innocence of newborn babes. The *Tao Teh Ching* is replete with passages describing the sage as gentle, considerate, self-effacing and compassionate. On this background, many commentators have puzzled over certain sutras that appear to clash with the pervading humane tone of the *Tao Teh Ching*. For example:

> When Tao is lost, 'compassion' and 'justice' arise,
> Then 'knowledge' and 'wisdom' appear
> With hypocrisy in their wake

(18)

To understand this seeming contradiction, one must consider again the historical context of Lao Tse's writings, i.e. the Confucian Canon with its extensive inventory of *dos* and *don'ts* and assorted utilitarian incentives. Lao Tse considered such behavior-modifying ethics worthless. For him, ethical behavior must spring from a deeper, *natural* source. As Lao Tse saw it, *Tao* obviates unsatisfactory arbitrary concepts such as Justice or Compassion.

Equally, the *Tao Teh Ching* disparages the kinship-based, reward-laden Confucian code:

> When the Six Relations are lost,
> 'Kind fathers' and 'devoted sons' appear
>
> (18)

The 'Six Relations' represent **natural kinship**, deep loyalty that springs from *Tao* and requires neither justification nor exhortation nor reward. The imperatives of the Code, Lao Tse suggests, are only necessary when natural kinship is lost or disregarded. Here is what he says of the Confucian *Li*:

> When Tao is lost, 'compassion' arises,
> When 'compassion' is lost, Li arises,
> Li is the death of loyalty and honesty
> And the beginning of chaos
>
> (38)

In this context:

> Drop 'compassion', abandon 'justice',
> And people will find their true loyalties
>
> (19)

11.4.5. **The doctrine of Straw Dogs**

One passage of the *Tao Teh Ching* has baffled critics and admirers alike, prompting some to interpret Taoist ethics as a-moral, relativistic, harsh. The passage invokes the metaphor of *Straw Dogs*, the expendable sacrificial figurines burned as offering at ancestral altars *en lieu* of blood sacrifice:

> The world is not 'good',
> To it all things are Straw Dogs.
> The sage is not 'good',
> To him all people are Straw Dogs
>
> (5)

The impression of indifference, of moral neutrality, is further strengthened by the following description of the sage:

> He treats the good kindly,
> He treats the bad kindly...
> ...He believes the honest,
> He also believes the liar
>
> (49)

Again, echoes of early Christianity seem to reverberate here,[14] with the age-old confrontation between the mystic's paradoxical, natural a-morality, and organized religion's institutional, codified ethics. Lao Tse's seeming nihilism is grounded in his vision of the all-embracing *Tao*:

> Tao is a mystery, source of all,
> Treasure to the good,
> Refuge to the bad.
> Fine words may come at a price,
> Fine manners may be contrived,
> Though the bad be bad,
> They need not be rejected...
> ...Seek the guilty and then forgive
>
> (62)

And further:

> The executioner is often also killed,
> To presume to be one
> Is to presume to wield the Master Carver's axe:[15]
> Whoever wields the Master Carver's axe
> May chop his own hands
>
> (74)

Taoist ethics emerges here as non-judgemental as Christ's ('Let he who is without sin...'), and just as compassionate:

> I have three treasures:
> The first is love,
> The second moderation,
> The third humility
>
> (67)

---

14 'I have not come to call the righteous, but the sinners to repent'.
15 The Master Carver is used by both Lao Tse and Chuang Tse as metaphor for the sage. In the present context it is just as likely a metaphor for *Tao*.

Lastly, Lao Tse's seeming permissiveness and moral relativism are firmly grounded in his figure-ground, context-dependent, dialectic epistemology:

> How different is 'aye' from 'nay'?
> How different is 'good' from 'evil'?
>
> (20)
>
> Who knows the end?
> Who knows the norm?
> Norms soon become abnormal,
> Good turns into evil,
> So long have humans been misguided!
>
> (58)

11.5. Closure

The history of pragmatics has often yielded a curious mix of compelling intellectual triumph and spectacular media failure. This has to do, I believe, with an in-built hazard of all middle-ground positions: They never seem quite as attractive, quite as clear-cut, striking or *salient*, as the well-articulated, aggressive extremes.[16] The middle ground often is, as Lao Tse observed, socially murky, dull, unattractive:

> All the people have plenty,
> I alone have nothing,
> Like a fool, muddled, befogged....
> ...All the people are smug and clever,
> I alone am dim, dull,
> Aimless as the sea, forever drifting
>
> (20)

The way 'great philosophical questions' have always been formulated, in reductionist terms, invites extreme responses. When one asks: "Is it the chicken or is it the egg that came first?", one *presupposes* that either one or the other must have come first, that complex interactions can and must be reduced to neat, linear, cause-and-effect scripts.[17] It is an old story.

In epistemology, traditional rationalism and empiricism have both insisted on an either-or solution to the ontology of percepts and concepts, Kant's middle ground notwithstanding. In semantics, extreme Platonists and avid Wittgensteineans have both sought pure answers to

---

16 The fact that the middle also catches the flak from both extremes is an added hazard.
17 As Alfred North Whitehead observed: "...philosophical truth is to be sought in the presuppositions of language rather than in its expressed statements..." (1938, p. vii)

the puzzle of natural categories, rejecting a compromise through which both categoriality and gradation are preserved -- in the appropriate context. In the empirical study of cognition, both Chomsky and Skinner have insisted on a reductionist rendition of the interaction between mind and input, whereas the facts point toward a context-mediated mix.

In linguistics likewise, one is told that only law-like generalizations are worthy of the name; that grammars that are not context-free will bog us in contextual mire; that failure to demonstrate that *all* features of grammar are functionally motivated must entail failure to argue for functional motivation for *some* or *most*.

In the philosophy of science, deductivists and inductivists share their abiding faith in extreme reduction, never mind the facts of doing real science, never mind abduction. In cultural anthropology, extreme universalists and extreme relativists struggle for exclusive dominion. In evolutionary biology, extreme Lamarckians and extreme mutatio-selectionists still act as each other's deadly foils. In artificial intelligence, top-down (deductive, linear) and bottom-up (inductive, parallel) processing are presented as exclusive alternatives rather than natural complements. And so it goes.

What falls by the wayside, in each case, is the vast empirical evidence suggesting that living organisms have long ago, perhaps from the very start, opted for interactive, hybrid, pragmatic solutions. That they are capable of a wide range of behavioral responses. That their adaptive-context demands -- indeed rewards -- *selective* access to what Mayr has called 'open programs'.

The position of pragmatics in the intellectual arena is just as frustrating today as it must have been in Lao Tse's or Aristotle's time. As then, the pragmatist must put up with a certain measure of murk that comes with the territory, a whiff of Wittgenstein's 'friction'. As then, the pragmatist must resist, against considerable odds, the seductive clarity of reductionist answers; or rather, of reductionist questions.

BIBLIOGRAPHY

Achinstein, P. (1965) "The problem of theoretical terms", in B. Brody (ed., 1970)

Adams, M.J. (1979) "Models of word recognition", **J.V.L.V.B.**, 16: 277-304

Adler, M. (1967) **The Difference of Man and the Difference it Makes**, NY: World Publ. Co.

Ackrill, J.L. (tr. & ed., 1963) **Aristotle's Categories and De Interpretatione** Oxford: Clarendon Press

Allen, R.E. (ed., 1966) **Greek Philosophy: Thales to Aristotle** NY: Macmillan/The Free Press

Andersen, H. (1983) "A map of the territory", paper read at the **Symposium on Iconicity in Syntax**, Stanford University, June, 1983 (ms)

Anderson, A. S.C. Garrod and A.J. Sanford (1983) "The accessibility of pronominal antecedents as a function of episodic shift in narrative text", **Quarterly J. of Experimental Psychology**, 35A: 427-440

Anderson, J.R. and G.H. Bower (1973) **Human Associative Memory**, Washington, DC: Winston

Anderson, J.R. and R. Paulson (1978) "Interference in memory for pictorial information", **Cognitive Psychology**, 10: 178-202

Anderson, R.C. and J.W. Pichert (1978) "Recall of previously unrecallable information following a shift in perspective", **J.V.L.V.B.**, 17: 1-12

Andrade, E.N. (1954) **Sir Isaac Newton: His Life and Work**, Garden City, NY: Doubleday

Anttila, R. (1977) **Analogy; State of the Art Report no. 10**, The Hague: Mouton

Aristotle, **Categories**, in J.L. Ackrill (tr. & ed., 1963)

Aristotle, **De Anima**, in R. McKeon (ed., 1941)

Aristotle, **De Generatione Animalium**, in R. McKeon (ed., 1941)

Aristotle, **De Interpretatione**, in J.L. Ackrill (tr. & ed., 1963)

Aristotle, **De Partibus Animalium**, in R. McKeon (ed., 1941)

Aristotle, **De Sophisticis Elenchis**, in R. McKeon (ed., 1941)

Aristotle, **Ethics (Ethica Nichomanchea)**, in R. McKeon (ed., 1941)

Aristotle, **Metaphysics**, tr. by R. Hope, Ann Arbor: University of Michigan Press (1952)

Aristotle, **Posterior Analytic**, in R. McKeon (ed., 1941)

Aristotle, **Prior Analytic**, tr. by Jenkinson, ed. by Ross, Oxford: Oxford University Press

Aronson, D. and S. Ferres (1983) "Lexical categories and reading tasks", J. of Experimental Psychology: Human Perception and Performance, 9

Aronson, D. and H.S. Scarborough (1976) "Performance theories for sentence encoding: Some quantitative evidence", J. of Experimental Psychology: Human Perception and Performance, 2

Ascher, J.J. and R. García (1969) "The optimal age to learn a foreign language", Modern Language Journal, 8

Attneave, F. (1957) "Transfer of experience with a class-schemata to identification learning of patterns and shapes", J. of Experimental Psychology, 54

Attneave, F. (1959) Application of Information Theory to Psychology, NY: Holt

Austin, J. (1962) How to Do Things with Words, Cambridge: Cambridge University Press

Bach, E. (1965) "Structural linguistics and the philosophy of science", Diogenes, 51

Baggish, H. (1983) "Confessions of a former cultural relativist", Anthropology, 83/84

Baldwin, J.M.A. (1896) "A new factor in evolution", American Naturalist, 30

Bartlett, F. (1932) Remembering: A Study in Experimental and Social Psychology, Cambridge: Cambridge University Press

Bartsch, R. (1984) "Norms, tolerance, lexical change, and context-dependence of meaning", J. of Pragmatics, 8.3

Bates, E. (1976) Language in Context: The Acquisition of Pragmatics, NY: Academic Press

Bateson, G. (1972) Steps to an Ecology of Mind, NY: Ballantine Books

Bateson, G. (1979) Mind and Nature: A Necessary Unity, NY: Bantam

Becker, A.L. (1979) "Communication across diversity", in A.L. Becker and A.A. Yengoyan (eds) The Imagination of Reality, Norwood, NJ: Ablex

Bentivoglio, P. (1983) "Topic continuity and discontinuity in discourse: A study of spoken Latin-American Spanish", in T. Givón (ed., 1983a)

Berlin, B. and P. Kay (1969) Basic Color Terms: Their Universality and Evolution, Berkeley: U.C. Press

Bever, T.G., J.A. Fodor and W. Weksel (1965) "Is linguistics empirical?", Psychological Review, 72

Bickerton, D. (1975) "Creolization, linguistic universals, natural semantax and the brain", University of Hawaii Working Papers in Linguistics, Honolulu (ms)

Bickerton, D. (1981) Roots of Language, Ann Arbor: Karoma

Bickerton, D. (forthcoming) Language Evolution

Bierwisch, M. (1967) "Some semantic universals of German adjectives", Foundations of Language, 3.1

Blofeld, J. (1958) The Zen Teachings of Hunag-Po, NY: Grove Press

Bloomfield, L. (1922) "Review of Sapir's Language", The Classical Weekly, 18

Bloomfield, L. (1926) "A set of postulates for the science of language", **Language**, 2

Bloomfield, L. (1933) **Language**, NY: Holt, Rinehart and Winston

Bolinger, D. (1952) "Linear modification", in his **Forms of English**, Cambridge: Harvard University Press (1965)

Bolinger, D. (1954) "Meaningful word-order in Spanish", **Boletín de Filología, Universidad de Chile**, vol. 8

Bolinger, D. (1977) **The Forms of Language**, London: Longmans

Bolinger, D. (1978a) "Intonation across languages", in J. Greenberg *et al* (eds) **Universals of Human Language**, vol. 2, **Phonology**, Stanford: Stanford U. Press

Bolinger, D. (1978b) "Yes and no questions are not alternative questions", in H. Hiż (ed.) **Questions, Synthese Language Library**, #1

Bolinger, D. (1984) "The inherent iconicity of intonation", in J. Haiman (ed., 1984)

Bonner, J.T. (1980) **The Evolution of Culture in Animals**, Princeton: Princeton University Press

Bonnet, C. (1764) **Contemplations de la Nature**, vol. 2, Amsterdam: Marc-Michel Rey

Bradshaw, J.L. and N.C. Nettleton (1981) "The nature of hemispheric specialization in man", **Behavior and Brain Science**, 4

Bransford, J. and Franks, J.J. (1971) "Attraction of linguistic ideas", **Cognitive Psychology**, 2

Broadbent, D.E. (1958) **Perception and Communication**, London: Pergamon Press

Broadbent, D.E. (1977) "Levels, hierarchies, and the locus of control", **Quarterly J. of Experimental Psychology**, 29

Brody, B. (ed., 1970) **Readings in the Philosophy of Science**, Englewood Cliffs, NJ: Prentice-Hall

Bromberger, S. (1966) "Why questions", in B. Brody (ed., 1970)

Brown, P. and S. Levinson (1978) "Universals of language usage: Politeness Phenomena", in E. Goody (ed., 1978)

Brown, P. and S. Levinson (1979) "Social structure, group and interaction", in K. Schere and H. Giles (eds) **Social Markers in Speech**, Cambridge: Cambridge University Press

Buchler, J. (1939) **Charles Peirce's Empiricism**, London: Kegan Paul

Bybee, J. (1985) **Morphology: A Study of the Relation Between Meaning and Form**, TSL vol. 9, Amsterdam: J. Benjamins

Cairns, H.S. and J. Kamerman (1975) "Lexical information processing during sentence comprehension", **J.V.L.V.B.**, 14

Carnap, R. (1923) "Über die Aufgabe der Physik", **Kantstudien**, 28

Carnap, R. (1934) **Der Logische Aufbau der Welt**, Tr. by R.A. George as **The logical structure of the world**, Berkeley: UC Press (1967)

Carnap, R. (1947) **Meaning and Necessity**, Chicago: University of Chicago Press

Carnap, R. (1956) "The methodological character of theoretical concepts", in H. Feigl and M. Scriven (eds) **Minnesota Studies in the Philosophy of Science**, vol. I

Carnap, R. (1958) **Introduction to Symbolic Logic and its Applications**, NY: Dover

Carnap, R. (1959) **The Logical Syntax of Language**, Patterson, NJ: Littlefield, Adams & Co.

Carr, T. (1985) "Perceiving visual language", in L. Kaufman, J. Thomas and K. Boff (eds) **Handbook of Perception and Human Performance**, NY: J. Wiley

Carroll, J.B. (1953) **The Study of Language**, Cambridge: Harvard University Press

Cassierer, E. (1933) "La langue et la construction du monde des objets", **J. de Psychologie Normale et Pathologique**, 30

Chafe, W. (1970) **Meaning and the Structure of Language**, Chicago: University of Chicago Press

Chafe. W. (1976) "Givenness, contrastiveness, definiteness, subjects, topics and point of view", in C. Li (ed., 1976)

Chafe, W. (1979) "The flow of thought and the flow of language", in T. Givón (ed., 1979c)

Chafe, W. (ed., 1980) **The Pear Stories**, Norwood, NJ: Ablex

Chafe, W. (1987) "Cognitive constraints on information flow", in R. Tomlin (ed., 1987)

Chafe, W. and J. Nichols (eds, 1986) **Evidentiality: The Coding of Epistemology in Language,** Norwood, NJ: Ablex

Chase, W.G. and K.A. Ericsson (1981) "Skilled memory", in J. Anderson (ed.) **Cognitive Skills and their Acquisition**, Hillsdale, NJ: Erlbaum

Chase, W.G. and K.A. Ericsson (1982) "Skill and working memory", in G. Bower (ed.) **The Psychology of Learning and Motivation**, vol. 16, NY: Academic Press

Chase, W.G. and H.A. Simon (1973) "Perception in chess", **Cognitive Psychology**, 4

Chang, F. (1980) "Active memory processes in visual sentence comprehension: Clause effect and pronominal reference", **Memory and Cognition**, 8

Chisholm, W. (ed.) **Interrogativity**, TSL vol.4, Amsterdam: J. Benjamins

Chomsky, N. (1957) **Syntactic Structures**, The Hague: Mouton

Chomsky, N. (1959) "Review of Skinner's **Verbal Behavior**", **Language**, 35

Chomsky, N. (1964) "Current issues in Linguistics", in J. Fodor and J. Katz (eds) **The Structure of Language**, Englewood Cliffs, NJ: Prentice-Hall

Chomsky, N. (1966) **Cartesian Linguistics**, NY: Harper and Row

Chomsky, N. (1968) **Language and Mind**, revised edition [1972], NY: Harcourt, Brace and World

Chomsky, N. (1981) "On the representation of form and function", **The Linguistic Review**, 1: 3-40

Cirilo, R.K. and D.J. Foss (1980) "Text structure and reading time for sentences", J.V.L.V.B., 19

Clark, E. (1971) "What's in a word", in T. Moore (ed.) **Cognitive Development and the Acquisition of Language**, NY: Academic Press

Clark, H. (1970) "Linguistic processes in deductive logic", **Psychological Review**, 76.4

Clark, H. and B. Malt (1984) "Psychological constraints on language", in W. Kintsch *et al.* (eds.) **Methods and Tactics in Cognitive Science**, Hillsdale, NJ: Erlbaum

Claudi, U. and B. Heine (1984) "From metaphor to grammar: Some examples from Ewe", Köln: Institut für Linguistik, Universität zu Köln (ms)

Cocchiarella, N.B. (1965) **Tense and Modal Logic: A Study in the Typology of Temporal Reference**, PhD dissertation, U.C.L.A. (ms)

Cohen, A. and S. Nooteboom (eds, 1975) **Structure and Process in Speech Perception**, Heidelberg: Springer-Verlag

Cohen, N.J. and L.R. Squire (1980) "Preserved learning and retention of pattern analyzing skill in amnesia: Dissociation of knowing how and knowing that", **Science**, 210

Cole, P. (ed., 1978) **Pragmatics, Syntax and Semantics**, vol. 9, NY: Academic Press

Cole, P. (ed., 1981) **Radical Pragmatics**, NY: Academic Press

Cole, P. and J. Morgan (eds, 1975) **Speech Acts, Syntax and Semantics**, vol. 3, NY: Academic Press

Cole, R.A. and A.I. Rudnicky (1983) "What's new in speech perception? The research ideas of William Chandler Bagley, 1874-1946", **Psychological Review**, 90: 94-101

Coleman, L. and P. Kay (1981) "Prototype semantics and the English word *lie*", **Language**, 57.1

Collins, and M.R. Quillian (1969) "Retrieval time for semantic memory", J.V.L.V.B., 8:240-247

Cooreman, A. (1982a) "Transitivity, ergativity and topicality in Chamorro", BLS #8, Berkeley: University of California, Berkeley Linguistics Society

Cooreman, A. (1982b) "Topicality, ergativity and transitivity in narrative discourse: Evidence from Chamorro", **Studies in Language**, 6.3

Cooreman, A. (1985) **Studies in Chamorro Grammar and Discourse**, University of Oregon, Eugene, PhD dissertation (ms)

Cooreman, A., B. Fox and T. Givón (1984) "The discourse definition of ergativity", **Studies in Language**, 8.1

Corbett, A.T. and F.R. Chang (1983) "Pronoun disambiguation: Accessing potential antecedents", **Memory and Cognition**, 11

Cresswell, M.J. (1972) "The world is everything that is the case", **Australian Journal of Philosophy**, 50.1

Crouch, J.E. (1978) **Functional Human Anatomy**, 3rd edition, Philadelphia: Lea and Fabiger

Curtiss, S. (1977) **Genie: A Psycholinguistic Study of a Modern-Day "Wildchild"**, NY: Academic Press

Cutler, A. and D.J. Foss (1977) "On the role of sentence stress in sentence processing", **Language and Speech, 21**

Cuvier, G. (1828) **Le régne animal distribué d'apres son organization**, Paris: Fortin

Dahl, D.A. and J. K. Gundel (1982) "Identifying referents for two kinds of pronouns", **Minnesota Papers in Linguistics and Philosophy, 7**

Darwin, C. (1859) **The Origin of Species**, London: J. Murray

Darwin, C. (1871) **The Descent of Man, and Selection in Relation to Sex**, (Heritage Edition, 1971), Norwalk, Conn.: Heritage Press

Davison, A. (1975) "Indirect speech acts and what to do with them", in P. Cole and J. Morgan (eds, 1975)

Dawkins, R. (1976) **The Selfish Gene**, NY: Oxford University Press

de Beer, G.R. (1930) **Embryology and Evolution**, Oxford: Clarendon Press

DeLancey, S. (1984) "The analysis-synthesis-lexis cycle in Tibeto-Burman: A case study in motivated change", in J. Haiman (ed, 1984)

Dell, G., G. McKoon and R. Ratcliff (1983) "The activation of antecedent information during the processing of anaphoric reference in reading", **J.V.L.V.B.**, 22: 121-132

Denier van der Gon, J.J. and J.P. Thuring (1965) "The guiding of human writing movements", **Kybernetic, 2**

Derbyshire, D. (1985) "Topic continuity and OVS order in Hixkaryana", in J. Sherzer and G. Urban (eds) **Native South American Discourse** (ms, SIL-Dallas)

Derbyshire, D. and G. Pullum (1981) "Object initial languages", **I.J.A.L.**, 47.3

Derwing, B. (1973) **Transformational Grammar as a Theory of Language Acquisition**, Cambridge: Cambridge University Press

de Waal, F. (1982) **Chimpanzee Politics: Power and Sex among the Apes**, London: Unwin Paperbacks/Counterpoint

Diels, H. (1969) **Die Fragmenten der Vorsokratiker, herausgegeben von Walter Kranz**, 3 vols, Dublin and Zürich: Weidman

Dik, S. (1978) **Functional Grammar**, Amsterdam: North Holland

Dijk, T. van and W. Kintsch (1983) **Strategies of Discourse Comprehension**, NY: Academic Press

Donellan, K. (1966) "Reference and definite description", **The Philosophical Review**, 75.3

Dreizin, F. (1980) "The flavor of Russian negation: Some notes on and around", University of Haifa, Israel (ms)

DuBois, J. (1980) "Beyond definiteness", in W. Chafe (ed., 1980)

DuBois, J. (1985) "Self evident", in W. Chafe and J. Nichols (eds, 1985)

Eco, U. **The Name of the Rose,** tr. by W. Weaver, NY: Harcourt, Brace and World

Eckert, R. and D. Randall (1978) **Animal Physiology: Mechanisms and Adaptations,** NY: Freeman

Edgerton, R. (1978) "The study of deviance: Marginal man or Everyman", in G. Spindler (ed.) **The Making of Psychological Anthropology,** Berkeley: U.C. Press

Einstein, A. (1934) **The world as I see it,** tr. by A. Harris, NY: Covici and Friede

Eldredge, N. and S.J. Gould (1972) "Punctuated equilibria: An alternative to physical gradualism", in T.J.M. Schoopf (ed.) **Models in Paleobiology,** San Francisco: Freeman, Cooper & Co.

Elster, J. (ed., 1985) **The Multiple Self,** Cambridge: Cambridge University Press

Ericsson, K.A. (1985) "Memory skill", **Canadian J. of Psychology,** 39.2

Ervin-Tripp, S. (1974) "Is second language learning like the first?", TESOL **Quarterly,** 8.2

Feyerabend, P. (1970) "How to be a good empiricist -- a plea for tolerance in matters epistemological", in B. Brody (ed., 1970)

Feyerabend, P. (1975) **Against Method: An Outline of an Anarchic Theory of Knowledge,** NY: The Humanities Press

Fillmore, C. (1963) "The position of embedding transformations in grammar", **Word,** 19

Fillmore, C. (1968) "The case for the case", in E. Bach and R.T. Harms (eds) **Universals in Linguistic Theory,** NY: Holt, Rinehart and Winston

Fillmore, C. (1971) "How to know whether you're coming or going", in K. Hylgaard-Jensen (ed.) **Linguistik 1971,** Athenäum-Verlag

Firbas, J. (1966) "On defining the theme in functional sentence perspective", **Traveaux Linguistiques de Prague,** 2

Firbas, J. (1974) "Some aspects of the Czechoslovak approach to problems of functional sentence perspective", in F. Daneš (ed.) **Papers on Functional Sentence Perspective, Janua Linguorum,** sm 147, The Hague: Mouton

Fletcher, C.R. (1982) "Markedness and topic continuity in discourse processing", J.V.L.V.B., 21

Fodor, J. (1983) **The Modularity of Mind,** Cambridge: MIT Press

Foley, W. and R. van Valin (1985) **Functional Syntax and Universal Grammar,** Cambridge: Cambridge University Press

Fossberg, H. (1985) "Ontogeny of human locomotive control, I: Infant stepping, supported locomotion and transition to independent locomotion", **Experimental Brain Research,** 57

Fox, A. (1983) "Topic continuity in Biblical Hebrew", in T. Givón (ed., 1983a)

Fox, B. (1985) "Word order inversion and discourse continuity in Tagalog", in T. Givón (ed. 1985b)

Frost, N.A.H. (1971a) "Clustering of visual shape in the free recall of visual stimuli", **J. of Experimental Psychology,** 88

Frost, N.A.H. (1971b) **Interaction of Visual and Semantic Codes in Long-Term Memory**, PhD dissertation, U. of Oregon, Eugene (ms)

Futuyma, D.J. (1979) **Evolutionary Biology**, Sunderland, Mass.: Sinauer

Galambov, R. and C.T. Morgan (1960) "The neural basis of learning", in J. Field, H.W. Magoun and V.E. Hall (eds) **Handbook of Physiology**, vol. 3, section 1: **Neurophysiology**, Washington, DC: American Physiological Society

Ganong, W.F. (1980) "Phonetic categorization in auditory word perception", **J. of Experimental Psychology: Human Perception and Performance**, 6: 110-125

García-Marquez, G. (1975) **Cien Años de Soledad**, Buenos Aires: Editorial Sudamericana

Garfinkel, H. (1972) "Remarks on ethnomethodology", in J. Gumpertz and D. Hymes (eds) **Directions in Sociolinguistics**, NY: Holt, Rinehart and Winston

Garrod, S. and A. Sanford (1977) "Interpreting anaphoric relations: The integration of semantic information while reading", **J.V.L.V.B.**, 16: 77-90

Gazdar, J. (1979) **Pragmatics: Implicature, Presupposition and Logical Form**, NY: Academic Press

Geertz, C. (1972) "Linguistic etiquette", in J.B. Pride and J. Holmes (eds) **Sociolinguistics**, Harmondsworth: Penguin

Geertz, C. (1973) **The Interpretation of Cultures**, NY: Basic Books

Geertz, C. (1984) "Anti anti-relativism", **American Anthropologist**, 86

Gellner, E. (1982) "Relativism and universals", in M. Hollis and S. Lukes (eds, 1982)

Gernsbacher, M.A. (1985) "Surface information loss in comprehension", **Cognitive Psychology**, 17

Gernsbacher, M.A. (1987) "Conceptual anaphora in English: An experimental approach", University of Oregon, Eugene (ms)

Gernsbacher, M.A. and D. Hargreaves (1986) "Cognitive accessibility of sentence participants", University of Oregon, Eugene (ms)

Givón, T. (1966) "Leonard Bloomfield as a philosopher of language", University of California, Los Angeles (ms)

Givón, T. (1970) "Notes on the semantic structure of English Adjectives", **Language**, 46.4

Givón, T. (1971) "Historical syntax and synchronic morphology: An archaeologist's field trip", **CLS 7**, Chicago: University of Chicago, Chicago Linguistics Society

Givón, T. (1972) **Studies in ChiBemba and Bantu Grammar, Studies in African Linguistics**, Supplement 3

Givón, T. (1973a) "The time-axis phenomenon", **Language**, 49.4

Givón, T. (1973b) "Opacity and reference in language: An Inquiry into the role of modalities", in J. Kimball (ed.) **Syntax and Semantics**, vol. 2, NY: Academic Press

Givón, T. (1975a) "Serial verbs and syntactic change: Niger-Congo", in C. Li (ed.) **Word Order and Word Order Change**, Austin: University of Texas Press

Givón, T. (1975b) "Cause and control: On the semantics of interpersonal manipulation", in J. Kimball (ed.) **Syntax and Semantics**, vol. 4, NY: Academic Press

Givón, T. (1975c) "Focus and the scope of assertion: Some Bantu evidence", **Studies in African Linguistics**, 6.2

Givón, T. (1976a) "Topic, pronoun and grammatical agreement", in C. Li (ed., 1976)

Givón, T. (1976b) "On the VS word-order in Israeli Hebrew: Pragmatics and typological change", in P. Cole (ed.) **Studies in Modern Hebrew Syntax and Semantics**, Amsterdam: North Holland

Givón, T. (1977) "The drift from VSO to SVO in Biblical Hebrew: The pragmatics of tense-aspect", in C. Li (ed.) **Mechanisms for Syntactic Change**, Austin: U. of Texas Press

Givón, T. (1978a) "Definiteness and referentiality", in J. Greenberg *et al* (eds) **Universals of Human Language**, vol. 4: Syntax, Stanford: Stanford University Press

Givón, T. (1978b) "Universal grammar, lexical structure and translatability", in F. Guenthner and M. Guenthner-Reutter (eds) **Meaning and Translation**, London: Duckworth

Givón, T. (1979a) **On Understanding Grammar**, NY: Academic Press

Givón, T. (1979b) **Ute Dictionary**, Ignacio, Colorado: Ute Press

Givón, T. (ed., 1979c) **Discourse and Syntax, Syntax and Semantics**, vol. 12, NY: Academic Press

Givón, T. (1980a), "The binding hierarchy and the typology of complements", **Studies in Language**, 4.3

Givón, T. (1980b) **Ute Reference Grammar**, Ignacio, Colorado: Ute Press

Givón, T. (1981a) "Typology and functional domains", **Studies in Language**, 5.2

Givón, T. (1981b) "On the development of the numeral 'one' as an indefinite marker", **Folia Linguistica Historica**, 2.1

Givón, T. (1982a) "Logic vs. pragmatics, with human language as the referee: Toward an empirically viable epistemology", **Journal of Pragmatics**, 6.1

Givón, T. (1982b) "Tense-aspect-modality: The Creole prototype and beyond", in P. Hopper (ed.) **Tense and Aspect: Between Semantics and Pragmatics**, TSL vol. 1, Amsterdam: J. Benjamins

Givón, T. (1982c) "Evidentiality and epistemic space", **Studies in Language**, 6.1

Givón, T. (ed., 1983a) **Topic Continuity in Discourse: Quantified Cross-Language Studies**, TSL #3, Amsterdam: J. Benjamins

Givón, T. (1983b) "Topic continuity in spoken English", in T. Givón (ed., 1983a)

Givón, T. (1983c) "Topic continuity in discourse: An introduction", in T. Givón (ed., 1983a)

Givón, T. (1984a) **Syntax: A Functional-Typological Introduction**, Vol. 1, Amsterdam: J. Benjamins

Givón, T. (1984b) "Universals of discourse structure and second language acquisition", in W. Rutherford (ed.) **Language Universals and Second Language Acquisition**, TSL vol. 5, Amsterdam: J. Benjamins

Givón, T. (1984c) "Iconicity, isomorphism and non-arbitrary coding in syntax", in J. Haiman (ed., 1984)

Givón, T. (1984d) "Direct object and dative shifting: Semantic and pragmatic case", in F. Plank (ed.) **Objects**, NY: Academic Press

Givón, T. (1984e) "The speech-act continuum", in W. Chisholm (ed.) **Interrogativity**, TSL vol.4, Amsterdam: J. Benjamins

Givón, T. (1984f) "Prolegomena to discourse pragmatics", in C. Caffi (ed.) **Metapragmatics**, special issue of **J. of Pragmatics**, 8.4

Givón, T. (1985a) "The pragmatics of referentiality", in D. Schiffrin (ed.) **Meaning, Form and Use in Context**, Washington, DC: Georgetown University Press

Givón, T. (ed., 1985b) **Quantified Studies in Discourse**, special issue of Text, 5.1/2

Givón, T. (1987a) "Beyond foreground and background", in R. Tomlin (ed., 1987)

Givón, T. (1987b) "The pragmatics of word-order: Predictability, importance and attention", in E. Moravcsik *et al* (eds) **Typology and Language Universals**, TSL vol.16, Amsterdam: J. Benjamins

Givón, T. (1987c) "Serial verbs and the mental reality of 'event'", **Final N.E.H. Project Report**, University of Oregon, Eugene (ms)

Givón, T., W. Kellogg, M. Posner and P. Yee (1985) "The identification of referents in connected discourse: Automatic vs. attended processing", **Cognitive Science Working Papers**, University of Oregon, Eugene (ms)

Givón, T. and A. Kimenyi (1974) "Truth, belief and doubt in KinyaRwanda", **Studies in African Linguistics**, Supplement #5

Glazner, D., B. Fischer and D. Dorfman (1984) "Short term storage in reading", **J.V.L.V.B.**, 23

Goede von Aesch, A. (1941) **Natural Science in German Romanticism**, NY: Columbia University Press

Goffman, H. (1974) **Frame Analysis**, Cambridge: Harvard University Press

Goffman, H. (1976) "replies and responses", **Language and Society**, 5

Goguen, J. (1969) "The logic of inexact concepts", **Synthese**, 19

Goodall, J. (1965) "Chimpanzees of the Gombe reserve", in E. deVore (ed.) **Primate Behavior**, NY: Holt, Rinehart and Winston

Goody, E. (ed., 1978) **Questions and Politeness: Strategies in Social Interaction**, Cambridge: Cambridge University Press

Gordon, D. and G. Lakoff (1971) "Conversational postulates", **CLS 7**, Chicago: University of Chicago, Chicago Linguistics Society

Gould, S.J. (1977) **Ontogeny and Phylogeny**, Cambridge: Harvard University Press

Gould, S.J. (1980) **The Panda's Thumb**, NY: Pelican

Gould, S.J. and N. Eldredge (1977) "Punctuated equilibria: The tempo and mode of evolution reconsidered", **Paleobiology**, 3

Grace, G. (1986) "The intertranslatability postulate and its consequences", in his **Ethnolinguistic Notes**, 3.25, Honolulu: University of Hawaii at Manoa (ms)

Green, G. (1970) "Whimperatives: Schizophrenic speech acts", University of Michigan, Ann Arbor (ms)

Green, G. (1975) "How to get people to do things with words: The whimperative question", in P. Cole and J. Morgan (eds, 1975)

Greenfield, P. and L. Schneider (1977) "Building a tree structure: The development of hierarchic complexity and interrupted strategies in children's construction activity", **Developmental Psychology**, 13.4

Grice, H. P. (1968/1975) "Logic and conversation", in P. Cole and J. Morgan (eds, 1975)

Griffin, D.R. (1976) **The Question of Animal Awareness**, NY: Rockefeller University Press

Griffin, D.R. (1984) **Animal Thinking**, Cambridge: Harvard University Press

Grillner, S. (1975) "Locomotion in vertebrates -- central mechanisms and reflex interaction", **Physiological Review**, 55

Grossman, M. (1980) "A central processor for hierarchically-structured material: Evidence from Broca's aphasia", **Neuropsychologia**, 18

Gumperz, J. (1977) "Sociocultural knowledge in conversational inference", in M. Saville-Troike (ed.) **Linguistics and Anthropology**, Washington, DC: Georgetown University Press

Gumperz, J. (1982) **Discourse Strategies**, Cambridge: Cambridge University Press

Gurfinkel, V.S. and M.L. Shik (1977) "The control of posture and locomotion", in A.A. Gyikov, N.T. Tanov and D.S. Kosarov (eds) **Motor Control**, NY: Plenum Press

Haberland, H. (1985) "Review of Klaus Heinrich's **Dahlemere Vorlesungen I**, J. of Pragmatics, 9

Haberlandt, K. (1980) "Story grammar and reading time of story constituents", **Poetics**, 9

Haeckel, E. (1866) **Generelle Morphologie der Organismen: Algemeine Gerundzüge der Organischen Formen-Wissenschaft, Mechanisch begründet durch die von Charles Darwin reformierte Descendenz-Theorie,** (2 vol.), Berlin: Georg Reimer

Haiman, J. (1978) "Conditionals are topics", **Language**, 54

Haiman, J. (1979) **Hua: A Papuan Language of the Eastern Highlands of New Guinea**, Amsterdam: J. Benjamins

Haiman, J. (1980) "The iconicity of grammar: Isomorphism and motivation", **Language**, 56.3

Haiman, J. (1983) "Iconic and economic motivation", **Language,** 59

Haiman, J. (ed., 1984) **Iconicity in Syntax,** TSL vol.6, Amsterdam: J. Benjamins

Haiman, J. (1985) **Natural Syntax,** Cambridge: Cambridge University Press

Halliday, M.A.K. (1967) "Notes on transitivity and theme in English", **J. of Linguistics,** 3

Hallett, G. (1977) **A Companion to Wittgenstein's "Philosophical Investigations",** Ithaca: Cornell University Press

Hanson, R.N. (1958) **Patterns of Discovery,** Cambridge: Cambridge University Press

Hanson, R.N. (1961) "Is there a logic of scientific discovery?", in H. Feigl and G. Maxwell (eds) **Current Issues in the Philosophy of Science,** NY: Holt, Rinehart and Winston

Hargreaves, D. (1983) **Evidentiality in Newari,** MA Thesis, University of Oregon, Eugene (ms)

Haviland, J.B. (1986) "Complex referential gestures in Guugu Yimidhirr", Reed College, Portland, Oregon (ms)

Hawkins, H.L. (1969) "Parallel processing in complex visual discrimination", **Perception & Psychophysics,** 5

Hawkinson, A. and L. Hyman (1974) "Natural topic hierarchies in Shona", **Studies in African Linguistics,** 5

Heidegger, M. (1959) **Introduction to Metaphysics,** NY: Doubleday (1961 ppbk edition)

Heine, B. and M. Reh (1984) **Grammaticalization and Reanalysis in African Languages,** Hamburg: Helmut Buske Verlag

Heller, J. (1962) **Catch-22,** London: Transworld Corgi (1970 ppbk edition)

Hempel, C. (1945) "Studies in the logic of confirmation", **Mind,** LIV.1

Hempel, C. (1959) "The logic of functional analysis", in B. Brody (ed., 1970)

Hempel, C. (1966) **Philosophy of Natural Science,** Englewood Cliffs, NJ: Prentice Hall

Hempel, C. and P. Oppenheim (1948) "Studies in the logic of explanation", **Philosophy of Science,** XV reprinted in B. Brody (ed., 1970)

Herman, R., S. Grillner, P. Stein and D.G. Stuart (eds, 1976) **Neural Control of Locomotion,** vol. 18, NY: Plenum Press

Hertzberger, H. (1971) "Setting Russell free", Toronto, University of Toronto (ms)

Hetzron, R. (1971) "Presentative function and presentative movement", **Studies in African Linguistics,** Supplement #2

Hinton, G. (1986) "Learning in massive parallel networks", paper read at the **Office of Naval Research Conference,** Eugene, Oregon, (November 1986; ms)

Hinton, G. and S.J. Nowlan (1987) "How learning can guide evolution", Computer Science Dept., Carnegie Mellon University (ms)

Hinttika, J. (1967) "Individuals, possible worlds and epistemic logic", **Nôus**, 1

Hintzman, D.L. (1970) "Effects of repetition and exposure duration on memory", **J. of Experimental Psychology**, 83

Hintzman, D. (1983) "Schema abstraction in multiple trace memory model", University of Oregon, Eugene (ms)

Hintzman, D. and D.L. Ludlam (1980) "Differential forgetting of prototypes and old instances", **Memory and Cognition** 8

Hocart, A.M. (1937) "Kinship systems", in P. Bohanan and J. Middleton (eds) **Kinship and Social Organization**, NY: Natural History Press

Hollis, M. and S. Lukes (eds, 1982) **Rationality and Relativism**, Cambridge: MIT Press

Hopper, P. and S. Thompson (1980) "Transitivity in grammar and discourse", **Language**, 56.3

Hopper, P. and S. Thompson (eds, 1982) **Studies in Transitivity, Syntax and Semantics**, vol. 15, NY: Academic Press

Hopper, P. and S. Thompson (1984) "The communicative basis for lexical categories", **Language**, 60

Horn, L. (1972) **On the Semantic Properties of Logical Operators in English**, PhD dissertation, U.C.L.A. (ms)

Horton, R. (1982) "Tradition and modernity revisited", in M. Hollis and S. Lukes (eds, 1982)

Huang, F. (1985) "The numeral 'one' as an indefinite marker in Mandarin Chinese", University of Oregon, Eugene (ms)

Hume, D. (1739/1740) **A Treatise on Human Nature**, Oxford: Clarendon Press (1978)

Hyman, L. (1973) "How do natural rules become unnatural?" paper read at the **LSA Winter Conference**, San Diego, Dec. 1973 (ms)

Hyman, R. and Frost, N.A.H. (1975) "Gradients and Schema in pattern recognition", in P.M.A. Rabbitt and S. Dornic (eds) **Attention and Performance**, V, New York: Academic Press

Ibbotson, N.R. and J. Morton (1981) "Rhythm and dominance", **Cognition**, 9

Jackendoff, R. (1971) "Modal structure in semantic representation", **Linguistic Inquiry**, 2.4

Jelinek, E. (1986) "Yaqui minus control", in S. DeLancey and R. Tomlin (eds) **Pacific Linguistics Conference, II**, Eugene, Oregon: University of Oregon

Jespersen, O. (1924) **The Philosophy of Grammar**, NY: Norton [1965 edition]

Johnson, M. (ed., 1981) **Philosophical perspectives on metaphor**, Minneapolis: University of Minnesota Press

Johnson, P. (1983) **Modern Times: The World from the Twenties to the Eighties**, NY: Harper and Row

Johnson-Laird, P. (1983) **Mental Models**, Cambridge: Harvard University Press

Jorgensen, J. (1972) **The Sundance Religion: Power for the Powerless,** Chicago: University of Chicago Press

Karttunen, L. (1974) "Presupposition and linguistic context", **Theoretical Linguistics,** 1.2

Katz, J.J. (1972) **Semantic Theory,** NY: Harper and Row

Katz, J.J. (1976) "A hypothesis about the uniqueness of natural language", in S.R. Harnad, H.D. Steklis and J. Lancaster (eds) **Origin and Evolution of Language and Speech, Annals of the N.Y. Academy of Science,** 280

Katz, J.J. (1978) "Effability and translation", in F. Guenthner and M. Guentner-Reutter (eds) **Meaning and Translation,** London: Duckworth

Katz, J.J. and J. Fodor (1964) "The structure of a semantic theory", in J. Fodor and J.J. Katz (eds) **The Structure of Language,** Englewood Cliffs, NJ: Prentice-Hall

Katz, J.J. and P. Postal (1964) **An Integrated Theory of Linguistic Descriptions,** Cambridge: MIT Press

Kay, P. and C. K. McDaniel (1978) "The linguistic significance of the meaning of basic color terms", **Language,** 54.4

Keele, S.W. (1969) "The repetition effect: A memory dependent process", **J. of Experimental Psychology,** 80

Keele, S.W. (1972) "Attention demands on memory retrieval", **J. of Experimental Psychology,** 81

Keele, S.W. (1986) "Sequencing and timing in skilled action: An overview", **Technical Report 86-1,** Cognitive Science Program, University of Oregon, Eugene

Keele, S.W. and R. Ivry (1986) "Components of the motor program: The cerebellum as an internal clock", **Technical Report 86-7,** Cognitive Science Program, University of Oregon, Eugene

Keele, S.W., R. Ivry and R.A. Pokorny (1986) "Force control and its relation to timing", **Technical Report 86-4,** Cognitive Science Program, University of Oregon, Eugene

Keele, S.W., R.A. Pokorny, D.M. Corcos and R. Ivry (1985) "Do perception and production share common time mechanisms?", **Acta Psychologica,** 60

Keenan, E.L. (1969) **A Logical Base for a Transformational Grammar of English,** PhD dissertation, University of Pennsylvania (ms)

Keenan, E.L. (1971) "Two types of presupposition in natural language", in C. Fillmore and T. Langendoen (eds) **Studies in Linguistic Semantics,** NY: Holt, Rinehart and Winston

Keenan, E.L. (1975) "Some universals of passive in Relational Grammar", **CLS 11,** University of Chicago, Chicago Linguistics Society

Keenan, E.L. (1976) "Remarkable subjects in Malagsy", in C. Li (ed., 1976)

Keenan, E.L. (1978) "Some logical problems in translation", in F. Guenthner and M. Guenthner-Reutter (eds) **Meaning and Translation,** London: Duckworth

Keenan, E.O. and B. Schieffelin (1976) "Topic as a discourse notion: A study of topic in the conversation of children and adults", in C. Li (ed., 1976)

Kemp, J. **The Philosophy of Kant**, Oxford: Oxford University Press

Kim, A. H. (1986) "Semi-clausal modals in Korean verb morphology", University of Oregon, Eugene, Linguistics Colloquium, November, 1986 (ms)

Kim, A.H. (1987) "Korean honorification system and relevance theory", in S. De-Lancey and R. Tomlin (eds) **Pacific Linguistics Conference II**, Eugene, Oregon: University of Oregon

Kimura, D. (1979) "Neuromotor mechanisms in the evolution of human communication", in D.H. Stelkis and M.J. Raleigh (eds) **The Neurology of Social Communication in Primates**, NY: Academic Press

Kintsch, W, (1974) **The Representation of Meaning in Memory**, Hillsdale, NJ: Erlbaum

Kintsch, W. (1977) **Memory and Cognition**, NY: Wiley

Kintsch, W. and E. Green (1978) "The role of culture-specific schemata in the comprehension and recall of stories", **Discourse Processes**, 1: 1-13

Kintsch, W. and J.M. Keenan (1973) "Reading rate and retention as a function of the number of the propositions in the base structure of sentences", **Cognitive Psychology**, 5: 257-274

Kintsch, W. and T. van Dijk (1978) "Toward a model of text comprehension and production", **Psychological Review**, 85: 363-394

Kiparski, P. and C. Kiparski (1968) "Fact", in M. Bierwisch and K.E. Heidolph (eds) **Progress in Linguistics**, The Hague: Mouton

Klatt, D.H. (1979), "Speech perception: A model of acoustic-phonetic analysis and lexical access", **J. of Phonetics**, 7: 279-312

Koestler, A. (1967) **The Ghost in the Machine**, NY: Macmillan

Koestler, A. (1972) **The Case of the Midwife Toad**, NY: Random House

Krashen, S.(1972) "Lateralization, language learning and the critical period", **Language Learning**, 23.1

Krashen, S., S. Long and R. Scarcella (1979) "Age, rate and eventual attainment in second language acquisition", **TESOL Quarterly**, 13.4

Kripke, S. (1963) "Semantic considerations on modal logic", **Acta Philosophica Fennica**, 16

Kripke, S. (1972) "Naming and necessity", in D. Davidson and G. Harman (eds) **Semantics of Natural Language**, Dordrecht: Reidel

Kroeber, A.L. (1909) "Classificatory systems of relationships", reprinted in P. Bohannon and J. Middleton (eds, 1968) **Kinship and Social Organization**, NY: Natural History Press

Kroon, F. (1981) "Kant and Kripke on the identifiability of modal and epistemic notions", **Southern Journal of Philosophy**, 19.1

Kuhn, T. (1962) **The Structure of Scientific Revolutions**, Chicago: University of Chicago Press

Labov, W. (1972a) **Sociolinguistic Patterns**, Philadelphia: University of Pennsylvania Press

Labov, W. (1972b) "Rules for ritual insults", in D. Sudnow (ed.) **Studies in Social Interaction**, NY: The Free Press

Labov, W. (1972c) "Where do grammars stop?", in R. Shuy (ed.) **Georgetown Monograph on Language and Linguistics**, Washington, DC: Georgetown University Press

Labov, W. (1972d) "For an end to the uncontrolled use of linguistic intuitions", Paper read at the LSA meeting, Atlanta (ms)

Labov, W. (1975a) "The quantitative study of linguistic structure", in K.-H. Dahlstedt (ed.) **Proceedings of the Second International Conference on Nordic and General Linguistics**, Umeâ

Labov, W. (1975b) "Empirical foundations of linguistic theory", in R. Austerlitz (ed.) **The Scope of American Linguistics**, Lisse: Peter de Ridder Press

Labov, W. and J. Waletzky (1967) "Narrative analysis: Oral versions of personal experience", in J. Helm (ed.) **Essays on the Verbal and Visual Arts**, Seattle: U. of Washington Press

Laertius, Diogenes, **Lives of Eminent Philosophers**, vols 1,2, tr. by R.D. Hicks (1925), Cambridge: Harvard University Press

Lakoff, G. (1973) "Hedges: A study in the meaning criteria and the logic of fuzzy concepts", **J. of Philosophical Logic, 2**

Lakoff, G. (1977) "Linguistic gestalt", **CLS 13**, University of Chicago: Chicago Linguistics Society

Lakoff, G. (1982) "Categories and cognitive models", **Berkeley Cognitive Science Report**, no. 2, Berkeley: Institute for Human Learning, University of California

Lakoff, G. and M. Johnson (1980) **Metaphors We Live By**, Chicago: University of Chicago Press

Lamarck, J.-B. (1809) **Philosophie zoölogique, ou exposition des considérations relatives á l'histoire naturelle des animaux**, Paris; English tr. Hugh Elliot (1914), **The Zoological Philosophy**, London: Macmillan

Lamendella, J. (1975) **The Early Growth of Cognition and Language: A Neuropsychological Approach**, Cal. State University, San Jose (ms)

Lamendella, J. (1976) "Relations between the ontogeny and phylogeny of language: A neo-recapitulationist approach", in S.R. Harnad, H.D. Stelkis and J. Lancaster (eds) **The Origins and Evolution of Language and Speech**, NY: New York Academy of Science

Langacker, R. (1987) **Cognitive Grammar**, vol. I, Stanford: Stanford University Press

Leach, E.R. (1958) "Concerning Trobriand clans and the kinship category 'tabu'", in J. Goody (ed.) **The Development Cycle in Domestic Groups, Cambridge Papers in Social Anthropology**, 1, Cambridge: Cambridge University Press

Lees, R.B. (1957) "Review of Chomsky's **Syntactic Structures**", **Language**, 33

Levinson, S. (1983) **Pragmatics**, Cambridge: Cambridge U. Press

Levy, D. (1979) "Communicative goals and strategies: Between discourse and syntax", in T. Givón (ed., 1979c)

Levy, W.B. and O. Steward (1983) "Temporal continuity requirements for long-term associative potentiation/depression in the hippocampus", **Neuroscience** , 8

Lewis, D. (1972) "General semantics", in D. Davidson and G. Harman (eds) **Semantics for Natural Language**, Dordrecht: Reidel

Lewis, D. (1979) "Score keeping in language games", **J. of Philosophical Logic** , 8

Li, C.N. (ed., 1976) **Subject and Topic**, NY: Academic Press

Li, C.N. and S. Thompson (1976) "Subject and topic: A new typology for language", in C.Li (ed., 1976)

Lieberman, P. (1984) **The Biology and Evolution of Language**, Cambridge: Harvard University Press

Lindlahr, V. (1940) **You Are What You Eat**, NY: Lancer Books [1972 ppbk edition]

Linnaeus, C. (1753) **Species Plantarum**, Halmiae

Linnaeus, C. (1758) **Systema Naturae**, Stockholm

Lloyd Morgan, C. (1896) "On modification and variation", **Science,** 4

Loftus, E.F. (1980) Eyewitness Testimony, Cambridge: Harvard University Press

Longacre, R. (1964) **Grammar Discovery Procedures: A Field Manual**, The Hague: Mouton

Lounsbury, F.G. (1965) "Another view of the Trobriand kinship categories", in **Formal Semantic Analysis**, special issue of **American Anthropologist**, 67.5, part 2

Luce, P.A. and D.B. Pisoni (1984) "Speech perception: Recent trends in research, theory and applications", in H. Winitz (ed.), **Human Communication and its Disorders**, Norwood, NJ: Ablex

Lyons, J. (1977) **Semantics**, vol. 1,2, Cambridge: Cambridge University Press

Malinowski, B. (1926) "Anthropology", **Encyclopaedia Britannica**, London and NY: The Encyclopaedia Britannica, Inc.

Malinowski, B. (1932) **The Sexual Life of Savages**, 3rd edition, London

Malinowski, B. (1935) **Coral Gardens and Their Magic**, London

Malinowski, B. (1954) **Magic, Science and Religion, and Other Essays**, Garden City, NY: Doubleday Anchor Books

Mandler, J.M. (1978) "A node in the code: The use of a story schema in retrieval", **Discourse Processes**, 1: 14-35

Mandler, J.M. and N. Johnson (1977) "Remembrance of things parsed: Story Structure and recall", **Cognitive Psychology**, 9: 111-151

March, J. and H.A. Simon (1958) **Organizations**, NY: Wiley

Marslen-Wilson, W., L.K. Tyler and M. Seidenberg (1978) "Sentence processing and the clause boundary", in W.J.M. Levelt and G.B. Flores (eds) **Studies in the Perception of Language**, London: Wiley

Martin, J.G. (1972) "Rhythmic (hierarchic) versus serial structure in speech and other behavior", **Psychological Review,** 79.6

Mayr, E. (1959a) "Typological vs. population thinking", in Mayr (1976)

Mayr, E. (1959b) "Isolation as an evolutionary factor", in Mayr (1976)

Mayr, E. (1959c) "Agassiz, Darwin and evolution", in Mayr (1976)

Mayr, E. (1960) "The emergence of evolutionary novelties", in Mayr (1976)

Mayr, E. (1962) "Accident or design: The paradox of evolution", in Mayr (1976)

Mayr, E. (1970) **Populations, Species and Evolution,** Cambridge: Harvard University Press

Mayr, E. (1972) "Lamarck revisited", in Mayr (1976)

Mayr, E. (1974) "Behavior programs and evolutionary strategies", in Mayr (1976)

Mayr, E. (1976) **Evolution and the Diversity of Life,** Cambridge: Harvard University Press

Mayr, E. (1982) **The Growth of Biological Thought,** Cambridge: Harvard University Press

McKeon, R. (ed., 1941) **The Basic Works of Aristotle,** NY: Random House [22nd printing, 1970]

McKoon, G. and R. Ratcliff (1980) "The comprehension processes and memory structures involved in anaphoric reference", **J.V.L.V.B.,** 19: 668-682

McLeod, P., C. McLaughlin and I. Nimmo-Smith (1985) "Information encapsulation and automaticity: Evidence from visual control of finely timed actions", in M. Posner and O. Marin (eds, 1985)

Medin, D.L. and M.M. Schaffer (1978) "Context theory of classification and learning", **Psychological Review,** 85.3

Merton, T. (1965) **The Way of Chuang-Tse,** NY: New Directions

Midgeley, M. (1978) **Beast and Man: Roots of Human Nature,** Ithaca: Cornell University Press

Miller, G.A. and P. Johnson-Laird (1976) **Language and Perception,** Cambridge: Cambridge University Press

Mishkin, M., B. Malamut and J. Bachevalier (1984) "Memories and habits: Two neural systems", in G. Lynch, J.L. McGaugh and N.M. Weinberger (eds) **The Neurobiology of Learning and Memory,** NY/London: Guilford Press

Mithun, M. (1985) "Is basic word order universal?", in R. Tomlin (ed., 1987)

Montague, R. (1970) "Pragmatics and intensional logic", **Synthese,** 22; reprinted in D. Davidson and G. Harman (eds, 1972) **Semantics of Natural Language,** Dordrecht: Reidel

Morris, C. (1938) **Foundations of the Theory of Signs,** Chicago: University of Chicago Press

Morris, W. (ed., 1969) **The American Heritage Dictionary,** Boston: Houton and Mifflin

Neely, J.H. (1976) "Semantic priming and retrieval from lexical memory: Evidence for facilitatory and inhibitory processes", **Memory and Cognition**, 4: 648-654

Neely, J.H. (1977) "Semantic priming and retrieval from lexical memory: Roles of inhibitionless spreading activation and limited-capacity attention", **J. of Experimental Psychology: General**, 106: 226-254

Nissen, M.J. (1976) **Semantic Activation and Levels of Processing**, University of Oregon, Eugene: Unpublished PhD Dissertation (ms)

Nissen, M.J. and P. Bulleme (1986) "Attention requirements of learning: Evidence from performance measures", University of Minnesota, Minneapolis (ms)

Nola, R. (1986) "The status of Popper's theory of scientific method", Auckland University, New Zealand (ms)

Nooteboom, S.G. (1981) "Speech rate and segmental perception: The role of words in phoneme identification", in T. Myers, J. Laver and J. Anderson (eds), **The Cognitive Representation of Speech**, Amsterdam: North Holland

Ochs, E. (1979a) "Social foundations of language", in R. Freedle (ed.) **New Directions in Discourse Processing**, vol. 3, Norwood, NJ: Ablex

Ochs, E. (1979b) "Introduction: What a child can contribute to pragmatics", in E. Ochs and B. Schieffelin (eds, 1979)

Ochs, E. (1979c) "Planned vs. unplanned conversation", in T. Givón (ed., 1979c)

Ochs, E. and B. Schieffelin (eds, 1979) **Developmental Pragmatics**, NY: Academic Press

Oh, C.-K. and D. Dinnen (eds, 1979) **Presupposition, Syntax and Semantics**, 11, NY: Academic Press

Ortonyi, A. (ed., 1979) **Metaphor and Thought**, Cambridge: Cambridge University Press

Osgood, C. (1971) "Where do sentences come from?", in D. Steinberg and L. Jacobovitz (eds) **Semantics: An Interdisciplinary Reader in Philosophy, Linguistics and Psychology**, London: Cambridge University Press

Osgood, C. and T. Sebeok (eds, 1954) **Psycholinguistics: A Survey of Theory and Research Problems**, I.J.A.L. Memoir #10

Osgood, C., G. Suci and P. Tannenbaum (1957) **The Measurement of Meaning**, Urbana: U. of Illinois Press

Owen, R. (1841) **John Hunter's Observations on Animal Development, Edited, and his Illustrations of that Process in the Bird Described**, London: R. and J.E. Taylor

Paillard, J. (1960) "The patterning of skilled movement", in J. Field, H.M. Magoun and V.E. Hall (eds) **Handbook of Physiology**, vol. 3, section 1, **Neurophysiology**, Washington, DC: American Physiological Society

Paivio, A. (1971) **Imagery and Verbal Processes**, NY: Holt, Rinehart and Winston

Patterson, K.E. and A.J. Marcel (1977) "Aphasia, dyslexia, and the phonological coding of written words", **Quarterly J. of Experimental Psychology**, 29: 307-318

Pawley, A. (1966) **The Structure of Karam: A Grammar of a New Guinea Highlands Language**, ph.D. dissertation, Auckland University, Auckland, NZ (ms)

Pawley, A. (1976) "On meeting a language that defies description by ordinary means", Auckland University, Auckland, NZ (ms)

Pawley, A. (1987) "Encoding events in Kalam and English: Different Logics for reporting experience", in R. Tomlin (ed., 1987)

Payne, D. (1983) "Basic constituent order in Yagua clauses: Implications for word-order universals", in D. Derbyshire and G. Pullum (eds) **Handbook of Amazonian Languages**, vol. 1, Berlin: Mouton (ms)

Payne, D. (1985) "Information structuring in Papago", **Language**

Pearson, T.R. (1985) **A Short History of a Small Place**, NY: Ballantine

Peirce, C.S. (1931) **Collected Writings**, vol. 1, Cambridge: Harvard University Press

Peirce, C.S. (1934) **Collected Writings**, vol. 5, Cambridge: Harvard University Press

Peirce, C.S. (1940) **The Philosophy of Peirce**, J. Buchler (ed.) NY: Harcourt, Brace

Perfetti, C.A. and S.R. Goldman (1974) "Thematization and sentence retrieval", J.V.L.V.B., 13: 70-79

Piattelli-Palmarini, M. (ed.,1980) **Language and Learning: The Debate Between Jean Piaget and Noam Chomsky**, Cambridge: Harvard University Press

Pirozzolo, F.H. and K. Rayner (1977) "Hemispheric specialization in reading and word recognition", **Brain and Language**, 4: 248-261

Poeck, K. and W. Huber (1977) "To what extent is language a sequential activity?", **Neuropsychologia**, 15

Pollatsek, A. and T.H. Carr (1979) "Rule-governed and wholistic encoding processes in word perceptions", in P.A. Kolers, M.E. Wrolstad and H. Bonma (eds) **Processing Visible Language**, NY: Plenum

Popper, K. (1950) **The Open Society and its Enemies**, vol. 1: **In the Spell of Plato**, London: Rutledge and Kegan Paul

Popper, K. (1959) **The Logic of Scientific Discovery**, revised edition (1968), NY: Harper and Row

Popper, K. (1974) **The Philosophy of Karl Popper**, ed. by P.A. Schlipp, La Salle, Ill.: Open Court

Popper, K. and J. Eccles (1977) **The Self and Its Brain**, London: Rutledge & Kegan Paul

Posner, M.I. (1969) "Abstraction and the process of recognition", in G.H. Bowers and J.T. Spence (eds) **The Psychology of Learning and Motivation**, vol. 3, NY: Academic Press

Posner, M.I. (1985) "Hierarchically distributed networks in neuropsychology of selective attention", **Cognitive Science Working Papers**, TR-85-I, University of Oregon, Eugene

Posner, M. (1986) "Empirical studies of prototypes", in C. Craig (ed.), **Categorization and Noun Classification**, TSL vol. 7, Amsterdam: J. Benjamins

Posner, M.I. and S. W. Boies (1971) "Components of attention", **Psychological Review**, 78

Posner, M. and S. Keele (1968) "On the genesis of abstract ideas", J. of Experimental Psychology, 77

Posner, M. and S. Keele (1970) "Retention of abstract ideas", **J. of Experimental Psychology**, 83

Posner, M.I. and R. Klein (1971) "On the function of consciousness", paper read at the **Fourth Conference on Attention and Performance**, University of Colorado, Boulder (ms)

Posner, M.I. and O.S.M. Marin (eds, 1985) **Attention and Performance**, XI, Hillsdale, NJ: Erlbaum

Posner, M.I. and C.R.R. Snyder (1974) "Attention and cognitive control", in R.L. Solso (ed.) **Information Processing and Cognition: The Loyola Symposium**, Hillsdale, NJ: Erlbaum

Posner, M. and R.E. Warren (1972) "Traces, concepts and conscious constructions", in A.W. Melton and E. Martin (Eds) **Coding Processes in Human Memory**, Washington, DC: V.H. Winston & Sons

Potter, M.C., V.V. Valian and B.A. Faulconer (1977) "Representation of a sentence and its pragmatic implications: Verbal, imagistic, or abstract?", **J.V.L.V.B.**, 16

Powell, A. (1971) **Temporary Kings**, NY: Popular Library (1986 paperback reprint)

Price, H.H. (1953) **Thinking and experience** NY: Hutchinson's University Press

Prince, E. (1979) "On the given/new distinction" , **CLS 15**, Chicago: University of Chicago, Chicago Linguistics Society

Prince, E. (1981) "On the inferencing of indefinite-this NPs", in A. Joshi, B. Webber and I. Sag (eds) **Elements of Discourse Understanding**, Cambridge: Cambridge University Press

Purtill, R.L. (1968) "About identity through possible worlds", **Nôus**, 2

Pylyshyn, Z.W. (1973) "What the mind's eye tells the mind's brain: A critique of mental imagery", **Psychological Bulletin**, 80

Quillian, M.R. (1968) "Semantic memory", in M. Minsky (ed.) **Semantic Information Processing**, Cambridge: MIT Press

Quine, W. van O. (1953) "Reference and modality", Ch. 8 of his **From a Logical Point of View**, Cambridge: Harvard University Press

Rafferty, E. (1987) "Word order in intransitive clauses in High and Low Malay of the Late 19th Century", in R. Tomlin (ed., 1987)

Ramsay, V. (1987) "Preposed and postposed 'if' and 'when' clauses in English discourse", in R. Tomlin (ed., 1987)

Rapoport, A, (ed., 1968) **Clausewitz's On War**, NY: Penguin Classics

Ratcliff, R. and G. McCoon (1980) "Automatic and strategic priming in recognition", **J.V.L.V.B.**, 20: 204-215

Reyburn, W.D. (1958) "Kaka kinship, sex and adultery", **Practical Anthropology**, 5.1., reprinted in W.A. Smalley (ed.) **Readings in Missionary Anthropology**, So. Pasadena, California: William Carey Library

Robinson, G.M. (1977) "Rhythmic organization in speech processing", **J. of Experimental Psychology: Human Perception and Performance**, 3.1

Robinson, G.M. and D.J. Solomon (1974) "Rhythm is processed by the speech hemisphere", **J. of Experimental Psychology**, 102.3

Rosch, E. (1973a) "On the internal structure of perceptual and semantic categories", in T. Moore (ed.) **Cognitive Development and the Acquisition of Language**, NY: Academic Press

Rosch, E. (1973b) "Natural categories", **Cognitive Psychology**, 4

Rosch, E. (1975) "Human categorization", in N. Warren (ed.) **Advances in Cross-Cultural Psychology**, London: Academic Press [1977]

Rosch, E. and B.B. Lloyd (eds, 1978), **Cognition and Categorization**, Hillsdale, NJ: Erlbaum

Rosch, E. and C.B. Mervis (1975) "Family resemblances: Studies in the internal structure of categories", **Cognitive Psychology**, 7: 573-605

Rosch, E., C.B. Mervis and W. Gray (1976) "Basic objects in natural categories", **Cognitive Psychology**, 8: 382-439

Ross, J.R. (1972a) "The category squish: Endstation Hauptwort", **CLS 8**, Chicago: University of Chicago, Chicago Linguistics Society

Ross, J.R. (1972b) "Act", in G. Harman and D. Davidson (eds) **Semantics of Natural Language**, Dordrecht: Reidel

Ross, J.R. (1973) "Nouniness", in D. Fujimura (ed.) **Three Dimensions of Linguistics**, Tokyo: TEC Corporation

Ross, J.R. (1974) "Clausematiness", in E.L. Keenan (ed.) **Semantics for Natural Languages**, Cambridge: Cambridge University Press

Rude, N. (1983) "Transitivity, topicality and direct object in Nez Perce discourse", **I.J.A.L.**, 52.2 (1987)

Rude, N. (1985) **Studies in Nez Perce Grammar and Discourse**, University of Oregon, Eugene, PhD dissertation (ms)

Rumelhart, D. (1977) "Toward an interactive model of reading", in S. Dorničh (ed.) **Attention and Performance VI**, Hillsdale, NJ: Erlbaum

Rumelhart, D. and A. Ortony (1977) "The representation of knowledge in memory", in R. Anderson, R. Spiro and W. Montague (eds), **Schooling and the acquisition of knowledge**, Hillsdale, NJ: Erlbaum

Russell, B. (1905) "On defining", **Mind**, 14

Russell, B. (1919) **Introduction to Mathematical Philosophy**, London: Allen and Unwin

Russell, B. (1948) **Human knowledge, its scope and limits,** NY: Simon and Schuster

Russell, E.S. (1916) **Form and Function: A Contribution to the History of Animal Morphology,** London: J. Murray

Rybarkiewicz, W. (1984) "Word-order flexibility in Polish", University of Oregon, Eugene (ms)

Sacks, H., E. Schegloff and G. Jefferson (1974) "A simplest systematic for the organization of turn-taking in conversation", **Language,** 50.4

Sadalla, E. and W.J. Burroughs (1981) **Food Preferences and Social Identity,** U.S. Science and Education Administration, Technical Report, Phoenix: Arizona State University

Sadock, J. (1970), "Whimperatives", in J. Sadock and A. Vanek (eds) **Studies Presented to R.B. Lees,** Edmonton: Linguistic Research

Sadock, J. and A. Zwicky (1985) "Speech act distinctions in syntax", in T. Shopen (ed.) **Language Typology and Syntactic Description,** vol. 1, Cambridge: Cambridge University Press

Saffran, E. and O.S.M. Marin (1977) "Reading without phonology: Evidence from aphasia", **Quarterly J. of Experimental Psychology,** 29: 515-525

Salisbury, M. (1986) "Negation and irrealis in Pukapukan", Auckland University, Auckland, N.Z. (ms)

Salkever, S. (1983) "Beyond interpretation: Human agency and the slovenly wilderness", in N. Haan, R.M. Bellah, P. Rabinow and W.M. Sullivan (eds) **Social Science as Moral Inquiry,** NY: Columbia University Press

Sapir, E. (1949) **Selected Writings of Edward Sapir,** ed. by D.G. Mandelbaum, Berkeley: U.C. Press

Saussure, F. de (1915) **Course in General Linguistics,** edited by C. Bally and A. Sechehaye, tr. by A. Reidlinger, NY: Philosophical Library (1959)

Schank, R. and R. Abelson (1977) **Scripts, Goals, Plans and Understanding,** Hillsdale, NJ: Erlbaum

Scheffler, H.W. (1972) "Kinship semantics", in B. J. Siegel (ed.) **Annual Review of Anthropology**

Scheffler, H.W. and F.G. Lounsbury (1971) **A Study in Structural Semantics: The Siriono Kinship System,** Englewood Cliffs, NJ: Prentice-Hall

Schieffelin, E. (1976) **The Sorrow of the Lonely and the Burning of the Dancer,** NY: St. Martin's Press

Schneider, W. (1985) "Toward a model of attention and the development of automatic processing", in M.I. Posner and O. Marin (eds, 1985)

Schneider, W. and A.S. Fisk (1983) "Attention theory and the mechanisms for skilled performance", in R.A. McGill (ed.) **Memory and Control of Action,** NY: North Holland

Schneider, W. and R.M. Shiffrin (1977) "Controlled and automatic human information processing, I: Detection, search and attention", **Psychological Review,** 84

Schmidt, R.A. (1975) "A schema theory of discrete motor skill learning", **Psychological Review, 82**

Schmidt, R.A. (1980) "Past and future issues in motor programming", **Research Quarterly for Exercise Sports, 51.1**

Scollon, R. (1974) **Conversations with a One-Year Old Child,** Honolulu: University of Hawaii Press

Scott, D. (1970) "Advice on modal logic", in K. Lambert (ed.) **Philosophical Problems in Logic,** Dordrecht: Reidel

Scriven, M. (1962) "Explanations, predictions and laws", in B. Brody (ed., 1970)

Searle, J. (1970) **Speech Acts,** Cambridge: Cambridge University Press

Searle, J. (1975) "Indirect speech acts", in P. Cole and J. Morgan (eds, 1975)

Searleman, A. (1977) "A review of right hemisphere linguistic capabilities", **Psychological Bulletin,** 84: 530-528

Serrés, E. (1860) **Principles d'embryologie, de zoögenie, et de teratogenie, Mém. Acad. Sci.,** 25:1-943

Shallice, T. and E.K. Warrington (1975) "Word recognition in a phonemic dyslexic patient", **Quarterly J. of Experimental Psychology,** 27: 187-199

Shapiro, D.C.A. (1977) "A preliminary attempt to determine the duration of a motor program", in D.M. Landers and R.W. Christina (eds) **Psychology of Motor Behavior and Sports,** vol. 3, Champaign, Ill.: Human Kinetics

Shapiro, D.C.A. (1978) **The Learning of Generalized Motor Programs,** PhD dissertation, University of Southern California, Los Angeles (ms)

Shapiro, D.C.A. and R.A. Schmidt (1980) "The schema theory: Recent evidence and developmental implications", in J.A.S. Kelso and J.E. Clark (eds) **The Development of Movement Control and Coordination,** NY: Wiley

Shapiro, D.C.A., R.F. Zernicke, R.J. Gregor and J.D. Diestel (1980) "Evidence for generalized motor programs using gait pattern analysis", **J. of Motor Behavior**

Shapiro, M. (1983) **The Sense of Grammar,** Bloomington: Indiana University Press

Shir, N. (1979) "Discourse constraints on dative movement", in T. Givón (ed., 1979c)

Short, T.L. (1981) "Semeiosis and intentionality", **Transactions of the Charles S. Peirce Society,** 17

Shroyer, S. (1985) "The demonstrative 'this' as an indefinite article in spoken English", in S. DeLancey and R. Tomlin (eds) **Proceedings of the First Pacific Linguistics Conference,** Eugene: University of Oregon

Silva-Corvalán, C. (1977) **A Discourse Analysis of Word Order in the Spanish Spoken by Mexican-Americans in West Los Angeles,** MA Thesis, UCLA (ms)

Simonds, P. (1974) **The Social Primates,** NY: Harper & Row

Skinner, B.F. (1938) **The Behavior of Organisms,** NY: Applton-Century-Croft

Skinner, B.F. (1957) **Verbal Behavior,** NY: Applton-Century-Croft

Slobin, D. (1973) "Cognitive prerequisites for the development of grammar", in C. Ferguson and D. Slobin (eds) **Studies in Child Language Development**, NY: Holt, Rinehart and Winston

Slobin, D. (1977) "Language change in childhood and history", in J. MacNamara (ed.) **Language Learning and Thought**, NY: Academic Press

Slobin, D. and A. Aksu (1982) "Tense, aspect and modality in the use of Turkish evidentials", in P. Hopper (ed.) **Tense and Aspect: Between Semantics and Pragmatics**, TSL vol.1, Amsterdam: J. Benjamins

Smalley, W.A. (1958) "Vocabulary and the preaching of the gospel", **Practical Anthropology**, 6.4., reprinted in W.A. Smalley (ed.) **Readings in Missionary Anthropology**, So. Pasadena: William Carey Library

Smith, E.E. and D. Medin (1981) **Categories and Concepts**, Cambridge: Harvard U. Press

Smith, J.L. (1980) "Programming of stereotyped limb movements by spinal generators", in G.E. Stelmach and J. Requin (eds) **Tutorials in Motor Behavior**, NY: North Holland

Smith, N.K. (tr., 1929) **Emanuel Kant's Critique of Pure Reason**, London/NY: Macmillan [1973 edition]

Sperber, D. (1982) "Apparently irrational beliefs", in M. Hollis and S. Lukes (eds, 1982)

Sperber, D. and D. Wilson (1988) **Relevance: Communication and Cognition**, Cambridge: Harvard University press

Spiro, M. (1978) "Culture and human nature", in G. Spindler (ed.) **The Making of Psychological Anthropology**, Berkeley: U.C. Press

Squire, L.R. and N.J. Cohen (1984) "Human memory and amnesia", in G. Lynch, J.L. McGaugh and N.M. Weinberger (eds) **Neurobiology of Learning and Memory**, NY/London: Guilford Press

Sridhar, S.N. (1980) **Cognitive Determination of Linguistic Structure: A Cross-Linguistic Experimental Study in Sentence Production**, PhD dissertation, University of Illinois, Urbana (ms)

Stein, P.S.G. (1978) "Motor systems, with specific reference to the control of locomotion", **Annual Review of Neuroscience**, 1

Strawson, P. (1950) "On referring", **Mind**, 59

Sun, C.-F. and T. Givón (1985) "On the so-called SOV word-order in Mandarin Chinese: A quantified text study and its implications", **Language**, 61.2

Sundberg, K. (1985) "Word-order in Klamath: The effect of topic continuity in determining pre- and post-verbal position", University of Oregon, Eugene (ms)

Syder, F. and A. Pawley (1974) "The reduction principle in conversation", Auckland University, Auckland, NZ (ms)

Szentagothai, J. (1977) "The neuron network of the cerebral cortex: A functional interpretation", **Proceedings of the Royal Society of London**, B, 201

Tesniére, L. (1959) **Eleménts de Syntaxe Structurale**, Paris: Klinksack

Thelen, E. (1984) "Learning to walk: Ecological demands and phylogenetic constraints", in P. Lipsitt and C. Rovee-Collier (eds) **Advances in Infancy Research,** vol. 3, Norwood, NJ: Ablex

Thomas, H. (1983) "The inferno of relativism", **Times Literary Supplement,** July 8, 1983

Thompson, S. (1973) "Resultative verb compounds in Mandarin Chinese: A case for lexical rules", **Language,** 49.2

Thompson, S. (1985) "Grammar and written discourse: Initial vs. final purpose clauses in English", in T. Givón (ed., 1985)

Thompson, S. (1987) "That deletion in English from a discourse perspective", BLS, Berkeley: University of California (ms)

Thurman, R. (1978) **Interclausal Relations in Chuave,** MA Thesis, University of California, Los Angeles, (ms)

Tomlin, R. (1987) "Linguistic reflections of cognitive episodes", in R. Tomlin (ed., 1987)

Tomlin, R. (ed., 1987) **Coherence and Grounding in Discourse,** TSL vol. 11, Amsterdam: J. Benjamins

Traugott, E. (1974) "Spatial expressions of tense and temporal sequencing: A contribution to the study of semantic fields", Stanford: Stanford University (ms)

Tsuchihashi, M. (1983) "The speech-act continuum: An investigation of Japanese sentence-final particles", **J. of Pragmatics,** 7.4

Tversky, B. (1969) "Pictorial and verbal encoding in a short-term memory task", **Perception and Psychophysics,** 6

Tversky, B. (1975) "Pictorial encoding of sentences in sentence-picture comparison", **Quarterly J. of Experimental Psychology,** 27

Tweedale, M. (1986) "How to handle problems about forms and universals in Aristotle's work", Auckland University, Auckland, NZ (ms)

van der Muelen, E.C. (1977) "A survey of multi-way channels in information theory: 1961-1976", **IEEE Transactions in Information Theory,** IT-23

van Lawick-Goodall, J. and H. van Lawick (1971) **Innocent Killers,** Boston: Houghton and Mifflin

Verhaar, J. (1985) "On iconicity and hierarchy", **Studies in Language,** 9.1

Verhaar, J. (1984) "Topic continuity in Indonesian discourse", St. Michael's Institute, Gonzaga University, Spokane, Wash. (ms)

von Wright, G.H. (1971) **Explanations and Understanding,** Ithaca: Cornell University Press

Waddington, C.H. (1942) "Canalization of development and the inheritance of acquired characters", **Nature,** 150

Waddington, C.H. (1953) "Genetic assimilation of an acquired character", **Evolution,** 7

Wald, B. (1973) **Tense Variation in Mombasa Swahili,** PhD dissertation, Colombia University (ms)

Wald, B. (1983) "Referents and topics within and across discourse units: Observations from contemporary English", in F. Klein-Andreu (ed.) **Discourse Perspectives on Syntax**, NY: Academic Press

Waley, A. (1934) **The Way and its Power**, London: Macmillan (reprinted 1958, NY: Grove Press)

Wallace, A.F.C. (1961) **Culture and Personality**, NY: Random House

Wallace, A.R. (1890) **Darwinism**, London: Macmillan

Welch, H. (1957) **Taoism: The Parting of the Way**, Boston: Beacon Press

Whitaker, H. (1983) "Toward a brain model of automatization: A short essay", in R.A. Magill (ed.) **Memory and Control of Action**, Amsterdam: North Holland

Whitehead, A.N. (1938) **Modes of Thought**, NY: Capricon Books (1958 ppbk edition)

Whiting, W.C., R.F. Zernicke, T.M. McLaughlin and R.J. Gregor (1980) "The recognition and correlation of human movement patterns", **J. of Biomechanics**, 13

Whorf, B.L. (1950) "An American Indian model of the universe", I.J.A.L., 16

Whorf, B.J. (1956) **Language, Thought & Reality: Collected Writings**, ed. by J.B. Carroll, Cambridge: MIT Press

Wierzbicka, A. (1986) "Does language reflect culture: Evidence from Australian English", **Language and Society**, 15

Winograd, T. (1970) **A Computer Program for Understanding Natural Language**, PhD Thesis, Dept. of Mathematics, MIT (ms)

Wittgenstein, L. (1918) **Tractatus Logico Philosophicus**, tr. by D.F. Pears and B.F. McGuinness, NY: The Humanities Press (1966)

Wittgenstein, L. (1953) **Philosophical Investigations**, tr. by G.E.M. Anscombe, NY: Macmillan

Woodruff, P. (1982) **Plato, Hippias Major**, Indianapolis: Hackett Publishing Co.

Wright, S. and T. Givón (1987) "The pragmatics of indefinite reference", **Studies in Language**, 11.1

INDEX